THE GLOBAL PROMISE OF FEDERALISM

Edited by Grace Skogstad, David Cameron,
Martin Papillon, and Keith Banting

The Global Promise of Federalism honours the life and work of Richard Simeon, one of Canada's foremost experts on federalism. It features a group of distinguished scholars of federalism from Canada and abroad who take up some of the fundamental questions at the heart of both Simeon's work and contemporary debates: Does federalism foster democracy? Can it help bring together divided societies? How do federations evolve and adapt to changing circumstances?

In the course of answering these questions, the chapters in this collection offer a comparative perspective on the challenges and opportunities facing well-established federations, such as Canada and Australia, as well as new federal and quasi-federal systems in Europe, Africa, and Asia. They examine the interplay between federal values, such as trust and mutual recognition, and institutional design; the challenges facing post-conflict federations; and the adaptability of federal systems in the face of changing social, economic, and cultural contexts.

GRACE SKOGSTAD is a professor in the Department of Political Science at the University of Toronto.

DAVID CAMERON is a professor in the Department of Political Science at the University of Toronto.

MARTIN PAPILLON is an associate professor in the School of Political Studies at the University of Ottawa.

KEITH BANTING is a professor in the Department of Political Studies and the School of Policy Studies at Queen's University.

Richard Simeon

The Global Promise of Federalism

Edited by
Grace Skogstad, David Cameron,
Martin Papillon, and Keith Banting

Institute of Intergovernmental Relations
IIGR Queen's University

and

UNIVERSITY OF TORONTO PRESS
Toronto Buffalo London

ISBN 978-1-4426-2647-8

Library and Archives Canada Cataloguing in Publication

The global promise of federation / edited by Grace Skogstad,
David Cameron, Martin Papillon, and Keith Banting.

This book honours the legacy of Richard Simeon, one of the most
prominent federalist scholars in the world and a long-time member
of the Department of Political Science at the University of Toronto.
Includes bibliographical references.
ISBN 978-1-4426-2647-8 (pbk.)

1. Federal government – Case studies.   I. Skogstad, Grace, 1948–,
author, editor of compilation   II. Cameron, David, 1941–, author,
editor of compilation   III. Papillon, Martin, 1971–, author, editor of
compilation   IV. Banting, Keith G., 1947–, author, editor of compilation

JC355.G56 2013   321.02   C2013-906897-X

University of Toronto Press acknowledges the financial assistance to its
publishing program of the Canada Council for the Arts and the Ontario
Arts Council.

Canada Council **Conseil des Arts**
for the Arts **du Canada**

University of Toronto Press acknowledges the financial support of the
Government of Canada through the Canada Book Fund for its publishing
activities.

Contents

Acknowledgments   vii

1 The Global Promise of Federalism   3
GRACE SKOGSTAD, DAVID CAMERON, MARTIN PAPILLON, AND
KEITH BANTING

2 Federalism and Democracy: A Critical Reassessment   17
THOMAS O. HUEGLIN

3 Is There a Political Culture of Federalism in Canada? Charting an
Unexplored Territory   43
FRANÇOIS ROCHER AND PATRICK FAFARD

4 A Problem of Trust: Can Federalism Silence the Guns?   69
MARIE-JOËLLE ZAHAR

5 Designing a Durable Federation: The Case of Cyprus   99
JOHN McGARRY

6 The Constitutional Jurisprudence of Federalism and the Theocratic
Challenge   139
RAN HIRSCHL

7 Ideology, Identity, Majoritarianism: On the Politics of
Federalism   166
ALAIN NOËL

 8 Adaptability and Change in Federations: Centralization, Political
    Parties, and Taxation Authority in Australia and Canada   188
    LUC TURGEON AND JENNIFER WALLNER

 9 Living with Contradictions in Federalism: Goals and Outcomes of
    Recent Constitutional and Financial Reforms in the Spanish *Estado
    autonómico*   214
    CÉSAR COLINO

10 Spatial Rescaling, Federalization, and Interest Representation   236
    MICHAEL KEATING

11 *Engagé* Intellectuals, Technocratic Experts, and Scholars   259
    JAN ERK

12 Reflections on a Federalist Life   279
    RICHARD SIMEON

13 The Collected Works of Richard Simeon   294
    ANDREW MCDOUGALL

Contributors   311

Acknowledgments

This collection represents the collaborative effort of many individuals and institutions. It had its origins in a conference at the University of Toronto in September 2011 to honour the career of Richard Simeon. The conference was made possible by generous funding from the Social Sciences and Humanities Research Council of Canada under its Aid to Research Workshops and Conferences in Canada, the Queen's Institute of Intergovernmental Relations, and the Mowat Centre for Policy Innovation and the Department of Political Science at the University of Toronto. Gabriel Eidelman, Sari Sherman, Luc Turgeon, and Jenn Wallner all played an invaluable role in helping to organize the conference and in ensuring its success. So did several conference participants who acted as formal paper commentators and panelists during the conference: George Anderson, Sebastian Baglioni, Karlo Basta, Josh Hjartason, André Juneau, Jean Lachapelle, Christina Murray, Alexandre Paquin-Pelletier, Philippe Roseberry, Julie Simmons, and Ron Watts. Andrew McDougall has been a superb research assistant throughout, including preparing the bibliography of Richard's life works. We are grateful as well to our chapter contributors, the three anonymous reviewers of the manuscript, and the two publishers of this volume: the University of Toronto Press and the Institute of Intergovernmental Relations at Queen's University and its director, André Juneau.

THE EDITORS

THE GLOBAL PROMISE OF FEDERALISM

1 The Global Promise of Federalism

GRACE SKOGSTAD, DAVID CAMERON,
MARTIN PAPILLON, AND KEITH BANTING

This volume honours the life and work of Richard Simeon, and its contents perfectly reflect the man. The title of the book – *The Global Promise of Federalism* – clearly suggests the primary focus of the essays in this volume, but the spirit that lies behind the selection of the title is perhaps less evident on its face. The spirit is caught by turning the title into a question: what is the global promise of federalism? Neither the man nor the book reflects a triumphalist assumption in which federalism is a story of unblemished progress and advance, established federations consolidating and strengthening their federal arrangements and increasing numbers of new polities successfully introducing the federal idea into their constitutions and governing arrangements.

Richard Simeon and the other authors in this collection see the federal narrative quite differently. It is a story of trial and error, success and failure, stops and starts – incremental change and pragmatic adjustment in one case, transformation in another. Most federations are best understood as works in progress. Examples of success are matched by instances of failure; for every Spain, there is a Czechoslovakia, for every India, a Sudan. This is the real world of federalism – contingent, uncertain, dynamic.

But federalism's promise, mixed or not, is real. It has been employed as a way of organizing the state for more than two centuries. Historically, federalism was often praised as an institutional arrangement that contributes to democracy: as in the United States, the world's first federation; in post-war Austria and West Germany; or in the large but relatively homogeneous territory of Australia. Democracy remains part of federalism's global promise, but in the contemporary era interest in federalism has increasingly focused on its potential as a means of governing diverse and divided societies. Why have so many countries settled on this form of government? Why is there such interest in federalism today? Following the collapse of authoritarian regimes – the Soviet Union, the dictatorships in Spain and Iraq, and more recently the autocracies in the Arab spring countries – ethnic, religious, and linguistic identities have re-emerged. The political mobilization of these groups has generated a global search for mechanisms through which to manage diverse societies. Large numbers of countries with significant ethno-religious minorities – rich countries and poor countries alike – have asked whether federalism holds promise for them. Some countries suffering civil wars are doing so as well. In this context, federalism has emerged as a powerful idea about how to organize a divided society.

Today, there are well over two dozen federal systems around the world, containing more than 40% of the globe's population. Richard Simeon has studied and worked in many of them, bringing his distinctive brand of scholarship and genial curiosity to each. Like many Canadian political scientists of his generation, Richard was caught up in – one might almost say "consumed by" – the federal and constitutional crisis of his own country. For well over 30 years, from the 1960s until the late 1990s, Canadians struggled to adapt the political and constitutional order to a society that was rapidly changing, both in Quebec and in the rest of Canada. The national question – the existential matter of Quebec's status within or outside Canada – preoccupied Canadians for many years. Richard played his part as an engaged citizen and scholar throughout these decades. From the publication of his first (and, as he sees it, most important) book, *Federal-Provincial Diplomacy*, in 1972 to his appointment as director of the Queen's University Institute of Intergovernmental Relations, his membership on the Ontario Advisory Committee on Confederation, his management of federalism research on the Macdonald Commission, his role as an occasional adviser to Ontario premiers Davis, Peterson, and Rae, Richard's involvement was not simply that of the scholar in his study, but also that of a citizen fiercely concerned about and engaged in the fortunes of his country.

During this period, he taught at Queen's and then at the University of Toronto and produced a stream of publications on federalism and other matters that framed both academic debate and public policy discussion. Since he was a scholar, his participation was rooted in evidence and argument, in writing and speaking, but there is no question that his academic work during this time was animated by a passionate preoccupation with the welfare of his country. In a reflective moment, Richard in fact asked the question, of himself and others, of whether Canadian academics had been too close to the public and political process during these years, and he wondered aloud about what may have been lost from a scholarly point of view.[1]

Again, like many Canadian colleagues of his generation, when the sovereignist movement was on the wane in the late 1990s, Richard reactivated the comparative and international interests of his early career, continuing his teaching and writing on the Canadian federal experience, but adding to that a broader comparative agenda of teaching, consulting, advising, and publication. It took him all over the world. As we have seen, this was a time of growing international interest in federalism and other forms of decentralized government. Many countries were wrestling with the question of how to reconstitute themselves after civil wars, invasions, and political collapse; Canada's experiences – coping with a powerful sovereignist movement, accommodating itself to deep cultural pluralism engendered by high levels of immigration, responding to the demands for justice of indigenous peoples, engaging in substantial constitutional reform, which included an increasingly influential bill of rights – generated international attention. Richard was one of a substantial number of Canadians who sought to explain Canada to the world. His broadening comparative focus was reflected in his ongoing interest in the United States and in Canada-US studies, nurtured by his two years at Harvard as the Mackenzie King Fellow. Richard worked in and on South Africa during its democratic transition, on Iraq and Sudan under the auspices of the Forum of Federations, and – partly as a result of his role as an academic adviser to the Club of Madrid – on questions of regional integration in Spain and Scotland. Practice, teaching, and research were fused.

Over his distinguished career, Richard has examined many facets of federalism, including its ideological and cultural underpinnings, the interplay between federal societies and federal institutions, federalism's relationship to democracy, and the role of intergovernmental relations in the functioning of federations; the fiscal management of federations and the limits of federalism; and the constitutional design of new federations in post-conflict countries. His "federalist life," as Richard characterizes it in his contribution to this volume, has led him to appreciate the uncertainty, complexity, and variability of federal systems; they are, he says, "no universal solution to the problems of divided societies." Federal systems, he reminds us, are often second-best solutions, the outcome of negotiations between those who would prefer outright secession and independence and those who would rather retain a centralized, unitary state.

Such scepticism is shared by other scholars, who argue that federations in ethnically plural societies are unstable and likely to self-destruct (Elkins and Sides 2007; Roeder 2009; Feeley and Rubin 2008). Against this view, Christin and Hug (2012) argue that the record is likely to be more mixed, with some ethno-federal arrangements succeeding even while others do not.

If there is pessimism about federalism's prospects, there is more optimism about federal principles and values. Shared values of tolerance, recognition of the other, shared and dispersed power, non-majoritarian democracy, and autonomy and self-determination of territorially concentrated minority communities, are promoted as principles and values that allow divided societies to live in harmony. Coming to grips with the global promise of federalism thus requires us to pay attention to the degree to which federal values are instantiated in the political institutions of a federal system and embedded in the political culture of its citizens.

Understanding the relationship between federal values and federal institutions is an important endeavour and one to which the chapters that comprise this volume contribute. They collectively investigate very diverse federal and federalizing contexts: post-conflict countries contemplating federalism, like Cyprus; young federations with strong secessionist movements, like Spain; older, stable federations, like Canada and Australia; federations in Africa and Asia that are constitutional theocracies; and European countries in the process of devolving authority to meso-level territorial governments. Some chapters deal explicitly with the issue of whether certain values are prerequisites to establishing federal systems and/or whether federal systems can flourish in the absence of a supportive federal culture. Others address the relationship between federal values and federal institutions by turning their lens on the adequacy of different types of federal institutions to promote the federal principles and values on which the political system's legitimacy ultimately rests. And yet other chapters serve to demonstrate the complexity of the relationship between federal values and federal institutions by showing how federal institutions always interact with other institutions and factors in the local context to determine the relative priority given to federal values, compared with, for example, class-based values of equality/inequality.

Coming at federalism from different angles and through different lenses, the chapters that comprise this volume highlight certain matters, moments, and processes that are worthy of our attention if we want to understand the global promise of federalism. First, still on the values front, trust is crucial to the success of federations, even while the ability of federal systems to create trust and other supportive federal values is unclear. Directing attention to the role of federal institutions according to whether or not they engender a basic level of trust across the constituent communities and groups is thus an important line of enquiry for better understanding federalism's global promise. Second, the institutional design of federal systems at their founding is likely to be especially important to their ability to succeed. Accordingly, paying close attention to the period during which federal institutions are created and the extent to which they embody federal ideas from the outset should get us closer to understanding federalism's global promise. Third, the success of federal systems is closely related to their congruence with contextual (social, cultural, economic) factors and, accordingly, to their capacity to evolve as these contextual factors themselves shift. An important line of enquiry for federal scholars is thus mapping the differing capacity of federal systems to adapt in the face of changes in the societal, economic, and political context of federalism and to respond to the evolving understandings of federalism in the given country's constitutive political communities. And fourth, in its very eclecticism – some authors approaching federalism normatively, others adopting empirical approaches, all of them highlighting different factors that affect federalism's promise – the collection displays various traditions in the study of federalism and suggests the contribution they make to understanding its future prospects.

Federalism and Federal Values: The Importance of Trust and a Supportive Political Culture

Notwithstanding a tendency to focus on the requisite formal and informal institutions of federal systems, it is also clear that federal systems rest on certain ideals and values. The latter's absence poses obstacles to creating a federal system. Moreover, as Broschek (2010, 2) observes, once federations are created, a gap between the legitimating frameworks/values of federalism and the allocation of political authority in federal institutions creates endogenous pressures for change, which, if left unattended, will undermine the legitimacy of federalism itself.

Scholars tend to concur on the necessary values for federalism even while they wrestle with the "chicken and egg problem" of the relationship between these values and federal institutions. On his list of five prerequisites for federalism to operate effectively in multicultural contexts, Watts (2004, 15–16) includes "underlying shared values and objectives, trust [and] the development of a political culture emphasizing sharing and cooperation and fostering respect for cultural norms and structures and the rule of law." Yet as Cameron (2009, 313) observes, in countries that have been at civil war "trust cannot be established, shared values cannot be created, and political cultures cannot be changed directly and in the immediate term." In his view, these values usually can be developed only during the peace process – when warring parties opt for peace and federalism over the less desirable alternative of going back to war.

The causal relationship between democratic values and federalism is also not straightforward. Watts's list of prerequisites for federal systems includes liberal democratic values (Cameron 2009, 313), while others see federalism as a promoter of democracy, for example, by giving minorities a voice they would not otherwise have and the tools to engage in meaningful debate (Scott 2011, 185, 195; see also Burgess and Gagnon 2010, 12).

Contending that plural societies need institutions that build in a dialogical form of non-unitary governance, Thomas Hueglin argues in Chapter 2 that certain kinds of federal institutions are well equipped to play this role. More specifically, institutions of cooperative or executive federalism that build in an intergovernmental dialogue across central and constituent governments are a good example of dialogical institutions of non-unitary governance. In contrast to majority rule and parliamentary institutions, cooperative or executive federalism as practised in Canada pluralizes public reason as a dialogue among equal participants, as does the European Union through its subsidiarity principle: all EU legislative drafts must be a matter of wide consultation among all institutionalized actors, including national parliaments. By contrast, the American style of judiciary federalism provides a poor model for pluralist societies, in Hueglin's view, because it does not build an intergovernmental dialogue directly into its institutional design.

The constituent ingredients and presence of a political culture of federalism in Canada are the subject of Chapter 3. François Rocher and Patrick Fafard's survey of Canadian citizens' attitudes leads them to conclude that Canadians do not have a particularly strong political culture of federalism. As evidence, they point to Canadians' weak grasp of the division of powers, their poor knowledge of how a federation should operate, and their disinclination to support asymmetry to accommodate diversity in multinational federations. In an argument reminiscent of Broschek (2010), Rocher and Fafard conclude that, over the longer term, the weakness, if not the absence, of a political culture of federalism in Canada may mean the ongoing weakening of the federal character of Canada. Their findings, the authors conclude, demonstrate that while federations may be a response to pre-existing societal values, the lived reality of a federation can in turn shape and alter these values.

Trust, observes Marie-Joëlle Zahar in Chapter 4, is likely to be in short supply among communal groups that have been at war with one another and who have little reason to believe that agreements reached through political negotiation will be honoured. What is needed to build trust within and across communities, she argues, is meeting citizens' and communities' security needs. These security needs are twofold: deterrence (persuading groups not to return to violence by restoring the state's monopoly on the legitimate use of force) and assurance (ensuring that the state will not use its force against citizens and communities). Drawing on the experience of several post-conflict countries, Zahar argues that federations are likely to fare better than either majoritarian unitary structures or power-sharing arrangements in meeting citizens' security needs and thus in also building trust between elites and followers as well as between communities.

In her view, citizens and communities are likely to believe that their security will be better protected in a federation; the central government, by restoring the state's monopoly on the legitimate use of force, can deter groups from returning to violence, and the governments of the federal units can use their control over public safety to assure people that the state will not use its force against citizens and communities. Neither majoritarian nor power-sharing systems can provide both deterrence and assurance. Majoritarian systems can deter groups returning to violence, but are not able to offer assurance to the other groups that the power of the state will not be used against them. Power-sharing systems may provide assurance that the state will not use force against its citizens, but they are prone to fail on deterrence, owing to policy inaction or blockage and the absence of both a coherent political authority and an effective central command structure. Notwithstanding her guarded optimism about federalism's trust-building capacity, Zahar cautions that "the promise of federalism is not without qualifiers"; it is how institutions and people within them operate over time that will determine whether trust is fostered.

The Importance of Founding Institutions

Institutionalist scholars have documented that early institutional choices are likely to prove highly resistant to change as a result of path-dependent effects. The lasting effect of early institutional choices is likely magnified in federal systems; their constitutional amendment formulae usually require high thresholds of agreement for change, and efforts to change power-sharing arrangements are likely to be divisive occasions, as the example of Canada illustrates. These observations remind us that the institutional design of a federation at its founding is likely to have a major impact on whether the federation will survive and be regarded as legitimate over the longer term.

Getting federal institutions "right" at the outset is no easy task. As Vermeule (2009) observes, when designing a constitution, it is important to remember that a society may not be able to get an "ideal" constitution; it may have to settle for inferior institutions when setting up its system. Similarly, institutions that look optimal at the outset may change in unexpected and undesirable ways. Vermeule (2009, 2) advocates a systemic approach that focuses on the properties of the aggregate system, rather than on its individual, institutional components.

In Chapter 5, John McGarry adopts just such an approach in his appraisal of the prospects for federalism in Cyprus. Turkish Cypriots and Greek Cypriots have agreed that any shared political future should be federal. While they also agree in principle on a pluralist federation – a federation that includes a degree of self-government and recognition of more than one official culture – they do not yet agree on its crucial details. Concerns about the fragility of pluralist federations have led to a search for micro-institutional arrangements that are consistent with a pluralist federation but compensate for its centrifugal tendencies by emphasizing an overarching identity and political union. McGarry considers four micro-institutional arrangements that have been proposed to counteract pluralist federations' centrifugal tendencies: first, an electoral system at the federal level that rewards moderates and encourages cooperation; second, engineered internal boundaries of heterogeneous communities that run across ethnic groups rather than around them; third, a *negotiated* constitutional clause that prohibits secession; and fourth, a redistributive program to breakaway regions that purchases solidarity.

Drawing on the experience of Cyprus as well as several other countries, McGarry suggests caution in expecting these four institutions to actually emerge and suggests other options. An electoral system that rewards moderates is unlikely to be included in a peace agreement, or taken seriously in negotiations, unless moderates are already in a reasonably strong political position or the electoral system is imposed from the outside. Given that these conditions are not likely to be present, McGarry suggests an electoral system that gives all sizable political parties, including radical parties, incentives to work within the system. Instead of drawing new internal boundaries that divide communities and create cross-cutting cleavages, which he believes are unlikely to meet the approval of either ethnic/linguistic minorities or majorities, McGarry proposes autonomy arrangements that are based on existing internal boundaries. In place of a negotiated constitutional clause that prohibits secession, McGarry advocates that, where one part of the state has broken away de facto but not de jure, the most productive way to proceed during negotiations may be to park disputes over sovereignty and secession or territorial integrity, rather than try to negotiate a constitutional clause prohibiting secession. Focusing on constitutional bans does more harm than good because it distracts from the cooperation that is needed to keep pluralist federations together. And finally, while a redistributive program to breakaway regions that purchases solidarity may be forthcoming from wealthy parties, deprived minorities are more likely to place core political and security concerns ahead of material advantages. In an argument reminiscent of those who argue that trust is a prerequisite to federalism, McGarry observes that solidarity payments are likely to be given unconditionally only when there is some significant level of pre-existing solidarity. In his sobering analysis, McGarry, while acknowledging the importance of good institutional design, also recognizes the need to reconcile institutional arrangements with the tolerances and proclivities of the parties to the conflict.

In Chapter 6, Ran Hirschl examines the interplay between values and federal institutions in a different context, namely, in what might be called federal theocracies. Constitutional theocracies, several of them federal, are home to about one in seven people across the globe. In these systems, a divine authority is the ultimate source of sovereignty, power, and legitimacy; not only is religion a basis of collective identity – as it is in many secular states – but it is also granted a formal constitutional status, putting certain religious directives above the constitutional order. The result, Hirschl observes, is a secular-religious divide, as anti-theocratic interests seek to tame the spread of religious fundamentalism and to defuse attempts to establish a constitutional theocracy.

Can federalism be an institutional arrangement to contain religious fundamentalism? Drawing on examples from four constitutional theocracies that are also federations – Nigeria, Malaysia, Indonesia, and Pakistan – Hirschl demonstrates how opponents of theocratic government have successfully drawn on federalism-based constitutional jurisprudence to contain religion and its traditional interlocutors. Courts, most notably those with final review powers, have used constitutionally enshrined principles of federalism to block the expanded ambit of religious law, as well as to advance secularizing solutions to religion and state problems. Moreover, although constitutional courts in both unitary and federal polities tend to resist radical religion, in Hirschl's view, courts in federal systems may be better equipped than their counterparts in unitary states to blunt the demand for more religion in public life. Calls for theocratic governance can be accommodated within sub-national units and confined to that level while leaving intact the status of constitutional law and courts across the state as a whole.

An Institutional Capacity to Evolve

The fate of federal systems is shaped, importantly, not only by the path-dependent effects of their inaugural institutions and principles, but also by the interactions over time of these same federal institutions and principles with other contextual factors. For many federalism scholars, it is the interaction of federal institutions with their changing social environment that is most important (Livingston 1952; Erk 2008). For other scholars, the most important contextual factors are other institutions, for example, the political party system (Riker 1964) or courts of judicial review (Cairns 1971). The general proposition that unites these scholars is that federal institutions must have the capacity to evolve in tandem with contextual shifts if they are to retain their legitimacy and endure. An important line of enquiry for federalism scholars is thus mapping the multiple ways in which the social and political context of federalism can change and the resulting consequences for federations.

Four chapters in this volume pursue such an enquiry and develop the theme of the contextually specific nature of the evolution of federal systems. In an essay that draws on his personal recollections, Alain Noël in Chapter 7 sets out to demonstrate that social cleavages structure the lines of political conflict in multinational federations. He identifies three such cleavages, which pervade debates about federalism in Canada and Quebec: class divisions over social change and distributive issues, religious or identity differences, and the division between national majorities and national minorities. Noël makes three basic arguments. First, these social cleavages and their interactions give rise to very different debates about federalism and different politics in Quebec and the rest of Canada. For example, support for federalism in Quebec tends to be associated with the ideological right, who have defended inequality and the status quo, while the left has largely supported sovereignty. In Canada, by contrast, the left has historically leaned toward a centralized federation, while the right has favoured provincial autonomy, associating it with less government. Second, identity issues pervade politics in multinational federations; for example, the Canadian social identity lends support to a centralized federation with the capacity to fund social policies that redistribute wealth across the country, whereas in Quebec, the welfare state is strongly associated with a strong provincial state. Third, notwithstanding the importance of cleavages of class and identity, the majority's exercise of power usually allows it to prevail over the minority. The resulting non-egalitarian relationships between majorities and minorities, in his view, not only contribute to the inherently conflictual character of multinational federations, but also limit their global promise.

In Chapter 8, Luc Turgeon and Jenn Wallner argue a different contextual factor – the political party system – has had an important impact on the evolution of the Australian and Canadian federal systems. Using the allocation of taxation authority as a measure of the relative centralization-decentralization of a federal system, they observe that Australia, created as a decentralized federation, has become more centralized over time, while Canada, designed as a centralized federation, has experienced fluctuations in centralization and decentralization, but has gravitated to a decentralized form. Turgeon and Wallner argue that the difference in the two countries' centralization-decentralization trajectory reflects the relative strength of their left-wing parties, which tend to favour centralization over decentralization. In Canada, they argue, regionally based parties, combined with the absence of a powerful leftist political party at the national level, helped provinces to acquire considerable taxation autonomy. By contrast, the electoral strength of the Labor Party and its preference for a centralized federation account for the much smaller taxation autonomy of Australian states relative to the Commonwealth government. Their argument – that left-wing parties are agents of centralization in federations – is consistent with Noël's observation of the politics of the left in English-speaking Canada but contrasts with his contention that the left in Quebec supports decentralization and provincial autonomy.

The Spanish federation is a relatively new one, beset with regional tensions. In Chapter 9, César Colino discusses recent constitutional and financial reforms in Spanish federalism aimed at increasing the powers, fiscal resources, and autonomy of the autonomous communities and the impact of these same reforms on the goals of equitable treatment of citizens, recognition and accommodation of diversity, and procedural democracy. He argues that reforms in the funding arrangements relating to the Spanish autonomous communities and amendments to their regional statutes of autonomy were affected by the intervention of the Constitutional Court, the Spanish central government, and the ongoing financial crisis; the overall outcome is that the goal of equity took priority over the accommodation of diversity and democracy. The result, says Colino, is not only that nationalists in Catalonia were not appeased, but that the reforms increased their permanent dissatisfaction and provided further justification for their need for independence.

A different approach to understanding the interactive effects of federal/federalizing institutions with contextually specific institutions and values is taken by Michael Keating in Chapter 10. Keating examines whether – and, if so, how – interest groups and policy communities adapt as authority is transferred from the central state to an intermediate or "meso" level of government. Focusing on the United Kingdom, Italy, France, and Spain, he documents how interest groups adapt their organizational structures to mirror those of the territorial government. Territorial lobbying, strongest where there is a historic identity, is more prominent in Spain, Italy, and the UK (Scotland and Wales) than in France. However, he also finds that the territorialization of groups is limited by path-dependency and is subject to political contestation, in many cases, between the sectoral and territorial perspectives of interest groups. New cleavages and alliances emerge at the regional level as the policy agenda shifts. Shifting territorial scales or levels do not dissolve class or sectoral cleavages or replace the politics of conflict and compromise with those of consensus and collaboration, but it does transform them. While federalizing tendencies in Europe are thus accompanied by a federalization of policy systems and policy arenas, there is no clearly defined hierarchy of arenas. Territorial policy systems are open, with unequal constraints on different groups. The boundaries of the new arenas themselves remain the objects of contestation.

Federalism from Theory to Practice

A final theme that emerges from this collection is that a theoretically eclectic approach provides important payoffs when it comes to understanding the factors that are important to federalism's success or failure. Such an approach includes attention to both the normative and empirical traditions in federalism and the "comparative turn" of which Richard Simeon has been an integral part. But there remains the issue of the federalism scholar: what is his or her role if the promise of federalism is to be realized?

In the penultimate essay in this collection, in Chapter 11, Jan Erk tackles this question by pointing to the pitfalls in translating a theoretical understanding of federalism into ready-made solutions in the designing of real-life federations. Erk warns that the institutionalist bias predominant in the federalism literature may lead scholars to underplay contextually specific, extra-institutional, non-codified, and structural factors that often play a key role in the success or failure of federalism. While Erk sees a role for *engagé* intellectuals in political action, he cautions that the analytical expertise of technocratic experts may fall short in addressing real-life problems. When it comes to designing new federations, he believes the erudition and prudence of all-round scholars is more valuable than the expertise of technocratic experts.

In Chapter 12, we give the final word – on this issue and on federalism – to the engaged intellectual to whom this volume is dedicated: Richard Simeon.

NOTE

1 Simeon (1989) praised Smiley's eclecticism but argued that his "wrestling with contemporary events" could also limit the scope of analysis, the ability to develop more general theory, and the capacity to draw on and contribute to the comparative literature.

REFERENCES

Broscheck, Jörg. 2010. Federalism and Political Change: Canada and Germany in Historical-Institutionalist Perspective. *Canadian Journal of Political Science* 43(1):1–24.

Burgess, Michael. 2006. *Comparative Federalism: Theory and Practice.* London: Routledge.

Burgess, Michael, and Alain-G. Gagnon, eds. 2010. *Federal Democracies.* Routledge Series in Federal Studies. London and New York: Routledge.

Cairns, Alan C. 1971. The Judicial Committee and its Critics. *Canadian Journal of Political Science* 4(3):301–45.

Cameron, David. 2009. The Paradox of Federalism: Some Practical Reflections. *Regional and Federal Studies* 19(2):309–19.

Christin, Thomas, and Simon Hug. 2012. Federalism, the Geographic Location of Groups, and Conflict. *Conflict Management and Peace Science* 29(1):93–122.

Elkins, Zachary, and John Sides. 2007. Can Institutions Build Unity in Multi-Ethnic States? *American Political Science Review* 101(4):693–708.

Erk, Jan. 2008. *Explaining Federalism: State, Society, and Congruence in Austria, Belgium, Canada, Germany, and Switzerland.* New York: Routledge.

Feeley, Malcolm, and Edward Rubin. 2008. *Federalism: Political Identity and Tragic Compromise.* Ann Arbor: University of Michigan Press.

Livingston, Walter S. 1952. *Federalism and Constitutional Change.* Oxford: Clarendon Press.

Riker, William H. 1964. *Federalism: Origin, Operation, Significance.* Boston: Little, Brown.

Roeder, Philip. 2009. Ethnofederalism and the Mismanagement of Conflicting Nationalisms. *Regional and Federal Studies* 19(2):203–19.

Scott, Kyle. 2011. *Federalism: A Normative Theory and Its Practical Relevance.* New York: Continuum.

Simeon, Richard. 1989. We Are All Smiley's People: Some Observations on Donald Smiley and the Study of Federalism. In *Federalism and Political Community: Essays in Honour of Donald Smiley,* edited by David P. Shugarman and Reg Whitaker. Peterborough: Broadview Press.

Vermeule, Adrian. 2009. System Effects and the Constitution. *Harvard Law Review* 123(1):4–72.

Watts, R.L. 2004. Federal Co-Existence in the Near East: General Introduction. Paper presented at the Jean Nordmann Foundation colloquium on Federalism: Tool for Conflict Management in Multicultural Societies with Regard to the Conflicts in the Near East, Fribourg.

2 Federalism and Democracy: A Critical Reassessment

THOMAS O. HUEGLIN

Ultimately judgments about how democratic the [intergovernmental nego-
tiating] process is depend on the observer's own conceptions of democratic
representation. If he prefers a system in which a majority will be elected and
then govern with relatively few restrictions, the system is undemocratic ... If,
however, he believes that a multiplicity of checkpoints enhances the chances
for rational decision-making and for maximizing consent ... then it is more
democratic.

Simeon (2006, 296)

I want to argue that cooperative and "executive" federalism are dialogical forms of non-unitary governance that provide a more legitimate –
and often more effective – form of political accommodation in complex
plural societies than unitary majoritarian parliamentary democracy. In
doing so, I take issue with the usual complaints about federalism as
undemocratic. These complaints are overdrawn – if not misplaced – because they tend to measure the imperfect reality of federalism against
the idealist assumption that majority rule and parliamentary accountability somehow bring about the rational convergence of a plurality of
particular interests into a reasonable common public good.

The chapter therefore begins with a critique of democratic theory.
In the first section, the intellectual roots of the rational convergence
assumption are traced back to Rousseau's general will and Locke's
representative government. In both instances, there is an untenable presumption of social homogeneity as the precondition for rational convergence. The second and third sections deal with two major theoretical
responses to this presumption: pluralism and civil society theory. In

either case, the legitimate convergence of societal plurality into public reason remains unsuccessful because the dialogue between pressure groups or social movements and the institutions of representative democracy lacks principled institutional design and therefore remains skewed in favour of the more powerful or better organized.

The second part of the chapter then suggests that cooperative or executive federalism may be a closer approximation of rational convergence because it provides an institutional design that pluralizes public reason as a dialogue among equal participants. The fourth section, however, begins with a review of American judiciary federalism as lacking a significant cooperative dimension, suggesting that Canada and the European Union provide more instructive examples. In the fifth section, Canadian executive federalism is re-examined as a form of intergovernmental dialogue that can effectively filter pluralist competition into reasonable public policy. And in the sixth section, the European principle of subsidiarity is suggested as a guide for the rational allocation of powers in plural systems of divided and share rule.

Democracy's Fallacies: Locke and Rousseau

In his *Second Treatise*, Locke provides the formula that has become the bedrock of liberal democratic practice ever since: representative government and majority rule. And in the *Social Contract*, Rousseau conjures up the vision that forever sustains the very possibility of popular sovereignty: the general will of the people as the indispensable foundational vision without which a society, any society, cannot exist in democratic peace and stability. The underlying rationale for both is rational convergence, the assumption that the plurality of selfish human interests can be brought into harmony, that it can find expression as the unified will of the people.

In Rousseau's vision of the general will, this rational convergence is presumed a priori. If only human beings can be brought to search for their real selves (from behind a veil of ignorance about the vicissitudes of their real existences, to borrow from a more modern reincarnation of the same vision), then the general will can come to the fore and prevail. The beauty of this vision is its fallacy. Human beings do not exist a priori. They exist only within the confines of their real lives. Any political theory that does not take into consideration these confines ignores the passion and power driving them. And what goes for the general will in the real world is often nothing more than cheap populism.

The pre-eminent task then is to organize politics in such a way as to constrain passion and power so that, in John Stuart Mill's terms, harm is minimized and happiness is advanced. This is not a matter of human nature. Whether human beings gregariously strive for the good life, as Aristotle thought, or whether man acts as man's wolf, as Hobbes held against him, almost entirely depends on institutional design, and on the organized way of life it provides. To this extent, Marx was entirely right: existence determines consciousness.

Locke has no illusions about rational convergence anchored a priori in the human condition. It needs to be organized. Human beings will consent to forming a "Body Politick," and they will submit to majority rule, but they will do so only if they are represented in such a way as to ensure that their selfish interests cannot be violated, "distinctly," and for each part of the people "in proportion to the assistance, which it affords to the publick" (1980, 82–3). By assistance to the public Locke means taxes. This conditionality for representation and majority rule is Locke's fallacy.

For our appreciation of this fallacy it is entirely irrelevant whether Locke meant to limit representative government to the propertied classes and therefore was, as C.B. Macpherson famously argued, a theorist of possessive individualism. What matters is only the conditionality itself. Following the logic of Locke's argument, majority rule is acceptable, and rational convergence can occur, only when what is represented are homogeneous interests. Anticipating the American slogan of no taxation without representation a century later, Locke reduces the plurality of interests and passions to the one of property protection – however narrowly or widely understood. Then and only then, when the purpose of representative government is reduced to the protection of one common cause, can it be assumed that majority rule becomes synonymous with rational convergence. Only then is it rational to assume, as Hobbes did, that human beings would agree "to conferre all their power and strength upon one Man, or upon one Assembly of men, that may reduce all their Wills, by plurality of voices, unto one Will" (1992, 120).

One can only wonder why it is that Locke's formula has endured for so long when it is patently obvious that the conditionality of social homogeneity is so much at odds with social reality. Three possible explanations come to mind. The first one is that majority rule is practical and, in a purely numerical sense, less offensive than minority rule. But this is not a very satisfactory answer. As Tocqueville already observed, it is the "moral authority of the majority" that sanctions its untouchable status in representative democracy, not just the larger number (2003, 289). More is not only more but is also better. Practicality simply has been given the halo of morality.

The second explanation leads back to Rousseau's general will. Combined with a vision, however nebulous, of an a priori predisposition to rational convergence embedded in human beings, majority rule becomes more palatable. This explanation is even less satisfactory. If there were such a thing as a priori rational convergence, why would one have to resort to majority rule in the first place? The great French dilettante was opposed to it for good reason (1968, 112). The only plausible reason is practicality. We are back to square one.

The third explanation has been preformulated by Tocqueville again: "All parties are ready to acknowledge the rights of the majority because they are all hoping to be able one day to exercise them to their own advantage" (2003, 290). This opens the question of political pluralism as a road to rational convergence.

Pluralism: The Rational Convergence That Never Happened

In 1942, Schumpeter famously debunked the classical doctrine of representative democracy as a normative hoax by postulating what he claimed to be an empirically grounded and therefore realistic definition of the democratic method: "the democratic method is that institutional arrangement for arriving at political decisions in which individuals acquire the power to decide by means of a competitive struggle for the people's votes" (1976, 269).

One may take issue with both Schumpeter's characterization of classical democratic theory and the extent of realism underlying his own definition (Held 1987, 164–85; Schmidt 2000, 181–95). But his definition was realistic enough to send shock waves through the theoretical democracy establishment. Effectively, Schumpeter denied the existence of a direct transmission belt between popular will and government action. Democracy appeared reduced to the periodical election of competing elites. The most sustained answer in rescue of representative democracy came from political pluralism.

Based on their own perception of empirically grounded realism, pluralists argued that the people's will does not manifest itself just in individualized electoral acts, but through the organization of society into interest groups, associations and parties, which in turn exercise – more or less – powerful influence upon government action. Competing elites, in other words, cannot simply get on with business as usual; they have to listen to a plurality of voices before making their selective choices. And, in particular, the parliamentary game of government and opposition will ensure the overall balance of the governmental process.

The classic locus of political pluralism is Dahl's polyarchy: citizens formulate and express their preferences through individual as well as collective action; government action results from weighing these preferences without discrimination (1971, 2). There are two variants in this kind of pluralist theory about how governments are supposed to convert the plurality of preferential pressures into public reason (Wolff 1968, 128–9). One is a "referee theory," according to which the government lays down general rules and then enforces adherence to them. This is the pluralist version of the liberal "night watch" state. It relocates the entire question of rational convergence back into society itself, except, that is, for common agreement about the general rules. For these rules, however, no new convergence mechanism is introduced or added. In fact, by taking on the seemingly neutral role of arbiter, the state does exactly what it pretends not to do: take sides. Its rational objectivity is "spurious," as Marcuse observed, like that of the newscaster who "reports the torture and murder of civil rights workers in the same unemotional tone he uses to describe the stock market or the weather" (1969, 98). Instead of guiding plural action into public reason, the institutions of government only administer the status quo as measured by the normal distribution of behavioural conformism (see Arendt 1998, 41–2).

According to Arendt, the only remedy for this "failure of institutions" still is the plurality of voluntary associations (1972, 102). Their collective action, from pressure group politics all the way to civil disobedience, forces government into action. This points to the other or "vector-sum" theory of pluralism (Wolff 1968, 128–9). Government is seen as the focal point for plural pressures, responding to them by "combining" or "resolving" them "into a single social decision." Yet this second version of pluralist theory only reiterates the classical assumption of rational convergence by means of compromise, without taking into consideration the inequalities of power and influence. Nothing is said about an organized and equally weighted way of deliberation: converging the plurality of voices into inclusive and balanced political action.

Dahl was very much aware of these pluralist pathologies, "stabilizing inequalities, deforming civic consciousness, distorting the public agenda, and alienating final control over the public agenda by the citizen body" (1982, 166). Here we come one step closer to the core of the problem. Dahl's unquestioned assumption is that the end result of the process must be a single, unified public agenda. This constrains inclusive deliberation outside the normal distribution of public opinion. Public reason remains reduced to compromise among those voices, which are, in Tocqueville's words, "ready to acknowledge the rights of the majority because they are all hoping to be able one day to exercise them to their own advantage" (2003, 290).

If this is rational convergence, then it is rational convergence reduced to the sphere of behavioural conformism. What is outside this sphere is not included. We are not a single step ahead of Locke. Arendt suggested that civil disobedience is the logical extension of pluralism under such conditions of democratic institutional failure. This, "politicizing the nonpolitical" (Chambers and Kopstein 2006, 367), also lies at the heart of civil society theory.

Civil Society to the Rescue?

That functioning democracy requires active citizenship beyond the ritual of periodical elections has been a triviality since ancient Greece. In the language of Solon and Pericles, an "idiot" was someone who did not participate in public affairs. Yet the discourse on civil society as the state's vigilant counterpart took on renewed saliency only after 1989, when it became common currency that communism had been brought down by its own citizen movements. Coinciding with a growing awareness about both political disengagement among those with potential majority status under the bell curve of normal distribution and mounting frustration among the outliers with "deviant" behavioural characteristics due to cultural background, gender, sexual orientation, physical disability, or even geographical remoteness, political theory rediscovered the publicly engaged citizen.

Precisely because of the institutional failure of representative majoritarian democracy to provide satisfactory levels of rational convergence, civil society was called upon to fill the void. Defined as a "sphere apart from the state," it would have to engage "in a creative and critical dialogue with the state," generating and sustaining a public sphere in which "ideas, interests, values, and ideologies" would be "voiced and made politically effective" (Chambers and Kopstein 2006, 369).

Chambers and Kopstein have mapped the possible scope and dimension of civil society's public engagement: as associational autonomy apart from the state, as resilient and unconventional opposition against the state, as a separate public sphere in dialogue with the state, as a school of civic engagement in support of the state, as new forms of governance in partnership with the state, and as non-governmental networks of vigilance in the process of globalization beyond the state (ibid., 364–78). While all these possible and existing forms of civic engagement point to organized and active civil society as the indispensable counterpart or even precondition of democracy in progress, little if anything is said about institutional design. As Chambers notes, moving "the heart of democracy away from the vote and into the public sphere" is not meant to and does not create "an alternative to representative democracy." In fact, it creates only a "two-tiered view of democratic politics," with those engaged in formal representative institutions as "strong publics," and those active in informal deliberative civil society as "weak publics." How those two spheres are supposed to interact remains "vague" at best (2003, 311).

Habermas, one of the most prominent voices in the deliberative civil society theory discourse, talks eloquently about a "functioning public sphere" providing for "general accessibility of a deliberative process whose structure grounds an expectation of rationally acceptable results," even though this public sphere is not supposed to "entirely replace conventional procedures for decision-making and political representation" (2004, 546). Civil society as a functioning public sphere, in other words, remains outside the formal political sphere where, when all the deliberations are over, binding decisions are made in the end. Whether or not these binding decisions are rationally acceptable does not depend on any kind of institutional design making civil society part of the process. On the contrary: the assumption is that civil society can play its part only if it remains a resource of vigilance apart from the unaltered institutions of the representative liberal democratic state.

According to Moore, it is particularly this "Habermasian strain" in the civil society debate that "emphasizes the need to distance deliberative processes from political power" (2006, 32). Yet none of the variants surveyed by Chambers and Kopstein indicates any kind of structural integration. Civil society may oppose, dialogue with, or support political power. But so long as its role is to function as a vigilant and critical counterpart of that power, it must not become part of it. If it opposes the state, it defies its procedural norms. If it supports the state, it may become an accomplice to its procedural deficiencies. In between, as

Chambers and Kopstein emphasize, it is the dialogical form of critical interaction with the state that strengthens democracy (2006, 370).

But the problem of rational convergence remains. The responsiveness of the state and its mechanisms of representative democracy entirely depends on how "effective" civil society actors such as social movements are (ibid.). As in pluralism, the dialogue is skewed in favour of the more powerful and better organized. In fact, again, this is not dialogue at all, but only the continuation of pluralist competition with (slightly) other means.

A truly dialogical form of political discourse can be defined instead as a symmetrical and balanced engagement among two or more equal participants. Its outcome is not unity as a victory of the better argument, as Bickford holds against Habermas (1996, 17), but a "higher-order unity, that is, a unity that encompasses both self and other in a situation of mutual understanding" (Lindahl 2008, 109). As Lindahl emphasizes, dialogues are necessarily bounded dialogues in that they "would be pointless" if plurality was not held together by something "deemed to be in common" (ibid., 108). "To conserve plurality, but to achieve a form of unity in which a plurality of perspectives can recognize themselves as being part of a whole," Lindahl asserts, is impossible as an unconstrained dialogue (ibid., 110).

The question of democratic authenticity in complex plural societies, of how a plurality of wills can ever become transformed into unity of action, can now be restated: Rational convergence cannot ever be achieved in full, as a state of democratic uniformity. At the same time, it cannot ever be entirely absent as long as diverse societies exist and continue to exist locally, regionally, nationally, or even globally. Instead, it has to be rescued into the dialogical form itself, as the procedural form "in-between" (ibid., 115) that allows reconciling unity and diversity. This is a different kind of rationality, not that of Descartes, for whom there "there is only one truth concerning any matter" (2005, 121), but that of his early critic Vico, who postulated against him that "human choice, by its nature most uncertain, is made certain and determined by the common sense of men with respect to human needs or utilities" (1984, 63).

This suggests that democratic authenticity is located in the dialogical form itself. It is not enough to engage representative democracy in a dialogue with the needs and aspirations of civil society; the dialogue has to become the principal form itself. One of the traditional political forms of reaching common sense through non-majoritarian dialogue is federalism.

A System without a Precedent

In simplest terms, federalism is generally understood as a political form that divides powers among different levels of government. In more procedural terms, it is also commonly referred to as a system of divided and shared rule. In substance, it is an institutional design meant to provide the constituent members of a larger union with the necessary autonomy to regulate their own distinct affairs and to give them a co-deciding voice in the regulation of general or common affairs by the union government.

We live in a world of deepening sociocultural diversity and ethnic division within and across conventional nation-state boundaries and in a globalizing world with rapidly intensifying socio-economic interdependence. Both are in desperate need of new forms of governance with at least a semblance of legitimacy and stability. One would think that federalism ought to be front and centre in the minds of the political theorist as well as the engineer. Yet one of the most authoritatively voluminous recent publications on political theory, *The Oxford Handbook of Political Theory* (Dryzek, Honig, and Phillips 2006), does not mention it once. And an admittedly cursory review of the ever-expanding literature on globalization and global governance reveals that the situation is not much different there.

One major reason for these omissions is easy to detect. Federalism almost exclusively has been associated with the American model and its image of a highly centralized federal superstate. Exploring possibilities for democratic globalization, for example, Moore rejects federalism because the "fundamental idea of federalism ... is to transform the people into *a* people" – as evidenced by the "central model" of the United States (2006, 26–7).

To invalidate this view by pointing out that American federalism is a case of exceptionalism may be annoyingly trivial. But it is possible to argue that the transformation of the American people into *a* people had little to do with federalism. It came about because of "the clear interlocking of republican with liberal preoccupations" (Held 1987, 65). As James Madison once remarked, the American system was meant to be "a system without a precedent" (Taylor 2009, 185). Madison was referring to the idea of a "compound republic" (*The Federalist*, No. 51), which was meant to undercut the autonomy of distinct communities by multiple checks and balances, not to protect their autonomies (Diamond 1961; Hueglin 2003). Federalism in this scheme played an auxiliary, not a principal role (Beer 1994, 279).

More important, it is also possible to argue that American federalism itself has not become a precedent for subsequent federal unions elsewhere – notwithstanding the fact that key constitutional elements were imitated almost everywhere. The key difference is what LaCroix has called a "judiciary-centred solution to the problem of authority:" The framers "cobbled together" a structure that "refined the ideology of multiplicity," with the supremacy clause as the lynchpin that would require the courts to play the role of "mediating agents between the national and state governments" (2010, 171–2). As Alexander Hamilton wrote: "Controversies between the nation and its members or citizens can only be properly referred to the national tribunals" (*The Federalist*, No. 80).

What sets American federalism apart from most other federations, then, albeit to varying degrees, is the lack of a dialogical form directly built into institutional design and operation. It is the difference between judicial or legal federalism and procedural or intergovernmental federalism. This may come as a surprise, since so much of the American discourse on federalism is couched in terms of intergovernmental relations.

But what passes for intergovernmental relations in the United States typically means "cooperation and coordination" among federal, state, and local bureaucrats "in the implementation of intergovernmental policies and programs." In sharp contrast, the legislative formulation of such policies and programs is characterized by "impositions of federal dictates on state and local governments under what Kincaid has called a regime of "coercive or regulatory federalism" (2011, 37–8).

According to its original design, of course, it was the American Senate that, as the true "federal" institution, was meant to provide for intergovernmental accommodation and balance (*The Federalist*, No. 39). Yet this changed with the XVIIth Amendment, of 1913, which introduced popular senate elections and thus "brought to an end any sense in which senators might have been viewed as representing state interests" (Dinan 2006, 321).

In short, the states, at least as of now and for a variety of historical reasons (Kincaid 2012), do not play any significant role in co-determining federal legislation, and there is no institutionalized or informal system of bargaining that would open up important policy decisions to an intergovernmental dialogue. The states are just one lobby group among many others in Washington, D.C., and are by no means the most important one (Kincaid 2011, 37).

These critical observations are not meant to undervalue the strength and legitimacy of American federalism its own right. The states have been comparatively weak players in this system because at least since the decline of the historical north-south divide they do not represent "distinct societies." And the presidential form with its checks and balances precludes the kind of executive federalism that is facilitated in parliamentary systems where government leaders command majority support and loyalty. A more dialogical form of federalism therefore has to be retrieved from federal experiences elsewhere. Particularly instructive examples are found in Canada and the European Union.

Who Is Dialoguing? Governments v. Societies

Canadian federalism, routinely criticized as malfunctioning, inefficient, and lacking democratic legitimacy, is a remarkable case of federal success, having held together an impossible country for more than 150 years. To keep it that way requires a constant dialogue between the two levels of government. If Canadians are *a* people, then they are so primarily by means of an ongoing conversation.

This is so for a number of reasons. The most obvious one is the cultural divide between Quebec and the rest of (English) Canada. Almost equally important has been the economic divide between the manufacturing central provinces and the resource-based west – to which now must be added the newly discovered oil riches in the east. For these reasons, Canadian provinces have evolved as powerful players in a dramatically decentralizing federal system. Judicial interpretation did play a significant role in this evolution as well, but at least since the 1960s, the Supreme Court of Canada as the "umpire" in intergovernmental disputes has been "overshadowed by the dominance of intergovernmental negotiation and compromise." Dialogue replaced court challenges, which were avoided "except as a tactic of last resort" (Baier 2012, 79, 82).

One may argue, of course, that the dialogue failed spectacularly when it counted most. In the case of Quebec, this dialogue has always been contentious and fractured, and after the 1995 referendum it was replaced by a rare instance of judicial federalism, the 1998 constitutional *Reference re Secession of Quebec*, followed by the federal government's unilateral Clarity Act of 2000. And in the case of the west, attempts to reach common ground on energy policy have been all but abandoned after an ill-fated attempt to forge a national energy program during the

1980s. Indeed, while one of the most authoritative volumes on Canadian federalism in recent years affirms that "the clash between central Canadian and hinterland interests continues" (Stevenson 2012, 32), energy policy as an issue of intergovernmental preoccupation is not mentioned once (Bakvis and Skogstad 2012).

But at least the Quebec story can be told differently: the constitutional reference as well as, but more so than, the Clarity Act actually do not end the conversation but will put the dialogue on separation on a more principled trajectory – should that ever be necessary. More important, the narrow focus on western resources and Quebec nationalism detracts from other areas of dialoguing, negotiation, and compromise, which account for remarkable pan-Canadian success regardless of political grandstanding and constitutional rigidity. The most obvious is social policy.

As only a cursory look at the evolution of social policy and the Canadian welfare state more generally reveals, and despite all duly noted deficiencies, Canadian intergovernmentalism has been creative, productive, and successful (Banting 2012). The results have been rationally acceptable in large part precisely because of the intergovernmental "institutional filters through which wider political and economic pressures flow" (ibid., 161). It is no exaggeration to say that the kind of federation Canada is today has been shaped far more, and far more constructively, by intergovernmental dialogue than by majoritarian grandstanding in the nation's parliament.

The dialogue predominantly takes place among governments. For this reason, Cairns once argued that Canadian federalism might serve governmental rather than societal interests (1977). It is an argument that has overshadowed the Canadian debate on federalism for more than three decades, and it has done more harm than good. Of course, it contains a valid argument and concern: what is known in Canada as "executive federalism" – meetings of first ministers making deals behind closed doors – may be driven by political expediency rather than societal need. But the argument has contributed to quick dismissals of executive federalism as undemocratic instead of focusing on efforts to make it more democratic. Given the path-dependent inevitability of executive federalism in Canada (Brock 1995), this is unfortunate. As Papillon and Simeon (2004) have argued, despite their pivotal role in shaping the federation, first ministers' conferences in Canada have remained its weakest institutional link.

It is actually quite unclear what undemocratic means in the context of executive federalism. The often invoked catchword is accountability. The first ministers in the Canadian federation are elected as government leaders accountable to their elected parliaments. If these parliaments routinely pass whatever deal is put before them, then this is a problem of majoritarian democracy, not of federalism. In comparison with the pathologies of pluralist pressure politics as well as with the uneven and unstructured access of civil society groups, the intergovernmental process almost appears to be a poster child of principled discourse and equality. And if the question can be raised of whether the governments of Canadian federalism properly represent their societies rather than selfish power interests, then the same question must also be asked about the relationship between leadership and rank and file in pressure groups, civil society, and lobby groups more generally. By comparison, the governments of federalism at least remain tied to formal structures of democratic control more directly.

The pluralist chorus not only sings with a strong upper-class accent, as a former president of the American Political Science Association once put it (Schattschneider 1960), it also makes for a cacophony of infinite voices. What federalism provides as an institutional design is that it bundles the infinite variety of voices into a limited number of choices. The final outcome is more likely than unfiltered pluralist pressure politics to produce "rationally acceptable results" (Habermas 2004, 546).

One just needs to compare health care in the United States and in Canada. In the United States, the recent health care reform by the Obama administration was driven by everything but federalism – unless one accepts, as Americans do, that it constitutes meaningful federalism when representatives of the National Governors Association or the National Conference of State Legislatures, purportedly "among the most important vehicles" for the advancement of state interests, "occasionally testify at congressional hearings or draft letters to congressional leaders expressing state concerns" (Dinan 2011, 400). The result was everything but rationally acceptable. Challenged as unconstitutional by three state-initiated lawsuits with support from twenty-eight states as well as by some twenty private legal actions, the matter eventually ended up where it always ends up: before the Supreme Court (Joondeph, 2011).

In Canada, on the other hand, universal health care evolved through an intergovernmental process of ongoing deliberation. Surely one can see this process as one of competing governmental interests. Surely, however, one can also see it as that kind of procedural "in-between," mediating, as it were, between the plural voices of people and Canada's fragile identity as *a* people. The comparison again is not meant to demonstrate or prove the superiority of Canadian over American federalism. Canada simply is a federation with a more powerful centrifugal dynamic, which necessitates a more collaborative style of governance. The comparative point is that this intergovernmental dimension in Canada points to an alternative model of federalism more attuned to fragmented societal realities elsewhere.

Democracy is by definition a unitary concept: somehow the plurality of wills must be transformed into unity of decision and action. Majoritarian democratic theory assumes that this can be achieved by the weight of numbers. Pluralist democratic theory does not change this assumption. It only explains how the plurality of wills is transmitted by means of organized interest competition. Civil society theory in turn seeks to add voices outside the institutionalized political process.

The intergovernmental dimension of federalism bundles voices and thus both reduces and channels pluralist competition. This is a structural argument that meets Madison's idea of the compound republic from the other end, so to speak. Madison thought that majorities had to be broken up by a multilevel plural design of institutions. Federalism was to have a de-concentrating effect on society. But under conditions of pluralist competition, the institutions of federalism become "institutional filters" for that competition (Banting 2012, 161). Federalism has a concentrating effect on society. The formulation of public reason is left neither to the anarchical conditions of pluralist pressure politics, nor to a tyranny of the majority. Instead, the process of rational convergence is located somewhere in the in-between.

Whether that in-between is primarily occupied by governmental interests or, as famously proposed by Livingston (1952) and reaffirmed by Erk more recently (2008), functioning federalism needs strong sociological underpinnings, is actually a rather moot point. First of all, the question of whether governments represent people in more than just a formal sense can be raised for all systems and regimes, parliamentary democracy included. So it is not really more of a problem in a federal system than in any other. In fact, I would argue that the Canadian disaffection with executive federalism primarily stems from a historically unfounded and rather naïve faith in the democratic virtues of the parliamentary system.

Secondly and more important, form does not always follow function. It may well be that houses should be built in such a way as to serve best their intended purposes or functions. But many people buy homes that are available or affordable at the time and then adapt to their design or form in practical or even ingenious ways. Following recent theories of historical institutionalism (Broschek 2012), Canadian federalism had its beginning at a critical juncture, when economic modernization and political stability were not possible without federalism. The constitutional form Canadians gave it was a combination of Westminster parliamentarianism with a weak government-appointed senate as a second chamber and a division of powers that, contrary to original intentions, played into the hands of provincial governments. It turned out to be a constitutional form that only poorly served the diversity as well as unity needs of the country. But by following a course of path-dependent evolution, Canadians learned to work around the constitutional form by engaging in an ongoing intergovernmental dialogue.

A standard argument in the arsenal of those who dislike executive federalism is that it dominates Canadian politics only because the senate, appointed by the federal government on a wildly uneven regional rather than equal provincial basis, fails to give the provinces an effective voice in federal legislation. This is the interstate v. intrastate federalism argument (Smiley and Watts 1985, 4).

However, this may be another argument misguided by naïve assumptions about what a strong second chamber can accomplish. If the societal dimension of federalism is shallow, or overridden by strong sentiments of nationalism, as in the American case, the second chamber will likely become an additional forum of national policy formation. If they are deep, as in Canada, a strong second chamber may render the national process of policy formation dysfunctional. The German *Bundesrat*, arguably the most successful or perhaps even the only successful case of strong intrastate federalism, "works" because regional divisions are not particularly deep – although they have gained depth since reunification, and because of Germany's distinctive system of "administrative federalism" (Hueglin and Fenna 2006, 62): the *Länder* administer most federal laws and therefore have an interest in passing legislation in a timely and effective manner. Under conditions of deep diversity such as ethnic divisions, or for the purpose of multinational governance in an age of globalization, in any case it seems that intergovernmental dialogue must inevitably be an essential part of the institutional design.

The argument is not that executive federalism as practised in Canada did not have the kinds of problem its critics have been quick to point out ever since Smiley put it authoritatively for them: secrecy behind closed doors, low levels of citizens' participation in public affairs, weakened government accountability, territorial bias regarding the public agenda, as well as government growth and conflict (1979). The argument is only that it is an illusion to think that these are problems only or even predominantly associated with executive federalism. In fact, one may distil from some of the literature the impression that the root cause of all the problems attributed to executive federalism lies rather with the unreformed deficiencies of the parliamentary system itself (Franks 1999; Cameron 2004). And while it is entirely useful to think about how executive federalism might be complemented by inter-parliamentary institutions of cooperation in a federal system (Cameron 2004), it seems equally if not more important to focus on democratizing mechanisms of the intergovernmental process itself (Simmons 2008).

A distinction needs to be made between the accusation that executive federalism is undemocratic and the accusation that it is not democratic enough. The former accusation is untenable. Federalism is more than just a constitutional division of powers. It also and essentially rests on the entirely democratic assumption that spatial collectivities in a larger union have a right to pursue their particular collective interests and, in doing so, to be represented by their democratically elected governments. The intergovernmental dialogue provides an entirely legitimate forum for the articulation and cooperative coordination of such interests. The democratic problem is not so much how to conduct that dialogue as it is what it ought to be about. Procedural transparency and more citizens' inclusion does not lead to a more rational convergence of diverse interests into common public reason unless there is a more principled understanding, among societies as well as governments, about what in fact ought to be particular and what ought to be common or universal in a federal system of divided and shared rule.

What's the Dialoguing About?

So far, so good: cooperative federalism can provide a successful formula of how to transform the infinity of plural voices into a more limited set of choices. Of course, the same also can be said about unitary political systems so long as a cooperative rather than an adversarial political culture prevails (Lijphart 1999, 275–300). But the point is that such a political culture cannot be taken for granted in increasingly complex plural societies, let alone in the context of globalization with its demands for new mechanisms of stable and efficient governance.

There is at least one characteristic of federalism that unitary systems of any kind cannot emulate. Federalism lowers the threshold for rational convergence by pluralizing what is rationally acceptable in the first place. It does so by constitutionally dividing powers among different levels of government allowing for sub-national policy variation.

This, too, has been criticized more often than not, either as too rigid, too entangled, or inefficient government duplication more generally. Moreover, the historical pattern of power distribution, centralizing economic and security policies while leaving social and cultural policies to the constituent member units, has become obsolete, at least in part. In an age of globalization and migratory mobility, social policy, and income security in particular, ought to be seen as general concerns for all citizens alike and hence be treated as such, by national or even transnational policy standards. On the other hand, given the local and regional impact of economic globalization, trade and commerce powers might become more decentred.

Constitutions are hard to change, and they should be, because they reflect a carefully negotiated original agreement among the constituent members of a federation. In some of these federations, notably the United States, constitutional change is well nigh impossible, and judicial review remains the only option for systemic adaptations to time and circumstance. But even in federations where constitutional change happens quite regularly, such as Germany, wholesale efforts at recalibrating the division of powers have met with only limited success (Scharpf 2009). In Canada, again, the "inappropriateness of the constitution to contemporary problems and the inflexibility of amendment" (Simeon 2006, 41) have been the principal reasons why federalism turned to extra-constitutional intergovernmental agreements, classically described and analysed by Richard Simeon as federal-provincial diplomacy.

This does not mean that federal constitutions have lost their significance. They still remain the principal expression of a principled commitment to plurality and power sharing among equal partners. This is precisely what distinguishes federalism from all other forms of pluralist and multilevel governance. But the systemic nature of federalism has undergone change. What Simeon described in 1972 as an "add-on" to constitutional federalism (ibid., 327), has now taken on systemic character in its own right. In line with a "dominant tide" in modern federalism more generally, Canada has moved, in the words of the Supreme Court of Canada, "toward a more flexible view of federalism that accommodates overlapping jurisdiction and encourages intergovernmental cooperation" (*Reference re Securities Act* 2011, 57).

The dominant tide that Canada's highest court has discerned may be only a belated recognition that constitutions are "incomplete" original contracts and therefore are "important not because they solve the assignment problem, but because they structure the ongoing intergovernmental contracting process" (Rodden 1999, 37, 38). What has changed, then, is not so much the underlying rationale and dynamic of Canadian federalism as the perception of it. Canadian federalism is no longer seen as a predominantly constitutional design based on power separation guaranteed by judicial review. Instead, a more procedural perception of federalism is gaining ground, characterized by intergovernmental bargaining. It therefore may be appropriate to speak of a gradual transition from constitutional to treaty federalism (Hueglin 2000). And insofar as the legal separation of powers in a complicated world of sociocultural as well as socio-economic diversity no longer is as simple as it appeared to the American framers or Canadian founding fathers several centuries ago, the Canadian case may in fact gain model character for federalism more generally.

Not quite yet, though. What Canadians likely object to most about executive federalism is its unprincipled exercise: "Rolling the dice," one former prime minister put it in one of his more unfortunate statements. When it comes to negotiations about fundamental issues of power and authority, where policy needs are inevitably intertwined with political expediency – the desire to get re-elected, the philosophical recourse to dialogue as the procedural form-in-between quickly rings hollow. Majoritarianism and legal constitutionalism at least have the advantage of principled certainty. But if the former falls short of legitimately accommodating diversity, and the latter fails to adjust to time and circumstance, the principles themselves they are based on lose meaning. A principled form of intergovernmentalism then becomes federalism's last best stand. But can such a principle be found?

The Meech Lake Accord of 1987, a quid pro quo of recognizing Quebec's distinct place in the federation in return for modest upgrades to provincial powers, including a constitutional veto and participation in senate appointments, was the most spectacular failure of Canadian intergovernmentalism. The political classes, urged on by academics as well as a disgruntled public, meant to do better in a second round by resorting to more inclusive and direct methods of democracy: more public consultation and a national referendum. But the Charlottetown

Agreement of 1992 failed just as miserably. Just what the principle was this second deal was supposed to be based on remained largely a mystery to experts and public alike.

Yet federalism provides such a principle, and it is in fact one of the oldest principles of political practice in human history. It is called subsidiarity. This may come as a surprise again. The idea and principle of subsidiarity is generally known only in the context of the European Union, which must be regarded as an unconventional federation at best. Moreover, even though subsidiarity is now recognized as a procedural centrepiece in European Union governance, it has remained a contested concept because it seems to suggest only *how* powers ought to be assigned instead of assigning them with legal certainty (Peterson 1996). In more conventional conceptualizations of federalism based on the American model, it is a concept largely unknown if not outright alien (Levy 2007).

In fact, this is not so. When the American framers crafted the first modern federal constitution in 1787, they very much thought about how to divide powers. The idea was to assign to the federal government economic and security powers common to all American citizens. In turn, they left most social powers to be dealt with by the state governments according to local tradition and circumstance. This pattern of dividing powers was repeated in the creation of most federations following the American example. The underlying rationale is nothing other than subsidiarity: while centralizing powers over matters held at the time to be common to all, the constituent members of a federation should retain all powers necessary for the regulation of their own affairs in particular ways. However, when this formula was written in constitutional stone, it was transformed from a concept of procedural guidance into one of legal certainty.

Unwittingly, the American framers drew on a tradition most of them rejected, the tradition of governance in the Holy Roman Empire of the Middle Ages. When the Frankish King Charles (Charlemagne) was crowned emperor in 800, the other kings contested his and his successors' supremacy claims. Around 1200, the formula *rex imperator in regno suo* was developed to give expression to the reality of a divided and overlapping power relationship between emperor and other territorial rulers: a king was to have as much power and authority over his realm as the emperor had over the whole. This is exactly what Madison rejected as "imbecility in the government" (*The Federalist* No. 20): the idea of shared sovereignty.

But it is an imbecility only as a concept of legal certainty. For mediaeval rulers, it was a concept of prudent political practice. The emperor knew and understood that governance of the "whole" required a cooperative dialogue. Thus, in 1244, when Emperor Frederic II summoned the imperial princes to a council in the upper Italian city of Verona, he did so by using, perhaps for the first time, an old Roman law formula, which gave a principled expression of when and how shared sovereignty should be exercised: *quod omnes tangit, ab omnibus approbetur* – what pertains to all must be approved by all (Hofmann 1974).

At least implicitly, these two formulas contain the essence of subsidiarity, a "presumption of power allocation at the lowest possible level" (Hueglin 2007, 202) based on a conceptual distinction between what is particular in a plural polity and what is common to all. A federalist dialogue – whether designed in interstate or intrastate fashion – is the appropriate mode for making this decision on an ongoing basis according to time and circumstance. This is why subsidiarity belongs in the toolbox of procedural or treaty federalism rather than legal or constitutional federalism. The question is whether it is a tool that can be operationalized constructively.

In Europe, after initial scepticism, subsidiarity as the key procedural mechanism for Union governance is no longer in dispute. Article 5/3 of the post-Lisbon Consolidated Version of the Treaty on European Union now reads: "Under the principle of subsidiarity, in areas which do not fall within its exclusive competence, the Union shall act only if and in so far as the objectives of the proposed action cannot be sufficiently achieved by the Member States, either at central level or at regional and local level, but can rather, by reason of the scale or effects of the proposed action, be better achieved at Union level" (*Official Journal* 2010). As stipulated in Protocol No. 2, appended to the Lisbon Treaty, all draft legislative acts under the principle of subsidiarity now require wide consultation among all institutionalized actors, including the national parliaments. Draft acts have to contain detailed assessments of their quantitative and qualitative impact upon member states, regions, and citizens. The compatibility of each act with the principle of subsidiarity requires formal approval by the Council (55%) and the European Parliament (majority of votes). Whereas Parliament, Council, Commission, and member states can appeal all legislative acts before the European Court of Justice for infringement of the principle of subsidiarity, the Committee of the Regions can do so in matters where it has a right of consultation. As the court has wisely declared in one of its landmark decisions, it cannot and will not adjudicate the political wisdom of a legislative act itself, but it can and will render judgment as to whether "the relevant procedural rules have been complied with" (European Court of Justice 1998).

In Canada, such elaborate procedural specifications are far from intergovernmental reality, although one of the most authoritative compendiums of constitutional law has long since mentioned subsidiarity as a "guideline for the division of responsibilities," offering "some useful ways of thinking about the Constitution" (Hogg 1988, 112). At least the Supreme Court of Canada has taken notice. In a 2001 decision it declared that "matters of governance are often examined through the lens of the principle of subsidiarity. This is the proposition that law-making and implementation are often best achieved at a level of government that is not only effective, but also closest to the citizens affected and thus most responsive to their needs, to local distinctiveness, and to population diversity" (*114957 Canada Ltée (Spraytech, Societé d'arrosage) v. Hudson (Town). 2001*, 3).

In doing so, the court at least echoes what lies at the core of the European understanding of subsidiarity: the adjudication of who should do what in a federal polity is not just a matter of legal power separation but follows from a sorting principle about who should do how much of what according to time and circumstance. This in turn requires an elaborate process of deliberation, consultation, and justification. By no means does this mean that the principle of subsidiarity is a new miracle formula for the rational convergence of plural interests into common public reason, or that the European Union should be regarded as a model federation with legitimacy superior to conventional federal states or even parliamentary democracies.

Certainly, concerns over a democratic deficit apply to the European Union as much as to other systems of executive governance, and perhaps more so, since the technocratic and regulatory apparatus of the Union is even more removed from "contestation for political leadership and argument over the direction of the policy agenda" (Follesdal and Hix 2006, 534). But it is precisely here that the subsidiarity mechanism provides an "enhanced inter-institutional dialogue" (Horsley 2012, 269), which can play "a promising role in structuring the democratic process" (Barber 2005, 315). In this way, subsidiarity can be appreciated as a procedural principle by which the intergovernmental dialogue becomes more accountable to public reason and even to judicial review.

Federal-Provincial Diplomacy – Another Postscript

As Richard Simeon argued in his classic 1972 study, *Federal-Provincial Diplomacy*, "what is democratic and what is not is mostly in the eye of the beholder (2006, 296). In a country like Canada, where "social and institutional patterns ... facilitate a pattern of federal-provincial relations" (ibid., 42), the parliamentary majoritarian exercise of democracy is of limited normative value. To the extent that these patterns become paradigmatic in a globalizing world of overlapping and conflicting identities, it is Canadian executive federalism that may gain model status, because in such a world, to quote Habermas more fully, "the democratic procedure no longer draws its legitimizing force only, indeed not even predominantly, from political participation and the expression of political will, but rather from the general accessibility of a deliberative process whose structure grounds an expectation of rationally acceptable results" (2004, 546).

Already in 1972, Simeon suggested as much, and he pointed to the European Union – then called the Common Market – as a particularly promising case for comparative insight (2006, 300). He also gave some indication of where the comparative value of the Canadian case is situated: in an intergovernmental process supplanting the government and opposition scheme of conventional democracies as well as the exclusive reliance on constitutional prescriptions; and in the possibilities of effective conflict management including the mitigation of ethnic conflict in particular (ibid., 278–97).

In his postscript to the 2006 edition of *Federal-Provincial Diplomacy*, Simeon raised the question whether the persistence of the social and institutional patterns he had first analyzed a generation earlier might warrant "a fundamental rethinking of our federal structure, in the division of powers, fiscal arrangements, and in the larger political framework" (332). Yet the question can also be raised of whether a hidden theme in his study, and part of its enduring legacy, is a need to rethink democracy.

REFERENCES

Arendt, Hannah. 1972. *Crises of the Republic*. New York: Harcourt Brace Jovanovich.

Arendt, Hannah. 1998. *The Human Condition*. Chicago: University of Chicago Press.

Baier, Gerald. 2012. The Courts, the Constitution, and Dispute Resolution. In *Canadian Federalism*, edited by Herman Bakvis and Grace Skogstad. Don Mills: Oxford University Press.

Bakvis, Herman, and Grace Skogstad. 2008. *Canadian Federalism*. Don Mills: Oxford University Press.

Banting, Keith G. 2012. The Three Federalisms Revisited: Social Policy and Intergovernmental Decision-Making. In *Canadian Federalism*, edited by Herman Bakvis and Grace Skogstad. Don Mills: Oxford University Press.

Barber, N.W. 2005. The Limited Modesty of Subsidiarity. *European Law Journal* 11(3):308–25.

Beer, Samuel. 1994. *To Make a Nation: The Rediscovery of American Federalism* Cambridge: Harvard University Press.

Bickford, Susan. 1996. *The Dissonance of Democracy*. Ithaca: Cornell University Press.

Brock, Kathy L. 1995. The End of Executive Federalism? In *New Trends in Canadian Federalism*, edited by François Rocher and Miriam Smith. Peterborough: Broadview Press.

Broschek, Jörg. 2012. Historical Institutionalism and the Varieties of Federalism in Germany and Canada. *Publius: The Journal of Federalism* 42(4):662–87.

Cairns, Alan C. 1977. The Governments and Societies of Canadian Federalism. *Canadian Journal of Political Science* 10(4):695–725.

Cameron, David. 2004. Inter-Legislative Federalism. In *Reconsidering the Institutions of Canadian Federalism*, edited by J. Peter Meekison, Hamish Telford, and Harvey Lazar. Kingston: Institute of Intergovernmental Relations.

Chambers, Simone. 2003. Deliberative Democratic Theory. *Annual Review of Political Science* 6:307–26.

Chambers, Simone, and Jeffrey Kopstein. 2006. Civil Society and the State. In *The Oxford Handbook of Political Theory*, edited by John S. Dryzek, Bonnie Honig, and Anne Phillips. Oxford: Oxford University Press.

Dahl, Robert A. 1982. *Dilemmas of Pluralist Democracy*. New Haven: Yale University Press.

Dahl, Robert A. 1971. *Polyarchy*. New Haven: Yale University Press.

Descartes, René. [1637] 2005. Discourse on the Method. In *The Philosophical Writings of Descartes*. Vol. 1. Cambridge: Cambridge University Press.

Diamond, Martin. 1961. The Federalist's View of Federalism. In *Essays in Federalism*, edited by George C.S. Benson. Claremont: Institute for Studies in Federalism.

Dinan, John. 2006. United States of America. In *Legislative, Executive, and Judicial Governance in Federal Countries*, edited by Katy Le Roy and Cheryl Saunders. Montreal: McGill-Queen's University Press.

Dinan, John. 2011. Shaping Health Care Reform: State Government Influence in the Patient Protection and Affordable Care Act. *Publius: The Journal of Federalism* 41(3):395–420.

Dryzek, John S., Bonnie Honig, and Anne Phillips, eds. 2006. *The Oxford Handbook of Political Theory*. Oxford: Oxford University Press.

Erk, Jan. 2008. *Explaining Federalism*. London: Routledge.

Federalist, The. 2001. Edited by George Carey and James McClellan. Indianapolis: Liberty Fund.

Follesdal, Andreas, and Simon Hix. 2006. Why There Is a Democratic Deficit in the EU: A Response to Majone and Moravcsik. *Journal of Common Market Studies* 44(3):533–62.

Franks, C.E.S. 1999. Parliament, Intergovernmental Relations and National Unity. Working Paper. Kingston: Institute of Intergovernmental Relations.

Habermas, Jürgen. 2004. The Postnational Constellation. In *The Global Transformation Reader*, edited by David Held and Anthony McGrew. Cambridge: Polity Press.

Held, David. 1987. *Models of Democracy*. Stanford: Stanford University Press.

Hobbes, Thomas. [1651] 1992. *Leviathan*. Cambridge: Cambridge University Press.

Hoffmann, Hasso. 1974. *Repräsentation*. Berlin: Duncker & Humblot.

Hogg, Peter. 1988. *Constitutional Law of Canada*. Student Edition. Scarborough: Carswell.

Horsley, Thomas. 2012. Subsidiarity and the European Court of Justice: Missing Pieces in the Subsidiarity Jigsaw? *Journal of Common Market Studies* 50(2):267–82.

Hueglin, Thomas O. 2000. From Constitutional to Treaty Federalism: A Comparative Perspective. *Publius: The Journal of Federalism* 30(4):137–52.

Hueglin, Thomas O. 2003. Federalism at the Crossroads: Old Meanings, New Significance. *Canadian Journal of Political Science* 36(2):275–94.

Hueglin, Thomas O. 2007. The Principle of Subsidiarity: Tradition – Practice – Relevance. In *Constructing Tomorrow's Federalism*, edited by Ian Peach. Winnipeg: University of Manitoba Press.

Hueglin, Thomas O., and Alan Fenna. 2006. *Comparative Federalism*. Toronto: University of Toronto Press.

Joondeph, Bradley W. 2011. Federalism and Health Care Reform: Understanding the States. Challenges to the Patient Protection and Affordable Care Act. *Publius: The Journal of Federalism* 41(3):447–70.

Kincaid, John. 2011. Political Coercion and Administrative Cooperation in U.S. Intergovernmental Relations. In *Varieties of Federal Governance*, edited by Rekha Saxena. New Delhi: Cambridge University Press.

Kincaid, John. 2012. The Rise of Coercive Federalism in the United States:

Dynamic Change with Little Formal Reform. In *The Future of Australian Federalism*, edited by Gabrielle Appleby, Nicholas Aroney, and Thomas John. Cambridge: Cambridge University Press.

LaCroix, Alison L. 2010. *The Ideological Origins of American Federalism*. Cambridge: Harvard University Press.

Levy, Jacob T. 2007. Federalism, Liberalism, and the Separation of Loyalties. *American Political Science Review* 101(3):459–77.

Lijphart, Arend. 1999. *Patterns of Democracy*. New Haven: Yale University Press, 1999.

Lindahl, Hans. 2008. Democracy, Political Reflexivity and Bounded Dialogues: Reconsidering the Monism-Pluralism Debate. In *Public Law and Politics*, edited by Emilios Christodoulidis and Stephen Tierney. Aldershot: Ashgate.

Livingston, William S. 1952. A Note on the Nature of Federalism. *Political Science Quarterly* 67(1):81–95.

Locke, John. [1690] 1980. *Second Treatise of Government*. Indianapolis: Hacket.

Marcuse, Herbert. 1969. Repressive Tolerance. In *A Critique of Pure Tolerance*, edited by Robert P. Wolff, Barrington Moore Jr, and Herbert Marcuse. Boston: Beacon Press.

Moore, Margaret. 2006. Globalization and Democratization: Institutional Design for Global Institutions. *Journal of Social Philosophy* 37(1):21–43.

Official Journal of the European Union 53. 2010. C 83. Available at http://eurlex.europa.eu/JOHtml.do?uri=OJ:C:2010:083:SOM:EN:HTML

Papillon, Martin, and Richard Simeon. 2004. The Weakest Link? First Ministers' Conferences in Canadian Intergovernmental Relations. In *Reconsidering the Institutions of Canadian Federalism*, edited by J. Peter Meekison, Hamish Telford and Harvey Lazar. Kingston: Institute of Intergovernmental Relations.

Peterson, John. 1996. Subsidiarity: A Definition to Suit Any Vision? *Parliamentary Affairs* 47(1):117–32.

Rodden, Jonathan. 1999. *Hamilton's Paradox: The Promise and Perils of Fiscal Federalism*. Cambridge: Cambridge University Press.

Rousseau, Jean-Jacques. [1762] 1968. *The Social Contract*. London: Penguin.

Scharpf, Fritz W. 2009. *Föderalismusreform*. Frankfurt: Campus.

Schattschneider, E. E. 1960. *The Semisovereign People: A Realist's View of Democracy in America*. New York: Holt, Rinehart and Winston.

Schmidt, Manfred. 2000. *Demokratietheorien*. Opladen: Leske + Budrich.

Schumpeter, Joseph A. 1976. *Capitalism, Socialism & Democracy*. London: Allen & Unwin.

Simeon, Richard. [1972] 2006. *Federal-Provincial Diplomacy*. Toronto: University of Toronto Press.

Simmons, Julie. 2008. Democratizing Executive Federalism: The Role of Non-

Governmental Actors in Intergovernmental Agreements. In *Canadian Federalism*, edited by Herman Bakvis and Grace Skogstad. Don Mills: Oxford University Press.

Smiley, Donald V. 1979. An Outsider's Observations of Federal-Provincial Relations Among Consenting Adults. In *Confrontation and Collaboration: Intergovernmental Relations in Canada Today*, edited by Richard Simeon. Toronto: The Institute of Public Administration of Canada.

Smiley, Donald V., and Ronald L. Watts. 1985. *Intrastate Federalism in Canada*. Toronto: University of Toronto Press.

Stevenson, Garth. 2012. The Political Economy of Regionalism and Federalism. In *Canadian Federalism*, edited by Herman Bakvis and Grace Skogstad. Don Mills: Oxford University Press.

Taylor, Quentin. 2009. "A System Without a Precedent": The Federalism of the *Federalist* Papers. In *The Ashgate Research Companion to Federalism*, edited by Ann Ward and Lee Ward. Farnham: Ashgate.

Tocqueville, Alexis de. [1835;1840] 2003. *Democracy in America*. London: Penguin.

Vico, Giambattista. 1984. *The New Science of Giambattista Vico*. Ithaca: Cornell University Press.

Wolff, Robert P. 1968. *The Poverty of Liberalism*. Boston: Beacon Press.

COURT RULINGS

114957 Canada Ltée (Spraytech, Société d'arrosage) v. Hudson (Town). 2001. 2001 SCC 40. Avalable at http://scc.lexum.org/en/2001/2001scc40/2001scc40.html

Reference re Securities Act. 2011. 2011 SCC 66. Available at http://scc.lexum.org/en/2011/2011scc66/2011scc66.html

United Kingdom of Great Britain and Northern Ireland v. Council of the European Union. 1998. European Court of Justice. (1998), C-150/94. Available at http://www.dkrnet.de/data/curia/jurispr/89–94/numdoc=61994J0150&lg=EN.htm

3 Is There a Political Culture of Federalism in Canada? Charting an Unexplored Territory

FRANÇOIS ROCHER AND PATRICK FAFARD

What is the optimal way to study and compare federations? For the most part they are analysed by focusing on how well federal institutions work in light of the division of powers, the degree of intergovernmental collaboration or competition, and, ultimately, the ability of multiple governments to govern effectively. Nevertheless, in order for federations to operate in a manner that results in policies and programs that are considered fair and just by both citizens and the federal partners, they must be evaluated and understood in light of the values they promote and their ultimate purpose: balancing self-rule and shared rule. The analysis of the operation of federal institutions and processes must be linked to an analysis of citizens' understandings of federalism and, perhaps most important, citizen preferences about the nature of the federal regime, not just the policies and programs that governments choose. Richard Simeon once suggested that the analysis of the success or failure of a federation "also has a normative dimension. Overall, federations need to be judged in terms of how well they promote – or obstruct – democracy, social justice, and the recognition and accommodation of difference in divided societies" (2011, 210). Thus, in addition to analysis of the division of powers and the institutionalization and effectiveness of intergovernmental relations, the strength or weakness of the political culture – that is, the values, norms and views underpinning citizens' views of federalism – is important in evaluating and comparing federations.

Yet much of the scholarly literature on federalism and federations has a strong institutionalist bias. This bias is particularly evident in Canada, where, as Richard Simeon and others have observed, a generation of scholars was preoccupied by the challenge of restructuring the federation, up to and including formal constitutional amendment in 1982 (Fafard and Rocher 2009; Simeon 2002). There has been a resurgence of late of the study of the implications of federalism for public policy, echoing the early contribution of Richard Simeon himself (Simeon 1972; Wallner 2010; White 2002). The focus remains on the institutions of federalism, however, either as a dependent or an independent variable. This institutionalist bias is also marked in the comparative study of federalism, where analysis often remains focused on the impact and reform of federal institutions and on processes of intergovernmental relations (Hueglin and Fenna 2006; Papillon 2008; Watts 1999). Notable exceptions to this trend are works that focus on the federal idea (Burgess 2006; Gagnon 2008; Rocher 2009; Hueglin 2011; Fafard and Rocher 2011).

This institutionalist bias and the associated neglect of the sociological dimensions of federalism and, in particular, the political culture of federations is particularly important when multinational federations such as Belgium, Switzerland, and, of course, Canada are considered. Accommodating and reflecting the multinational reality of Canada is at the heart of the Canadian federal project. For students of comparative federalism, it is precisely the multinational dimension that draws the most attention, and rightly so.

Thus, this chapter gives sustained consideration to what Simeon has called "cultural and attitudinal factors" that shape Canadian federalism. Specifically, it offers a detailed consideration of the existence, strength, and implications of a federal political culture in Canada. The chapter begins with a brief review of the literature on regional political cultures in the Canadian context and a somewhat longer discussion of the idea of a "culture of federalism." It reviews how the concept of a culture of federalism has been developed in Europe and elsewhere in order to offer a more complete account of the nature and dynamics of federalism in different countries and to propose a working definition of a culture of federalism. Following this discussion, the chapter operationalizes the concept of a culture of federalism, using the results of a public opinion survey conducted by the authors in 2007 to assess the existence, strength, and characteristics of the political culture of federalism in Canada. A short conclusion summarizes the paper and suggests areas for further research and reflection.

What Is a "Political Culture of Federalism?"

In an important and relatively early example of political culture research in Canada, Richard Simeon and David Elkins demonstrated that

Canadian provinces had distinct political cultures (Simeon and Elkins 1974). Political cultures varied across provinces in concert with other socio-demographic factors such as class, employment, and immigration status (Elkins and Simeon 1980; Henderson 2004). More recent analyses have debated whether regional political cultures in Canada have become more or less distinctive over time (Simeon 2002; Wiseman 2007).

While these analyses tell us much about the nature and diversity of political cultures within the Canadian federation, they pay surprisingly little attention to beliefs and attitudes *about* federalism and federations, or, what others have called the political culture of federalism. To be sure, Simeon and others have acknowledged the importance of public opinion and the social context in shaping governments' preferences as they enter into intergovernmental negotiations (Simeon 2006, 233–6; Simeon and Robinson 1990), but work on the views and values that underpin Canadians' understandings of their federation remains scant. This reflects, to some extent, the more general pattern among political scientists who share an interest in federalism. It also reflects the reality that the presence and indeed the strength of a culture of federalism are hard to measure and in "an unexplored area, a blank that we have tentatively called *a federal political culture*" (Duchachek 1987, 346). It is this relatively unexplored territory that is our focus in this chapter.

The political culture of federalism – as the modes of representation of federalism, its ideational dimensions – shapes how political actors and citizens perceive the federal political regime and defines their preferences in a federal context. The notion of culture refers to a set of ways of thinking and of grasping reality and is constituted by norms, values, and codes which contribute to guiding actions as well as developing judgments regarding different social objects. Culture, thus defined, is expressed through symbols and preferences, both individual and collective. It contributes to enhancing communication and to strengthening solidarity within a group. It helps in defining expectations, wishes, and needs. In doing so, it allows for a "meaning" with regard to the preferences and behaviours that must be shared. It is in this spirit that the notion of "political culture" can be understood as a "set of attitudes, beliefs and sentiments which give order and meaning to a political process and which provide the underlying assumptions and rules that govern behavior in the political system. It encompasses both the political ideals and the operating norms of a polity" (*International Encyclopedia of the Social Sciences* 1968). The concept of a political culture of federalism can be derived from this definition, since some of these attitudes, beliefs, and sentiments will focus on a particular dimension of the political arrangement, namely, its federal character.

There is a long tradition of conceiving of a federation first and foremost as a mode or an institutional principle of organization (Vile 1977, 13–14). However, the preferences for a federal type of system must also be understood in light of the ends that are being pursued. Hence, William S. Livingston insisted that sociological aspects also be taken into consideration, since the

> discussions on federal government frequently miss the point, for they tend to concentrate on powers, jurisdictions, "balances" and other legal questions; but the primary requirements for federalism are diversities among the peoples of a nation and diverse values of the people within the society. There is accordingly a psycho-sociological complex of values in any society which determines the shape and character of political and governmental institutions. Federalism, no less than other forms of governments, is a response to the values of the society. (1968, 138)

Recognition of the sociological character of federations led Preston King to argue for the need to distinguish between federation and federalism. The first term focuses specifically on institutional dimensions, while the second refers to normative elements. Both aspects must be present for a society to qualify as being federal (King 1982). As two prominent students of federalism have put it: "in any given society, the relation between federation and federalism is the one that exists between *structure* and *culture*. If the two concepts can be distinguished for analytical purposes, they, in reality, complement each other, one beckoning the other: they are in fact two facets of the same reality" (Delmartino and Deschouwer 1994, 14–15). This call to distinguish between structure and culture is, at first glance, quite straightforward. However, while they are distinct, they are also inherently interdependent, which makes analysis that much more challenging.

Broadly speaking, federation – that is to say, the *structural dimension* – refers to a particular form of relations linking individuals, groups, and political entities in a limited but permanent union to achieve common objectives, while maintaining the integrity of the respective parties. A federal political system is constituted by multiple governments and, consequently, a division of powers meant to protect the existence, integrity, and authority of the respective governments (Watts 1999). The notion of balance between the constitutive elements of the whole, or of the orders of government, is at the heart of the federal idea. According to Frank Delmartino and Kris Deschouwer (1994, 14), a federation is "a form of politico-institutional structuration which offers the constitutive elements explicit guarantees of self-management over their own matters and of co-management of those of the State, and which renders this balance between centre and periphery inherent to the conduct of public affairs." Or, in the words of Carl Friedrich (1974, 54), "we can properly speak of federalism only if a set of political groupings coexists and interacts as autonomous entities, united in a common order with an autonomy of its own." Thus, at the centre of federal institutions there are two complementary imperatives: the principle of the autonomy of federated entities (or self-management) coupled with the principle of cooperation in the achievement of common objectives (or co-management).

The structural dimension of a federation is not implemented in a political vacuum. It rests specifically on a shared comprehension of the goals being pursued by a political regime: notably, the norms, values, preferences, and political ideals that constitute its cultural dimension. Thus, the autonomy of subnational units is justified for a variety of reasons. In all federations, subnational units' relative independence and autonomy is deemed to be critical to allow the expression of local preferences, to foster innovation or, according to some, to allow for beneficial competition (Breton 1995). In multinational federations in particular, the emphasis is often on equity. As noted by philosopher Daniel Weinstock, the principle of equity, which lies at the heart of a democracy's normative justification, does not provide for permanent minorities in an organized political space. Yet the presence of national minorities that seek to ensure their viability can constitute just such a permanent minority. In his words, "the fairness that underpins democracy does not tolerate the existence of such minorities; they too should be able – without the need for special measures – to achieve what the members of the majority can achieve, that is, constitute a majority at least on certain issues that affect their interests very directly" (Weinstock 2001, 79). This argument valorizes the principle of autonomy and, by extension, of self-determination within a multinational federal political space.

The recognition and preservation of diverse collectivities within federations requires specific institutional accommodations that aim to achieve this initial objective. Analysts often refer to the fact that federalism strives to reconcile unity and diversity within a given political space or society. These two ideals, which on the surface may appear contradictory, can be reconciled if the political system, and the institutions around which the system is built, favour the maintenance and the renegotiation of a balance, deemed acceptable by the political actors, between the imperatives of unity and diversity. Regardless of how these ideals are pursued, the starting point is that different communities recognize the value of preserving their diversity as well as their need for solidarity, and they support the creative tension between the dynamics of autonomy and cooperation.

In order for the federal experience to work effectively, its different components (states, groups, collectivities) must abandon the idea that the concentration of power into a single government constitutes the best way to govern. In other words, federal diversity must be valued, promoted, and respected. The pluralism of identities and preferences must take precedence over concerns about costs and a certain level of "inefficiency" that is lessened in unitary states. Respect for plural identities is more easily accepted when the federal culture is strong (Hueglin 1987, 34). In other words, federalism constitutes a response to the values present in societies that are characterized mainly by an important diversity: a broad pluralism.

The presence of a political culture of federalism is reflected by openness to specific legal and constitutional accommodations of diversity. The "federal society" is not understood solely as an aggregate of undifferentiated individuals who maintain relations only as a result of formal rules and procedures. Rather, a federal society is one where citizens accept a specific structuring of social relations that reflects the federal idea. In multinational federations, the political culture should reflect the presence of a territorially circumscribed national minority, which requires the means to ensure its survival. This is the idea expressed by Bruno Théret (2005, 112) when he states that "federalism is in fact, fundamentally, a 'structurally holistic' principle of specific rights, which both compete with and complement individual rights. A federation is a system of relations between collective entities – primarily those linking the federal state and the federated entities, but also those linking the federated entities amongst themselves."

A federal culture calls for respect for the value of diversity, but it also implies a double loyalty to each order of government and a shared identity. Without this loyalty to both orders of government, no federation can continue to exist. The loyalty that is expressed towards the federal state as the integrator of solidarities is just as important as the reinforcement of collective autonomies. For Delmartino and Deschouwer (1994, 12), "far from being imposed by (institutional) force, this loyalty is the natural consequence of the realization that all citizens contribute to the global social state at various levels, without having one of these prevail over the other." The corollary to the principle of autonomy (and of the sharing of competencies, which gives it meaning) is that neither of the two orders of government can pretend to speak on behalf of all citizens or on behalf of the entire political community. Neither the federal state nor the federated states, taken individually, can, in return, claim the right to represent the collectivities (federal or federated) exclusively. The division of powers then requires a double loyalty. There is no element of competition between the orders of government, but rather an element of complementarity. To account for the totality of the needs of individuals and of federated communities (be they defined by region, language, religion, or culture), it is necessary to take into consideration *all* orders of government. Furthermore, the presence of a shared identity, the federal identity, does not imply the abandonment of other sources of collective identities. The latter, however, must not be perceived as a threat to the achievement of federal interests, and, conversely, the federal identity must respect and be open to citizens belonging to different communities (e.g., distinct regional preferences in Australia and the United States, linguistic and national minorities in Canada and Belgium).

As such, the legitimacy of a federation is to a large extent the result of its capacity to meet the normative principles of federalism. This reality is all the more important when the origin of the federal system is interpreted as the result of an agreement, a pact, or a reciprocal accord. The recourse to the pact argument, as a source of legitimacy, is invoked mostly in situations where discussions concerning the future of the federation jeopardize the compromise as perceived by any one or other of the political actors (Frankel 1986; Sabetti 2000). A federation's legitimacy is reinforced by the correspondence or fit between the presence of a federal culture and the institutions that are intended to maintain it. The absence of a federal culture and deficiencies in the operation of federal institutions can only lead the federation into a profound crisis. This crisis takes the form of disagreements not over ad hoc choices, but rather, and more fundamentally, over the very conditions for the perpetuation of the federal union.

If, as we suggest, *structure* and *culture* are interdependent, they cannot be analysed separately. Although a number of studies do discuss one or the other, few works on the political culture of federalism pay

Table 3.1
The Multidimensional Nature of a Political Culture of Federalism

	Strong	Weak
Sociocultural preferences	Autonomy Double loyalty/identification	Subordination Single loyalty/identification
Operational preferences	Cooperation Asymmetry	Unilateralism Symmetry

attention to both. Duchacek (1987) and Cole, Kincaid, and Rodriguez (2004, 215) point out that one reason why the empirical study of federal political culture is a "blank" (to use Duchacek's term) is because different authors operationalize the term in varying ways. This operationalization is often limited to measuring the level of support for the division of powers, in contrast to that of a unitary state or, in the case of multinational federations, to analysing support for sociological pluralism versus linguistic, ethnic, and religious uniformity. If these indicators allow us to measure a certain degree of openness with regard to diversity, they are a far cry from a full account of the constitutive dimensions of a federal culture.

Thus, unlike Kincaid and Cole (2004, 2011), for example, we argue that the political culture associated with federalism cannot be measured simply though an analysis of support for the structural aspects of federalism. We suggest instead combining the sociocultural dimensions, that is to say, the attitudes of citizens towards diversity, with preferences as to the structural or, perhaps more accurately, the operational dimensions, such as attitudes toward the division of powers and support for asymmetry. Table 3.1 outlines the different components that must, in our view, be taken into account. In order to capture the complexity of a political culture of federalism, we distinguish the sociocultural and operational preferences of citizens with respect to the federation, although both are inextricably linked. For each dimension, we identify those aspects that allow us to observe the presence of a "strong" or a "weak" federal culture. It is the combination of these different dimensions that enables us to observe the nuances that are generally absent in the literature. We analyse the strengths and the weaknesses of the federal culture in Canada in terms of the possible tension between the sociocultural and the operational dimensions of federalism.

Canadians' Understanding of Federalism

The presence of a federal culture within the Canadian political community presupposes that Canadian citizens have a good understanding of their political system and a reasoned and informed judgment on the activities and choices of different orders of government. Overlapping jurisdiction seems to be a fundamental reality in the evolution of the Canadian federation. While certain governments insist on the respect of the competencies enumerated in the British North America Act, 1867, for their part citizens often have difficulty in attributing specific responsibilities to each order of government.

With the help of a national survey[1] we measured the level of public understanding of how the Canadian federation operates. Our survey shows that an important majority of citizens (70%) have difficulty knowing which order of government is responsible for what. Citizens acknowledge confusion in allocating responsibility to each order of government. We also assessed whether citizens attribute to the correct order of government certain responsibilities that one would expect to be well understood. For areas such as national defence, the postal service, and the Mint, the exclusive responsibility of the federal government is without question, as is the power of provincial governments in matters of elementary and secondary education. Indeed, Alberta, Ontario, and Quebec do not have their own currency and there is no federal department of education. To better understand citizens' understanding of the division of powers and federalism, we developed an index built around questions concerning which order of government is responsible for each of these domains. We considered those able to correctly attribute these four domains to the appropriate order of government to have a solid basic knowledge of the sharing of responsibilities. Those who obtained two or three correct answers were deemed to have a moderate knowledge, and those who were able to correctly attribute one or none of these domains were defined as having a weak knowledge of the division powers.

Table 3.2 suggests that less than one Canadian in two (45.8%) possesses a solid basic knowledge of the sharing of responsibilities, a little more than one in three has a moderate knowledge (36.2%), and close to one in five Canadians has a weak or non-existent knowledge (18%). Quebec citizens are best informed and those in the Atlantic provinces are the least informed, with a gap of almost 20 percentage points separating these two regions. A solid understanding increases with age

Table 3.2
Canadians' Understanding of Who Does What in the Federation (percentage of respondents)

	Region					
	Atlantic	Quebec	Ontario	Prairies	B.C. & Terr.	Total
Strong	35.6	54.6	44.0	38.8	49.3	45.8
Moderate	37.0	29.0	37.8	44.2	33.8	36.2
Weak	27.4	16.4	18.1	17.0	16.9	18.0
Total	100.0	100.0	100.0	100.0	100.0	100.0
N	73	238	386	165	136	998

Table 3.3
Gender Differences in Understanding of Who Does What (percentage of respondents)

	Gender		
	Male	Female	Total
Strong	53.1	38.8	45.8
Moderate	34.3	37.8	36.1
Weak	12.7	23.3	18.1
Total	100.0	100.0	100.0
N	490	510	1000

(36% for those under 35; 54% for those 55 and older) and with level of education (33% for those with an elementary and secondary education; 59% for those who have a university background). As shown in Table 3.3, gender is particularly significant: almost 15 percentage points separate men and women with a solid understanding of the sharing of responsibilities between orders of government.

Another way of measuring the knowledge of citizens of federalism is determining their attachment to the general principle of autonomy or *self-rule*. When asked a hypothetical question about which order of government should be assigned certain responsibilities, survey respondents privileged, to varying degrees, joint government intervention, regardless of the issue at hand (Table 3.4). If a federation is characterized by the principle of a clear division of powers, as per the classic definition of Kenneth C. Wheare (1963, 10), this principle is not one to

Table 3.4
Canadians' Understanding of Who Does What by Policy Area (percentage of respondents)

	Negotiation of trade agreements	Environment	Integration and settlement of immigrants	Promotion of the arts	Social welfare
Exclusively provincial	7.0	7.1	9.4	36.5	27.5
Exclusively federal	40.9	9.7	31.0	6.4	14.0
Shared	50.1	82.0	58.6	53.3	56.7
Don't know	2.0	1.3	1.1	3.8	1.7
Total	100.0	100	100	100	100
N	1000	1000	1000	1000	1000

Q: If you could modify the sharing of responsibilities between the federal and provincial governments, which among the following responsibilities, should be exclusively provincial, federal or even shared?

which Canadians are very attached. For example, only 41% of respondents wished to see the negotiation of international trade agreements remain, as they are now, an exclusively federal responsibility. More specifically, a significant number of those surveyed wanted provinces to intervene more in areas that fall under the exclusive authority of the federal government, notably in the areas of foreign affairs, national defence, and employment insurance (Table 3.5). A third would like provincial governments to have more responsibility in foreign affairs, and more than one-half would like it in employment insurance. It is also surprising to note that approximately a quarter of respondents wanted provinces to intervene less in areas (foreign affairs and defence), where in reality they exercise no responsibility and, in the case of defence, say and do almost nothing. In summary, there are no domains in which citizens do not favour intervention by the two orders of government. The principle of *shared-rule* clearly outweighs the principle of *self-rule*, even in domains that clearly fall under the jurisdiction of the central government, such as national defence.

This relatively weak understanding of how the federation operates may reflect a preference for a functional and instrumental approach to the state. Our survey results suggest that citizens want, first and foremost, effective and efficient government where costs are kept under

Table 3.5
Support for Giving Provinces More Responsibility (percentage of respondents)

	Foreign Affairs	Defence	Employment Insurance
More responsibility	32.6	27.4	53.5
No change	40.9	43.7	34.6
Less responsibility	23.5	25.6	9.9
Don't know	3.0	3.2	2.1
Total	100.0	100.0	100.0
N	1000	1000	1000

Q: For each of the following areas I would like you to tell me if the [name of provincial] government should have more responsibility. What about for … ?

control. For example, a significant number of Canadians would appear to have no objection to having the Canadian passport issued by their provincial government, despite its being a document that attests to Canadian citizenship. In fact, 56% would support this possibility if it were to lead to greater efficiency.[2] This scenario even enjoyed support from nearly two-thirds of Quebec respondents. And support for a provincial role in passports was quite robust. About 90% of respondents who were favourable to this change remained so even after they were reminded that the passport is proof of Canadian citizenship and also serves to control access to borders.[3] In the same manner, a majority of those surveyed (54%) approved of a scenario where their health insurance card would be issued by the federal government.[4] Conversely, in Quebec such a change was rejected by 61% of the respondents. Once again, support for a federal role in health card distribution was quite robust: 87% of those in favour remained so even after being reminded that their health card controls access to the health care system and aims to control cost increases.[5] In summary, whether it is a federal or provincial prerogative, a surprising majority of Canadians place a great deal of emphasis on efficiency at the expense of a federal perspective on the Canadian political and institutional reality.

These results do not allow for a comprehensive understanding of how Canadians truly understand their federation. They nevertheless suggest that the division of powers between Ottawa and the provinces is not well understood by many Canadians. A number of respondents indicated that they have difficulty in grasping the present sharing of responsibilities. In some areas where one would expect a good under-standing of "who does what" (notably, national defence, postal serv-ice, and elementary and secondary education), a significant number of Canadians were unable to correctly identify the responsible order of government. On the other hand, it would appear that many Canadians are ready to transform certain functions that are at the heart of the fed-eral arrangement (citizenship and access to health care) when the im-peratives of efficiency come into conflict with the federal institutional structure. The combination of what citizens know (or do not know) and the importance given to managerial principles (effectiveness, efficiency, and control of costs) necessarily has a major impact on the nature of the political culture of federalism in Canada. In effect, how can we even speak of a political culture of federalism when a significant number of citizens have but a minimal comprehension of the federation as a sys-tem of political organization?

Mapping the Political Culture of Federalism in Canada

Earlier we argued that a more complete analysis of the political culture of federalism requires careful attention to both structural and socio-cul-tural dimensions. The structural dimension of a federal political culture refers to the views and attitudes of citizens with respect to the structure of the federation, that is, how governments do or do not work together and the extent to which asymmetrical arrangements are deemed legiti-mate. The sociocultural dimension of a federal political culture refers to citizens' views and attitudes with respect to diversity, identity, and the fundamental nature of the federation.

The Sociocultural Dimension

In order to understand better the *socio-cultural dimension* of Canada's federal political culture, we asked respondents how they identify them-selves. In light of the analysis presented earlier, we would expect that as citizens of a mature federation, Canadians would identify themselves more or less equally with Canada and with their province or region. However, fully 64% of respondents in the survey identified themselves as Canadian only, slightly more than 20% identified themselves equally as a Canadian and as a resident of their province, and 16% identified themselves mainly with their province. The results were quite different in Quebec, where 44% of respondents identified primarily with their province, 35% had a dual identification, and only 21% identified themselves as "mainly Canadian." These results suggest that divided loyalties, one of the key elements we previously identified with a political culture of federalism, are relatively weak in Canada. This conclusion echoes an argument we have made elsewhere (Fafard, Rocher, and Côté 2010).

Similarly, our definition of a federal political culture suggests that if such a culture is strong, citizens will value provincial autonomy and reject the subordination of provincial governments to the federal government, especially in areas of provincial jurisdiction. We asked respondents a series of questions about provincial autonomy and federal supervision. For example, almost two-thirds (62.8%) of respondents agreed that in areas such as education and health the provinces "should be able to act without interference from the federal government." This result held across the country, although, perhaps not surprisingly, the view was more strongly held among Quebec respondents (70%) than among those in the rest of Canada (61%).

To further probe support for autonomy, we asked respondents whether, in their view, federalism aims to "accommodate diversity, for example, of Québec and Aboriginal peoples." Support for this conception of federalism would, we submit, suggest a strong federal political culture, especially in a multinational federation. More than 70% of respondents agreed with this characterization of federalism and support ran as high as 79% in British Columbia. The notable exception was in Quebec, where slightly over 60% of respondents shared this view. Identity plays a key role in explaining this variation. In Quebec, respondents who identified mainly with their province were less likely to agree that federalism (in Canada) accommodates diversity (53%) and this figure fell to 40% among those who voted for the Bloc Québécois in the 2006 election. The difference between Canadians generally and BQ supporters in particular when it comes to their understanding of the nature of federalism is to be expected insofar as Bloc supporters effectively reject many of the core notions of federalism, those that concern striking a balance between orders of government and multiple identities. In other words, the Bloc Québécois electorate is largely made up of individuals who favour Quebec independence or nationalists who support a very strong decentralization of powers to the detriment of the principle of federal solidarity. These nationalists do not appear to have a strong federal culture, in spite of the fact that they are strongly in favour of the principle of provincial autonomy. These results suggest significant variations in the federal political culture of Quebecers, based on their political identity and partisan preferences.

We also considered views on provincial autonomy versus subordination by asking respondents whether they agreed or disagreed with the statement that the federal government should exercise oversight and control of provinces. We purposefully used quite strong language, asking if Ottawa should have the ability to "supervise and control" the activities of provincial governments for areas under provincial jurisdiction, such as education and auto insurance. Surprisingly, 59% of our respondents agreed with this statement, and even in Quebec a very slim majority supported the notion of federal control. In much the same vein, 90% of respondents agreed that the federal government should be "capable of defining national standards so that all people are treated the same."

How can we explain respondents' simultaneous support for the ability of provinces to act without interference and the notion of federal supervision and control? To understand this apparent contradiction we can draw on other data from the survey with respect to identity and knowledge.

Support for the subordination of provinces (i.e., federal supervision and control) falls to only 46% among those who identify primarily with their province. Similarly, support in Quebec for federal supervision and control falls to only 40% among those who primarily identify with Quebec. While both figures are still surprisingly high in absolute terms, the downward shift as we control for identity does suggest that the results are not as contradictory as they may appear.

Moreover, support for the subordination of provincial governments is negatively correlated with an understanding of federalism. As indicated in Table 3.6, respondents with a strong or good understanding of the division of powers were far less likely (44%) to express support for federal supervision and control compared with those with a moderate (70%) or weak understanding (72%). Not understanding even the most basic aspects of "who does what" between Ottawa and the provinces (e.g., the armed forces are a federal government responsibility) is an indicator of a weak understanding of the workings of the federation and suggests a weak attachment to a federal political culture

In summary, the strength of Canada's political culture of federalism varies along different sociocultural dimensions. Although one would expect multiple loyalties in a federal political community, in Canada, a majority of citizens display an identity and a loyalty that is primar-

Table 3.6
Knowledge and Support for the Subordination of Provinces (percentage of respondents)

Subordination of provinces	Basic knowledge of the division of powers			Total
	Strong	Moderate	Weak	
Disagree	54.6	28.5	22.1	39.3
Agree	44.3	70.1	72.4	58.7
Don't know	1.1	1.4	5.5	2.0
Total	100.0	100.0	100.0	100.0
N	458	361	181	1000

Q: The federal government should have the ability to supervise and control the activities of provincial governments in certain areas like elementary and secondary education or auto insurance.

ily, if not exclusively, "national." Outside Quebec, the primary identity is with the federal community as a whole, with important variations between Ontario (82%) and the Atlantic (58%). In Quebec by contrast, identity is strongly Quebec-oriented (44%), even if a third of respondents (35%) state that they are equally a Canadian and a Quebecer. In both cases, but in opposite ways, the lack of multiple identities suggests a relatively weak political culture of federalism. That being said, Canadians still subscribe to the principles of diversity and provincial autonomy. Surprisingly it is in Quebec where we find the lowest level of support for these principles, even though they are endorsed by a majority. Canadians who have little or no interest in participating in the Canadian federation hold a weaker federal identity. Even more surprising are the relatively high levels of support for the principle of subordination, as reflected in the willingness to have the federal government exercise supervision and control in some areas of provincial jurisdiction. There is a gap between Canadians who have a solid basic knowledge of federalism, and who are for the most part opposed to this subordination, and Canadians who have no knowledge of the modus operandi of the federation and unequivocally support federal government subordination and control.

The Structural Dimension

In order to tap the *structural dimension* of Canada's federal political culture, we asked a series of questions pertaining to whether and how

Table 3.7
Regional Breakdown of Views on Government Collaboration / Unilateralism (percentage of respondents)

Collaboration/ Unilateralism	Region					
	Atlantic	Quebec	Ontario	Prairies	B.C. & Terr.	Total
Ottawa establishes objectives	1.4	3.4	2.6	1.8	0.7	2.3
Ottawa establishes objectives after consulting provinces	20.3	9.2	20.8	12.7	22.6	16.9
Federal/provincial collaboration on objectives	52.7	45.0	58.2	63.9	53.3	54.9
Provinces consult each other to establish objectives	9.5	8.8	6.0	10.2	6.6	7.7
Each province establishes its own objectives	9.5	31.1	10.1	9.0	13.9	15.4
Don't know	6.8	2.5	2.3	2.4	2.9	2.8
Total	100.0	100.0	100.0	100.0	100.0	100.0
N	74	238	385	166	137	1000

Q: Canada faces new challenges. When it comes time to develop common objectives to confront these challenges, which of the following five processes, in your opinion, will be more appropriate?

governments work together. We expected a strong political culture of federalism to manifest itself as a preference for intergovernmental collaboration over unilateralism (be it by Ottawa or the provinces) as well as a willingness to allow asymmetrical intergovernmental arrangements, something that we would argue is normal and inevitable in a multinational federation such as Canada.

With respect to collaboration versus unilateralism, we asked respondents how they thought governments should respond to new challenges (Table 3.7). Their choices ranged from federal unilateralism (i.e., the federal government establishes objectives for the whole country) to collaboration (i.e., the federal government and the provincial governments work together) to provincial unilateralism (i.e., each provincial government establishes its own objectives). What is striking is the very weak support for federal unilateralism and the strong support for collaboration. Just over half of respondents (55%) preferred collaboration, and this result was quite constant across the country, from a low of 45% in Quebec to a high of 64% on the Prairies (of course, the national average would be higher save for the weak support in Quebec). Support in Quebec for provincial unilateralism, not surprisingly, is strongest among sovereigntists and what we may call "autonomistes"; almost half of the respondents who voted for the Bloc Québécois in the 2006 election expressed support for provincial unilateralism. This suggests that a political culture of federalism is relatively weak among an important group of Quebec residents insofar as a preference for "going it alone" is inconsistent with the principle of shared rule.

To probe further the structural dimension of Canada's federal political culture, we asked respondents their views on asymmetrical arrangements between Ottawa and the provinces. In a multinational federation such as Canada, a certain amount of asymmetry is normal and desirable (Kymlicka 1998; Milne 2005). Slightly fewer than 60% of our respondents disagreed that the Government of Quebec should be more autonomous from the federal government compared with other provincial governments. Disagreement was particularly strong west of the Quebec/Ontario border, rising to just over 70% in Ontario and on the Prairies. Similarly, just over half (52%) of our respondents agreed that the federal government "should continue to reach specific agreements with the Government of Québec" that are different from those with other provinces. However, support varied widely across the country from a low of 38% on the Prairies to 44% in Ontario and a high of 80% in Quebec. At first glance, these results might suggest that this aspect of the federal political culture is not particularly strong in some parts of Canada, notably on the prairies, where just over one-third of respondents supported asymmetrical arrangements. We conclude that even though Canadians value intergovernmental collaboration – which seems to us to be a good indicator of a strong political culture of federalism – they are globally opposed to asymmetrical arrangements as a necessary condition of a well-functioning multinational federation. However, in order to nuance this finding, as we did with the sociocultural dimension, we were interested to see what impact identity and knowledge of federalism had on the results.

Beginning with identity, as indicated in Table 3.8, support for asymmetry is quite high (75%) among those who identify primarily with their province. More important perhaps, more than two-thirds (68%)

Table 3.8
Identity and Support for Asymmetry (percentage of respondents)

	Identities			
Asymmetry	Mainly Canadian	Equally Canadian & Province	Mainly Province	Total
Disagree	55.4	31.0	23.4	45.3
Agree	41.7	68.0	75.3	52.5
Don't Know	2.9	1.0	1.3	2.3
Total	100	100	100	100
N	617	197	156	972

Identities – Q: How do you identify yourself?
Asymmetry – Q: The federal government should continue to reach specific agreements with the Government of Quebec in areas such as immigration and health care that differ from those signed by other provincial governments.

of the respondents who identify more or less equally with Canada and their province expressed support for asymmetry (and this figure reaches almost 90% among Quebec respondents who profess a shared identity). We interpret this result as evidence that support for asymmetry is part of inculcation into a federal political culture.

Turning to knowledge of federalism and the division of powers, we see that the general lack of enthusiasm for asymmetry does not vary among respondents with a strong or even a moderate understanding of the division of powers. As indicated in Table 3.9, both strong and moderately knowledgeable respondents were more or less evenly divided on the merits of asymmetrical arrangements for Quebec. Curiously, however, support for such asymmetrical arrangements actually rose to over two-thirds (68%) among respondents with a weak understanding of the division of powers. The 20% of respondents with a weak understanding of federalism were inclined equally to support federal supervision and control of provinces, the ability of provinces to act without interference from Ottawa, asymmetry for Quebec, and national standards set by the federal government. This finding suggests that a weak understanding of the structural dimensions of federalism weakens one's federal political culture: approximately one-fifth of Canadians are open to calls from Ottawa or the provinces to proceed in ways that are inimical to the balance inherent in federal arrangements.

Table 3.9
Federalism Knowledge and Support for Asymmetry (percentage of respondents)

Asymmetry	Knowledge			Total
	Strong	Moderate	Weak	
Disagree	48.5	49.2	44.7	44.7
Agree	50.2	47.8	65.2	52.1
Don't Know	1.3	3.1	8.3	3.2
Total	100	100	100	100
N	458	360	181	999

Asymmetry – Q: The federal government should continue to reach specific agreements with the Government of Quebec in areas such as immigration and health care that differ from those signed by other provincial governments.

Conclusion

In this chapter, we have argued that the relationship between societies and federations is, in fact, reciprocal. Assuming that the initial choice of federation is a response to societal values, we believe that the lived reality of federation can in turn influence (more and less) societal values. This reciprocal effect is what Cairns (1977, 724) called "the moulding effect of institutions on political behaviour." More precisely, we have tried to show that just because Canada is a federation does not necessarily mean that Canadians possess a particularly strong culture of federalism.

The weakness of federalism as a constituent part of Canadian political culture is demonstrated first and foremost by evidence that a large number of Canadians have a weak grasp, at best, of the division of powers and a vague understanding of how a federation operates. In this sense, it is perhaps better to speak not of the strength or weakness of the political culture of federalism but of its presence or absence. The presence/absence of Canada's federal political culture is further demonstrated by distinguishing between two complementary dimensions, notably, citizen views about the nature of the federation (the socio-cultural dimension) and how the federation operates in practice (the structural and institutional dimensions).

When we looked at the sociocultural dimension of Canada's political culture of federalism, our expectation was that, as residents of a mature federation, Canadians would identify themselves more or less equally with Canada and with their province or region. This proved not to be the case. In our survey, slightly more than 20% identified themselves equally as Canadians and as residents of their province, a figure that rose to 35% among Quebec respondents. Similarly, we expected that, pursuant to our definition of a federal political culture, citizens would value provincial autonomy and reject the subordination of provincial governments to the federal government, especially in areas of provincial jurisdiction. Our results suggest that respondents simultaneously support the ability of provinces to act without interference and the notion of federal supervision and control. This finding suggests that, when we focus on the sociocultural dimension, there is little evidence of a robust political culture of federalism. And whereas we previously had argued that the political culture of federalism is stronger in Quebec than in the rest of Canada (Fafard, Rocher, and Côté 2010), our more recent analysis suggests that this support masks significant variations among Quebecers with different conceptions of their political identity and different partisan preferences.

The structural dimension of Canada's political culture of federalism was measured through the views and attitudes of citizens with respect to the structure of the federation: how governments work together (or not), and the perceived legitimacy of asymmetrical arrangements to be legitimate. Our general conclusion is that on this structural dimension, there is a reasonably strong political culture of federalism in Canada. But there are some important caveats to this generalization. One is that Canadians do not support asymmetry, a disconcerting finding in a multinational context where such arrangements are, we argue, essential. A second has to do with the very strong support for intergovernmental collaboration. The latter may reflect a more generalized preference for cooperation and collaboration over unilateral action, be it by Ottawa or a provincial government. Indeed, in a federation we would expect citizens to want their governments to collaborate as an expression of the very nature of federalism. However, the observed preference for collaboration may also reflect a weak understanding of federalism or at least the division of powers (i.e., ignorance about who does what may lead to a preference for collaboration).

Is there a difference between Canadian elite and mass public opinion when it comes to federalism and federation? We are not aware of any comprehensive analyses of elite opinion that would allow a detailed answer to this question. However, there are at least three reasons to believe that elites are more likely to be supportive of at least some aspects of federalism and federation.

First, the data cited here suggest that understanding of both the normative and the structural dimensions of federalism increases with level of education. To the extent that elites are better educated, we would expect them to have a stronger understanding of the responsibilities of both orders of government as well as the importance of shared rule for the effective functioning of the federation. Second, as we have shown elsewhere, with the exception of Quebec, federal and provincial public servants have a rather functional view of federalism and are generally supportive of intergovernmental collaboration (Fafard and Rocher 2011). However, more important might be the impact of what Robert Young and others have called "province-building" and the associated pattern of strong support among local economic elites for strong, autonomous provincial governments (Young, Faucher, and Blais 1984; Stevenson 2004). The critical role of provincial governments in promoting economic development means that economic actors are inclined to build alliances with "their" provincial governments that, in turn, may have the effect of strengthening the political culture of federalism at the elite level.

What significance should we attribute to the provisional conclusion that Canada's political culture of federalism is not particularly strong or, at best, its strength is variable across the country? Does it reflect a basic lack of understanding of the nature of the Canadian federation? Or is it an amorphous preference for governments to "get along?" In our view, the results of our analysis are significant in at least two respects. In the short to medium term, the weakness of the political culture of federalism in Canada allows political actors to feel less constrained by the limits of federal structures (i.e., the division of powers). Politicians and the governments they lead, along with other non-governmental actors, can and do take advantage of the fact that Canadians are often quite unaware of even the most basic aspects of federalism. This public ignorance increases political leaders' capacity to act in ways that are inimical to the federal idea (e.g., a federal invasion of areas of provincial jurisdiction; a provincial decision to disengage with the federal government and try to act unilaterally or at least independently).

In the longer term, the weakness if not the absence of a political culture of federalism in Canada may mean the ongoing weakening of the federal character of Canada. If, as we suggest here, Canadians do not really understand federalism and the tradeoffs and choices inherent in a federation as a form of government, why have a federation at all? While there is no inherent reason why a federation cannot, over time, evolve into a more or less unitary state (or the reverse if one considers contemporary Belgium), the underlying reasons why Canada is a federation have not disappeared. Regional diversity and the multinational character of Canada remain and, because they do, a political culture supportive of this type of federation is required to reflect and manage these fundamental realities of Canadian politics and government.

NOTES

1 The views of Canadians are drawn from the results of a poll of a total of 1000 nationally representative Canadian adults. Interviews were conducted by TNS Canada Facts between 20 September and 14 October 2007. The survey results for all of Canada are considered accurate to 3.1 percentage points, 19 times out of 20. In contrast, regional and provincial results need to be interpreted with caution, since the small sample size means that the confidence interval is larger than 5.0. The detailed results of this survey are available from the authors.
2 The survey question was "Assuming that it would be quicker and more efficient, my passport should be issued by the Government of [name of province the respondent is from]."
3 The survey question was "Some people insist that a passport is evidence of citizenship and also helps control access to Canada's borders. Given this, to what extent do you agree that your passport should be issued by the Government of [insert name of province the respondent is from]?"
4 The survey question was "Assuming that it would be quicker and more efficient, my health card should be issued by the Government of Canada."
5 The survey question was "Some people insist that a health insurance card serves to control access to the provincial health care system and to manage the growth of costs. Given this, to what extent do you agree that the Government of Canada should issue your health card?"

REFERENCES

Bakvis, Herman, and Grace Skogstad. 2008. Canadian Federalism: Performance, Effectiveness, and Legitimacy. In *Canadian Federalism: Performance, Effectiveness, and Legitimacy*, edited by Herman Bakvis and Grace Skogstad. 2nd ed. Don Mills: Oxford University Press.

Breton, Albert. 1995. *Competitive Governments*. New York: Cambridge University Press.

Burgess, Michael. 2006. *Comparative Federalism: Theory and Practice*. London: Routledge.

Cairns, Alan C. 1975. Political Science in Canada and the Americanization Issue. *Canadian Journal of Political Science / Revue canadienne de science politique* 8(2):191–234.

Cairns, Alan C. 1977. The Governments and Societies of Canadian Federalism. *Canadian Journal of Political Science / Revue canadienne de science politique* 10(4):695–726.

Cole, Richard L., John Kincaid, and Alejandro Rodriguez. 2004. Public Opinion on Federalism and Federal Political Culture in Canada, Mexico, and the United States, 2004. *Publius* 34(3):201–21.

Delmartino, Frank, and Kris Deschouwer. 1994. Les fondements du fédéralisme. In *Le fédéralisme : Approches politique, économique et juridique*, edited by André Alen. Brussels: De Boeck-Wesmael.

Duchacek, Ivo D. 1987. *Comparative Federalism: The Territorial Dimension of Politics*. New York: Holt Rhinehart and Winston.

Elkins, David J., and Richard Simeon. 1979. A Cause in Search of Its Effect, or What Does Political Culture Explain? *Comparative Politics* 11(2):127–45.

Elkins, David J., and Richard Simeon. 1980. *Small Worlds: Provinces and Parties in Canadian Political Life*. Toronto: Methuen.

Fafard, P., and F. Rocher. 2009. The Evolution of Federalism Studies in Canada: From Dependent to Independent Variable. *Canadian Public Administration* 52(2):291–311.

Fafard, Patrick, and François Rocher. 2011. Clients, Citizens and Federalism: The Views of Governments. In *The State in Transition. Challenges for Canadian Federalism*, edited by Michael Behiels and François Rocher. Ottawa: Invenire Books.

Fafard, Patrick, François Rocher, and Catherine Côté. 2010. The Presence (or Lack Thereof) of a Federal Culture in Canada: The Views of Canadians. *Regional & Federal Studies* 20(1):19–43.

Frenkel, Max. 1986. *Federal Theory*. Canberra: Centre for Research on Federal Financial Relations.

Friedrich, Carl. 1974. *Limited Government: A Comparison*. Englewood Cliffs: Prentice Hall.

Gagnon, Alain-G. 2008. *La raison du plus fort. Plaidoyer pour un fédéralisme multinational*. Montreal: Québec-Amérique.

Henderson, Ailsa. 2004. Regional Political Cultures in Canada. *Canadian Journal of Political Science / Revue canadienne de science politique* 37(03):595–615.

Henderson, Ailsa. 2010. "Small Worlds" as Predictors of General Political Attitudes. *Regional & Federal Studies* 20(4–5):469–85.

Hepburn, Eve. 2010. Small Worlds in Canada and Europe: A Comparison of Regional Party Systems in Québec, Bavaria and Scotland. *Regional & Federal Studies* 20(4–5):527–544.

Hueglin, Thomas O. 1987. Legitimacy, Democracy, and Federalism. In *Federalism and the Role of the State*, edited by Herman Bakvis and William M. Chandler. Toronto: University of Toronto Press.

Hueglin, Thomas O. 2011. A Certain Degree of Social Homogeneity: Wicked Problems and Federal Possibilities in an Age of Globalization. In *The State in Transition. Challenges for Canadian Federalism*, edited by Michael Behiels and François Rocher. Ottawa: Invenire Books.

Hueglin, Thomas O., and Alan Fenna. 2006. *Comparative Federalism: A Systematic Inquiry*. Toronto: University of Toronto Press.

International Encyclopedia of the Social Sciences. 1968. *Encyclopedia.com*. 12 March 2012. Available at http://www.encyclopedia.com

Kincaid, John, and Richard L. Cole. 2011. Citizen Attitudes toward Issues of Federalism in Canada, Mexico, and the United States. *Publius: The Journal of Federalism* 41(1):53–75.

King, Preston. 1982. *Federalism and Federation*. London: Croom Helm.

Kymlicka, Will. 1998. *Multinational Federalism in Canada: Rethinking the Partnership*. In *Beyond the Impasse*, edited by Guy Laforest and Roger Gibbins, Montreal: Institute for Research on Public Policy.

Livingston, William S. 1968. Canada, Australia and the United States: Variations on a Theme. In *Federalism: Infinite Variety in Theory and Practice*, edited by Valerie Earle. Itasca: F.E. Peacock.

Milne, David. 2005. *Asymmetry in Canada: Past and Present*. Kingston: Institute of Intergovernmental Relations, School of Policy Studies, Queen's University.

Papillon, Martin. 2008. Is the Secret to Have a Good Dentist? Canadian Contributions to the Study of Federalism in Divided Societies. In *The Comparative Turn in Canadian Political Science*, edited by Linda A. White, Richard Simeon, Robert Vipond, and Jennifer Wallner. Vancouver: UBC Press.

Rocher, François. 2009. The Quebec-Canada Dynamic or the Negation of the Ideal of Federalism. In *Contemporary Canadian Federalism. Foundations, Traditions, Institutions*, edited by Alain-G. Gagnon. Toronto: University of Toronto Press.

Sabetti, Filippo. 2000. Covenant Language in Canada: Continuity and Change in Political Discourse. In *The Covenant Tradition: From Federal Theology to Modern Federalism*, edited by Daniel J. Elazar and John Kincaid. Lanham: Lexington Books.

Simeon, Richard. 2002. *Political Science and Federalism: Seven Decades of Scholarly Engagement*. Kingston: Institute of Intergovernmental Relations.

Simeon, Richard. [1972] 2006. *Federal-Provincial Diplomacy: The Making of Recent Policy in Canada*. Toronto: University of Toronto Press.

Simeon, Richard. 2011. Preconditions and Prerequisites: Can Anyone Make Federalism Work? In *The Federal Idea: Essays in Honour of Ron Watts*, edited by Thomas J. Courchene, John R. Allan, Christian Leuprecht, and Nadia Verelli. Kingston and Montreal: McGill-Queen's University Press.

Simeon, Richard, and David J. Elkins. 1974. Regional Political Cultures in Canada. *Canadian Journal of Political Science / Revue canadienne de science politique* 7(3):397–437.

Simeon, R., and I. Robinson. 1990. *State, Society, and the Development of Canadian Federalism*. Toronto: University of Toronto Press in cooperation with the Royal Commission on the Economic Union and Development Prospects for Canada and the Canadian Government Publishing Centre, Supply and Services Canada.

Stevenson, Garth. 2004. *Unfulfilled Union: Canadian Federalism and National Unity*. Montreal: McGill-Queen's University Press.

Théret, Bruno. 2005. Du principe fédéral à une typologie des fédérations: quelques propositions. In *Le fédéralisme dans tous ses États : Gouvernance, identité et méthodologie – The States and Moods of Federalism. Governance, Identity and Methodology*, edited by Jean-François Gaudreault-Desbiens et Fabien Gélinas. Cowansville: Les Éditions Yvon Blais.

Vile, M.J. 1977. Federal Theory and the "New Federalism." In *The Politics of "New Federalism,"* edited by D. Jaensch. Adelaide: Australasian Political Studies Association.

Wallner, Jennifer. 2010. Beyond National Standards: Reconciling Tension between Federalism and the Welfare State. *Publius: The Journal of Federalism* 40(4):646–71.

Watts, Ronald L. 1999. *Comparing Federal Systems*. Kingston: Institute of Intergovernmental Relations, Queen's University.

Weinstock, Daniel. 2001. Towards a Normative Theory of Federalism. *International Social Science Journal* 53(167):75–83.

Wheare, Kenneth C. 1963. *Federal Government*. 4th ed. London: Oxford University Press.

Wiseman, Nelson. 2007. *In Search of Canadian Political Culture*. Vancouver: UBC Press.

Young, R.A., P. Faucher, and A. Blais. 1984. The Concept of Province-Building: A Critique. *Canadian Journal of Political Science / Revue canadienne de science politique* 17(04):783–818.

4 A Problem of Trust: Can Federalism Silence the Guns?

MARIE-JOËLLE ZAHAR

Peace-building practitioners often argue that federalism is particularly well suited to achieve three important objectives: manage diversity, balance self- and shared-rule, and build trust. The literature on federalism has extensively addressed the manner in which federalism provides for the management of diversity (Gagnon and Tully 2001; Ghai 2000; Saunders 2003). It has also spent much time and effort disentangling the mechanisms that provide for self- and shared-rule, and it has thought extensively about the difficulties and tensions associated with attempts to maintain a precarious equilibrium between attempts to enhance autonomy and efforts to maintain and consolidate unity (Watts 1998; Henrard 2002; Tillin 2007). However, as federal solutions "go global" – that is, as federal models and mechanisms are being touted as a solution for those countries, mostly, but not exclusively, in the global South and attempting to transition from war to peace – the ability of federalism to generate trust appears particularly under-theorized (Bhatt and Murshed 2009; Gromes 2010).

This contribution asks how and under what conditions federalism can assist in overcoming the mistrust that civil war specialists identify as the major stumbling block in preventing the sustainability of peace agreements. As a corollary, I consider whether federalism should be expected to fare better than other modes of governance at generating trust.[1] I argue that federal systems are better than majoritarian unitary structures or power-sharing arrangements in helping to address the absence of trust as countries move from civil war to peace. This is because citizens and communities are more likely to believe that their security will be protected in a federation where the central government can deliver deterrence (the ability to prevent anyone but the state from using violence) and the federal units can offer assurance (the ability to persuade citizens that the power of the state cannot be used illegitimately against them because of the exercise of local control over public safety). Having laid out a conceptual argument explaining why federal systems are preferred by international actors as the better institutional set-up to ease a transition from war to peace, I address the difficulties of new institutions, unaided, to generate trust and overcome the dangers of backsliding and collapse that threaten any transition from violence. I close with conclusions for the engagement of international actors in new post-conflict federations.

A Problem of Trust

In the scholarship on civil wars, trust is identified as a central problem at two crucial stages: the initiation of violence and the transition from war to peace. Accounting for the role of mistrust in initiating violent conflict, Fearon convincingly argued that wars can start because of a credible commitment problem when there are bargains to be made between opposing sides, but when one or more sides would have an incentive to renege on the deal. Such a bargaining context exists when a stronger party is negotiating with a weaker one. Describing the relationship between insurgents and governments, Fearon and Laitin argue that the capability gap described above is a fundamental fact of insurgency (Fearon and Laitin 2003). In other words, governments that negotiate with aggrieved groups in their midst have no incentive to abide by the compromises that they make at the negotiating table, knowing that they have the means to enforce their preferred option. Fully cognizant of this fact, the aggrieved group will thus find it rational to start a war today rather than wait another day and provide the government with the opportunity to weaken it further. In the first instance, insurgents might stand a fighting chance; in the second instance, their growing weakness relative to the government ensures that their ability to get heard, let alone survive, diminishes by the day. In recent times, nowhere has this been as clearly demonstrated as in the events unfolding in Syria, where a clearly weaker opposition has taken up weapons against the Syrian armed forces. Three decades went by between the Hama massacre of 1982 and the uprising of 2011. In 1982 the regime of President Hafiz al-Assad carried out a scorched earth operation against Sunni opponents. In the three decades since, opponents have sought to engage peacefully with the regime in their attempts to bring about limited political openings. The glimmer of hope they may have experienced with the accession to power of his son and successor, Bashar al-Assad, in 2000 would soon die down. In the past decade, the new president has proceeded to concentrate more power in the hands of an ever-narrowing circle of close family members and allies. Demonstrations against the Assad regime began in a peaceful manner; however, in the face of the regime's refusal to engage (and probably emboldened by the success of regime opponents elsewhere in the Middle East), regime opponents eventually came to the conclusion that violence was the only way, in spite of the then clear and overwhelming military superiority of regime forces. The situation in Syria also illustrates the difficulty of reaching a compromise when parties have very little trust in one another. At the beginning of the failed mission of United Nations (UN) special envoy, Kofi Annan, to find a negotiated way out of the crisis, one of the major stumbling blocks to a negotiated outcome was the opposition's lack of faith in the credibility of the Assad regime's commitments.

Trust also figures prominently in analyses of the transition from war to peace; the fragility of these transitions is framed in terms of a credible commitment problem (Walter 1997, 2001). Drawing upon realist approaches to international relations, scholars have made much of the fact that, at the onset of civil war, subnational groups face a security dilemma. Deprived of a higher authority to protect them, societal groups behave in the same way as states do in an anarchical system. They deeply mistrust one another's intentions and take whatever means necessary to protect themselves from impending threats to their survival (Posen 1993; Rose 2000). At the end of a conflict, mistrust prevents leaders, who might otherwise want to put their weapons down, from disarming and demobilizing. Indeed, leaders who remain unconvinced of the commitment of their opponents to the peace process fear that they might disarm in good faith and find themselves exposed and their security threatened. In Northern Ireland, this mistrust resulted in a drawn-out process of demobilization and disarmament that lasted well over a decade and, at several key points, threatened to unravel the gains of the Good Friday Agreement (MacGinty 1999; Mitchell 2008; Smyth 2004).

Overcoming the Credible Commitment Problem

The credible commitment problem stands in the way of successful transitions from war to peace. It raises the spectre of a relapse into violence, a spectre associated with the emergence of spoilers (Stedman 1997). Nor have some of the solutions proposed to overcome the problem been satisfactory.

Walter's (1997) pioneering work on this issue argues that only an external guarantor can mitigate the existing lack of trust and act as an arbiter in ensuring that both parties to a peace agreement make good on their commitments. This prescription makes the success of war-to-peace transitions dependent on the presence and commitment of third-party guarantors. While it is the case that such parties may or may not be interested and available to step in and help bring a given conflict to an end, even when they do, no third-party guarantor can or does stay long enough to help rebuild trust. The reality of international politics is such that the commitment of external parties is often limited and their ability to stay the course is hampered by competing priorities and domestic pressures for early exit (Durch 2006). From Afghanistan and Iraq to Libya, several recent examples illustrate this contention. Second, this approach focuses only on inter-elite dynamics, forgetting that the lack of trust among communities can go a long way towards narrowing the margin of manoeuvre of the elites (Tsebelis 1990). In locales where third-party guarantors decided to stay the course, their presence on the ground and their commitment to see the transition through have not always been sufficient to iron out difficulties. Nowhere is this more evident than in the limits of international peace building in the Balkans (Bougarel, Helms, and Duijzings 2007; Chandler 1998, 1999; Yordán 2003).

In seeking to address the obvious limitations of peacekeeping deployments as a solution to the credible commitment problem, civil war analysts have turned to the literature on power sharing (Lijphart 1991). They have developed and tested the intuition that power sharing might compensate for the lack of trust in the short term by giving the various parties to a peace agreement constitutionally guaranteed rights and representation (McGarry and O'Leary 2004; Sisk and Stefes 2005; Wolff 2007). Distrustful actors, this body of work argues, might come to an agreement if the terms of this agreement increase their security; this is precisely what power sharing provides. The power-sharing literature thus provides a potential explanation for the prevalence of federal solutions to the transition from war to peace, particularly as many of these solutions do not simply divide power between a centre and units but include, as well, elements of power sharing at the centre between the various political masters of the day (hence the contention, at the beginning of this contribution, that the definitions of federalism and power sharing that I am using are "pure" ideal types). Indeed, recent iterations of this literature have argued that, the more dimensions of power sharing (military, political, territorial, and economic) there are in a peace agreement, the more likely the agreement is to endure (Hartzell and Hoddie 2007). Yet there are those who argue that power sharing does not overcome the lack of trust. Instead, it freezes a situation and creates obstacles on the road to peace and democracy (Roeder and Rothchild 2006; Zahar 2008). This is the context in which federalism is being suggested and implemented as an institutional solution meant to ease the transition from war to peace.[2]

Building Trust: What Role for Institutions?

For peace to be endogenously sustainable, trust needs to be built not only between elites but also among elites and their followers and between communities. The literature sees trust "as both a type of behavior and an underlying disposition" (Nooteboom 2007, 30). According to Deutsch, trust is a behaviour consisting of actions that (1) increase one's vulnerability to (2) the actions of another not under one's control and (3) in a situation where the worst outcome prevails when one suffers a penalty because the other has abused one's vulnerability (Deutsch 1962; cited in Nooteboom 2007, 30). Others have described trust as an expectation of reciprocity (Ostrom and Walker 2005) or "a type of expectation that alleviates the fear that one's exchange partner will act opportunistically" (Bradach and Eccles 1984, 104; quoted in Noteboom 2007, 30).

It has already been suggested that the mixed version of federalism that policymakers often propose as a way out of violence can contribute to creating inter-elite trust. As political negotiation replaces violence, leaders have more reason to believe that agreements will be honoured if the agreements provide for their security. Power-sharing agreements (sharing power at the centre, whether or not that is complemented by other dimensions of power sharing, such as a federal division of power between a centre and units) provide wartime elites with constitutionally guaranteed rights and representation. But can federalism create trust between elites and followers (also labelled intra-community trust)? Can it contribute to creating trust between communities? In what follows, I sketch out the contours of an argument that links state institutions to trust in the specific context of transitions from war to peace. I then put federalism, power sharing, and unitary majoritarian systems to the test of the argument, to probe which of these three types of institutional arrangements is more likely to generate trust as states and societies move away from war and attempt to establish the foundations for lasting peace.

A lot has been written on the link between institutions and trust. It can be argued that the notion of political trust is meaningless (Hardin 1999) because trust "implies specific knowledge about the likelihood of trustworthy behavior by someone else," something that cannot extend to citizens' attitudes towards the political system (Hooghe and Zmerli 2011, 3). However, most of the research on the topic attempts to link the two concepts and can be broadly divided into two main bodies of literature: research that argues institutions can build trust (Cook, Hardin, and Levy 2005; Cook, Levy, and Hardin 2009; Levi 1997) and research that argues that trust is prior and that, in its absence, institutions cannot perform optimally (Almond and Verba 1963; Inglehart 1997; Putnam 1993).

For cultural theories, trust is exogenous, originating outside the political sphere in "the long-standing and deeply seeded beliefs about people that are rooted in cultural norms and communicated through early-life socialization" (Mishler and Rose 2001, 31). From that perspective, building trust is a path-dependent process that takes time. As scholars who have studied transitions from communism to democracy argue, this perspective leads us to expect that "there is little that can be done in the short run to cultivate trust in new democratic institutions" (ibid., 33). Moreover, the cultural perspective expects people who trust each other to cooperate more readily and to form informal as well as formal associations (Putnam 1993, 1995). It is this interpersonal trust that is ultimately "projected onto political institutions, creating a civil culture" (Almond and Verba 1963; cited in Mishler and Rose 2001, 34). Building upon this research, one can extend the argument to transitions from war to peace. In such contexts, cultural theories would expect institutions to be unable to generate trust. They would also expect to see intra-community rather than inter-community cooperation or, in the language of students of civil society, they would hypothesize that bonding associations will be both more common and more efficient than bridging associations.

Institutional theories are of particular relevance when we examine claims that federalism can provide an institutional way out of the credible commitment problem generated by the lack of trust that is common at the end of a civil war. These theories argue that trust is politically endogenous. They contend that "state institutions encourage cooperation by providing third-party enforcement to insure personal safety and the security of exchange" (Cook, Levy, and Hardin 2009, 4). This body of analysis suggests that "the more the state demonstrates the reliability and neutrality of its institutions, the more it is able to facilitate the establishment of personal trustworthiness by allowing individuals to begin relationships with relatively small risks as they learn about each other, and by providing insurance against failed trust" (ibid., 4). The literature also argues that well-performing institutions generate trust, whereas untrustworthy ones yield mistrust. As Mishler and Rose rightly note, "this is not to deny the reality of early-life cultural influences. On the contrary, insofar as political institutions persist and perform relatively consistently over successive generations, political socialization and institutional performance should exert very similar and reinforcing effects on trust in institutions" (31). In other words, the institutional literature investigates the role of institutions in building horizontal trust among individuals as well as vertical trust between citizens and the state.

What expectations does the institutional literature hold for state institutions created on the morrow of a transition from war to peace? For this literature, trust is generated as a result of two mechanisms: repetition (in game-theoretic terms, iterated or multiple-shot games) and reciprocity. Extending the logic to the context of transitions from war to peace, one can argue that the new institutions are still untested. They cannot really claim to have established a pattern of repetition, nor have they provided proof of reciprocity. There is little indication, prima facie, that institutional performance could be a generator of trust in such conditions. Nor, as discussed earlier in this contribution, can political socialization help, at least not in the sense of rebuilding trust among communities.

Building Trust in Times of Transition

Although the literature does not expect newly created institutions to be able to generate trust among elites and followers and between communities, the rest of this chapter develops precisely such an argument, although one extremely circumscribed in scope. In this section, I argue that state institutions can contribute to building trust if, and only if, they are perceived to contribute minimally to the maintenance of order and security.

Recent research on political trust has emphasized the importance of context (Zmerli and Hooghe 2011). This research argues, among other things, that experience is key in generating citizens' trust in their political institutions. Thus, Rose and Mishler argue that the notion of a fatal legacy of communist socialization is a myth and that citizens in post-communist countries can learn to trust as they accumulate experience in how they are being governed. Similarly, research on the impact of peacekeeping suggests that, even on the morrow of drawn-out and particularly violent civil wars, the deployment of peacekeeping forces will have an impact on the dynamics between protagonists. The deployment of even small and relatively militarily weak peacekeeping missions functions as a cooperation mechanism that alters incentives, alleviates fear and mistrust, prevents accidental escalation to war, and shapes political procedures to stabilize peace (Fortna 2008). Drawing upon the insights of this research, one can build a minimal version of the argument linking post-war institutions to trust. In this minimal version, institutions, though untried and untested, nevertheless generate experiences that affect citizens' political trust. Since the maintenance of order and stability is the primary indicator of a successful transition from war to peace, this provides the baseline against which citizens judge the performance of new state institutions.

State institutions create trust in their ability to maintain order and stability by sending two sets of signals to communities, thus contributing to rebuild vertical trust between the state and society. If inter-elite cooperation can be constrained by popular pressure, then the more vertical trust is built between the state and society, the more communities will allow their elites to compromise. Scholars have acknowledged the importance of the elites' relative freedom to manoeuvre for the smooth functioning of power-sharing arrangements (Lijphart 1969, 1977, 1991). They have also argued that, in divided societies, community support for elites depends on two factors: the availability of options and information (Tsebelis 1990). In line with the experiential literature on trust, I therefore argue that the ability of state institutions to maintain order and stability provides citizens with information that translates into support for inter-elite cooperation to maintain and enhance the efficient functioning of the institutions.

The first set signals to communities that *the state will not allow anyone to use violence against them* (Saideman and Zahar 2008). In line with the Weberian understanding of the state as the repository of the monopoly of legitimate violence, the state seeks to deter groups and individuals from resorting to weapons in the pursuit of given objectives, whatever these may be. In so doing, the state fulfils its role of protecting citizens and prevents the development of the so-called security dilemma, which has been linked to the outbreak of civil war (Posen 1993; Rose 2000). To be able to fulfil this deterrence role credibly, the state needs to send information to the effect that it is (1) willing and (2) able to use violence against any group that contravenes the rules (Martin-Brûlé 2012). However, deterrence alone does not necessarily generate trust. It may generate a disposition by groups and individuals not to disobey the rules, but that can be the outcome of a straightforward calculus of cost-benefits and self-interest. Thus, trust needs to go beyond deterrence if it is not to be conflated with power (Maguire, Nelson, and Hardy 2001). Organizational theorists looking at the issue have argued that trust needs to include notions of goodwill or benevolence (see the special issue of *Organization Studies*, 2001). In earlier work, Stephen Saideman and I developed the notion of assurance or the second set of signals necessary to generate trust, whereby the state signals to communities that *it will not use violence against them* (Saideman and Zahar 2008). The first set of signals, deterrence, revolves around the state's military and security capabilities and the decisions regulating their role and the conditions of their deployment; in other words, deterrence is organically linked to the ability to ensure national security. The second set of signals, assurance, focuses more specifically on the normative architecture of the military and security forces, including, but not limited to, considerations regarding the nature of civil-military relations and others captured under the rubric of security sector reform and dealing with issues of public security/safety.

The discussion above yields four distinct expectations. If and when state institutions send signals of both deterrence and assurance, the experience of citizens and groups will likely generate political trust. When neither is present, the state's inability to provide order and security will generate high mistrust and the ground will be fertile for a relapse into violence. When the state deters but fails to assure, it generates compliance in response to power, but that acquiescence, as discussed earlier, should not be mistaken for trust. Finally, when the state assures but does not deter, its ability to credibly maintain order and security is always open to be tested, particularly by groups that secure the ability to build sufficient military might. Though groups might not distrust the state's intentions towards them, they will have little faith in its ability to protect them from one another and will likely seek alter-

Table 4.1
Deterrence, Assurance, and Trust

	Deterrence	No Deterrence
Assurance	Benevolent / Capable State *Trust in State's ability and willingness to protect*	Benevolent / Weak State *Mistrust of State ability to protect*
No Assurance	Authoritarian / Capable State *Trust in State's ability but not in its willingness to protect*	Authoritarian / Weak State *Mistrust of State willingness and ability to protect*

native measures to protect themselves. In the last scenario, one should expect the emergence of informal and extra-legal communal policing structures such as vigilantes, militia groups and other such self-help security structures.

Building Trust: The Promise of Federalism

If the lack of trust is such an obstacle to peace, and if federalism is being touted as a solution to societies emerging from war, then federalism should be able to contribute to restoring trust. This might well be the unspoken assumption (one might even say hope) of external actors who intervene in transitions from war to peace; theoretically, however, there is no compelling argument linking federalism to trust. In fact, Riker's foundational work on federalism suggests that this is a choice borne out of a bargain between politicians desiring to expand their territorial control but unwilling to use force to this effect and others willing to accept the bargain because of some external military-diplomatic threat or opportunity (1964, 12). This description of the origins of federalism does not fit the conditions of the set of countries under investigation. On the one hand, civil war is about the use of force in an attempt to expand territorial control or take over the government; on the other, the federal solution is not freely chosen by the parties but is suggested, even imposed, by outside interveners as a way to stop the killing. Some specialists argue that federalism requires a basic level of societal trust to function, what some would call "vouloir vivre ensemble" (Simeon and Conway 2001, 362). But this societal will to coexist is often absent on the morrow of violent conflict. Other specialists suggest that federalism functions well when officials at the federal and subnational levels "share common values and speak a similar vocabulary as a result of a common training in a particular profession or discipline" (Dupré 1985, 5). In such instances, one sees the formation of intergovernmental networks characterized by trust relationships. However, this argument holds limited sway in the context of post-war countries, which are more often than not characterized by a dearth of human resources, particularly where conflicts have been enduring and societies torn apart. The alternative argument developed in the preceding section proposes that federalism may create experiential trust by laying the foundations of a state better equipped than most to deliver deterrence and assurance.

Is federalism better equipped to send deterrence and assurance signals than power sharing or majoritarian unitary rule (which has been linked by some to the most sustainable outcomes in war to peace transitions; see Duffy Toft 2009)? This section discusses security provisions under all three institutional arrangements in an attempt to assess whether federalism is better at creating experiential trust in the ability of the state to maintain order and stability while protecting its citizens. Before doing so, I briefly sketch out the contours of security management in post-conflict countries.

Post-Conflict Security Management

In the context of a transition from war to peace, security management is driven by a core principle: ensuring the security of people. Fuelled by research that emphasizes that the security of the state is not the same as the security of people and that, in fact, state security sometimes obtains at the expense of citizens (Buzan 1991), security sector reform was intended to create "a responsible, accountable and effective security sector" (Sedra 2010, 3) that would engender conditions "conducive to development, poverty reduction and democracy" (OECD/DAC 2005). During a transition from war to peace, security sector reform is the sum of all activities intended to reform security provision by the state and its agencies in such a way as to uphold several key norms and principles. Alongside the notion that security ought to be people centred, these include principles such as the primacy of the rule of law, democratic accountability and oversight, transparency, civilianization, as well as operational effectiveness, among others (Sedra 2010, 5–7). Although security sector reform includes political, institutional, economic, and societal dimensions, only the first two will be of concern to us here (Chanaa

2002). The political dimension of security sector reform is "intended not just to ensure civilian governance, but liberal, democratic civilian control." Its institutional dimension focuses on reform and capacity building; "it is a process of professionalization aimed at increasing operational effectiveness, rationalizing bureaucratic structures, eliminating corruption, and institutionalizing international standards" (Sedra 2010, 4). It is important to emphasize that, while the values and dimensions of security sector reform highlighted by these standard definitions can also be extended to areas such as the functioning of political institutions at large (thus running the risk of conflating security sector reform with democratic consolidation), security sector reform concerns the way in which these values and dimensions affect internal policing or public safety as well as the ethos of the military and, subsequently, the issue of civil-military relations.

As the state strives to rebuild its deterrent capability, demobilization and disarmament of non-state actors is an important component of this process and one that does not need further elaboration (Ball and van de Goor 2006; Pouligny 2004). Equally important is the clear demarcation between national and public security. In times of civil war, the armed forces are often deployed internally to fight insurgents. They are also involved in practices such as interrogation and military trials of rebels. Rebuilding the state's deterrent capability is in part premised on redesigning the role of the armed forces and their rules of engagement. It also requires the development of democratic oversight mechanisms so that the armed forces remain an instrument in the hands of elected civilian leaders. However, as discussed earlier, this also involves rebuilding the state's monopoly over the use of legitimate violence in ways that would allow the state to deter would-be insurgents credibly. Such restructuring requires the development of appropriate procurement, training, and capacity strategies to provide the army with tools to carry out its obligations. Last but not least, rebuilding the state's deterrent capability requires the design of political decision rules that empower political authorities to use the army if and when it is needed.

As discussed earlier, the state not only needs to be able to deter, but also must assure. This may involve elements such as the representation of societal diversity in the state's security services, something that is usually achieved through the reintegration of some former non-state combatants in the armed forces or the police (Glassmyer and Sambanis 2008; Hartzell and Hoddie 2006; Knight 2011). Assurance also involves the democratic consolidation of the work of the security services or what has been discussed earlier under the broader label of security service reform.

Restoring the Monopoly of Legitimate Violence and Deterring Challengers

How efficient would federal arrangements, power sharing and/or majority rule be in helping the state regain the monopoly of legitimate violence and rebuild its capability to deter violence? Of course, the answer depends on a host of factors that vary widely from one case to the other. Deterring violence takes on a very different meaning depending on whether one looks at Bosnia, a country in the Western Balkans, at Lebanon, a country sandwiched between Syria and Israel, or at the Democratic Republic of Congo, a country sharing international borders with nine other states and whose civil war was described as Africa's first world war because of the extensive – and sometimes direct – involvement of neighbouring states and their armies in the conflict. Rebuilding a country's ability to deter violence also depends on the success of disarmament, demobilization, and reintegration programs, which, as the literature shows, varies widely (Muggah 2009; Duclos 2010). Last, but not least, the outcome of efforts to rebuild a country's deterrence capacity on the morrow of civil war depends in large part on the availability of resources and assistance to this effect. The case of the Lebanese army is illustrative. Whereas rebuilding Lebanon's armed forces was a relatively low priority task for outsiders – with the exception of Syria – until 2006, this became a key priority of western powers after the Israel-Hezbollah war of summer 2006. Subsequently, the United States and France, among others, provided extensive backing to this effect in an attempt to counter Hezbollah's military dominance in the country (Barak 2009; Gates 2010; Nerguizian 2009).

However, ceteris paribus, an important part of the answer lies in decisional rules regulating the deployment of the state's military capabilities in times of threat. On this issue, both majoritarian systems and federal arrangements are expected to score better than power-sharing institutions. Power-sharing arrangements enshrine the principle of inclusive decision-making. This is intended as an assurance measure to communities that no decision will be taken against their will. In practice, it often translates to instruments such as minority vetoes or decisional rules requiring a supermajority for key decisions to be adopted in government. For example, the Bosnian Constitution (an annex to the Dayton Peace Agreement) provided safeguards for the vital interests of the Bosniak, Croat, and Serb peoples by setting out stringent majority requirements for the adoption of constitutional modifications.[3] Moreover, should any of the three constituent people consider a proposed decision of the Parliamentary Assembly or the presidency destructive to its vital interest, the constitution spells out detailed procedures to contain potential escalation (Articles IV-3-e, IV-3-f, and V-2-d) (Zahar 2002).

Because, in war-to-peace transitions, power-sharing arrangements are often structured along ethnic lines,[4] inclusive decision rules often translate into paralysis. This paralysis severely impedes the ability of the state to reassert its monopoly over the legitimate use of force; it also weakens the state's ability to deter. Nowhere is this more evident than in the recent history of Lebanon. When in 2008 and for the first time since the end of the civil war, the Hezbollah used its weapons against co-nationals in a 48-hour struggle prompted by a deepening political crisis with their domestic rivals, the government was unable to deploy the army. The latter stood on the sidelines of the first serious challenge to the state's monopoly over the use of legitimate violence; more important, it unilaterally decided to overturn two governmental decisions,[5] which had triggered the violence, thus taking a serious stab at the notion of civilian control of the military (Zahar 2009). Indeed, while the reconstruction of Lebanon's army sought to increase its representativeness (Salloukh 2005),[6] "the force remains risk averse and acutely aware of the need to preserve cohesion and cross-sectarian unity" (Zahar 2009, 123). The reasons for the Lebanese Armed Forces' decision have been variously interpreted; regardless of the motives, what became clear to all factions on 12 May 2008 was that the Lebanese state did not possess a deterrent force against either internal or external challengers to its monopoly over the use of legitimate violence.

Bosnia and Herzegovina provides an interesting case to study because of the evolution of the country's institutional arrangements and their impact on the state's ability to restore monopoly over legitimate violence as well as to build a credible deterrent against would-be challengers. Initially, the Dayton Peace Agreement established a weak central government and the two Entities (Republika Srpska and the Bosniak-Croat Federation) retained separate defence ministries and armed forces. Although federal systems usually locate the responsibility for national security with the central authorities, the Dayton Peace Agreement provided for only a weak Standing Committee on Military Matters (Vetschera and Damian 2006; Kaldor 2003). That the Bosnian state did not have a monopoly over the use of legitimate violence was evident; the international community had to introduce confidence-building measures based on Europe's Cold War experience to decrease the level of mistrust (Keridis and Perry 2004, 262; Drewienkiewicz 2003, 31–2). Beginning in 2000, internationals began to exert pressure to reduce the autonomy of the Entities and build strong central state institutions, thus effectively changing the basis of the Dayton Accords (Donais 2005, 55–9). A Defence Reform Commission, established by the Office of the High Representative, was entrusted with recommending military reforms that would allow Bosnia to join NATO's Partnership for Peace program. The commission drafted a law calling for a Bosnian ministry of defence, establishing a single command structure, a joint staff, and a single budget. Operational and administrative control of the armed forces would be vested in the collective presidency.[7] Still, the forces themselves would remain separate and the defence departments of the Entities remained responsible for recruitment and training (Caparini 2004, 152; Vetschera and Damian 2006, 34). Although it can be argued that the state has finally reasserted monopoly over the use of legitimate force, the process of integration is ongoing and raises concerns about the ability of Bosnia and Herzegovina to effectively deploy its armed forces as a deterrent against would-be challengers.

In comparison with systems based on the principle of power sharing, federal and unitary majoritarian systems usually place the management of national security threats squarely in the ambit of the central state authorities. In the United States, a federal country established after a bloody civil war, the Constitution grants Congress the power to declare war. The South African Constitution and the New Defence Act of 2002 similarly ensured that the South African National Defence Forces be solely responsible for the defence and protection of the country (Section 11, Article 200 (2)) under the oversight of parliament. The fact that white officers remained in post during the transition ensured the continued efficiency of the army and the credibility of its deterrent capability (Petersen and Staniland 2008).

Angola and Mozambique are two of the few post-conflict settings where majoritarian unitary institutions were maintained at the end of the war. In Angola, the army secured a military victory over UNITA (Union for the Total Independence of Angola). In Mozambique, the Rome Accords provided for limited reintegration of RENAMO (Mozambican National Resistance) fighters within the national army as well as for the demobilization of the ruling FRELIMO (Mozambican Liberation Front) and of RENAMO. Protocol IV of the Rome Accords stated that each branch of the new Mozambican armed forces would have an equal number of government forces and RENAMO cadres. Though not explicitly stated in the text of the Protocol, this was expected to apply all the way to the top (Coelho 1998; cited in Brown and Zahar 2008, 79). Although observers acknowledge the existence of serious concerns on the part of political opponents of the two regimes about the nature of the peace that was established in both countries, the governments' control of their armed forces is such that no one expects dissatisfied parties to challenge the state's monopoly over the use of legitimate violence (Brown and Zahar 2008; Lundin 2000; Manning 2002; Ngolo 2006; Nunda 2006; Weinstein 2002).

This brief survey of cases suggests that, all else being equal, majoritarian unitary systems and federal systems where central authorities are not selected according to the dictates of communal power sharing are best equipped to restore the state's monopoly over the use of legitimate violence. Post-conflict countries that adopt power-sharing arrangements fare worst on this score. Although a single case study cannot serve as a basis for generalization, the Bosnian experience suggests that federal systems where power is shared not only between a centre and units but at the centre between the communal leaders of the units will likewise experience snags and that progress in such instances entails the steadfast commitment of outsiders. Although I have not discussed these other cases, both the experience of the Sudan during the Comprehensive Peace Agreement and the experience of Iraq post-2003 seem to concur with this finding.

Assuring Groups Within

As discussed earlier, the state's deterrent power alone does not necessarily generate trust. It can merely generate compliance. For trust to obtain, the post-conflict institutional arrangements must not simply deter the use of force; they must assure citizens that the state will not use force against them. Of federal, power sharing and majoritarian unitary arrangements, which is most likely to signal assurance and why?

In unitary states, the same levels of government that provide national security have command and control of the reins of public safety. However, public safety provision can be either centralized or decentralized, even in unitary systems. In the last 30 years, for example, both France and Italy have seen "a significant rise in local police forces" (Roché 2011,

12). For their part, federal systems tend to delegate the responsibility for public safety to their constituent units, although here as well the degree of centralization vs. decentralization varies greatly; Spain provides an example of centralization, whereas the United States and Switzerland are at the opposite end of the spectrum. As for power-sharing arrangements, they are not usually associated with a specific method of managing public security. Instead, much depends on whether they are centralized (in which case they behave much like unitary systems) or decentralized (in which case they behave like federal systems but with important qualifiers).[8]

In the context of transitions from war to peace, the state can signal assurance in a number of ways. First and foremost, it can do so by changing the composition of the police forces so that they reflect the diversity in society. Next, the state can signal assurance by professionalizing its public safety institutions, thus ensuring their accountability and their transparency. This is the main objective of security sector reform. Assurance, much like deterrence, varies, depending on a host of factors. For example, the nature of the conflict and the manner in which the war ended can affect the government's willingness to change the composition of the police forces. In Iraq, the brutality of Saddam Hussein's regime contributed to the decision to purge the post-Saddam government, including the police forces, of members of the Ba'ath Party. As a result, however, Sunni representation in the police was almost absent. When in 2009 the United States of America transferred responsibility for the Sunni Awakening Movement, which had been instrumental in the fight against al-Qaida in Iraq, to the Iraqi authorities, the reluctance of Prime Minister Nouri al-Maliki to integrate Awakening militiamen in the Iraqi security forces highlighted the weight of the past (Zahar 2009, 187–8). Likewise, the nature of assistance in the reform of the security sector varies widely and it can impact the ability of the state to assure. In the early 2000s, the U.S. Plan Colombia, although framed as assistance to the security sector, resulted in the militarization of the Colombian state's management of internal opposition. Cognizant of these variations, I argue that, ceteris paribus, federal arrangements provide the most reliable set of signals intended to assure communities on the morrow of civil conflict. In terms of their ability to assure, unitary centralized states are expected to fare the worst.

The representation of society's diversity in its armed forces and in the police is a first step towards assuring citizens. As discussed earlier, the composition of the officer corps of the Lebanese Armed Forces changed drastically between 1992 and 2004. In Mozambique, the Rome Accords provided for the integration of RENAMO rebels in the armed forces and the police. In South Africa, the South Africa National Defence Forces composition changed as Statutory and Non-Statutory Forces were integrated into a single military establishment.[9] However, the decision to maintain white officers at their command posts went a long way to assure the white minority during the transition process. Yet in and by itself, the representation of diversity is insufficient to provide assurance. Two problems arise in this connection: the reversibility of the move and the gap between theory and practice.

The representation of diversity in the public safety agencies is intended to convey the message that the state is keen on protecting its people, all of its people. Nevertheless, mechanisms to this effect can easily be reversed. Mozambique provides a telling tale. As the ruling FRELIMO consolidated power and as the line between party and state became progressively blurred,[10] it reneged on its commitments under Protocol IV of the Rome Accords concerning the integration of RENAMO combatants in the armed forces. RENAMO commanders were increasingly being retired or taken off active duty, thus increasing FRELIMO's relative proportion of active soldiers. Further, "At FRELIMO's insistence, the role and composition of the police and security forces [had been] excluded in the Rome Accords, effectively leaving the police and state security forces in FRELIMO's hands" (Brown and Zahar 2008, 81). In comparison, the 1979 Nigerian Constitution enshrined the "federal character, " a principle that sought to ensure that appointments to public service institutions fairly reflect the linguistic, ethnic, religious, and geographic diversity of the country. According to Nnoli (1998, 151), this has meant historically balancing the North and the South – Igbo, Yoruba, Hausa-Fulani – and this trinity as a whole against other minority groups. Section 197(2) of the Constitution provided: "The composition of the officer corps and other ranks of the armed forces of the Federation shall reflect the federal character." In practice, application of the principle in the federal civil service and in the military has "amounted to a confused balancing of the merit principle and the quota system, based essentially on states of origin. This has had adverse consequences for both institutions in terms of discipline, morale, and overall effectiveness and efficiency" (Adamolekun et al. 1991, 75).

Where security sector reform either has not been implemented or has partially failed, for whatever reason, representativeness alone will be insufficient to generate assurance. Although the Lebanese security services are undoubtedly more representative today than they were before the war, the behaviour of security forces and the lack of mechanisms of civilian oversight mean that a majority of Lebanese see the security agencies as a potential source of insecurity (Gaub 2011; Zahar 2002). In such conditions, whether federal or unitary, decentralized systems might have a slight advantage over centralized systems in that they bring public safety management closer to the people, thus increasing the opportunity for civilians to develop ways to engage with and affect the behaviour of the police and other security agencies. In Afghanistan, two such experiments were attempted: the Afghan National Auxiliary Police (ANAP) from 2006 to 2008, and the Afghan Social Outreach Program (ASOP) after 2008. Both sought to bring policing closer to the local level in an attempt to address the proverbial shortcomings of the Afghan National Police, widely known for its corruption and its contribution to the insecurity of Afghan citizens. Afghans fear and resent a force whose members have been involved in extortion, illegal taxation, kidnappings, and bank robberies (Rubin 2007). Although the impulse behind both programs sought to draw upon local structures to protect communities, program design and implementation were problematic in a number of ways. Their members were drawn from local militias, thus contradicting the government's demobilization efforts and threatening its monopoly over the means of violence. Further, the fact that ANAP and ASOP were implemented in Pashtun areas but not in other areas caused non-Pashtun militias, which were disarmed under Afghanistan's disarmament, demobilization, and reintegration program, to worry. Last but not least, the vetting and accountability procedures were not sufficiently strong to shield ANAP and ASOP from the factionalism and corruption that beset the Afghan National Police (Sedra 2008, 199). Comparative analysis of other cases, including Burundi, Haiti, and South Sudan, suggests that although the space for police reform has indeed increased and while surveys suggest that citizens acknowledge improvements in police performance, nevertheless concerns about police forces and their ability to assure are rooted in problems of efficiency and accountability (Baranyi and Salahub 2011, 57). Many, notably among the South Sudanese, perceive local authorities as the primary providers of security, but these results highlight the gap between theory and practice.

Concluding Thoughts: Back to Practice ... and Policy

This contribution began with an empirical observation: federal solutions are increasingly being adopted around the world as the institutional arrangement most likely to bring states and societies out of war. Policy-makers tout the ability of federalism to overcome the credible commitment problem. However, no one has unpacked the assumption that federalism can substitute for or generate trust where none is present.

Starting from the premise that trust is created through experience, I have developed an argument based on a minimalist approach to political trust as the citizens' belief that the state will be able to deter threats and that it will also refrain from using force against them. This initial probe has drawn upon the experience of several post-conflict countries to assess the performance of federal arrangements in contrast to power sharing or majoritarian unitary systems. The evidence culled from the various cases suggests that federalism does indeed hold a promise. As a system that attempts to simultaneously build in and build out, federalism allows the central state to restore monopoly over the legitimate use of violence and to build a deterrent capability while at the same time allowing units to manage public safety in ways that assure wary citizens because of the proximity between the population and the security forces and agencies. In comparison, majoritarian systems are more likely to fall under the control of dominant groups delivering deterrence but failing to assure other groups that the state will not use violence against them. Post-conflict power-sharing systems, with their community-based, representational guarantees and veto points, may score well on the assurance principle, but are prone to fail on the deterrence side, because of the likelihood of policy blockage, inaction, and the absence of a coherent political authority and an effective central command structure.

Of course, the promise of federalism is not without qualifiers. Much depends not only on theory but on practice. As the institutionalist literature tells us, trust is best fostered by institutions operating over time, where the institutions and the people who operate them behave predictably and consistently in accordance with the norms and practices that compose the institutional architecture. New post-conflict institutions cannot claim the benefits from iterated interactions and history of reciprocity. Indeed, as illustrated in the examples used throughout this contribution, new institutions have often failed in practice, either because they have been captured or because they have proven inefficient and thus incapable of meeting the challenges thrown their way. New federal institutions are thus equally vulnerable as power sharing or majoritarian unitary systems. However, if the preliminary results of this probe are borne out in more detailed and extensive analysis, ceteris paribus, federal systems hold a much stronger promise of bringing countries out of war than other forms of institutional arrangements. This has implications for policy and international practice in peace-building and post-conflict reconstruction settings.

This contribution has compared federal systems understood as systems where power is divided between a centre and units, with power sharing and majoritarian unitary systems. Of the three, two institutional set-ups are intended to address the credible commitment problem. Federal systems create ethnic units where communities and their wartime leaders retain sub-national control over themselves and their home territories. Power sharing at the centre apportions power between wartime leaders. As discussed in the chapter, reality is messier.[11] Many federal arrangements include ethnic power sharing at the centre. But where they do, the dynamics of ethnic politics have worked to hamper the effective functioning of institutions (Simonsen 2005). In such instances, the assurance principle may have been satisfied but the deterrence principle was not. This suggests that, in line with the recommendations of Roeder and Rothchild (2006), international mediators should think twice about using power sharing as the only principle upon which to build the post-conflict institutions. Although power sharing might be needed to address the credible commitment problem, it needs to be accompanied by power dividing. Federalism provides an opportunity to do exactly that, with units organized around a principle of ethnic majoritarianism and a centre organized around a different majoritarian principle. As Philip Roeder has argued elsewhere (2006), multiple majoritarianism stabilizes the political game by drawing the focus of politics away from purely ethnic concerns.

Because they are fragile and untested, the new institutions established on the morrow of civil war will not be able to achieve sustainable peace without foreign support and assistance. Several authors have already weighed in on the incoherence and lack of political will that often characterize efforts at security sector reform (Chanaa 2002; Nathan 2004). International interveners can and should play a key role in shielding the new institutions from factionalism or corruption and in assisting them in becoming efficient and meeting the expectations of citizens. Nowhere, however, are the stakes made clearer than in Mark Sedra's assessment of the situation in Afghanistan:

> Security sector reform is both a microcosm of the state building process and the key to its success. Many of the same challenges that have afflicted

the SSR process encompass the entire state building project, whether it is in the area of coordination or ownership. The stakes for SSR are particularly high, as development, reconstruction, and institution building in Afghanistan will be hard pressed to move forward until a secure environment is provided. The population will question the legitimacy of the state unless the government can provide that most basic public good: security. (2008, 213)

In conclusion, if institutions can generate trust by providing security to citizens and if, as this contribution has argued, federal institutions are best equipped to do so, while power sharing is most appropriate to address the credible commitment problem, then it is incumbent upon foreign interveners to draw the implications for their practice as they engage in designing institutions and carrying out security sector reforms in countries transitioning from war to peace.

NOTES

1   The chapter compares federalism with power-sharing and unitary majoritarian systems. For the purposes of the argument, I define federalism as a set of institutions that divide powers between a centre and units. Power sharing refers to the division of power at the centre between various constituent groups of a polity. Majoritarian unitary systems centralize power. However, these are ideal types and I readily acknowledge, for example, that there exist a number of federal arrangements that include power-sharing institutions. The intent here is to identify which specific institutions, decision rules, and procedures are most likely to contribute to building trust.

2   In the debate between supporters and detractors of power sharing, the question has been raised as to whether the weaknesses identified by critics are inherent in the model or whether they are the consequence of a specific form of power sharing, namely, the sharing of power between ethnic groups. Although the question is legitimate and its answer important, it is also important to note that ethnic power sharing is overwhelmingly predominant in the context of war to peace transitions.

3   Under Article X, a decision of the Parliamentary Assembly, including a two-thirds majority of those present and voting in the House of Representatives, is necessary to amend the Constitution.

4   For example, the Dayton Peace Agreement equally divided power in Bosnia and Herzegovina between Bosniaks, Serbs, and Croats. Iraq's post-2003

structure is premised on sharing power between Kurds and Arabs. Sudan's Comprehensive Peace Agreement divided power between the North and the South, understood as representing respectively Sudan's Arab and Muslim populations and its Non-Arab and Non-Muslim denizens.

5 The head of airport security, Lebanese Armed Forces (LAF) General Shoukeir, whom the government accused of being too close to Hezbollah, was dismissed and the Hezbollah's telecommunication network was dismantled .

6 Between 1991 and 2004, the sectarian distribution of the officers' corps shifted from being predominantly Christian Maronite in composition to including approximately 47% Christian (including non-Maronite) to 53% Muslim officers.

7 The presidency of Bosnia is a collective position with one representative from each of the three constituent peoples.

8 The qualifiers concern the constitutional guarantees that enshrine the powers of units in a federation. In other instances, the decentralization of powers can easily be revoked.

9 "Statutory Forces" refers to the White South African Defense Force and to the Bantustan Forces. "Non-Statutory Forces" refers to MK ("Spear of the nation"), the armed wing of the African National Congress and to the Azanian People's Liberation Army, the armed wing of the Pan-Africanist Congress (Higgs 2000).

10 The international community's insistence on dealing with the state as the key recipient of international assistance without acknowledging the blurring of lines between state and party has resulted in a growing capability gap and power asymmetry between the ruling party and the opposition.

11 Another dimension of this messy reality is the problem of minorities within minorities. With regard to this problem, a non-ethnic federal centre would allow minorities within minorities to play a role and be represented at the centre, an option that is unavailable where all levels of government have been designed around the major ethnic groups, effectively precluding the meaningful participation of other communities (the Jewish and Roma communities of Bosnia and Herzegovina or the Christian communities of Iraq) in the country's political life.

REFERENCES

Adamolekun, Ladipo, John Erero, and Basil Oshionebo. 1991. "Federal Character" and Management of the Federal Civil Service and the Military. *Publius: Federalism in Nigeria: Toward Federal Democracy* 21(4):75–88.

Almond, Gabriel A., and Sydney Verba. 1963. *The Civic Culture: Political Attitudes and Democracy in Five Nations*. Princeton: Princeton University Press.

Ball, Nicole, and Luc van de Goor. 2006. *Disarmament, Demobilization and Reintegration: Mapping Issues, Dilemmas and Principles*. The Hague: Netherlands Institute of International Relations "Clingandael" / Conflict Research Unit.

Barak, Oren. 2009. *The Lebanese Army: A National Institution in a Divided Society*. New York: State University of New York Press.

Baranyi, Stephen, and Jennifer Erin Salahub. 2011. Police Reform and Democratic Development in Lower-Profile Fragile States. *Canadian Journal of Development Studies / Revue canadienne d'études du développement* 32(1):48–63.

Bhatt, Shiv Raj, and Syed Mansoob Murshed. 2009. Nepal: Federalism for Lasting Peace. *Journal of Law and Conflict Resolution* 1(6):121–40.

Bougarel, Xavier, Elissa Helms, and Ger Duijzings, eds. 2007. *The New Bosnian Mosaic: Identities, Memories and Moral Claims in a Post-War Society*. Aldershot: Ashgate.

Bradach, Jeffrey L., and Robert G. Eccles. 1984. Price, Authority, and Trust: From Ideal Types to Plural Forms. *Annual Review of Sociology* (15):97–118.

Brown, Stephen, and Marie-Joëlle Zahar. 2008. Committing to Peace: Soft Guarantees and Alternative Approaches to Power Sharing in Angola and Mozambique. *Journal of Peacebuilding and Development* 4(2):75–88.

Buzan, Barry. 1991. *People, States, and Fear: An Agenda for International Security Studies in the Post-Cold War Era*. 2nd ed. Boulder: Lynne Rienner.

Caparini, Marina. 2004. *Civil Society and Democratic Oversight of the Security Sector: A Preliminary Investigation*. Geneva: Geneva Centre for the Democratic Control of the Armed Forces.

Chanaa, Jane. 2002. *Security Sector Reform: Issues, Challenges and Prospects*. Adelphi Paper 344. New York: Oxford University Press.

Chandler, David. 1998. Democratization in Bosnia: The Limits of Civil Society Building Strategies. *Democratization* 5(4):78–102.

Chandler, David. 1999. The Limits of Peace-Building: International Regulation and Civil Society Development in Bosnia. *International Peacekeeping* 6(1):109–25.

Coelho, João Paulo Borges. 1998. Epilogue: "Purification" vs. "Reconciliation" among Ex-Combatants. In *The Mozambican Peace Process in Perspective*, edited by Alex Vines and Dylan Hendrickson. Accord/International Review of Peace Initiatives. Vol. 3. London: Conciliation Resources.

Cook, Karen S., Russell Hardin, and Margaret Levy. 2005. *Cooperation without Trust*. New York: Russell Sage Foundation.

Cook, Karen S., Margaret Levy, and Russell Hardin, eds. 2009. *Whom Can We*

Trust? How Groups, Networks, and Institutions Make Trust Possible. New York: Russell Sage Foundation.

Deutsch, M. 1962. Cooperation and Trust: Some Theoretical Notes. In *Nebraska Symposium on Motivation*, edited by M.R. Jones. Lincoln: University of Nebraska Press.

Donais, Timothy. 2005. *The Political Economy of Peacebuilding in Post-Dayton Bosnia*. London: Routledge.

Drewienkiewicz, John. 2003. Budgets as Arms Control – The Bosnian Experience. *RUSI Journal* 148(2):30–5

Duclos, Nathalie, ed. 2010. *L'adieu aux armes: parcours d'anciens combattants*. Paris: Karthala.

Duffy Toft, Monica. 2009. *Securing the Peace: The Durable Settlement of Civil Wars*. Princeton: Princeton University Press.

Dupré, J. Stefan. 1985. Reflections on the Workability of Executive Federalism. In *Intergovernmental Relations*, edited by Richard Simeon. Toronto: University of Toronto Press.

Durch, William J., ed. 2006. *Twenty-First Century Peace Operations*. Washington, D.C.: The United States Institute of Peace.

Fearon, James, and David Laitin. 2003. Ethnicity, Insurgency, and Civil War. *American Political Science Review* 97(1):75–90.

Fortna, Virginia P. 2008. *Does Peacekeeping Work? Shaping Belligerents' Choices after Civil War*. Princeton: Princeton University Press.

Gagnon, Alain-G., and James Tully, eds. 2001. *Multinational Democracies*. Cambridge: Cambridge University Press.

Gates, Robert M. 2010. Helping Others Defend Themselves: The Future of U.S. Security Assistance. *Foreign Affairs* 89(3):2–6.

Gaub, Florence. 2011. *Rebuilding Armed Forces: Learning from Iraq and Lebanon*. Carlisle: Strategic Studies Institute, U.S. Army War College.

Ghai, Yash. 2000. *Autonomy and Ethnicity: Negotiating Competing Claims in Multi-Ethnic States*. Cambridge: Cambridge University Press.

Glassmyer, Katherine, and Nicholas Sambanis. 2008. Rebel-Military Integration and Civil War Termination. *Journal of Peace Research* 45(3):365–84.

Gromes, Thorsten. 2010. Federalism as a Means of Peace-Building: The Case of Postwar Bosnia and Herzegovina. *Nationalism and Ethnic Politics* 16(3–4):354–74.

Hardin, Russell. 1999. Do We Want Trust in Government? In *Democracy and Trust*, edited by Mark Warren. Cambridge: Cambridge University Press.

Hartzell, Caroline A., and Matthew Hoddie. 2006. From Anarchy to Security: Comparing Theoretical Approaches to the Process of Disarmament Following Civil War. *Contemporary Security Policy* 27(1):155–67.

Hartzell, Caroline A., and Matthew Hoddie. 2007. *Crafting Peace: Power-Sharing Institutions and the Negotiated Settlement of Civil Wars*. University Park: Pennsylvania State University Press.

Henrard, Kristin. 2002. Post-Apartheid South Africa's Democratic Transformation Process: Redress of the Past, Reconciliation and "Unity in Diversity." *Global Review of Ethnopolitics* 1(3):18–38.

Higgs, James A. 2000. Creating the South African National Defence Force. *Joint Forces Quarterly* 18(3):45–50.

Hooghe, Marc, and Sonja Zmerli. 2011. Introduction: The Context of Political Trust. In *Political Trust: Why Context Matters*, edited by Sonja Zmerli and Marc Hooghe. Colchester: ECPR Press.

Inglehart, Ronald. 1997. *Modernization and Postmodernization: Cultural, Economic, and Political Change in 43 Societies*. Princeton: Princeton University Press.

Kaldor, Mary. 2003. Security Structures in Bosnia and Herzegovina. In *Governing Insecurity: Democratic Control of Military and Security Establishments in Transitional Democracies*, edited by Gavin Cawthra and Robin Luckham. London: Zed Books.

Keridis, Dimitrios, and Charles Perry, eds. 2004. *Defense Reform, Modernization, & Military Cooperation in Southeastern Europe*. Vol. 3 of the IFPA-Kokkalis Series on Southeast European Policy. Washington, D.C.: Institute for Foreign Policy Analysis.

Knight, Mark. 2011. Military Integration and War Termination. In *Monopoly of Force: The Nexus of DDR and SSR*, edited by Melanne A. Civic and Michael Miklaucic. Washington, D.C.: National Defense University Press.

Levi, Margaret. 1997. *Consent, Dissent, and Patriotism*. Cambridge: Cambridge University Press.

Lijphart, Arend. 1969. Consociational Democracy. *World Politics* 21(2):207–25.

Lijphart, Arend. 1977. *Democracy in Plural Societies: A Comparative Exploration*. New Haven: Yale University Press.

Lijphart, Arend. 1991. Constitutional Choices for New Democracies. *Journal of Democracy* 2(1):72–84.

Lundin, Irâe Baptista. 2000. Africa Watch: Will Mozambique Remain a Success Story? *African Security Review* 9(3):79–88.

MacGinty, Roger. 1999. Biting the Bullet: Decommissioning in the Transition from War to Peace in Northern Ireland. *Irish Studies in International Affairs* 10:237–47.

Maguire, Steve, Phillips Nelson, and Cynthia Hardy. 2001. When 'Silence = Death,' Keep Talking: Trust, Control and the Discursive Construction of Identity in the Canadian HIV/AIDS Treatment Domain. *Organization Studies* 22(2):285–310.

Manning, Carrie. 2002. *The Politics of Peace in Mozambique: Post-Conflict Democratization, 1992–2000*. Westport and London: Praeger.

Martin-Brûlé, Sarah-Myriam. 2012. Assessing Peace Operations' Mitigated Outcomes. *International Peacekeeping* 19(2):235–50.

McGarry, John, and Brendon O'Leary. 2004. *The Northern Ireland Conflict: Consociational Engagements*. Oxford: Oxford University Press.

Mishler, William, and Richard Rose. 2001. What Are The Origins of Political Trust? Testing Institutional and Cultural Theories in Post-Communist Societies. *Comparative Political Studies* 34(1):30–62.

Mitchell, Claire. 2008. The Limits of Legitimacy: Former Loyalist Combatants and Peace-Building in Northern Ireland. *Irish Political Studies* 23(1):1–19.

Muggah, Robert, ed. 2009. *Security and Post-Conflict Reconstruction: Dealing with Fighters in the Aftermath of War*. London: Routledge.

Nathan, Laurie. 2004. *Obstacles to Security Sector Reform in New Democracies*. Berlin: Berghof Research Center for Constructive Conflict Management.

Nerguizian, Aram. 2009. *The Lebanese Armed Forces: Challenges and Opportunities in Post-Syria Lebanon*. Washington, D.C.: Center for Strategic and International Studies.

Ngolo, E. 2006. ("Manuvakola") UNITA Member of Parliament and former leader of UNITA-Renovada, interview with authors, 22 February, Luanda. Quoted in Stephen Brown and Marie-Joëlle Zahar, Committing to Peace: Soft Guarantees and Alternative Approaches to Power Sharing in Angola and Mozambique. *Journal of Peacebuilding and Development* 4(2):75–88.

Nnoli, Okwudiba, ed. 1998. *Ethnic Conflicts in Africa*. Nottingham: CODESRIA.

Nooteboom, Bart. 2007. Social Capital, Institutions, and Trust. *Review of Social Economy* 65(1):29–53.

Nunda, G. 2006. General and Chefe do Estado Maior General Adjunto, Angolan Armed Forces, interview with authors, 25 February, Luanda. Quoted in Stephen Brown and Marie-Joëlle Zahar, Committing to Peace: Soft Guarantees and Alternative Approaches to Power Sharing in Angola and Mozambique. *Journal of Peacebuilding and Development* 4(2):75–88.

Organisation for Economic Co-operation and Development, Development Cooperation Directorate (OECD/DAC). 2005. Paris: The Paris Declaration on Aid Effectiveness. Available at http://www.oecd.org/development/aideffectiveness/34428351.pdf

Ostrom, Elinor, and James Walker, eds. 2005. *Trust and Reciprocity: Interdisciplinary Lessons from Experimental Research*. New York: Russell Sage Foundation.

Petersen, Roger, and Paul Staniland. 2008. Resentment, Fear, and the Structure of the Military in Multiethnic States. In *Intra-State Conflict, Governments and*

Security: Dilemmas of Deterrence and Assurance, edited by Stephen M. Saideman and Marie-Joëlle Zahar. London: Routledge.

Posen, Barry. 1993. The Security Dilemma and Ethnic Conflict. *Survival* 35(2): 27–47.

Pouligny, Béatrice. 2004. *Ils nous avaient promis la paix: Opérations de l'ONU et populations locales*. Paris: Presses de Sciences Po.

Putnam, Robert. 1993. *Making Democracy Work: Civic Traditions in Modern Italy*. Princeton: Princeton University Press.

Putnam, Robert. 1995. Bowling Alone: America's Declining Social Capital. *Journal of Democracy* 6(1):65–78.

Riker, William H. 1964. *Federalism: Origin, Operation, Significance*. Boston and Toronto: Little, Brown.

Roché, Sebastian. 2011. *Federalism and Police Systems*. Geneva: Geneva Centre for the Democratic Control of the Armed Forces.

Roeder, Philip. 2006. Power Dividing as an Alternative to Ethnic Power Sharing. In *Sustainable Peace: Power and Democracy after Civil Wars*, edited by Philip G. Roeder and Donald Rothchild. Ithaca: Cornell University Press.

Roeder, Philip G., and Donald Rothchild, eds. 2006. *Sustainable Peace: Power and Democracy after Civil Wars*. Ithaca: Cornell University Press.

Rose, William. 2000. The Security Dilemma and Ethnic Conflict: Some New Hypotheses. *Security Studies* 9(4):1–51.

Rubin, Barnett R. 2007. Saving Afghanistan. *Foreign Policy* 86(1):57–78.

Saideman, Stephen M., and Marie-Joëlle Zahar, eds. 2008. *Intra-State Conflict, Governments and Security: Dilemmas of Deterrence and Assurance*. London: Routledge.

Salloukh, Bassel. 2005. Syria and Lebanon: A Brotherhood Transformed. *Middle East Report* 236(4):4–13.

Saunders, Cheryl. 2003. Federalism, Decentralisation, and Conflict-Management in Multicultural Societies. In *Federalism in a Changing World: Learning from Each Other*, edited by Raoul Blindenbacher and Arnold Koller. Montreal and Kingston: McGill-Queen's University Press.

Sedra, Mark. 2008. Security Sector Reform and State Building in Afghanistan. In *Afghanistan: Transition under Threat*, edited by Geoffrey Hayes and Mark Sedra. Waterloo: Wilfrid Laurier University Press and The Centre for International Governance Innovation.

Sedra, Mark. 2010. *Security Sector Reform 101: Understanding the Concept, Charting Trends and Identifying Challenges*. Waterloo: The Centre for International Governance Innovation.

Simeon, Richard, and Daniel-Patrick Conway. 2001. Federalism and the Management of Conflict in Multinational Societies. In *Multinational Democracies*, edited by Alain-G. Gagnon and James Tully. Cambridge: Cambridge University Press.

Simonsen, Sven Gunnar. 2005. Addressing Ethnic Divisions in Post-Conflict Institution-Building: Lessons from Recent Cases. *Security Dialogue* 36(3):297–318.

Sisk Timothy, and Christoph Stefes. 2005. Power Sharing as an Interim Step in Peace Building: Lessons from South Africa for Other Divided Societies. In *Sustainable Peace: Power and Democracy after Civil Wars,* edited by Philip G. Roeder and Donald Rothchild. Ithaca: Cornell University Press.

Smyth, Marie. 2004. The Process of Demilitarization and the Reversibility of the Peace Process in Northern Ireland. *Terrorism and Political Violence* 16(3):544–66.

Stedman, Stephen J. 1997. Spoiler Problems in Peace Processes. *International Security* 22(2):5–53.

Tillin, Louise. 2007. Unity in Diversity? Asymmetry in Indian Federalism. *Publius* 37(1):45–67.

Tsebelis, George. 1990. *Nested Games: Rational Choice in Comparative Politics.* Berkeley and Los Angeles: University of California Press.

Tsebelis, George. 1995. *Veto Players: How Political Institutions Work.* Princeton: Princeton University Press and Russell Sage Foundation.

Vetschera, Heinz, and Matthieu Damian. 2006. Security Sector Reform in Bosnia and Herzegovina: The Role of the International Community. *International Peacekeeping* 13(1):28–42.

Walter, Barbara F. 1997. The Critical Barrier to Civil War Settlement. *International Organization* 51(3):335–64.

Watts, Ronald. 1998. Examples of Partnership. In *Beyond the Impasse: Toward Reconciliation,* edited by Roger Gibbins and Guy Laforest. Montreal: Institute for Research on Public Policy (IRPP).

Weinstein, Jeremy M. 2002. Mozambique: A Fading U.N. Success Story. *Journal of Democracy* 13(1):141–56.

Wolff, Stefan. 2007. Conflict Resolution between Power Sharing and Power Dividing, or Beyond? *Political Studies Review* 5(3):377–93.

Yordán, Carlos L. 2003. Society Building in Bosnia: A Critique of Post-Dayton Peacebuilding Efforts. *Seaton Hall Journal of Diplomacy and International Relations* 2: 59–74.

Zahar, Marie-Joëlle. 2002. Peace by Unconventional Means: Evaluating Lebanon's Ta'if Accord. In *Ending Civil Wars: The Implementation of Peace Agreements,* edited by Donald Rothchild, Steve Stedman, and Elizabeth Cousens. Boulder: Lynne Rienner.

Zahar, Marie-Joëlle. 2008. Power Sharing, Credible Commitment, and State (re)Building: Comparative Lessons from Bosnia and Lebanon. *Suedosteuropa* Special Issue: *Comparing the Balkans: War Legacies and State-Building in the Age of Globalisation* 56(1):35–57.

Zahar, Marie-Joëlle. 2009. Liberal Interventions, Illiberal Outcomes: The UN, Western Powers, and Lebanon. In *New Perspectives on Liberal Peacebuilding,* edited by Edward Newman, Roland Paris, and Oliver Richmond. Tokyo: United Nations University Press.

Zmerli, Sonja, and Marc Hooghe, eds. 2011. *Political Trust: Why Context Matters.* Colchester: ECPR Press.

5 Designing a Durable Federation: The Case of Cyprus

JOHN McGARRY

Since 1977, Turkish Cypriots and Greek Cypriots have agreed that any shared political future they may have should be federal. This chapter examines the question of how a Cypriot federation could be made durable. Such a federation must satisfy two conditions. First, the federation's institutional framework must be feasible. By feasible, I do not mean only that the framework must be compatible with "human psychology, human capacities generally, the laws of nature, and the natural resources available to human beings" (Buchanan 2004, 61), but that there are plausible circumstances in which it could be agreed to by the communities in question: the Greek Cypriots and Turkish Cypriots, and also Turkey, on whom the latter are largely reliant. The agreed procedural requirement that any settlement must be ratified in dual referendums among Greek Cypriots and Turkish Cypriots defines one key dimension of feasibility. Second, the agreed federal institutions must be operationally "functional," not just in the narrow sense of satisfying standards of administrative efficiency, but also in the broader and crucial sense of facilitating cooperation, stability, and unity rather than conflict, collapse, and break-up.

The chapter begins by showing that, of the two macro-institutional choices available, a national or pluralist federation, only the latter is feasible in Cyprus. Pluralist federations, however, are often criticized by national federalists and others as fragile in nature and as likely to be unstable or to break up (Bunce 1999; Roeder 2007; Snyder 2000). The chapter then assesses four micro-institutional choices that are seen as bridging the gap between national and pluralist federalism, and that are proposed as ways to counteract the centrifugal or "dysfunctional" tendencies in pluralist federations. My argument is that all four of these institutional choices face significant difficulties in Cyprus, and that this has lessons for other divided polities where federations exist or are under consideration.

The Macro-Institutional Choice: A National or a Pluralist Federation?

National and pluralist federations are ideal-types, but some actual federations fall clearly into either category. A national federation is a federation that is governed by the principles of a nation-state. There is thought to be one nation or people, coterminous with the state's boundaries and represented in the state's symbols, flag, national anthem, and public institutions. National federations promote a single public, or official, culture and a single language, although they may tolerate, to varying degrees, cultural diversity in the private (non-public) sphere (McGarry and O'Leary 2005, 2007; McGarry, O'Leary, and Simeon 2008; O'Leary and McGarry 2012). National federations either avoid giving territorial self-government to ethnic, linguistic, religious, or national minorities by ensuring that internal federal boundaries are drawn so that such minorities remain minorities at the regional level, or they do not give meaningful territorial self-government to minorities, by operating the federation as a centralized state. The United States is the most obvious example of the former, while the Russian Federation approximates the latter, particularly in the early 2000s, when Moscow appointed regional governors.

Within the federal executive branch, national federalists prefer a (single-person) presidency, elected by all the people, to represent the nation, or a parliamentary executive, operating on majoritarian principles and based on programmatic as opposed to ethnic parties. Some national federations, operating on liberal principles, champion a vision of individual rights in which the normative and legal response to ethnic diversity is to treat as equal and undifferentiated the entire citizenry, whose members cannot be discriminated against on the basis of their ethnicity. Other national federations, stressing republican principles of national unity, outlaw minority political parties or call for parties to be organized across the state before they can compete in national or even regional elections. The Russian Federation, for example, bans "racial, national or religious" political parties and requires parties to have regional branches of at least 100 members in over half of the subjects of the federation.[1] The United States can be seen as the paradigmatic national federation and the closest to the ideal type. Its model has been followed in some important respects in Germany, Austria, and Australia, and particularly across the various federations of Latin America, including Mexico, Brazil, and Argentina.

While national federations are different from unitary states in their institutional structure, they are similar in their mono-nationalist philosophy and practices. They are federations, not because of a desire to accommodate minority national communities, but for other reasons, including, as in the case of the United States, the need to accommodate previously existing "territorial" communities that share broadly similar cultures and identities and decide to unite to realize military and economic advantages (Riker 1964). National federations have also been championed because of their democratic advantages – they permit locally accessible government in geographically large countries (the U.S., Brazil, Australia) – or because of liberal advantages – they permit checks and balances that help protect against arbitrary power (the U.S. and post-1945 Germany).

Influenced by the example of the United States, including its success in integrating immigrants from diverse ethnic backgrounds into a single people (*e pluribus unum*), national federalists have promoted national federations throughout the world, including, most recently, in South Africa and Iraq. National federalism has also been proposed in Cyprus by some Greek Cypriots, who see it as the best alternative to the unitarism that Greek Cypriots espoused prior to the partition of Cyprus and the Makarios-Denktash "High-Level Agreement" of 1977.

A national federation for Cyprus squarely fails any feasibility test. There is little prospect of anything that approaches it being accepted by Turkish Cypriots. The Turkish Cypriots are not analogous to the immigrant communities that migrated as individuals to the United States and that were "accommodated" by American national federalist principles. Collectively *settled* in Cyprus in 1570 after the Ottoman victory over the Venetians, Turkish Cypriots have maintained separateness ever since, facilitated by their distinct language and religion and the fact they were the ruling class. At least since the independence of Cyprus in 1960, they have seen themselves as a distinct community or "people": partners with the Greek Cypriots and entitled to substantial community-based representation in common institutions but also to territorial autonomy and self-determination. Turkish Cypriots adhered to this position consistently from 1960 to 1974, when they lived in dispersed settlement patterns throughout the island. Since 1974, when Turkey partitioned Cyprus, the Turkish Cypriots have enjoyed 38 years of substantial autonomy. Indeed, in 1983 they declared the independence of the "Turkish Republic of Northern Cyprus" (TRNC hereafter), which is recognized only by Turkey. Turkish Cypriot views on their political future are not monolithic; there are important divisions between those who identify strongly with Turkey and those who see themselves as Turkish "Cypriots." However, there is no Turkish Cypriot constituency (or credible Turkish Cypriot politician) prepared to accept the institutions, state symbols, or public policies associated with a national federation or unitary state.

Any conceivable Cypriot federation will be pluralist in nature. The minimal criterion for a pluralist federation is that it has at least some internal boundaries that respect whatever national, ethnic, linguistic, or religious communities exist and in which the constituent units enjoy substantial autonomy. The provision of autonomy entails the official (public) accommodation of more than one distinct culture and often more than one language. By this standard, Canada, Belgium, India, Switzerland, Bosnia-Herzegovina, and Iraq are pluralist federations. Beyond this minimal criterion, pluralist federations often entail federal governments (and federal public sectors) that are inclusively representative of the federation's major constituencies. Bosnia-Hercegovina and Switzerland are governed by collective presidencies that are formally and informally inclusive, respectively. Belgium and Iraq have parliamentary executives that are formally and informally inclusive, respectively. Canada and India have traditionally been governed by dominant parties that are internally inclusive, although there has been a move, in India's case, towards inclusive multi-party coalitions in recent decades.

Pluralist federations protect individual rights, but they also protect the collective rights of minority national communities, such as language rights or rights to religious education, which are understood as important for individuals from such communities (Kymlicka 1995). Some pluralist federations are explicitly pluri-*national*, the pluri-national or multi-people character of the federation being reflected in the state's constitution, laws, and parliamentary declarations and in its flags and symbols. Unlike national federalists, who see the accommodation of multiple communities as a threat to the state's unity and as inconsistent with the development or maintenance of a single people, pluralist federalists see such accommodation as the only way in which a single state can be kept together and as the key to the achievement of an overarching identity. In 2004, Turkish Cypriots voted in overwhelming numbers for the UN's Annan Plan, which provided for a pluralist federation, though it was not the only one possible.

The Greek Cypriots do not embrace pluralist federalism. However, since Turkey's partition of Cyprus in 1974, mainstream Greek Cypriots political elites have accepted, as a "painful compromise," the principle of a "bi-zonal" federation in which the two zones are governed by the Turkish Cypriots and Greek Cypriots, respectively. They have also accepted the principle of a "bicommunal" federation, which implies a power-sharing federal executive. Therefore, there is agreement in principle on a pluralist federation for Cyprus but, as yet, no agreement on crucial details. In 2004, the Greek Cypriots overwhelmingly rejected the pluralist federation presented in the Annan plan.

Pluralist federations, however, are often criticized for their fragile nature. According to Jack Snyder, they have a "terrible track record" (2000, 327). The weaknesses of pluralist federations are usually ascribed to the fact that they focus too much on institutions that accommodate separate identities and give resources to secessionists, but not enough on institutions that build a common allegiance and strengthen unionists. This concern has led academics to suggest what they see as a middle ground compromise between national and pluralist federalism, that is, micro-institutional arrangements that are seen as consistent with some pluralist federalism, including some self-government and recognition of more than one official culture, but that seek to compensate for its centrifugal tendencies by emphasizing an overarching identity and political union (e.g., Brancati 2004; Hale 2008; Horowitz 1991, 2007). There are many such micro-institutional arrangements, but this chapter focuses on four prominent examples, all of which have been proposed in Cyprus and in the comparative academic literature for places like Cyprus:

- an electoral system for the federal executive that favours moderates and encourages co-operation;
- a multi-zonal federation that encourages cross-cutting cleavages and shifting alliances
- a negotiated constitutional clause that prohibits secession; and
- a redistributive program that purchases solidarity.[2]

These four arrangements are treated here in order.

An Electoral System that Rewards Moderates

The influential American political scientist Donald Horowitz prescribes a "single person" presidential executive[3] for divided polities, including federations, as long as the electoral system used for presidential elections encourages or requires candidates to reach out to (pool votes from) all salient communities (Horowitz 1991, 163–214; see also Brancati 2004, 16; Wimmer 2003, 122). This sort of electoral system is seen as rewarding moderate presidential candidates who make inter-ethnic appeals and is seen, consequently, as both "inclusive" of different communities and having a binding effect on the polity. Horowitz recommends two electoral systems in particular. The first involves a majoritarian system with geographical distribution requirements. This system is recommended where ethnic communities are territorially concentrated. The winner must win a majority of the vote overall plus a certain percentage in different regions of the country. Majority plus distribution electoral systems are used for presidential elections in the Nigeria federation, and in Kenya and Indonesia. The second electoral system is the "alternative vote," a majoritarian electoral system that allows voters to rank preferences. While the alternative vote would seem most likely to produce vote-pooling in a heterogeneous divided polity with no majority community, Horowitz claims that it can also facilitate moderation in a bipolar divided polity with a large majority community as long as there is party proliferation in the majority bloc. In this case, Horowitz argues, politicians from the majority community have incentives to reach out to minority voters to defeat rivals from their own (majority) community.[4] Horowitz contrasts his "centripetalist" approach with consociation; the latter relies on proportional (or communal) electoral systems that allow politicians to win office while appealing exclusively to their own ethnic community. Politicians elected by proportional electoral systems, Horowitz argues, are likely to be divisive in their political appeal, and their polity is likely to be unstable, or centrifugal.

A single person (or non-sharable) presidential executive is more characteristic of a national federation than a pluralist federation and does not meet the feasibility test in Cyprus. Turkish Cypriots are unlikely to ever accept it. Whether elected by one of Horowitz's preferred electoral systems, or any other democratic electoral system, the winner would be from one community in a context where there are very few people who have ties to both. As Greek Cypriots comprise around four-fifths of the electorate, it would almost certainly be a Greek Cypriot, even if a Greek Cypriot moderate, rather than a Turkish Cypriot. In the highly unlikely possibility that a Turkish Cypriot were elected, he or she would be chosen by Greek Cypriots and would not be representative of Turkish Cypriots.

Turkish Cypriots have consistently rejected the idea of a single-person presidency and have insisted on a formally consociational or "sharable" executive. After Cyprus became independent in 1960, Turkish Cypriots strongly supported the de facto *co*-presidency created by the 1960 constitution. The 1960 regime's executive is usually described as "presidential" because it included a (Greek Cypriot) president and (Turkish Cypriot) vice-president, but unlike the U.S. system, for example, the powers attached to both offices in Cyprus were virtually identical. Each executive was able to appoint proportions of the cabinet and to veto any decision of the legislature or cabinet in matters of foreign affairs, defence, or security. One Greek Cypriot critic went too far when he described the 1960 executive as "vice-presidential" (Polyviou 1975, 26), but it was clearly not the conventional single-person presidency recommended by Horowitz (1991, 205–14). During the negotiations that led to the Annan Plan, Turkish Cypriot negotiators proposed a formal co-presidency, but in the referendum on the Annan Plan, Turkish Cypriot voters endorsed a compromise option put forward by the UN in which there was to be a "presidential council" of six members, one-third of which was to be Turkish Cypriot. In recent years, Turkish Cypriot leaders have insisted on a "rotating" presidency, involving a Turkish Cypriot and a Greek Cypriot.

Greek Cypriot elites, by contrast, have been more open to a single-person presidency, reflecting the popularity of this option among majority communities. Archbishop Makarios, the president of Cyprus, proposed a single-person presidency (with no vice-president) during inter-communal negotiations that took place between 1968 and 1974 (Clerides 1992, 464), and the current orthodox archbishop, Chrystostomos II, supports a U.S.-style presidency.[5] However, since mainstream Greek Cypriot political elites now realize that a single-person presidency is a non-starter for Turkish Cypriots, they generally propose a variant of the 1960 executive model of a Greek Cypriot president and Turkish Cypriot vice-president. The two executives would be responsible for appointing cabinet ministers from their community, but neither would possess a veto. Even this relatively strong vice-presidency has been rejected by Turkish Cypriots, who see it as signalling a subordinate status for their community. In response to this Turkish Cypriot concern, the Greek Cypriot leader and president of Cyprus, Demetris Christofias, proposed in 2008 a rotating presidency, albeit, as we shall see, one elected in a particular way.

Horowitz's vote-pooling electoral systems are detachable from his preferred style of executive. It would be possible to elect a formally inclusive co-presidency or rotating presidency through either of his preferred vote-pooling electoral systems (where the presidency's Turkish Cypriot and Greek Cypriot members are either jointly elected on a single ticket or elected individually). This too would be wholly unacceptable to Turkish Cypriots, as either of Horowitz's "majoritarian" electoral systems would mean that the winning candidates, including the Turkish Cypriot, would be far more dependent on Greek Cypriot votes than Turkish Cypriot votes. It would be possible, indeed, under the "Alternative Vote" for the Turkish Cypriot member of a rotating or co-presidency to be elected with little or no Turkish Cypriot support. Any candidate who won 62.5% of the Greek Cypriot vote (assuming an 80:20 GC/TC ratio) would be elected, even if that candidate received no support from Turkish Cypriots. A qualified majority with a distributive requirement (e.g., the winning candidate would have to obtain a majority overall of Cyprus plus at least 25% in each of the Greek Cypriot, and Turkish Cypriot federal zones) would mean that the Turkish Cypriot candidate would need some Turkish Cypriot votes, given that the two zones are currently ethnically homogeneous, but he or she would still need more Greek Cypriot than Turkish Cypriot votes to win an overall majority (assuming uniform turnout across both communities).[6] Fearful of having to depend on Greek Cypriot votes for election, Turkish Cypriot elites have generally rejected any form of integrated electoral system and have insisted instead on "communal" elections, in which Turkish Cypriot leaders are elected exclusively by Turkish Cypriot voters.[7] This is the way that all Turkish Cypriot politicians have been elected since the independence of Cyprus in 1960. Like rational politicians everywhere, they fear shifting to an electoral system different from the one that put them in power.

Centripetalist-minded thinkers in Cyprus are fully aware that there is little prospect of Turkish Cypriots accepting (qualified) majoritarian electoral systems of the sort proposed by Horowitz, but they are also aware that communal electoral systems preclude vote-pooling. This has led local centripetalists to propose a *sui generis* centripetal electoral system geared to Cypriot realities. In this system, known locally as *weighted cross-voting*, elections for the Turkish Cypriot and Greek Cypriot members of the presidency would be largely communal, but partly integrated. The Greek Cypriot member of the presidency would be elected by all the island's voters (approximately 80% Greek Cypriot, 20% Turkish Cypriot). The Turkish Cypriot member would also be elected by the island's voters, but in this case, the Greek Cypriot share of the vote would be "weighted" so that it was exactly equivalent to the Turkish Cypriot share of the island's electorate (i.e., the electorate for the Turkish Cypriot member would be approximately 20% Greek Cypriot, 80% Turkish Cypriot). The advantage for Cyprus of weighted cross-voting over Horowitz's recommended electoral systems is that it would give each community a small and *equal* share of influence over the election of the other community's leader. Although different in detail from what Horowitz prescribes, weighted cross-voting has the same centripetalist intent. That is, it seeks to reward moderate ethnic politicians who can attract support from other communities as well as their own.[8]

Weighted cross-voting has been discussed in Cyprus since the late 1980s, but it became the official position of Greek Cypriot leader Christofias in September 2008, when he tied it to his offer of a rotating presidency. The centripetalist logic of the system appears to have appealed to Christofias, a Marxist, as necessary to reward political moderates and to bind a federal Cyprus together and as more likely to be accepted by Turkish Cypriots than any of the more integrated electoral formulae previously proposed by Greek Cypriots.[9] Weighted cross-voting also had political partisan advantages for Christofias. He led AKEL (*Anorthotikó Kómma Ergazómenou Laoú* / Progressive Party of Working People), the most moderate of all of the Greek Cypriot parties on the Cyprus problem and the party thought to be the most likely to win support from Turkish Cypriots. Christofias's embrace of this modified centripetalist formula, and the Turkish Cypriot reaction to it, allows us to assess its feasibility in the Cypriot context.

The Greek Cypriot proposal had some attractions for Mehmet Ali Talat, the Turkish Cypriot leader and "president" of the "Turkish Republic of Northern Cyprus" (TRNC), from 2005 to 2010. Like Christofias, Talat is a Marxist, a political moderate, and a trade union leader, who had previously cooperated with Christofias. In January 2010, the press confirmed that Talat was prepared to abandon communal voting and accept weighted cross-voting. In addition to supporting weighted cross-voting for ideological reasons (as division transcending), Talat may have had partisan motives for supporting it. His party, the CTP (*Cumhuriyetçi Türk Partisi* / Republican Turkish Party), is AKEL's equivalent in the Turkish Cypriot community and the party best placed to win Greek Cypriot votes.

Talat's decision to support cross-voting caused an immediate furore among right-wing Turkish Cypriot parties. Dervis Eroglu, the leader of the largest Turkish Cypriot party, the UBP (*Ulusal Birlik Partisi* / National Unity Party), denounced the step in a lengthy letter to the Turkish prime minister, Tayyip Erdogan.[10] Eroglu reputedly wrote that even 0.01% of cross-voting would be unacceptable. Serdar Denktash, the leader of the Turkish Cypriots' third-largest party, the Democratic Party (*Demokrat Parti*; DP hereafter), also strongly opposed weighted cross-voting and formed an electoral alliance with Eroglu, hitherto a rival, to oppose it. Eroglu was subsequently elected "president" of the TRNC in April of 2010, becoming the leader of, and chief negotiator for, the Turkish Cypriot community. He eventually rejected weighted cross-voting, reverting to the traditional Turkish Cypriot insistence on communal elections. Under pressure from the Greek Cypriot side, which accused him of intransigence and of backing away from previous "agreements" between the sides, Eroglu indicated in early 2012 that he would be prepared to "negotiate" weighted cross-voting in the context of an international conference that involved Turkey.[11] This condition, however, was one that his Greek Cypriot interlocutor had hitherto consistently rejected, on the basis that internal matters should be settled by the two communities' leaders alone. Christofias predictably rejected Eroglu's offer and, as yet, there is no agreement on how to elect the presidency of a united Cyprus.

Eroglu had two reasons for objecting to weighted cross-voting: the partisan and the principled. Eroglu's UBP is a conservative and nationalist party that has very little possibility, for the foreseeable future, of winning support among Greek Cypriot voters. Accepting weighted cross-voting would put the UBP at a significant disadvantage, as it would mean that Greek Cypriot voters would comprise 20% of the electorate for the Turkish Cypriot candidate for Cyprus's presidency. Turkish Cypriot "presidential" elections have normally been decided by much smaller margins. The UBP is also a nationalist party, founded by Rauf Denktash, the Turkish Cypriot leader who proclaimed the independence of the TRNC in 1983. It has traditionally insisted that Turkish Cypriots are a separate people, and it correctly sees weighted cross-voting, which requires a partly integrated electorate, as inconsistent with this thinking.[12]

While Greek Cypriots support integrated elections in principle, the main Greek Cypriot opposition party, the right of centre DISY (*Dimokratikós Sinayermós* / Democratic Rally), criticized weighted cross-voting as designed to help AKEL. DISY's deputy chair, Averoff Neophytou, announced that cross-voting was concocted by AKEL to "keep the left governing Cyprus forever."[13] All of the other Greek Cypriot opposition parties arc against weighted cross-voting, though they tend not to disaggregate it from "rotation" (which provides for a Turkish Cypriot to be president of all of Cyprus for part of the time), which they particularly dislike. These opposition parties – DIKO, EVROKO, EDEK and the Greens[14] – tend to prefer an integrated electoral system of the conventional majoritarian type, which would give a decisive role to Greek Cypriots.

The key point of this Cypriot story is that even the modest centripetalist mechanism proposed by Christofias faces a serious acceptance problem. Conceived as a method for promoting moderation in a deeply divided polity, it is likely to be put on the table only when one of the parties to the negotiations is a moderate party, and it is likely to be included in a settlement only when moderates are dominant in both communities. When radicals dominate ethnic communities, a common occurrence in deeply divided polities emerging from conflict, they will likely be unwilling to propose or accept centripetalism because it gives an advantage to moderates. Where radical leaders dominate, they are more likely to agree on consociational (proportional or communal) elections, precisely because the latter guarantee such leaders a share of seats without requiring them to appeal to voters across communal lines (see McGarry and O'Leary 2009, 62). This criticism of centripetalism is different from, though consistent with, the influential criticism of the "alternative vote" by Fraenkel and Grofman (2006). They have shown, using Fiji as a case study, that for the alternative vote to benefit moderate parties, there must already be a moderate electorate. My criticism is concerned not with how voters respond to a centripetalist electoral system once it has been adopted, but with a prior and equally important question: how do electoral systems that favour ethnicity-transcending political elites get negotiated and accepted in the first place.

While agreement on weighted cross-voting has been elusive so far, it is not out of the question that it could be accepted by Eroglu in future. If this happens, it is likely to be the result of pressure from Ankara, which is less interested in weighted cross-voting than in other aspects of the Cyprus problem, including its territorial and security aspects, and that might decide that weighted cross-voting is a price that has to be paid to remove a problem that damages Turkey's international diplomacy and that poses an obstacle, though not the only one, to its ambitions to join the European Union.

Even if weighted cross-voting is adopted, it may not be operationally functional in the way assumed by its advocates. One of the effects of its embrace by Christofias and Talat in early 2010 was a weakening of political moderates and of the prospects for a settlement. As we have seen, Talat's support for cross-voting led to an alliance of two right-wing parties, the UBP and DP, which contributed to Talat's election defeat and his replacement by a more nationalistic Turkish Cypriot leader.[15] On the Greek Cypriot side, the fear of exclusion under weighted cross-voting helps to explain the unwillingness of the largest Greek Cypriot party, DISY, to form a pro-settlement coalition, tacit or otherwise, with AKEL, although DISY and AKEL's negative relationship has multiple causes. The other smaller Greek Cypriot opposition parties are more nationalist than DISY and would likely be anti-settlement even without weighted cross-voting, but their opposition to a settlement is likely to have been reinforced by an electoral system that favoured moderates. The failure of a single Greek Cypriot party other than AKEL (which holds the support of only about 30% of the Greek Cypriot electorate) to back Christofias in the negotiations limited his room for manoeuvre, and contributed to his failure to reach a deal with Talat. Ironically, the embrace of an electoral system designed to help moderates may have contributed to the isolation of the main moderate party in each community, making it more difficult to reach a settlement of the Cyprus problem.

A presidential executive elected through weighted cross-voting may produce a similarly unproductive dynamic. In the post-settlement elections and afterwards, the radical (nationalist) parties on both sides would have heightened incentives to polarize the electorate on ethnic lines, including accusing the moderates from their own community of treachery and sell-out, as this would be likeliest way that these radical parties could triumph under Christofias's weighted cross-voting electoral system. A polarized climate would allow radical nationalist parties to win their community's seat on the presidency without reaching out across ethnic lines, as they would be able to rely on the lion's share of their own community's votes. If deprived of a stake in the executive, such parties would have incentives to adopt an obstructive or destructive role in the federal parliament (or in the parliaments and executives of the constituent states). If they did so, the polarized climate that resulted would make it difficult for moderates to work together.

These functionality and feasibility problems with centripetalism help explain why consociationalists recommend electoral systems that allow diverse community sentiments, including those of radicals, to be expressed rather than manipulatively suppressed and why they favour inclusive executive institutions that give a place to all sizable political parties willing to work within the system. Such institutions can provide institutional incentives for radical parties to be moderate, particularly if the latter's share of cabinet ministries or presidential council seats is linked to their vote share. This is what Northern Ireland's experience suggests. There, a 1974 power-sharing agreement restricted to moderates lasted less than five months, whereas the more inclusive institutions associated with the 1998 Good Friday Agreement have endured and have facilitated the moderation of Northern Ireland's erstwhile two radical parties, Sinn Fein and the DUP (McEvoy n.d.; McGarry and O'Leary 2009; Mitchell, Evans, and O'Leary 2009). An inclusive consociational electoral and executive system in Cyprus would provide radical parties with a stake in the settlement and reduce their incentive for opposing it.

Internal Boundary Engineering

Several academics argue that heterogeneous federations can be made durable if internal federal boundaries are constructed so that they run across (within) ethnic groups rather than around them (Dawisha and Dawisha 2003; Hale 2004; Horowitz 1991, 2007; Makiya 2003; Roeder 2009; Wimmer 2003). This internal boundary engineering draws its inspiration from the well-known cross-cutting cleavages thesis associated with S.M. Lipset (1960). Lipset argued that integrated polities need cleavages that are cross-cutting rather than congruent. From this perspective, a federation that draws its boundaries around ethnic communities risks disunity and instability because regional and ethnic divisions come to reinforce each other. If, by contrast, internal boundaries are drawn across ethnic communities, even if these communities each come to dominate certain regions, regional interests will intersect ethnic interests, promoting intra-ethnic divisions (sub-ethnic identities) and inter-ethnic alliances on cross-cutting matters, with centripetal effects. The cross-cutting cleavages thesis lies behind the broadly accepted view that two-unit federations are particularly susceptible to instability and break-up. In such cases, ethnic and regional boundaries are congruent rather than cross-cutting, which prevents shifting alliances and pits one community against the other on every inter-regional issue (Duchacek 1988; Watts, 2008). On the other hand, the existence of cross-cutting divisions is said to explain the stability of the world's most successful pluralist federations, including Canada, Switzerland, and India.[16] The thesis that internal boundaries can be engineered to promote cross-cutting divisions has influenced constitutional debates in a number of multi-ethnic settings where federation or autonomy is mooted, including Sri Lanka in the late 1980s, Bosnia-Herzegovina in the early 1990s,[17] and Iraq between 2003 and 2005.[18]

Some supporters of internal boundary engineering advocate the territorial division of ethnic communities regardless of the size of the community involved, or whether it is a majority or minority (Dawisha and Dawisha 2003). Those interested in preventing secession, such as Philip Roeder, tend to focus on drawing boundaries across minority homelands.[19] Others, such as Henry Hale, who are concerned with preventing the federation's domination by a large ethnic community, focus on dividing this dominant community (Hale 2004; 2008, 255). None of these sources has written on Cyprus, but their common analysis suggests it would be folly if a Cypriot federation were to be based on a single Greek Cypriot and a single Turkish Cypriot region. The general perspective suggests that Cyprus should have some form of multi-zonal or cantonal federation, in which territorial boundaries cut across ethnic boundaries. The anti-secessionist perspective suggests that the Turkish Cypriot community should be divided into more than one region. The anti-domination perspective suggests that it is the Greek Cypriot community, with 80% of Cyprus's population, that should be divided.[20] But are these boundary engineering strategies feasible and functional?

In their path is the long-standing consensus that a Cypriot federation should be bicommunal and "bizonal," a formula that has formed a consistent and central part of the agreed basis of negotiations in Cyprus since 1977 and through several changes of leadership on both sides.[21] Bizonality is not just the domestically agreed basis of the current talks. It is accepted by all relevant international actors, including Turkey, Greece, the U.K., the EU, the U.S., and the UN, and is reflected in numerous Security Council Resolutions going back to UNSCR 649 (13 May 1990). The international consensus behind bizonality may not itself be an insurmountable obstacle to internal boundary re-engineering, because most international actors would almost certainly be prepared to support change if the Greek Cypriots and Turkish Cypriots wanted it. However, there is no sign of this happening.

There is little possibility that Turkish Cypriot leaders would agree to divide their community across more than one federal unit. Turkish

Cypriot leaders reluctantly acknowledge that they will have to concede a substantial part of the TRNC's territory to the Greek Cypriot region as the cost of a settlement,[22] but this is different from agreeing that the Turkish Cypriot "community" should be divided across several regions. The consensus among both Turkish Cypriot and Greek Cypriot elites is that the vast majority of Turkish Cypriots (those who are not "original owners") living in areas transferred to the Greek Cypriots will have to relocate to the Turkish Cypriot region. No Turkish Cypriot leader has ever suggested that the territory left in the Turkish Cypriot zone could be divided into more than one federal region, whether that implies two or more regions in which Turkish Cypriots dominate, or a "third" mixed region, perhaps under federal control. There are sound efficiency reasons for their outlook. After the expected territorial adjustment, the Turkish Cypriot federal region will be around only 2,700 square kilometres in size, or 29% of the territory of Cyprus. It will also be small in population (c. 250,000) and in GDP. It will be difficult enough, though not impossible, for the Turkish Cypriots to achieve the economies of scale needed for the efficient production of public services within a region of this size, without its subdivision.

More important, the Turkish Cypriots have consistently claimed that they are a people with a right not just to self-determination, but to "collective" self-determination. In this respect, they are like other "national" communities, such as the Kurds of Iraq, the Québécois, the Scots, or the Irish. Even when the Turkish Cypriots were dispersed across Cyprus, whether in ghettoes and villages during 1960–63 or in the enclaves of the 1963–74 period, they "collectively" administered themselves under a single leadership. During the inter-communal talks that took place between 1968 and 1974, Turkish Cypriot elites never wavered from an insistence on collective autonomy, and any proposals for Turkish Cypriot "cantonal" areas were put forward on the condition that they would exist under the rubric of a single Turkish Cypriot authority.

Since the Turkish invasion of 1974, the Turkish Cypriots have governed an undivided territory, and cantonization is no longer attractive. This was eventually recognized by the Greek Cypriots, which explains why they (reluctantly) agreed to bizonality in 1977.[23] The Turkish Cypriot position now is roughly analogous to that of the Kurds in Iraq in 2003. The Kurds refused to divide their region when pressed and threatened withdrawal from constitutional negotiations, a refusal that destroyed any prospect for an Iraqi federation based on 18 governorates. Indeed, the TRNC has had none of the serious territorially based intra-ethnic divisions that marked the Kurdish self-government era be-tween 1991 and 2003 and that partly inspired the (mistaken) belief that a division of the Kurdish region was possible (Wimmer 2003, 124).[24] As a small minority in Cyprus, with living memories of the insecurity and deprivation that existed in scattered enclaves between 1963 and 1974, the Turkish Cypriots are not likely to relish the idea of a return to can-tonization, even if their cantons are contiguous. Nor are they likely to be inspired by the argument that this is needed for the unity of Cyprus, as opinion polls make it clear that the first preference of most Turk-ish Cypriots is for two independent states (Lordos, Kaymak, and Tocci 2009, Figure 5a). Even if the Turkish Cypriots were somehow to agree to their own territorial division, it is doubtful that Turkey would support this. Turkey appears to see the security of Turkish Cypriots, but also its own strategic interests, as linked to a single, defensible Turkish Cypriot region.

If there is to be a multi-zonal federation in Cyprus, then, it is likely to require a division of the Greek Cypriot region. This is also the only way to address Hale's concern about domination of the federation by a "core ethnic region." A division of the Greek Cypriot region would not address Roeder's concern about secession, at least not directly,[25] but it would allow for the possibility of cross-cutting cleavages and shift-ing alliances, as it would divide the Greek Cypriot majority in roughly the way that English-speaking Canadians and German-speaking Swiss have been divided. In principle, a division of the Greek Cypriot region could allow rotating alliances between different Greek Cypriot regions and the Turkish Cypriot region, of the sort that occurs between the lin-guistic communities in Canada and Switzerland. As the Greek Cypriots are far more interested in Cyprus's unity than the Turkish Cypriots are, and as they, like English Canadians, might come to see their need for "collective" self-determination as satisfied within federal institutions, it is probably more feasible to seek a subdivision of the Greek Cypriot region. It might also be thought that while Turkish Cypriots would be reluctant to divide the Turkish Cypriot region, they would hardly ob-ject if the Greek Cypriots adopted self-division.

Turkish Cypriots, however, may indeed object to multiple Greek Cypriot regions because bizonality has become central to the Turkish Cypriot notion of "partnership" in Cyprus. The Turkish Cypriots are well aware that they comprise only around one-fifth of Cyprus's popu-lation and that they cannot claim equality on demographic grounds, and so they have sought to claim it through the language of two communities and two "equal" constituent units in Cyprus.[26] This itself is not an insurmountable obstacle to the division of the Greek Cypriot region, as it may be possible to satisfy the Turkish Cypriot insistence on equality in other ways, but it does suggest that a division of the Greek Cypriot region would not be unconditionally accepted by Turkish Cypriots.[27]

Greek Cypriots are strong champions of Cyprus's unity, but persuading them to divide their region into several parts would require them to see their community's territorial and political cohesion as the obstacle to Cyprus's unity and the division of their territory as the solution. But that is decidedly not how Greek Cypriots explain the Cyprus problem. The obstacle to unity, in their eyes, is Turkish Cypriots' insistence on self-determination (and behind that, Turkey's historic aggression). This world view has been mainstream among Greek Cypriots since 1960, when fear of Turkish Cypriot secession informed their refusal to condone separate Turkish Cypriot municipalities. What Greek Cypriots fear about "bizonality," then, is not the existence of a united Greek Cypriot region, but the existence of a Turkish Cypriot region, particularly the united, ethnically homogeneous, and sealed region that Turkish Cypriots aspire to. Thus, when Archbishop Makarios proposed "cantonization" just after the Turkish partition of 1974, he had in mind the division of the region that was to be ceded to the Turkish Cypriots, while the Greek Cypriot remainder of the island would remain intact. His motives were the same as Roeder's: to reduce the prospects of a strong, united Turkish Cypriot region and to minimize the prospects of secession. Makarios gave up on the idea of dividing the Turkish Cypriots when his chief adviser, the future president, Glafkos Clerides, explained to him that cantonization was not possible in the new circumstances.[28]

A multizonal federation that divided the Greek Cypriot part of Cyprus would be very difficult to sell to Greek Cypriots unless it also divided the Turkish Cypriot region. Unsurprisingly, this is what those few Greek Cypriots who tout the centripetal benefits of multizonality recommend (Iacovidis 2011; Theophanous 2011). Among the Greek Cypriot public, federal division of any kind remains unpopular, and the dominant discourse is based on unitarism. Greek Cypriots constantly invoke the alleged inefficiencies (dysfunctionalities) of federations, in part because until recently they had achieved significant increases in their standard of living, including a high GDP, inward investment, and successful tourism, through the functionally proven structure of a unitary state.[29] From this perspective multizonality is even worse than bizonality, because it would deepen the problems and costs that arise from multiple administrations and bureaucracies.[30] Even a single Greek Cypriot federal region would be relatively small by international standards, even if it would be much larger than the Turkish Cypriot region.

A multizonal federation, whatever its alleged benefits, is probably even less feasible than weighted cross-voting. Unlike weighted cross-voting, multizonality has not been proposed by a serious politician on either side since the mid-1970s.[31] In any case, there are reasonable grounds for doubting whether a multizonal federation in Cyprus would deliver on its functional promise, that is, that it would promote sub-ethnic identities and cross-cutting inter-ethnic solidarities. A multizonal Cypriot federation would not be able to exploit sub-ethnic social cleavages based on linguistic differences (as in India), or religious differences (as in Switzerland), because religious, linguistic, and ethnic cleavages in Cyprus are reinforcing. Nor would there be significant geographic boundaries between the multiple Cypriot zones, as there are in Canada (distances) and in Switzerland (mountain ranges), or obvious differences in economic specialization. Cyprus's double-minority phenomenon – Turkish Cypriot fears arising from their minority status in Cyprus, and Greek Cypriot fears arising from their minority status in the region – would likely maintain the salience of the ethnic division ahead of any conceivable cross-cutting interests.[32] Any future construction of cross-cutting alliances will depend more on the success of cooperation within federal institutions than on the design of internal boundaries, and questioning the established consensus on bi-zonality is not likely to promote such cooperation.

A Constitutional Ban on Secession

A third suggested way to hold a federation together is to agree to a constitutional ban on secession or, more positively, a constitutional commitment to unity and territorial integrity. Such bans or commitments are seen as delegitimizing secessionist politics, while making it clear to other countries that seceding entities should not be helped or recognized. Several constitutions contain such prohibitions or pledges, including those of France, Turkey, Nicaragua, Spain, Ukraine, Nigeria, and Bosnia-Hercegovina. "The indissoluble unity of the Spanish nation, the common and indivisible country of all Spaniards" is hailed in Spain's 1979 Constitution.[33] Nigeria is both "indivisible" and "indissoluble" in the constitution of its Third Republic.[34] The Bosnia and Hercegovina constitution, negotiated at Dayton, Ohio, commits its parties to the state's "sovereignty, territorial integrity, and political independence" (see Watts 2008, 168–70).[35] Constitutional bans on secession or commitments to unity are in tension with the principles of pluralist federalism, but they can be at least partly reconciled with pluralist principles if they are agreed to in negotiations, do not entail material restrictions on peaceful secessionist politics, and are subject to constitutional amendment.[36]

In Cyprus, the tactic of prohibiting secession (or partition) has been favoured by some moderate Turkish Cypriots (e.g., Salih 1978, 30), but is particularly popular among Greek Cypriots. Greek Cypriots are preoccupied with fears that Turkish Cypriots want to divide Cyprus permanently and formally or informally unite their part of the island with nearby Turkey. These fears explain why Greek Cypriots opposed various Turkish Cypriot proposals for autonomy during 1960–74. Since Turkey's partition of Cyprus in 1974, and the unilateral declaration of independence by the TRNC in 1983, Greek Cypriots worry that Turkish Cypriots want to negotiate only to increase their prospects for formal recognition either by pinning the blame for the failure to reach agreement on the Greek Cypriots or by insisting on terms that facilitate secession. These Greek Cypriot fears were described by the UN secretary-general, Kofi Annan, in 2003 as "the Greek Cypriot nightmare" (UNSC 2003, para. 74). To address Greek Cypriot concerns, and at their insistence, the Annan Plan stated that the United Cyprus Republic would take the form of an "indissoluble partnership" and added that Cyprus was a member of the United Nations (a key marker of statehood) and had a "single international legal personality and sovereignty" (Art. 2.1. a). Article 1.6. of the Annan Plan ruled out "secession" and the "union of Cyprus in whole or in part with any other country or any form of partition."

Greek Cypriot worries about the secession of Turkish Cypriots have been equally salient in the negotiations that began in September 2008. At the outset the Greek Cypriots rejected even the Annan Plan's formulation that Cyprus should have a "single international legal personality and sovereignty," insisting instead, for greater clarity, that Cyprus should have a "single international legal personality and a single sovereignty" (Joint Statement, 1 July 2008). This formula, broadly agreed to by Turkish Cypriot leader, Talat, is part of the basis for the current talks. Greek Cypriots also insist that any Cypriot federation, should be "holding together" rather than "coming together," to use terms first laid out by Al Stepan; that is, the federation should be clearly seen as a continuation of, and creation of, the Republic of Cyprus, rather than created by two recognized entities that have decided to merge (Stepan 2001). The advantage of this is that it would make a united Cyprus look less like a confederation, whose parties can secede, and it would make it more clear in the event of a secession that the extant Republic of Cyprus would be recognized as the successor state, retaining its membership in international organizations, its treaties, and its ownership of lucrative offshore gas and oil resources.

The Greek Cypriot desiderata on secession and territorial integrity may appear to satisfy the feasibility test. The Annan Plan, which contained provisions outlawing secession, was ratified in a referendum by 66% of Turkish Cypriots, and Turkish Cypriots currently seem prepared to accept similar provisions to those in the Annan plan. But would a constitutional ban on secession or reinforcement of Cyprus's territorial integrity help its future federation to endure? Cyprus itself is surely an excellent example of the limitations of legal bans on state break-up. The 1960 Treaty of Guarantee, which had "constitutional force" under Article 181 of the Constitution of Cyprus, banned not just "union with any other State, or partition of the island," but any activity likely to promote them, whether direct or indirect (Treaty of Guarantee, Art. 1). This clause was aimed at least as much at the Greek Cypriots, the overwhelming majority of whom sought "*enosis*" (union) with Greece, as at those Turkish Cypriots who sought "*taksim*" (partition), possibly to be followed by union with Turkey. The constitutional ban and the ban on political activity did not prevent Greek Cypriots working for *enosis*, or Turkish Cypriots promoting *taksim*.

President Makarios was unable to publicly disavow *enosis*, even after he had decided by the late 1960s that it was impractical, as it was said to have a "mystic" popularity among his followers (Attalides 1980, chap. 6). The Greek Cypriot right openly campaigned for *enosis* from 1960 until 1974 and eventually, without concern for constitutional probities, launched a coup to achieve it in July 1974. The coup backfired and led to partition, because Turkey invaded within a week, using another section of the Treaty of Guarantee to justify its intervention. Turkish Cypriots had earlier created a less complete partition after the breakdown of law and order in December 1963, when they withdrew into dispersed enclaves throughout the island following Makarios's unilateral proposals to amend the independence constitution (Drousiotis 2008). The writ of the (Greek-Cypriot-controlled) Republic of Cyprus did not extend to these enclaves, which had their own security forces, taxation, and public services. Turkey's more serious partition of July and August 1974 was followed by the TRNC's declaration of independence in 1983.

The TRNC's failure to be recognized by any state but Turkey has had little to do with the legal ban on partition in the Treaty of Guarantee. Rather, the TRNC's failure to achieve recognition reflects the solid consensus in international law and practice that states cannot be permanently conquered or forcibly divided by other states. Even in the absence of external force, the world's states have been notoriously reluctant to recognize secessionist entities when the state's central authorities resist the secession, lest this create a precedent that affects them or undermines international stability. Virtually all cases of recognized independence in the post-Second World War period have occurred as a result of decolonization rather than unilateral secession, or they have occurred after the disintegration of states (in which there is deemed to be no extant central authority) or as a result of agreement on the part of central authorities. The exception is Bangladesh; Kosova's fate hangs in the balance. This international consensus against unilateral secession would have operated just as strongly in the case of Cyprus if the 1960 Treaty of Guarantee's ban on partition had never existed.

As events from 1960 to 1963 or from July to August 1974 suggest, whether a united Cyprus stays together is likely to depend far more on other factors, especially the success of power-sharing and federalism, and the stance of Turkey. If a reunited Cyprus were to break up, matters would be likely to revert to the status quo ante for the TRNC, that is, to de facto, but not de jure, partition. The TRNC would likely continue not to be recognized, particularly not by any member-state of the European Union, of which both Greece and the Greek-Cypriot-controlled Republic of Cyprus are members. There could be some exceptions to this among neighbourhood states won over by Turkey's increasing diplomatic and economic strength, but the international norm against the recognition of entities carved out by external force, and whose independence is contested by the state's central authorities, will limit recognition.[37] The maximum benefit that the Turkish Cypriots can reasonably expect, and perhaps only if blame for the failure to achieve a settlement falls squarely on the Greek Cypriots, is what has been described as the "Taiwan" scenario – a regime whereby other countries could legitimately trade and establish links with the TRNC, but that would fall short of recognized independence, including membership of the UN or EU (see Ker-Lindsay 2011, 100–11).[38]

A sceptic might conclude then that a ban on secession might meet the Hippocratic criterion for inclusion in a constitution; that is, it would "do no harm." A good case can be made, however, that the insistence on a ban on secession is harmful and counterproductive. The insistence of the Greek Cypriots on explicit constitutional language on "indissoluble" partnerships, "single sovereignty," "single international personality," "single citizenship," and the continuity of the Republic of Cyprus has prompted the Turkish Cypriots to propose the inclusion of other provisions that have the (intended) effect of undercutting or contradicting the Greek Cypriots' message. This is partly because, in inter-ethnic negotiations of this sort, one side wants to show to its followers that the negotiations are not one way and that it too has won "concessions." Turkish Cypriots also want to keep the option of secession open, not necessarily because they are determined on Turkish Cypriot independence at all costs (though some are), but because they want to keep open an "escape" route if constitutional politics break down as they did in 1963. Turkish Cypriots are prepared to accept Greek-Cypriot-inspired language on "indissolubility" only if there is compensating language that undermines it. In the negotiations on the Annan Plan between 2001 and 2003, the Turkish Cypriots sought and achieved language that recognized the "territorial integrity" of the constituent states, constituent state "anthems," "internal (constituent state) citizenship," that the constituent states could "sovereignly" exercise their responsibilities (within the limits of the constitution), and that the constituent states could make international agreements with other states in cultural and commercial matters.

Such concept-conflicts lead to virtually interminable, heated, and non-productive discussions on what is called "sovereignty," described by Kofi Annan as the "most contentious conceptual issue" in the negotiations that led to the Annan Plan (UNSC 2003, para. 73). These discussions do not just take up time, but polarize the atmosphere in negotiations, blocking progress on other issues. This is one of the reasons why discussions on the Annan Plan, which ultimately were futile, took three years, and why the negotiations that began in September 2008 lie currently suspended after over three years of talks. The unrecognized cost for the Greek Cypriots is that their insistence on an indissoluble Cyprus gets them nothing valuable, because even if there were no such language in a settlement, the international consensus against unilateral secession would still be there.

Focusing on constitutional bans on secession does harm, even if such bans are "agreed" rather than imposed, because they distract from what is necessary to keep pluralist federations together: cooperation within federal and consociational power-sharing institutions. Some Greek Cypriots understand this lesson: their history makes clear not just that bans on partition may not stop it, but that a failure to engage in consociational compromise and to respond generously to autonomy aspirations is injurious to both stability and unity.

Redistributive Federalism

A fourth celebrated way to bind federations is through redistributive or "equalization" programs that maintain an equitable standard of living and public services throughout the federation (Dawisha and Dawisha 2003, 38; Hale 2008, 255; Shah 2006, 29, 389; Treisman 1999). Such programs are often referred to as "solidarity" payments, because they are said both to express and to contribute to a sense of overarching community (Watts 2008, 109; Swenden, forthcoming). Equalization programs allow for the uniform standard of public services that one typically associates with a unitary state, but they are consistent with pluralist federalism, providing that (i) a significant share of the provided programs are the responsibility of the federative entities,[39] and (ii) transfers from the federal authorities to relatively deprived regions are mostly unconditional. In Canada, a noted pluralist federation, equalization coexists with significant decentralization, and transfers are either entirely unconditional or come with minor conditions, connected to access to programs and performance. One expert on fiscal federalism describes Canada's equalization program as providing the "glue that holds the federation together" (Shah 2006, 389).

However, redistribution does not always promote solidarity, as it always entails costs for part of the federation. All three of the former communist federations of Yugoslavia, the Soviet Union, and Czechoslovakia broke up in part because relatively wealthy regions did not want to share their wealth with less wealthy regions (Hale 2008, 7, 244–6). In Yugoslavia, the two wealthiest republics of Croatia and Slovenia were the first to secede, while in the USSR it was the Baltic republics and Ukraine that left first. In Czechoslovakia, the relatively wealthy Czechs arguably were the driving force behind the break-up, imposing economic changes on the poorer Slovaks that the latter were unwilling to accept (Innes 2001). Belgium's unity is threatened currently by the relatively prosperous Flemish, many of whom do not want to transfer resources to the Walloons. The latest crisis of government formation, which lasted a world-record 21 months, was settled only after Flemish parties achieved a transfer of competences and taxing capacity from the federal government to the regions, which has reduced the federal government's future ability to shift resources from Flanders to Wallonia (Swenden, forthcoming). The current economic crisis has also strengthened separatism in Spain, among the Basques and particularly the Catalans, both of whom are net contributors to the central government.

Arguably, redistribution causes such problems when a federation's relatively prosperous regions do not identify with the federation in question. In all of the cases discussed above, the richer community had its own distinct homeland/nationalist project that was separate from the state, even though some of them (the Flemish and Czechs) were ethnic majorities. National and economic interests could be seen as congruent in all of these cases. Cyprus, however, has the considerable advantage that its wealthiest community, the Greek Cypriots, strongly identifies with all of Cyprus as its homeland. In 2009, the GDP of the Greek-Cypriot-controlled part of Cyprus was $23.4 billion, while the GDP of the "TRNC" was $3.3 billion, or 14% of the Greek Cypriot amount. Greek Cypriot GDP per capita was $29,262, while Turkish Cypriot GDP per capita was $11,934, or 40% of the Greek Cypriot total.[40] This economic disparity has existed historically and, while it may be reduced in the context of a settlement that ends the Turkish Cypriots' isolation, it is likely to remain significant well into the post-settlement period.[41] This combination of Greek Cypriots'commitment to Cyprus's unity and their relative prosperity suggests that redistributive programs may be feasible.[42]

There is also direct evidence that Greek Cypriots are prepared to redistribute to Turkish Cypriots, under certain conditions. In 1989, the "National Council," an official political institution in the Republic of Cyprus that includes the president and the leaders of all political parties, unanimously endorsed a report that called for "fostering economic development with particular emphasis on redressing regional imbalances" (National Council 1989). The council undertook to support the establishment of a "central development fund" that would ensure the "balanced development of all areas of Cyprus and equal opportunities for all Cypriots." In the Annan Plan negotiations, from 2001 to 2004, the Greek Cypriot side agreed to a net transfer of resources from the Greek Cypriot state to the Turkish Cypriot state until the disparities between the two states had disappeared. According to Turkish Cypriot calculations, this would have amounted to roughly 25 million Cyprus pounds or US$50 million in the first year after a settlement (UNSC 2003, para. 124). In the negotiations that began in 2008 the Greek Cypriots agreed to provide a disproportionate amount of consumption tax revenue to the Turkish Cypriot state for a limited period of time, or until the gap between the two constituent states was substantially reduced. In addition, Greek Cypriot leaders routinely say that revenue from recently discovered and potentially lucrative offshore gas and oil deposits in Cyprus's Exclusive Economic Zone will be used to help the Turkish Cypriots in the context of a settlement. They point out that, as it has been agreed in the negotiations that natural resources are to be a federal responsibility, this revenue will be available to the federal authorities for redistributive purposes.[43] On the Turkish Cypriot side, there is some evidence that it is open to material inducements, including equalization payments, again under certain conditions. Indeed, one of the main attractions of a settlement from the Turkish Cypriot perspective is that it will end its current isolation and improve its material position. This helps to explain why a majority of Turkish Cypriots voted for the Annan plan in the 2004 referendum; the plan promises significant material benefits, including the discussed equalization payments and, even more significantly, accession to the EU.

Whether redistributive payments will play a productive bonding role cannot be answered in isolation. The conditions that are attached to such payments by the two communities need to be considered, and therein lies the rub. For the Turkish Cypriots, such payments, or other material benefits, are likely to be attractive only if they are offered in the context of strong political protections for the Turkish Cypriot community, that is, a significantly decentralized bizonal and bicommunal federation. This is clear from the Turkish Cypriots' history. From 1963 to 1974, the Turkish Cypriots endured significant isolation and material hardship rather than submit to a Greek Cypriot offer of minority rights within a unitary state. The Turkish Cypriots voted overwhelmingly for the Annan Plan in 2004, partly because of its clear material benefits, but also because it entrenched a reasonably robust form of bizonality and bicommunalism. Since 2004, in spite of their continuing isolation from the European Union and continuing hardship, the Turkish Cypriots have shown little sign of being prepared to compromise on the political achievements of the Annan Plan in return for material gains. Indeed, the Turkish Cypriots reacted to their continuing material isolation in 2010 by electing a relative hardliner as their leader. For the Turkish

Cypriots, equalization (or accession to the EU) has attractions only if it augments a strong form of pluralist federalism. In this respect, they are like minorities elsewhere, who place core political aspirations ahead of material interests (McGarry and O'Leary 1995, chap. 7).[44]

For the Greek Cypriots, material inducements to the Turkish Cypriots are seen, traditionally, as a way to extract concessions from Turkish Cypriots in other parts of the negotiations, including political, property, and territorial issues. One of the "winning" arguments of the Greek Cypriot leader, Tassos Papadopoulous, during the 2004 referendum campaign on the Annan Plan was that, if Greek Cypriots rejected the plan, they would get a better deal from the Turkish Cypriots (and Turkey) afterwards, as in that event, the Turkish Cypriot region would remain outside the EU until Turkish Cypriots agreed with the Greek Cypriots, presumably on terms more favourable to the Greek Cypriots than the Annan Plan offered. Now that oil and gas has been discovered in the Greek-Cypriot-controlled Republic of Cyprus's Exclusive Economic Zone, some Greek Cypriots believe it can be used as a lever to "nudge the Turkish side towards a less intransigent stance," in the words of Michalis Sarris, a former finance minister of the Republic of Cyprus and a member of the Economic Committee in the Cyprus negotiations.[45] The message delivered from Greek Cypriot elites to Turkish Cypriots is that the oil and gas revenue belongs to all Cypriots and that Turkish Cypriots can benefit from it, but only "in the context of a settlement." This was also the context in which the National Council made its offer on redistribution in 1989 and the context in which post-2008 Greek Cypriot negotiators offered to redistribute revenue from consumption taxes. At a minimum, the Greek Cypriots will want to ensure that equalization payments take place within the context of a "common economic market" in Cyprus in which the four (EU) freedoms of capital, people, services, and goods are assured. This, they will argue, is necessary if economic convergence is to be achieved between the two regions, without permanent Greek Cypriot subsidization of the Turkish Cypriots. The difficulty with this otherwise reasonable argument is that a common market, particularly one that is implemented quickly, is of profound concern to Turkish Cypriot leaders, who worry that it will lead to the much more numerous and wealthier Greek Cypriots dominating the economy and property regime, and perhaps even the political institutions, of the Turkish Cypriot region. This debate forms part of a difficult argument in the negotiations about "derogations" from the EU *acquis* in the event of a settlement and about whether such derogations should be temporary (and, if so, for how long) or permanent.

Redistributive payments have the potential to exercise a benign effect on a Cypriot federation, but it is unclear at this point if either side can accept the conditions that the other attaches to the offer or acceptance of such payments. The problem here is rather fundamental and relates to the conditions under which equalization works. For solidarity payments to work properly, that is, to be given without conditions, there may need to be some significant level of pre-existing solidarity, which makes it a little like vote-pooling, which seems to need pre-existing moderation to work. Indeed, one leading expert on the issue of solidarity payments argues that a common identity is needed to underwrite them (Miller 1995; also see Boadway 2004, 235; Shah 2006, 35).[46] That is a very different claim from the optimism that presumes that such payments can promote a common identity. In Cyprus, Greek Cypriots strongly identify with the island's territory and unity, but are far less keen on the Turkish Cypriots as either co-citizens or co-beneficiaries of a commonwealth. In their relations with Turkish Cypriots, the Greek Cypriots are more like Germans with respect to Greeks (or Greek Cypriots) in the context of the Eurozone crisis than they are like West Germans with respect to East Germans during Germany's reunification. Equalization can be agreed to by the Greek Cypriots, but only if it involves painful political concessions by the prospective recipients. Turkish Cypriots, of course, make it difficult for Greek Cypriots to be generous precisely by making it clear that they see themselves as a different people, not as fellow Cypriots.

Conclusion

Cyprus's experience with the four prescriptive proposals discussed here suggests some generalizable lessons. It is unlikely that an electoral system that benefits moderates will be included in a peace agreement or taken seriously in negotiations, unless moderates are already in a reasonably strong political position or the electoral system is imposed from the outside.[47] On the other hand, Cyprus, like Fiji, shows that moderate parties sometimes do occupy pivotal positions in deeply divided polities.

As there has been no experience of an operational centripetalist electoral system in a united Cyprus, it is difficult to assess its functional benefits, that is, to determine if it would deliver a strengthened moderate centre and weaker extremes. When a centripetalist electoral system was proposed in Cyprus's negotiations, however, it did not strengthen political moderates. The acceptance by the moderate Turkish Cypriot leader of weighted cross-voting helped to secure his election defeat at the hands of a hard line opponent. The election of a Turkish Cypriot hardliner has made it not just difficult to win acceptance of weighted cross-voting, but more difficult to secure an overall settlement acceptable to Greek Cypriots. On the Greek Cypriot side, Christofias's support for weighted cross-voting increased the resolve of hard line Greek Cypriot parties to oppose a settlement and made it difficult for his natural pro-settlement ally, DISY, to support one. One might reasonably anticipate that if the fear of exclusion under weighted cross-voting had these negative and obstructive effects before a settlement, it would have similar effects afterwards.

These problems with centripetalism explain why consociationalists advocate electoral and executive systems that are inclusive of all political parties willing to embrace constitutional politics. Consociationalists also seek to moderate radical parties, but rather than requiring such parties to moderate their appeal to win elections, an onerous and often unrealistic requirement, consociationalists seek to soften radical parties by giving them a stake in legislative and executive office and by offering them incentives to increase that stake if they adopt moderate politics. This implies proportional (or communal) electoral systems and executive composition rules that tie shares of ministerial portfolios to electoral success. Radical parties may still have reasons for refusing to compromise, but political exclusion will not then be one of them. Any problems associated with disparate parties in coalition can be mitigated, not just by provisions that tie shares in office to vote share, but by agreed dispute resolution mechanisms that alleviate abuses associated with vetoes and by a substantive degree of autonomy to regions controlled by each of the communities.

Cyprus also suggests that it is one thing to accept that the existence of cross-cutting cleavages, or the existence of territorial divisions within ethnic or linguistic communities, is conducive to political stability but another thing altogether to engineer such features if they do not exist already. The territorial structure of English-speaking Canada and of French-speaking or German-speaking Switzerland has had moderating effects on these two federations, but these territorial divisions arose without constitutional design.[48] Once communities are self-governing within a single undivided region, it is difficult to imagine such communities agreeing to divide themselves, particularly if they are minorities within the federation. Anyone who thinks otherwise should ask themselves if the Québécois or the Scots would agree to divide their homelands into multiple regions of Canada and the U.K., respectively, for the purpose of holding these states together. The most frequently cited example of such internal boundary engineering by Horowitz – that of Nigeria in the 1960s, when its three-unit federation was converted into twelve states – was not agreed to by the Hausa-Fulani, Yoruba, or Ibo communities (each of whom dominated one of the original three units) but was implemented by a military dictatorship, which conquered secessionist Biafra. Fresh territorial subdivisions are therefore not a viable strategy for peacefully reintegrating breakaway regions into a federal political system, a lesson that should be useful for Moldova (Transnistria), Georgia (South Ossetia and Abkhazia), Azerbaijan (Ngorno-Karabakh), and Somalia (Somaliland and Puntland). Majority communities may be more open to their own territorial subdivision – particularly as part of a strategy for uniting the state, as majorities are less likely to have security fears and may think that their desire for collective self-determination can be satisfied within federal or central institutions. But, as Cyprus shows, majorities may also prefer to remain territorially united even if they are prepared to concede autonomy to minorities, something that is also true for the English, Moldovans, and Georgians. In these circumstances, the most feasible territorial prescription is not the drawing of new internal boundaries that divide communities, but autonomy arrangements that are based on existing internal boundaries (McGarry 2012).

Cyprus is testimony to the deeply contested nature of sovereignty disputes during attempts to thaw "frozen conflicts," where one part of the state has broken away de facto but not de jure (Bahcheli, Bartmann, and Srebrnik 2004). In such conflicts, the breakaway region, which ordinarily will have ceaselessly proclaimed its sovereignty since the break-up, is likely to abandon this status in negotiations only under very considerable duress. The rump state, which will have just as consistently denied the breakaway region's sovereign status and proclaimed its sovereignty over all of the state's territory, is similarly unlikely to retract its position, as its aim is to prevent a recurrence of break-up, particularly one that would allow, this time, the de jure recognition of the breakaway region. For the state's authorities to insist during negotiations that the representatives of the breakaway region agree to the state's "indivisibility" and "single sovereignty" is very likely to produce either unproductively lengthy negotiations and a stalemate, or lead the breakaway region's representatives simultaneously to recognize the state's territorial integrity and contradict this through other inconsistent constitutional proposals. In these circumstances, which have occurred in Cyprus (and may occur in other frozen conflicts in Moldova, Georgia, Azerbaijan, and Somalia), the most sensible way to proceed may be to park disputes over sovereignty and secession or territorial integrity. The recognition is in any case protected by the international consensus against unilateral secession, while the breakaway region's representatives are freer to explore power-sharing provisions.

Cyprus's experience also allows us to put into perspective the utility of "solidarity" payments as a tool for facilitating settlements in deeply divided polities. Wealthy parties to negotiations may be prepared to offer such payments, particularly if they are committed to the state's unity, but they are also likely to seek a price; that is, "solidarity" payments in deeply divided settings are unlikely to be offered out of "solidarity," but rather amid hard bargaining. Cyprus also suggests that deprived minorities are unlikely to place material advantages, whether from solidarity payments or even more valuable membership of prestigious material clubs, ahead of core political and security concerns. Walker Connor's warning about the "unwarranted exaggeration of the influence of materialism in human affairs" should never be forgotten (1994, 144).

ACKNOWLEDGMENTS

I would like to thank the Trudeau Foundation and the Social Sciences and Humanities Research Council of Canada for funding my research. I'm also indebted to the following for advising me and answering my questions: Stephen Bourke, Michael Keating, Neo Loizides, Margaret Moore, Brendan O'Leary, Yiannis Papadakis, Nicos Trimliklionitis, and Ron Watts. They bear no responsibility for how I've used their help.

NOTES

1 On Political Parties – Federal Law No. 95-FZ of July 11 2001, Art. 3.2. Accessed online at http://www.democracy.ru/english/library/laws/ parties_fz95_eng/page1.html#P9_1378
2 The second, third, and fourth of these mechanisms are usually specific to federations, while the first applies to divided polities in general.

3 This system is understood to comprise a powerful president and a weak, dependent vice-president, elected on a single ticket.

4 The preferential element of the Alternative Vote, it is claimed, facilitates inter-ethnic transfers in divided polities. While minority voters will usually prefer to give their first preference vote to candidates from their own community, they may be prepared, it is thought, to give lower-preference votes to moderate leaders of other communities, particularly as doing so will not detract from the prospects of their own candidate, who will normally have little prospect of being elected.

5 As the archbishop put it recently, in the context of Barack Obama's tenure of the American presidency, the Turkish Cypriots should have as good a chance of winning a presidential election in Cyprus as African Americans have in the United States (Archbishop Says He will take Position on 2013 Presidential Elections, *Alithia*, 13 June 2011). He did not mention that it had taken African Americans over two centuries to achieve this distinction, or that it was unlikely to become a regular occurrence. For another Greek Cypriot academic who supports a U.S.-style presidency, see Theophanous (2011).

6 As the two federal units will not remain homogeneous after a settlement, it is possible that in future the Turkish Cypriot candidate could be elected exclusively by Greek Cypriot votes even with Horowitz's majority-plus distribution formula. The only way to prevent this would be either to require that Greek Cypriots living in the Turkish Cypriot federal region could not vote at the federal level, or to increase the distribution threshold required for election above 25%. The latter would increase a risk that exists with all majority-plus distribution formulae: there may be no winner.

7 The Lebanese electoral system, which is endorsed by Horowitz, combines ethnic quotas with an integrated (common) election. However, in Lebanon, the rival communities are much closer in population size than they are in Cyprus (Emerson and Tocci 2002, 15). The Lebanese system also produces inauthentic representatives – pliable Maronites allied with Shia, pliable Druze allied with Sunnis, and so on.

8 When weighted cross-voting, or variations of it, have been proposed in Cyprus, it has been argued that it would ensure that the elected candidates from each community would have to "seriously take into account both communities' interests and concerns" (National Council 1989) and that "it would make it advisable for politicians of both communities to appeal also to members of the other community for their votes. Until now there has been no advantage in so doing. [Weighted cross-voting would] give a premium to all politicians to develop policies that would appeal to members of the other community. Not all would. Those that did would be rewarded

by receiving voters from the other community which at the margins would affect the outcome of elections" (Friends of Cyprus 1995).

9   Greek Cypriots had previously proposed integrated electoral systems in which Turkish Cypriot votes were "weighted" so that they constituted more than their actual 20% of the population. In all of these proposals, however, the Greek Cypriot electorate would have exercised a more decisive say in the election of the Turkish Cypriot candidate than in the weighted cross-voting system proposed by Christofias, which limited the Greek Cypriot share of the electorate for the Turkish Cypriot candidate to 20%.

10 *Rota Gazetesi*, 19 December 2009. Available at http://rotagazetesi.com/index.php?option=com_content&task=view&id=12975&Itemid=41

11 *Cyprus Problem*: They Take Convergences out of the Fridge – Close on Governance, Economy, *Phileleftheros*, 28 October 2012.

12 UBP circles suggested that weighted cross-voting posed an "existential" threat to the Turkish Cypriots, as it could lead to the election of a Turkish Cypriot "leader" with only minority support among Turkish Cypriots. *Rota Gazetesi*, 19 December 2009. Available at http://rotagazetesi.com/index.php?option=com_content&task=view&id=12975&Itemid=41

13 Resigning Is Christofias's Only Option, *Phileleftheros*, 4 September 2011.

14 DIKO (*Dimokratikó Kómma* / Democratic Party); EDEK (Kinima SosialdimokratonMovement for Social Democracy); EVROKO (Evropaiko Komma/European Party); and the Greens (*Kinima Oikologon Perivallontiston* / Ecological and Environmental Movement).

15 Talat may well have lost anyway, given the dismal performance of the Turkish Cypriot economy, and disillusionment among Turkish Cypriots who voted "yes" in 2004 on Talat's recommendation, but without any end to their isolation.

16 Canada's longevity is seen as resulting in part from the division of English-speaking Canadians into nine provinces (and three territories). This division has reduced the salience of an English Canadian identity and promoted cross-cutting alliances between particular English-speaking provinces and Quebec on common (cross-cutting) economic interests (McGarry 2005, 97). Switzerland's endurance is seen as partly flowing from the fact that its linguistic cleavage is cross-cut by religious and urban-rural divides. German Catholic (or Protestant) cantons, for example, can combine with French Catholic (or Protestant) cantons on religious issues, helping to soften the salience of the linguistic cleavage (Roeder 2009; Watts 2008, 180; Wimmer 2003, 124). India's survival has been linked to the intersection of its potentially explosive religious divide with linguistic and other issues,

a consequence, it is said, of Nehru's decision to draw federal boundaries within the religious communities, and (reluctantly) to base India's states on language (Roeder 2005, 67). Although few would describe Nigeria as a successful federation, its durability since the disastrous civil war of the late 1960s has been traced to the reorganization of its internal boundaries, one result of which was to subdivide the large Hausa-Fulani, Yoruba, and Ibo communities into multiple federal regions, which apparently undermined destructive pan-Hausa-Fulani, Yoruba, and Ibo ideologies (Horowitz 1985, 604–13; 1991, 217–19; 2007, 961–2).

17 In Bosnia-Herzegovina, in the early 1990s, Cyrus Vance and David Owen warned against a tripartite federation made up of Bosniak, Serb, and Croat units, and instead recommended "cantonization," that is, boundaries that divided each of these ethnic communities into several federal regions.

18 Several academics warned against a tripartite federation made up of Kurdish, Shia Arab, and Sunni Arab regions and recommended a federation based on Baathist Iraq's 18 administrative "governorates," the effect of which would have been to subdivide each of Iraq's three large communities into multiple entities (Dawisha and Dawisha 2003; Council on Foreign Relations 2003; Makiya 2003; Wimmer 2003, 124).

19 Roeder recommends "various forms of cantonization or federalism that divide ethnic communities" as a way to prevent the consolidation of national identities "on the periphery" and to block "the conflation of political agendas into a conflict over alternative nation-state projects" (2009, 217).

20 If the Greek Cypriot region remained undivided, it would comprise around 60–70% of Cyprus's population and over 70% of its territory and would possess more than 80% of its wealth. This would make it a "core ethnic region" much more dominant than any of Hale's examples.

21 The consensus on two regions, each controlled by one community, exists alongside a disagreement on the exact meaning of "bizonality." Greek Cypriots advocate a "soft" bizonality in which there is freedom of movement between the two zones. Greek Cypriot refugees are able to return to their property, buy other property, vote in the northern federal unit, and so on. Turkish Cypriots prefer a "hard" bizonality in which the internal boundary is less permeable, the Turkish Cypriots are in a large majority, and so on.

22 The TRNC, declared in 1983 but established as a result of Turkey's invasion in 1974, comprises just over 36% of Cyprus's territory. As Turkish Cypriots make up around only 20% of Cyprus's population, there is an understanding that they will have to give up territory, at least 7% of the island's total, as part of the cost of a settlement. It is widely thought that

Turkey deliberately captured more territory than it sought to retain for the Turkish Cypriots, in order to strengthen its hand in negotiations.

23 Since the 1970s, mainstream Greek Cypriot political elites have abandoned any idea that the Turkish Cypriot region in a united Cyprus could be divided, although they occasionally propose Greek Cypriot enclaves and federal parks within the Turkish Cypriot zone, apparently to disrupt the territorial contiguity of the Turkish Cypriot region and to encourage more Greek Cypriots to move there.

24 Wimmer believed that Iraq provided the opportunity for dividing the Kurds across different regions because they were already divided into two "chiefdoms" (2003, 124).

25 Hale argues that the division of the dominant group's territory can reduce support for secession among minorities.

26 Smaller national communities in bipolar contexts often prefer to see themselves as involved in dualist partnerships rather than as having just one federal region among the majority's several regions. For example, the Parti Québécois's desire for "sovereignty-association" is for a dualist association between Quebec and the "rest of Canada." If a majority community has more regions than a minority, the minority may demand an "asymmetric" status for its region, that is, explicit constitutional recognition of the minority community as a "nation," or for its region as a "national homeland," or some such formula that indicates that it has a status superior to or distinct from each of the majority's several regions.

27 This argument can be contrasted with Hale's position that minorities are likely to resent a large "core ethnic region" and likely to support its division. This may be true in many circumstances. In Cyprus, the Turkish Cypriots do not appear to think the division of the Greek Cypriot region would advantage them, possibly because they do not think such a division would make any substantial difference to the unity of Greek Cypriots.

28 Karamanlis, the moderate Greek prime minister after the restoration of democracy, also argued that multizonality was not in the interests of the Greek Cypriots, because Turkish Cypriots living in discontiguous cantons would produce ethnic strife and invite future military action by the Turkish army (Hatzivasiliou 1992, 160–2).

29 This chapter was written before the catastrophic banking crisis that befell the Republic of Cyprus in March 2013. There are no signs yet that this crisis has reduced Greek Cypriot support for unitarism.

30 Ironically, one of the Greek Cypriot academics who discusses the advantages of multizonality also criticizes the alleged inefficiencies of multiple government bureaucracies (Theophanous 2011).

31 The third-place candidate in the Republic of Cyprus presidential elections of February 2013, George Lillikas, proposed a multizonal federation based on the "American, Australian or German" model that would divide both the Turkish Cypriots and the Greek Cypriots (see Towards a United States of Cyprus, Fuelled by Natural Gas, *Kathimerini*, 27 January 2013). Lillikas is the first presidential candidate in the history of the Republic of Cyprus to take such a position.

32 Thus, Turkish Cypriots were capable of maintaining a high degree of communal solidarity when they were dispersed in enclaves across Cyprus prior to 1974, because of antagonistic relations with Greek Cypriots.

33 Constitution of Spain, Article 2. Accessed at http://www.servat.unibe.ch/icl/sp00000.html

34 Constitution of the Federal Republic of Nigeria, 29 May 1999, Article 2(1). Full text available at http://www.nigeria-law.org/ConstitutionOfThe FederalRepublicOfNigeria.htm

35 The General Framework Agreement for Peace in Bosnia and Herzegovina, initialled in Dayton on 21 November 1995 and signed in Paris on 14 December 1995, Annex 4, Article 3(2)(a). Full text available at http://www .intstudies.cam.ac.uk/centre/cps/documents_bosnia_dayton.html

36 Actual constitutional bans or commitments to territorial integrity are often not the result of a negotiated agreement and in some cases (Turkey and Ukraine) are beyond constitutional amendment.

37 It is possible to imagine a scenario in which, if the United States wanted Turkey to recognize what is currently the Kurdistan region of Iraq, it might offer recognition of the TRNC in return. Such a step does not appear to be likely in the foreseeable future and would certainly fracture U.S. relations with Greece, although these are not as prized as they once were.

38 Hopeful Turkish Cypriots talk also of a "Kossovo" scenario, that is, a scenario where the TRNC is recognized by many states but not enough to entitle it to membership of the United Nations (Sozen 2012). This seems optimistic. It would require the TRNC to be recognized by 65 states, including the U.S. and a majority of the EU members, including five of its six largest states.

39 Equalization can also be provided directly by federal authorities, administering "region-blind" social programs that disproportionately benefit deprived regions. Such federal programs are generally considered by minorities that control deprived regions as a second-best option.

40 All figures are in U.S. dollars. Sources: Statistical Service (GC); State Planning Organization (TC); IMF (exchange rates).

41 A settlement will end the Turkish Cypriots' isolation, but Greek Cypriots

will either receive large chunks of their property in the north back, or be compensated for it. Greek Cypriot territory will also increase by around 8% of the island's total. Plausibly, a settlement will likely produce a peace dividend, in tourism and property prices, for both sides of the island.

42 The March 2013 financial crisis in the Republic of Cyprus has reduced the feasibility of redistribution, although the Greek Cypriot region is likely to remain relatively prosperous compared with the Turkish Cypriot region.

43 When lucrative oil and gas resources are a competence of the federal regions, or a shared competence, as in Canada and Iraq, it can make equalization programs considerably more difficult.

44 The Anatolian settlers who have moved to Cyprus are more likely than the Turkish Cypriots to have their preferences shaped by material considerations. Material inducements are more likely to be successful in persuading the former to return to Turkey than to persuade Turkish Cypriots to abandon a robust pluralist federalism.

45 *Cyprus Mail*, 27 November 2011.

46 "A national consensus on the standard of equalization is critically important for the sustainability of any equalization program" (Shah 2006, 35). "[Redistribution] involves a high degree of solidarity nationwide among rich and poor regions, and that solidarity may not exist in decentralized federations with heterogeneous regions" (Boadway 2004, 235).

47 The adoption of a vote-pooling electoral system in Fiji in 1997, seen by Horowitz as a triumph for centripetal theory, was agreed to by a governing coalition of moderate political parties (Fraenkel and Grofman 2006, 632). The decision to use the alternative vote for a presidential election in Republika Srpska in 2000 was not taken by the local political parties, but was imposed on them by the OSCE (Bose 2002, 218–22). The majority plus geographical distribution electoral system that has been used for presidential elections in Nigeria since 1979 was implemented during a military dictatorship.

48 The division of Jura in 1978 is an exception.

REFERENCES

Attalides, Michalis. 1980. *Cyprus: Nationalism and International Politics*. New York: St. Martin's Press.

Bahcheli, Tozun, Barry Bartmann, and Henry Srebrnik, eds. 2004. *De Facto States: The Quest for Sovereignty*. Abingdon and New York: Routledge.

Boadway, Robin. 2004. The Theory and Practice of Equalization. *CESifo Economic Studies* 50(1):211–54.

Bose, Sumantra. 2002. *Bosnia after Dayton: Nationalist Partition and International Intervention*. London: Hurst.

Brancati, Dawn. 2004. Is Federalism a Panacea for Post-Saddam Iraq? *Washington Quarterly* 25(2):7–21.

Buchanan, Allen. 2004. *Justice, Legitimacy, and Self-Determination: Moral Foundations for International Law*. Oxford: Oxford University Press.

Bunce, Valerie. 1999. *Subversive Institutions: The Design and the Destruction of Socialism and the State*. Cambridge: Cambridge University Press.

Clerides, Glafkos. 1992. *My Deposition*. Vol. 4. Nicosia: Alithia.

Connor, Walker. 1994. *Ethnonationalism: The Quest for Understanding*. Princeton: Princeton University Press.

Council on Foreign Relations and the James A. Baker III Institute for Public Policy of Rice University. 2003. Guiding Principles for U.S. Post-Conflict Policy in Iraq: Report of an Independent Working Group (Co-sponsored by the Council on Foreign Relations and the James A. Baker III Institute for Public Policy of Rice University. Accessed 18 February 2012. Available at http://bakerinstitute.org/publications/guiding-principles-for-u-s-post-conflict-policy-in-iraq

Dawisha, Adeed, and Karen Dawisha. 2003. How to Build a Democratic Iraq. *Foreign Affairs* 82(3):36–50.

Drousiotis, Makarios. 2008. *The First Partition: Cyprus, 1963–64*. Nicosia: Alfadi.

Duchacek, Ivo. 1988. Dyadic Federations and Confederations. *Publius* 18(2):5–31.

Emerson, Michael, and Nathalie Tocci. 2002. *Cyprus as Lighthouse of the Eastern Mediterranean: Shaping Re-unification and EU Accession Together*. Brussels: Centre for European Policy Studies.

Fraenkel, Jon, and Bernard Grofman. 2006. Does the Alternative Vote Foster Moderation in Ethnically Divided Societies? The Case of Fiji. *Comparative Political Studies* 39(5):623–51.

Friends of Cyprus. 1995. Report No. 38. Accessed 18 February 2012. Available at http://www.peace-cyprus.org/FOC/

Hale, Henry. 2004. Divided We Stand: Institutional Sources of Ethnofederal State Survival and Collapse. *World Politics* 56(2):165–93.

Hale, Henry. 2008. *The Foundations of Ethnic Politics: Separatism of States and Nations in Europe and the World*. Cambridge: Cambridge University Press.

Hatzivasiliou, Evanthis, ed. 1992. Constantinos Karamanlis: Archive, Events and Documents, Vol. 9 (Restoration of Democracy, Period B, 4 September 1971 – 21 October 1977). Athens: C.G. Karamanlis Foundation and Ekdotike Athenon.

Horowitz, Donald L. 1985. *Ethnic Groups in Conflict*. Berkeley: University of California Press.

Horowitz, Donald L. 1991. *A Democratic South Africa? Constitutional Engineering in a Divided Society*. Berkeley: University of California Press.

Horowitz, Donald L. 2007. The Many Uses of Federalism. *Drake Law Review* 55:953–66.

Iacovidis, Sava. 2011. What Federation for Cyprus? Accessed 18 February 2012. Available at http://www.sigmalive.com/simerini/politics/interviews/369448

Innes, Abby. 2001. *Czechoslovakia: The Short Goodbye*. New Haven: Yale University Press.

Joint Statement by Cypriot Leaders. 1 July 2008. Available at http://www.uncyprustalks.org/nqcontent.cfm?a_id=2575

Ker-Lindsay, James. 2009. A History of Cyprus Peace Proposals. In *Reunifying Cyprus: The Annan Plan and Beyond*, edited by Andrekos Varnava and Hubert Faustmann. London: I.B. Tauris.

Ker-Lindsay, James. 2011. *The Cyprus Problem: What Everyone Needs to Know*. Oxford: Oxford University Press.

Kymlicka, Will. 1995. *Multicultural Citizenship: A Liberal Theory of Minority Rights*. Oxford: Oxford University Press.

Kyriakides, Stanley. 1968. *Cyprus: Constitutionalism and Crisis Government*. Philadelphia: University of Pennsylvania Press.

Lipset, Seymour M. 1960. *The Political Man: The Social Bases of Politics*. Garden City: Doubleday.

Loizides, Neophytos. 2013 (forthcoming). *Cyprus: Federal and Consociational Failures and Prospects*. Philadelphia: University of Pennsylvania Press.

Lordos, Alexandros, Errol Kaymak, and Nathalie Tocci 2009. *A People's Peace in Cyprus: Testing Public Opinion on the Options for a Comprehensive Settlement*. Brussels: Centre for European Policy Studies.

Makiya, Kanan. 2003. A Model for Post-Saddam Iraq. *Journal of Democracy* 14(3):5–12.

McEvoy, Joanne. n.d. Power-Sharing Executives: Co-operation and Conflict in Bosnia, Macedonia and Northern Ireland. Unpublished manuscript.

McGarry, John. 2005. Canadian Lessons for Iraq. In *The Future of Kurdistan in Iraq*, edited by Brendan O'Leary, John McGarry, and Khalid Salih. Philadelphia: University of Pennsylvania Press.

McGarry, John. 2012. Asymmetric Autonomy in the United Kingdom. In *Multinational Federalism*, edited by Michel Seymour. London: Palgrave.

McGarry, John, and Brendan O'Leary. 1995. *Explaining Northern Ireland: Broken Images*. Oxford: Wiley-Blackwell.

McGarry, John, and Brendan O'Leary. 2005. Federation as a Method of Ethnic Conflict Regulation. In *From Power-Sharing to Democracy: Post-conflict Institutions in Ethnically Divided Societies*, edited by Sid J.R. Noel. Montreal and Kingston: McGill-Queen's University Press.

McGarry, John, and Brendan O'Leary. 2007. Federations and Managing Nations. In *Multinational Federations*, edited by Michael Burgess and John Pinder. London: Routledge.

McGarry, John, and Brendan O'Leary. 2009. Power-Shared after Death of Thousands. In *Consociational Theory: McGarry-O'Leary and the Northern Ireland Conflict*, edited by Rupert Taylor. London: Routledge.

McGarry, John, and Brendan O'Leary. 2011. Territorial Approaches to Ethnic Conflict Settlement. In *The Routledge Handbook on Ethnic Conflict*, edited by Karl Cordell and Stefan Wolff. London: Routledge.

McGarry, John, Brendan O'Leary, and Richard Simeon. 2008. Integration or Accommodation? The Enduring Debate in Conflict Regulation. In *Constitutional Design for Divided Societies: Integration or Accommodation?* edited by Sujit Choudhry. Oxford: Oxford University Press.

Miller, David. 1995. *On Nationality*. Oxford: Oxford University Press.

Mitchell, Paul, Geoffrey Evans, and Brendan O'Leary. 2009. Extremist Outbidding in Ethnic Party Systems is Not Inevitable: Tribune Parties in Northern Ireland. *Political Studies*. 57(2):397–421.

National Council. 1989. *Greek Cypriot Proposals*. Nicosia: National Council.

O'Leary, Brendan, and John McGarry. 2012. The Politics of Accommodation and Integration in Democratic States. In *Ethnicity and Politics*, edited by Adrian Guelke and Jean Tournon. Berlin: Budrich Press.

Polyviou, Polyvios. 1975. *Cyprus: The Tragedy and the Challenge*. Washington: The American Hellenic Institute.

Riker, William H. 1964. *Federalism: Origin, Operation, Significance*. Boston: Little, Brown.

Roeder, Philip. 2005. Power-Dividing as an Alternative to Ethnic Power-Sharing. In *Sustainable Peace: Power and Democracy after Civil Wars*, edited by Philip Roeder and Donald Rothchild. Ithaca: Cornell University Press.

Roeder, Philip. 2007. *Where Nation-States Come From: Institutional Change in the Age of Nationalism*. Princeton: Princeton University Press.

Roeder, Philip. 2009. Ethnofederalism and the Mismanagement of Conflict Nationalisms. *Regional and Federal Studies* 19(2):203–19.

Salih, Halil Ibrahim. 1978. *Cyprus: The Impact of Diverse Nationalism on a State*. Tuscaloosa: University of Alabama Press.

Shah, Anwar, ed. 2006. *The Practice of Fiscal Federalism: Comparative Perspectives*. Montreal and Kingston: McGill-Queen's University Press.

Snyder, Jack. 2000. *From Voting to Violence: Democratization and Nationalist Conflict*. New York: W.W. Norton.

Sozen, Ahmet. 2012. Heading Towards the Defining Moment in Cyprus: Public Opinion vs. Realities on the Ground. *Insight Turkey* 14(1):109–29.

Stepan, Alfred. 2001. *Arguing Comparative Politics*. Oxford: Oxford University Press.

Swenden, Wilfried. Forthcoming. Belgium and the Crisis of Governability, 2007–2011: Rebooting Territorial Pluralism? In *Assessing Territorial Pluralism*, edited by John McGarry and Richard Simeon. Vancouver: UBC Press.

Theophanous, Andreas. 2011. Which Federation for Cyprus? Accessed 18 February 2012. Available at http://www.onalert.gr/default.php?pname=Article&catid=10&art_id=4691

Treisman, Daniel S. 1999. *After the Deluge: Regional Crises and Political Consolidation in Russia*. Ann Arbor: University of Michigan Press.

United Nations Security Council. 2003. Report of the Secretary-General on his Mission of Good Offices in Cyprus, S/2003/398. 1 April.

Watts, Ronald L. 2008. *Comparing Federal Systems*. Montreal and Kingston: McGill-Queen's University Press.

Wimmer, Andreas. 2003. Democracy and Ethno-Religious Conflict in Iraq. *Survival* 45(4):111–34.

6 The Constitutional Jurisprudence of Federalism and the Theocratic Challenge

RAN HIRSCHL

Contrary to what many liberals predicted or wished for, not only has religion not vanished, but it has instead gained a renewed momentum worldwide. From the fundamentalist turn in predominantly Islamic polities to the spread of Catholicism and Pentecostalism in the global south, to the rise of the Christian Right in the United States, it is hard to overstate the significance of the religious revival in late twentieth- and early twenty-first-century politics. As of 2013, approximately half of the world's population, perhaps more, live in polities where religion continues to play a key role in political and constitutional life. India, Turkey, and Indonesia are merely a few examples. Within that religion-laden hemisphere, approximately a billion people live in polities, national or sub-national, that feature key elements of what I have termed elsewhere "constitutional theocracy" (Hirschl 2010).

In the past four decades, at least 30 of the world's predominantly Muslim polities, from Mauritania to Oman to Pakistan, declared Shari'a (Islamic law) "a" or "the" source of legislation (meaning that legislation must comply with principles of that religion). The more recent new constitutions of Afghanistan (2004), Iraq (2005), as well as the Constitutional Declaration of Libya (2011) reflect a dual commitment to principles of Shari'a and to principles of human rights, constitutional law, and popular sovereignty. As recent developments in Tunisia and Egypt indicate, this type of constitutionalism is not likely to vanish following the so-called Arab Spring. In several other countries precepts of Islam have been incorporated into the constitution, penal code, and personal-status laws of sub-national units, most notably in 12 Nigerian states, Pakistan's North-West Frontier Province, and Indonesia's Aceh, to varying degrees in two Malaysian states, and to an increasing extent in Russia's

Chechnya and Dagestan. In half a dozen Indian states, to pick another example, strict restrictions on conversion from Hinduism have been introduced into law by the Hindu nationalist Bharatiya Janata Party (BJP). In countries such as Israel (Judaism) or Sri Lanka (Buddha Sasana), religious affiliation is closely entangled with legal definitions of ethnicity, nationality, and citizenship. Granted, Malaysia or Israel is a world apart from Iran or the Vatican in how lax or rigid the actual translation of religious principles into public life is. But in virtually all these countries religion not only plays a key collective-identity role but also is granted a formal constitutional status, serves as a source of legislation, whether symbolically or practically, and, more important, enjoys jurisdictional autonomy in matters extending from education and personal-status law to essential omnipresence in every aspect of life, law, and politics.

In this chapter, I examine how federalism jurisprudence in the nonsecular world has responded to this wave of religiosity and assess the efficacy of federalism in containing the spread of religious fundamentalism and in defusing calls for incorporation of religious precepts into law in the increasingly large number of polities facing popular resurgence of religion. I begin by identifying the unique challenges posed by the worldwide theocratic surge toward spatial power-sharing mechanisms. I then proceed to examine innovative, federalism-based structures and interpretive modes developed by governments, legislatures, and constitutional courts in religion-laden polities to temper the challenge of theocracy. Illustrations are drawn from recent federalism jurisprudence from India, Nigeria, Malaysia, Indonesia, and Pakistan. Taken as a whole, these examples suggest that (i) beyond promoting diversity within regional boundaries, federalism-based jurisdictional boundaries in religion-laden settings have been drawn upon by those who object to theocratic government, to contain religion and its traditional interlocutors, spread a notion of state-controlled, institutionalized religion, or advance secularizing solutions to religion and state problems; and (ii) although constitutional courts in both unitary and federal polities tend to resent radical religion, courts in federal systems may be better equipped to deal with religious fundamentalism than their counterparts in unitary states, in particular, in settings where calls for theocratic governance are confined within clearly defined sub-national units.

The Theocratic Challenge to Spatial Power-Sharing Mechanisms

A voluminous body of literature on constitutional design and engineering suggests that when constitution-drafting is seen as a pragmatic, rather than principled, matter, it can be employed to mitigate tensions in ethnically divided polities through the adoption of federalism, secured representation, and other trust-building and power-sharing mechanisms.[1] The literature on constitutional design of this kind, often referred to as "consociationalism" (or "accommodation-centred") emphasizes the significance of joint-governance institutions, mutual veto points, power-sharing mechanisms, and the like (Lijphart 2004). In its more strategic, "centripetal" (or "integrationist") guise this brand of scholarship advocates the adoption of institutions that would make the political process more attractive to recalcitrant stakeholders, encourage moderation, and defuse the causes of strife by providing incentives to vote across group lines (Horowitz 1985). From Nepal to Lebanon and to Bosnia and Herzegovina, dozens of constitutions worldwide reflect such a "second-order," power-sharing, and problem-solving form of constitutionalism that is driven not by ideational platforms or expressive aspirations but by political necessities.

Surprisingly, however, although there are many examples of discussions of the mitigating potential of constitutional power-sharing mechanisms to ease rifts along national, ethnic, or linguistic lines, scholars of comparative constitutional design have given little attention to the increasing divisions along secular/religious lines per se (i.e., not in association with ethnic divisions). Constitutional treatment of religion in the non-western world comes in three basic configurations: strong establishment of a single religion with little regard to minority religions (e.g., much of the Islamic world); selective accommodation of religion in certain areas of the law – here the general law is secular, but a degree of jurisdictional autonomy is granted to religious communities, primarily in matters of personal status and education (e.g., Kenya, Senegal, India); overarching constitutional principles alongside limited autonomy to sub-national units with respect to religion (e.g., Nigeria, Malaysia).

From an analytical standpoint, the secular/religious divide differs in at least five respects from these more obvious and more commonly addressed markers of identity. First, and perhaps most important, there is a fundamental (and many argue irreconcilable) tension between the rule of state law and the rule of God. Whereas the rule of state law rests on the notion that the law is sovereign and the people of a given polity are the sources of power and legitimacy of that polity's law, a rule-of-God perception of the good sees the divine authority as the ultimate source of sovereignty, power, and legitimacy. It thus regards certain religious directives as standing above the politcal or constitutional order. Put differently, the theocratic challenge reflects conflicting claims concerning the foundations of the legal and political order. Such claims go beyond standard demands for autonomy and the assertion of difference that characterize ethnic group conflict. The groups in conflict do not want autonomy, constitutional guarantees, or protection from the state; rather, they seek to reshape the state's core institutions in a way that is in line with their conception of justice and, as is often the case, in line with their own material interest. The theocratic challenge is thus a challenge to the very secular foundations of the modern state. Any power-sharing, compromise-based constitutional pact is unlikely to find a principled (as opposed to pragmatist or consequentalist) common ground between these two conflciting views.

Second, more than any other divisions along ascriptive or imagined lines, the secular/religious divide cuts across nations otherwise unified by their members' joint ethnic, linguistic, and historical origins. In this sense the secularism/religiosity factor or other closely associated distinctions, such as universalism versus parochialism, are closer in nature to less visible categories, such as income deciles, social class, or cultural milieu, than they are to other kinds of markers such as race, gender, or ethnicity. Nationalist Catalans, the Flemish, and Quebecers see themselves as autonomous people with a unique cultural heritage, language, and history that are distinct from those of Spaniards, Walloons, or anglophone Canadians, respectively. By contrast, most cosmopolitan *and* traditionalist Egyptians define themselves as members of the same nation, speak the same language or dialects of it, treasure the pharaoh dynasty, and share the same ancestral ties. However, some Egyptians are close adherents of religious directives, while others follow them more casually. These differences, however important they seem, are in most cases differences of degree, not of kind.

Third, federalism typically recognizes group identities that are territorial in nature. However, the territorial boundaries of the secular/religious divide are often blurred. Although residents of certain regions within a given country may be more prone to hold theocratic views than residents of other regions, this divide is not neatly demarcated along territorial lines, as is often the case with ethnic or linguistic boundaries. Proponents of theocratic governance may reside in rural towns or in blue-collar neighbourhoods on the outskirts of large urban centres, but they may also reside within a few bus stops of bastions of modernism such as art galleries, universities, posh hotels, shopping malls, and government buildings. Thus, the secular/religious divide manifests itself in a wide range of situations in everyday life, from the sidewalk to the market and from schools to workplaces. This is in stark contrast to, say, Cyprus, where the territorial divide between the Greeks and the Turks is clearly demarcated. Territory-based power-sharing mechanisms or any other kind of joint-governance structures that are based on the allocation of powers or goods according to region may not be an efficient means for analysing, let alone reducing, tensions along secular/religious lines.

Fourth, accounts of religion and state tend to assume firm identities and fixed group affiliations, although in reality this is not always the case (Brubaker 2004; Brubaker and Cooper 2000). This is particularly true with respect to religious faith. To begin with, people have multiple identities beyond their faith-based affiliation. Feminist philosopher Judith Butler notes: "I identify, for example, as a Lesbian and as Jewish. But I have additional identities: I am a peculiar philosopher, a short person, and a woman who is getting old. Lesbian and Jewish clearly does not define everything that I am" (2004). More important, membership in a group is in some instances voluntary and self-professed, whereas in others it is determined by laws external to the group, and in still other cases it is imposed by intra-group practices and traditions. Religious labels such as "Jewish," "Christian," or "Muslim" do not tell us much, because there are a variety of schools, from very moderate to ultra-conservative, within each of these categories. At certain times one school may enjoy greater support or become more dominant than others, but as the political kaleidoscope shifts, other voices within each religious community become more prevalent, and different aspects of that religion are emphasized. Thus, identity and group affiliation are not primordial. They are to a large extent politically constructed by a dynamic interplay between intra-group politics and the political context within which that group operates. And religiosity as a marker of identity may be brought to the fore or relegated to lesser status as coalitions shift, elites transform, and interests change. The Zionist movement, for example, drew on aspects of Orthodox Judaism to support its cause in the years before and after the establishment of Israel. But as Orthodox Judaism fulfilled its historic role and new challenges of membership in the global community emerged, Orthodox Judaism became more of a burden than an asset for many Israelis. This holds true in smaller-scale, non-theocratic settings as well. In their recent study of the shifting dimensions of ethnicity in the Romanian-Transylvanian city of Cluj-Napoca, Rogers Brubaker and his co-authors show how groups use ethnic or nationalist symbols to announce their presence and promote their interests (2008). When such markers of identity exhaust their effectiveness, they are gradually replaced with others.

One might add the numerous intra-faith struggles and interpretive debates that question the validity of labels such as "Jewish," "Christian," or "Muslim" identity. Intra-religion splits and intense rivalry, theological, political, economic, and otherwise, have come to dominate much of the history of religion. The split between the western and eastern Churches in the eleventh century, the emergence of the Anglican Church, and the Reformation and the Counter-Reformation are only a few obvious examples. Today the Christian world is divided into several established Churches and dozens of smaller sects, some distinctly more conservative than others. Even within established Churches – the current rift within the Anglican Church is only one illustration – internal interpretive and political divides are fierce and plentiful. The Jewish world is divided; Orthodox Judaism remains hegemonic (although not unchallenged) in Israel, whereas Reform and Conservative branches of Judaism are distinctly more popular in the Diaspora. The Muslim world is divided into two major branches – Sunni and Shi'a – but also draws on several traditional interpretive schools within Islamic law and features a wide variety of sects and subdivisions, from radical Wahhabism to spiritual Sufism. Therefore, group identities not only are dynamic and fluid but also are contested from within, because intra-group struggles may emerge over who should speak for the group and on what basis. These problems, one would expect, intensify with formal state recognition of some or all aspects of religion, as intra-group contestation emerges over who officially serves as the community's voice, who represents its "authentic" precepts and traditions, or who "owns" the community's constitutive meta-narratives.

Fifth, the assumption that whole peoples of a given faith share unified interests is, at best, highly questionable. The spread of religious fundamentalism in the developing world is sometimes wrongfully depicted as a phenomenon that is near monolithic, all-encompassing, or free of fierce internal opposition (Huntington 1996). More religiosity in the public sphere or in the political domain serves the interests of some at the expense of others. It poses a clear and present danger to the cultural propensities, world views, interests, and policy preferences of many, ranging from most of the urban intelligentsia and the majority of the managerial classes to the strong statist bureaucracy and powerful industries (e.g., tourism, banking, international trade) and economic stakeholders. It would be an understatement to say that theocratic governments are not the type of regime that finds favour with supranational trade and monetary bodies. The secular/religious divide and the struggle over the nation's aspirational commitments more generally are not free of large-scale distributive-justice aspects and material interests because, more often than not, support for religious parties emanates from occupiers of the polity's periphery, real or imagined. Furthermore, principles of theocratic governance often stem from alternative sources of authority and legitimacy that constitutionalism may regard as exogenous and even threatening to overarching state authority. The holistic nature of theocratic governance itself is not, prima facie, conducive to constitutional compromise, power-sharing pacts, separation of powers, checks and balances, relative judicial independence, and other essentials of modern constitutionalism. With few exceptions, theocracy has been and remains detested by the military – a symbol of modern nationalism in many developing polities. The powerful Turkish, Pakistani, and Algerian militaries are only three of many examples that come to mind here. The prospect of theocratic government has potentially far-reaching power-shifting implications, both symbolic and material. Most of all, runaway theocratic governance beyond state control poses a major threat to established religious interests, the "official" state-endorsed version of religion, with its publically funded and monitored set of institutions, leaders, and interpretive hierarchy.

From this uneasy alliance of anti- or a-theocratic interests and forces, a coalition emerges that seeks to tame the spread of religious fundamentalism and defuse attempts to establish a full-fledged theocracy. It comprises secularist or moderately religious political leaders and parties; statist bureaucrats; powerful economic stakeholders, corporations, and the managerial classes; judges and jurists; the established religious apparatus; and, at times, the nationalist military. Each of these groups brings to the table its own world views, interests, and communities of reference, and at times there is an embedded distrust between two or more of them, for example, between state bureaucrats and free marketeers, or between supporters of political liberalization and the military (think Turkey or Pakistan). But the threat of theocratic governance drives these groups to leave their animosity toward each other for better days and to collaborate tacitly so as to keep their eyes on the religious ball, so to speak. At the same time, as support for religious parties and policies increases, religious talk of some kind – and it had better come across as genuine – becomes ever more essential to maintaining some of these elites' popular legitimacy and political hegemony.

A range of constitutional strategies have been developed by those who wield political power and represent the groups and policy preferences that defy principles of theocratic governance to hedge or mitigate the impact of religiosity on politics and public policy. This is done in different ways in different places because of variance in different countries' constitutional legacy, political culture, and power struggles. But taken as a whole, these forms of constitutional ingenuity allow non- or anti-theocratic elites and leaders to talk the talk of commitment to religious values without walking much of the actual walk of that commitment. Let us consider a few examples of such ingenuity in federalism jurisprudence in a few religion-laden settings.

Hedging the Theocratic Challenge via Centralizing Federalism Jurisprudence

In most federal democracies that adhere to constitutional separation of religion and state, supreme courts have drawn upon their overarching jurisdictional supremacy to advance a constitutional vision that is considerably less religious than that of the society within which they operate. As many observers acknowledge, American constitutional jurisprudence continues to uphold a formally secular political order in one of the most religious societies in the west. European constitutional courts (e.g., the Spanish Constitutional Court and the German Federal Constitutional Court) regularly draw on their designation as the supreme interpreters of the constitution with respect to all laws and regulations of the national and regional governments in their respective polities to promote secularizing or religion-neutral policies in settings that until not too long ago were among the most religious in Europe (lest we forget, Spain had an official policy of National Catholicism until 1978).

Less well known is the Supreme Court of India's effective advocacy of a secularist vision of the Indian Constitution amid a markedly religious setting and increased political presence of Hindu and Muslim religiosity. The 42nd Amendment (1976) inserted into the preamble to the Indian Constitution the words "socialist" and "secular" so that it reads: "We, the people of India, having solemnly resolved to constitute India into a sovereign, socialist, secular democratic republic." The Supreme Court has since held that secularism is indeed part of the basic structure (i.e., a foundational pillar) of India's constitutional order (*S.R. Bommai v. Union of India* 1994). Likewise, the Supreme Court of India has sounded a clear voice for uniformity and standardization in the hotly contested domain of personal status laws (see, generally, Jacobsohn 2003; Khosla 2012). In a series of blatant statements over the past few decades, the court called upon the government to implement Article 44 of the Indian Constitution ("The State shall endeavour to secure for the citizens a uniform civil code throughout the territory of India").[2] To pick one example, in *Sarla Mugdal v. Union of India* (1995), a case that involved married Hindu men who were converting to Islam in order to practice polygamy, which is legal under Muslim personal law, Justice Kuldip Singh wrote: "Those who preferred to remain in India after the partition, fully knew that the Indian leaders did not believe in two-nation or three-nation theory and that in the Indian Republic there was to be one Nation – Indian nation – and no community could claim to remain a separate entity on the basis of religion ... The Successive Governments till-date have been wholly remiss in their duty of implementing the constitutional mandate under Article 44 of the Constitution of India" (ibid.). In the *Vallamattom* case (2003) – a successful challenge to the constitutionality of section 118 of the Indian Succession Act that prohibited bequests to religious or charitable organizations made less than a year prior to the grantor's death – the then chief justice of India, V.N. Khare, stated: "Article 44 provides that the State shall endeavor to secure for the citizens a uniform civil code throughout the territory of India. The aforesaid provision is based on the premise that there is no necessary connection between religious and personal law in a civilized society ... It is a matter of regret that Article 44 of the Constitution has not been given effect to. Parliament is still to take steps for framing a common civil code in the country. A common civil code will help the cause of national integration by removing the contradictions based on ideologies" (ibid.).

In the American, Spanish, or Indian settings, however, religion-taming jurisprudence is what the formal secular constitutional order warrants. Surprisingly, in federal settings that defy the Franco-American model of separation of religion and state, constitutional jurisprudence pertaining to religion has not taken an altogether different direction. Let us explore a few illustrative examples.

Malaysia

The Constitution of Malaysia (1963) establishes Malaysia as a unique form of Islamic state where "Islam is the religion of the Federation; but other religions may be practiced in peace and harmony in any part of the Federation" (Article 3), and where "every person has the right to profess and practice his religion and to propagate it" (Article 11.1). Further, "every religious group has the right to manage its own religious affairs" (Article 11.3), while state law (and, in the Federal Territories of Kuala Lumpur and Labuan, federal law) "may control or restrict the propagation of any religious doctrine or belief among persons professing the religion of Islam" (Article 11.4). The pragmatist state establishment has adopted a mainstream Islam Hadhari doctrine (a moderate or "civilizational" Islam), which the religious opposition sees as based on a watered-down, compromised, secularized understanding of Islam.

To add a further complication, Malaysian law draws on religious ascriptions to establish what has been termed "ethnic democracy," where, despite the existence of some ethnic power-sharing mechanisms and an accompanying façade of interracial harmony, Malay political dominance is ensured. Ethnic Malays (*Bumiputra*, or "sons of the soil"), generally Muslim, are granted constitutionally entrenched preferential treatment in various aspects of public life over members of other ethnic groups (Article 153 of the constitution). Malay citizens who convert out of Islam are no longer considered Malay under the law and hence forfeit the Bumiputra privileges afforded to Malays under Article 153.

In the face of the growing Islamization, Malaysia's constitutional division of powers between the federal and state governments has been used to effectively block religious parties-led governments in the states of Kelantan and Terengganu from instituting Qur'an- and Sunna-based *hudood* and *qisas* (retaliation) law as the basis for their criminal code. Although the Kelantan State Assembly passed the Syariah (Malay for "Shari'a") Criminal Enactment in 1993, it has yet to be implemented, mainly because criminal law is in federal hands. According to the Federal Constitution, Syariah courts do not have jurisdiction over offences "except in so far as conferred by federal law"; state authorities can only legislate for Islamic offences, "except in regard to matters included in the Federal List" (e.g., criminal law and procedure). What is more, Article 75 provides: "If any State law is inconsistent with a federal law, the federal law shall prevail and the State law shall, to the extent of the inconsistency, be void." Finally, item 4(k) in the list of matters falling under federal jurisdiction provides: "Ascertainment of Islamic Law and other personal laws for purposes of federal law" is a federal matter.

The religious-secular duality embedded in the Malaysian legal system is further reflected in the changing jurisdictional interrelation between the civil and Syariah courts. Muslims (and non-Muslims who marry Muslims) are obliged to follow the decisions of Syariah courts in matters concerning their religion, most notably marriage, inheritance, apostasy, conversion, and custody. Historically, the civil and Syariah courts existed side by side in a dual court structure established at the time of Malaysia's independence, with the prevalent understanding that Syariah courts were subordinate to the civil courts and that the common law was superior to other laws. In the landmark case *Che Omar bin Che Soh* (1984) the Federal Court, then known as the Supreme Court of Malaysia, ruled that the common law had not been ousted or otherwise affected by the introduction of the Federal Constitution, and that it would allow secular courts to resolve legal issues, even where the parties to the case were Muslims. However, in 1988 an amendment to the constitution, Article 121(1A), was introduced; it provided that civil courts "shall have no jurisdiction in respect of any matter within the jurisdiction of the Syariah Courts."

Even after the 1988 amendment the civil court system continued to view Syariah courts as subordinates and, at any rate, subject to general principles of administrative and constitutional law. The civil courts consistently interpreted the jurisdictional boundaries between the two court systems so as to prevent the expansion of the Syariah court system. Likewise, the Malaysian Bar Council has continued to argue that Article 121(1A) does not exclude the supervisory review power of the Federal Court.

However, because Islam has become a major political force in Malaysia, taking an all-out anti-Islamist stand on the question of jurisdictional boundaries is no longer a feasible option for the court. It opted instead for a dual approach of respecting Syriah courts' jurisdiction in matters assigned to them, at the same time maintaining for the Federal Court overarching jurisdiction in all matters constitutional, religious or otherwise.

The *Lina Joy* case (2007) raised the question of Syariah courts' jurisdictional authority over apostasy in a case of conversion out of Islam. Ms Lina Joy, who was born Azalina Jailani, claimed to have converted from Islam to Christianity and argued that conversion was protected by the right to freedom of religion under Article 11 of the Constitution, and that she had the right to convert to Christianity without being designated as apostate. However, the National Registration Department refused to change her name or her religious status as they appeared on her identity card on the grounds that the Syariah court had not granted permission for her to renounce Islam. In other words, Lina Joy questioned the hierarchy of three core tenets of Malaysian constitutional order: Shari'a court jurisdiction over conversion, individual religious freedoms, and the ethnic issue (conversion out of Islam questions one's Bumiputra status). Following a long legal battle, the case reached the Federal Court of Malaysia, which ruled in May 2007 that approvals of conversions out of Islam fall under the exclusive jurisdiction of the Syariah court system. In other words, the court refused to limit the jurisdictional boundaries of Syariah courts in Malaysia, even at the cost of infringing on general principles of freedom of religion or formal gender equality.

But only two months later the Federal Court sent a somewhat different message in the *Latifa Mat Zin* case (2007), an inheritance dispute that raised the question whether the applicable law was the Islamic law of gifts *(hibah)* or the federal law of banking or contract. Although the court sided with the claimant, holding that Islamic law should apply in the particular situation under dispute, it also stated clearly: "In case an application to the syariah court is resisted on the ground that the syariah court has no jurisdiction in the matter, let me answer that question right now. Interpretation of the Federal Constitution is a matter for this court, not the syariah court. [If] this court says that the syariah court has jurisdiction, [then] it has" (*Latifa Mat Zin v. Rosmawati Binti Sharibun* 2007).

The court's cautious navigation through this politically charged jurisdictional quagmire continued in the *Subashini* case (2007). The originally Hindu husband of a Hindu woman converted to Islam in 2006 and went on to convert their elder son as well. The husband then applied to the Syariah court to dissolve the couple's civil marriage and to obtain custody of both their sons. The Federal Court held that the civil court has jurisdiction over marriage and divorce, as well as over custody of children in a civil marriage, even when one spouse has converted to Islam, since the original marriage took place when both parties were Hindus. At the same time, the court held that the consent of only one parent was sufficient for a conversion of the children to be lawful. To support its ruling, as well as to increase the legitimacy of this and several other contested decisions, the court cited several solicited opinions of respected religious scholars. These opinions and their authors' academic credentials (including their post-secondary degrees, the institutions of higher learning they attended, and their main publications), were cited in great detail by the court, presumably in order to signal the court's respect for sacred law. At any rate, the court granted a partial victory to each side of the dispute, compounding the jurisprudential ambiguity. Or, to be more colloquial, it threw each side a chewy bone, while jurisprudential wishy-washiness reigned. What better way to maintain the court's legitimacy while avoiding the possible wrath of influential stakeholders from both sides?

With respect to its overarching review authority, the Federal Court of Malaysia has effectively asserted its exclusive authority as the ultimate interpreter of the constitution even in religion-related laws, inter alia through the effective "sanctification" of the hitherto largely symbolic Article 4(1) of the constitution, which declares that the federal constitution is the supreme law.

In its ruling in the *Abdul Kahar bin Ahmad* case (2008), to pick another example, the Federal Court dismissed in a decisive tone an argument that the 1988 amendment and, in particular, Article 121(1A) conferred jurisdiction on Syariah courts to interpret the constitution in matters falling under the jurisdiction of such courts. The Federal Court stated: "The constitutionality of any law, whether a law made by Parliament or by the Legislature of a State ... is a matter for this court to decide, not the Syariah High Court ... Interpretation of the Federal Constitution is a matter for this Court, not the Syariah court. If this court says that the Syariah Court has jurisdiction, then it has ... Article 121(1A) was not inserted to oust the jurisdiction of this Court in matters that rightly belong to it ... The entire realm of the constitutionality of state law, however Syariah based it may be, can be decided only by the Federal Court."

Although the power to create and punish offences against the precepts of Islam has been assigned by the constitution to the states, Syariah courts have jurisdiction only over persons professing the religion of Islam. Further, the enactment of *hudood* as state law runs counter to Article 11 (freedom of religion), which has been interpreted to protect individuals against prosecution on the basis of choice of religion. What is more, Article 8 provides that every citizen is equal before the law, hence rendering the blanket application of *hudood* laws arguably unconstitutional because they discriminate against non-Muslims and women. Finally, as the Malaysian Federal Court – the country's peak court since 1985 – has observed on numerous occasions, Malaysian public law is secular, and unless the Federal Constitution is amended to reflect the Syariah law as the supreme or basic law, this remains the case. The Federal Constitution has not been amended to reflect that position. Article 4(1) still declares that the Federal Constitution is the supreme law.

The supremacy of the Federal Constitution, and the Federal Court's guard of it, have served repeatedly as a basis for lower-court rulings that block religion-based radicalization in the country's hinterlands. In 2013, to pick a recent example, the High Court of Malaya in Ipoh (Perak) voided the Muslim conversion certificates of three Hindu minors, as the certificates had been issued based on a unilateral request of the children's originally Hindu, now convert-to-Islam, father and without their Hindu mother's knowledge or consent (*M. Indira Gandhi v. Pengarah Jabatan Agama Islam Perak*). The court cited principles of natural justice, breach of Perak legislation, which required the children to be present at the time of the purported conversion ceremony, Malaysia's obligation under international law, and most important, the Federal Constitution as prescribing a mother's equal right to raise her children according to her faith. Specifically, the court held that the right to "life" and "liberty" protected by the Constitution's Article 5, and the right to practice one's religion protected by Article 11(1), included within it a right to determine one's child's religious upbringing and education.

In short, the Malaysian Federal Court system has used constitutionally enshrined principles of federalism to block attempts to expand the ambit of Shari'a law. Operating within an increasingly Islamic political environment, it has been wrestling with the harmonization of constitutional and Shari'a law on a case-by-case basis. And while it has been sending mixed messages with regard to the scope and nature of the 1988 constitutional amendment that established the exclusive jurisdiction of Syariah courts in personal-status matters, it has also asserted its authority vis-à-vis the religious establishment as the sole and ultimate interpreter of Malaysia's Federal Constitution.

Nigeria

A brief analogy may be drawn here between Malaysia and Nigeria. Nigeria is the most populous country in Africa, with approximately 140 million inhabitants. Although it is a secular state with no established state religion, Islam and Christianity play a key role in Nigerian collective identity, alongside various indigenous religions. Nigeria's 36 states include 19 states in northern Nigeria and 17 states in southern Nigeria, with traditional Muslim dominance in the north and Christian dominance in the south. Filling a gap left by the near collapse of local and federal services in the 1980s and 1990s, as well the economic decline throughout most of the country (oil-rich regions being the exception), new Muslim groups stepped into the breach in the predominantly Muslim north, just as Evangelical and Pentecostal churches did in the mainly Christian south; millions of Nigerians have converted to Pentacostalism over the last three decades alone. Shari'a courts existed in Nigeria, a former British colony, but were limited to areas of family and personal law. Even after independence criminal courts continued to function under inherited British common law (Bose 2004; Laitin 1982). In the late 1980s Islamic parties started to garner massive political support in northern Nigeria. Since 1999, twelve northern state governments, led by Zamfara State and its proactive governor at that time, Alhaji Ahmed Sani, have enacted legislation or executive decrees that establish Shari'a criminal law, accompanied by an implicit threat of civil war in opposition to then President Olusegun Obasanjo.[3]

Anticipating federalism-based resistance to the Islamization of criminal law in these states, Sani and proponents of the move argued that because Islam is a faith, "only those who believe in that faith will either determine something is wrong or something is right" (BBC News 2002). This has led to the introduction of penalties such as amputation or death by stoning for serious criminal offences. Granted, the partial introduction of Shari'a is a vote-winner, not merely a reflection of a genuine doctrinal shift. However, it has posed serious challenges to human rights standards in a country that professes secularism (Bolaji 2009). This in turn led, inter alia, to the infamous *Safi yatu Hussaini* and *Amina Lawal* cases. In the *Safi yatu Hussaini* case (decided in March 2002) the Shari'a Court of Appeal of Sokoto State relied on procedural grounds to quash the conviction of Safi yatu Hussaini by a lower Shari'a court for the offence of *zina* (adultery) and her sentence to *rajm* (death by stoning) for giving birth to a child as a single woman (*Safi yatu Hussaini Tungar Tudu v. Attorney-General Sokoto State* 2002). In the twin case, *Amina Lawal*, a divorced woman was accused of bearing a child outside marriage, which was classified as adultery. She was sentenced to death by stoning in March 2002 by lower Islamic Shari'a courts in the northern state of Katsina. In September 2002, under immense pressure from domestic and international human rights organizations and Nigeria's federal government, Katsina's Shari'a Court of Appeals voted (4–1) to quash the case on the basis that the lower Shari'a courts failed to follow rules of procedure laid down by Islamic law itself, Shari'a-based state criminal law, and some of the federal constitution's provisions protecting due process (*Amina Lawal v. The State* 2003). This self-restraint of top Shari'a courts is not atypical. In fact, despite the new Islamic criminal provisions in sub-national units in countries such as Nigeria, Pakistan, and Libya, the higher criminal courts in these countries have never actually allowed the draconian punishment of stoning to be implemented (Otto 2009).

But the main counter-religious weapon in Nigeria has been the constitution. As in Malaysia and to some extent Pakistan, Nigerian judicial attempts to contain religious law have been centred on principles of federalism and the ultimate superiority of the constitution over the laws of any sub-national unit. Although the 1999 constitution allows states to grant additional jurisdiction to their local courts, the adoption of Shari'a can criminalize actions deemed permissible by the constitution and its bill of rights, and the accompanying penalties almost always violate protections set out in the same document (Marshall 2005, 126). Furthermore, the constitution establishes Nigeria as a secular state, and Article 10 explicitly forbids governments at any level from adopting an official religion (Iwobi 2004; Nmehielle 2004). The constitution also provides for freedom of religion and the right of all citizens to practise their religion. Any law enacted in the country that conflicts with the constitution is void to the extent of its inconsistency. Much as in Malaysia and Pakistan, the general tenet in Nigeria has been that as a supreme law, the Nigerian Constitution is endowed with a higher status, over and above any other legal rules in operation in that polity. Shari'a legislation and practice in the northern states must therefore comply with the provisions of the constitution (Nwauche 2008, 576).

Another interesting analogy to Malaysia is the occasional strategic judicial resort to blurriness, deference, or even sheer silence when the courts are torn between their judicial preferences and political realities, or when the political stakes are high but courts are not entirely clear about which way the political wind is blowing. Caution appears logical under these circumstances. A case in point is the Supreme Court of Nigeria's "non-ruling" in the recent *Kano State v. Nigeria* case (2007). As part of the imposition of Shari'a law in the northern states, the state of Kano created a Hisba Board, very similar in nature to the entity that would have been created in Pakistan's North-West Frontier Province (NWFP) had the Islamization bill become law (see the previous discussion of Pakistan). This created a parallel *hisba* police, the aim of which was to enforce Islamic morality in instances where no "official" crime had been committed. In February 2006 the federal government declared the Hisba Board and its "morality police" unacceptable on constitutional grounds. Federal authorities followed suit with arrests of Hisba Board members for national security concerns and alleged links to Iran and Libya. Kano State then petitioned the Supreme Court, asking for a ruling on the constitutionality of the *hisba* law. Specifically, Kano officials sought a declaration that the Hisba Board was "legal, lawful, and constitutional" (*Attorney-General of Kano State v. Attorney-General of the Federation* 2007).

Given the very high political stakes, the court chose to avoid the wrath of both Islamists and the federal government by framing the Kano State petition as focusing on the detention of *hisba* corps members, as well as on its jurisdictional competence with respect to the identity of the party, rather than the constitutionality, of the Hisba Board itself. Once the petition had been framed as centring on these arrests, not on the principled question of Shari'a morality, the court could declare that it had no original jurisdiction over state claims against the federal inspector of police (who issued the detention writs). The inspector of police, the Supreme Court reasoned, was "unfortunately not a recognized party subject to the original jurisdiction of this court" (ibid). Whereas in *Subashini* (discussed earlier) the Malaysian Federal Court resorted to the "everyone-gets-something" strategy, in Kano State the Supreme Court of Nigeria chose to avoid a direct engagement with the issue at stake. Shrewd courts and judges, then, are political not only in the sense that they may opt to expand the ambit of their influence when the political sphere appears amenable to such expansion, but also in the sense that they may resort to restraint or deference when the risks or costs of a clear-cut ruling seem particularly high. Strategic accounts of judicial behaviour could not have asked for stronger confirmation.

Indonesia

Indonesia has one of the largest Muslim populations in the world; approximately 90% of its roughly 250 million citizens identify as Muslim. One of the five core precepts of the *Pancasila* (the foundational national philosophy) established by the Indonesian Constitution (1945, reaffirmed 1959) is that "the state shall be based on the belief in the one and only God." However, the constitution does not establish Islam as the sole state religion; Buddhism, Catholicism, Hinduism, Islam, Protestantism, and, as of 1998, Confucianism enjoy equal status as state-recognized religions. In addition, freedom of religion is guaranteed by

Chapter 10 of the constitution. The *Pancasila* has always been viewed by orthodox Muslim groups as an effort to subordinate Islam to a secular state ideology, a "civil religion" of sorts promoted by a regime in order to contain religion.

In 2001, following the rise of intense secessionist impulses in the state of Aceh, the historical stronghold of Islam in Southeast Asia, the federal government agreed to grant Aceh special autonomy. Federal laws 44/1999 and 18/2001 provided the legal basis for Aceh to apply certain aspects of Shari'a without contested aspects of Islamic criminal law and procedure. Federal authorities, meanwhile, have used the procedure of presidential decrees – essentially executive orders by Jakarta – to limit the codification and implementation of certain controversial aspects of Shari'a law in Aceh.

Established in 2003, the Indonesian Constitutional Court (*Mahkamah Konstitusi*) has the power to ensure compliance of all legislation with principles of the Indonesian constitution. It is hardly surprising that the court has quickly emerged as a key centralizing player in the struggle between the state and radical Islam.[4] The Indonesian Constitutional Court response to the increasing calls for more Islam in public life has been twofold: (i) distinction between acts of devotion or worship of God (*ibadah*) and relations between humans (*mu'amalah*) – unlike the former realm, the second may be subject to strict government regulation (i.e., polygamous marriage may be banned by state law, even though many hard line clerics in Indonesia maintain it should be allowed, e.g., *Polygamy Case* 2007); and (ii) exclusive endorsement of the institutionalized, federally supported version of Islam via the *Pancasila* and of state-endorsed Shari'a courts as the only permissible interpretative authorities.

Two recent landmark rulings illustrate this approach. The Indonesian Religious Courts Law lists a number of areas (e.g., marriage, divorce, inheritance, trusts, gifts, and Islamic finance) over which Shari'a tribunals have jurisdiction. In the *Religious Court Law Case* (2008), the Constitutional Court unanimously rejected a claim made by a religious student who argued that the state-imposed limitation of the jurisdiction of religious courts to particular civil matters is unconstitutional because it prevents his full observance of Islam. The court held that expanding the list of subject matter falling within the jurisdiction of religious courts is within the exclusive prerogative of the federal government and is not something the court is permitted to do (Butt 2010, 297). A powerful statement by the court was this:

The Court is of the opinion that the Applicant's argument does not accord with the understanding of the relationship between religion and the
state in Indonesia. Indonesia is not a religious state which is based only
on one religion; but Indonesia is also not a secular state which does not
consider religion at all. It does not hand over all religious affairs entirely
to individuals and the community. Indonesia is a state which is based on
the Almighty God. Islamic law is indeed a source of national law. But it is
not the only source of national law, because in addition to Islamic law, cus-
tomary law, western law and other sources of legal tradition are sources of
national law. Therefore, Islamic law can be one of the sources of material
for law as part of formal government laws. Islamic law, as a source of law,
can be used together with other sources of law, and, in this way, can be the
material for the creation of government laws which are in force as national
law. (Cited in ibid.)

Justice Muhammad Alim's note sums it up nicely: "in this Republic
of Indonesia, the highest law is the 1945 Constitution, not the Quran.
As Muslims, we consider the Quran to be the highest law but ... the national consensus is that the Constitution is the highest law" (ibid., 298).

In 2010 and again in 2013, the Indonesian Constitutional Court went
on to uphold the legality of the country's controversial 1965 Blasphemy
Law (*Blasphemy Law Case I* and *Blasphemy Law Case II*). The law officially
acknowledges six religions, as stated above. It prohibits religious interpretation and activities that deviate from the basic teachings of any of
these denominations. This has been used to clamp down on "unoffi-
cial" Islamic voices ranging from the Ahmadiyah sect (whose members
have been persecuted in parts of the Islamic world) to militant Wahhabism. Proponents of western-style religious freedoms and advocates
of religious minority rights argued that the law in its current form, and
in particular the criminalization of certain religious beliefs, infringes
upon basic individual and group rights, and violates the International
Covenant on Civil and Political Rights. Drawing on a "war on terror"
impulse (Bali and other parts of Indonesia have been targets of bomb-
ings tied to Islamic militants), the government argued that the law must
be upheld to avoid interpretation-at-will by keeping the process of religious interpretation under official check. Court rulings of a similar
nature have protected "official religion" from competitors in dozens of
other settings from Tajikistan to Vietnam.

Another telling example of the centralizing effect of religion-related laws in Indonesia is the religious-court reform; over 200 million

of its citizens identify as Muslims. During the 1980s the hitherto non-standardized Islamic court system was integrated into the national judiciary, with all the government supervisory powers that such incorporation entails (Cammack 2007). The Religious Judicature Act of 1989 established municipal and provincial Shari'a courts' jurisdiction over Muslim litigants in certain civil matters specified by the act, mainly marriage, inheritance, and charitable foundations (*waqf*), generally subject to ordinary (non-religious) civil procedure norms. But alongside the formal recognition of Islamic courts' power, educational requirements and judicial appointment procedures were introduced so as to transfer the locus of power from local strongmen to government officials. Whereas in the past judges were recruited locally, under the current system judges are hired through nationwide recruitment and undergo a process of training and socialization in Jakarta before being sent into the field (Cammack 2007, 162). As a result, judges appointed under the new standards have very different training and backgrounds from their predecessors. The vast majority of judges on Islamic courts – almost 90% by one count – have degrees from one of Indonesia's State Islamic Institutes, and many also possess a university degree. What is more, the number of religious-court judges with both university training and graduate training has been consistently increasing because additional education is a major factor in promotions (Cammack 2007, 161). The reform also increased the number of female judges serving on Islamic courts from roughly 5% in the early 1980s to roughly 20% today.[5]

Pakistan

A different illustration of religion-containing constitutional jurisprudence comes from Pakistan. The process of "Islamization" of Pakistani law goes back to 1973 and has known many twists and turns. Its pinnacles have been the 1978–1980 establishment of a Shari'at court system at the provincial and federal levels, the Shari'at Appellate Bench (SAB) at the Supreme Court, and the introduction in 1985 of a set of amendments to the constitution, effectively stipulating: "All existing laws shall be brought in conformity with the Injunctions of Islam as laid down in the Holy Qur'an and Sunna, in this Part referred to as the Injunctions of Islam, and no law shall be enacted which is repugnant to such Injunctions." In theory, this means that legislation must be in full compliance with principles of Shari'a. The Supreme Court of Pakistan, however, has begged to differ.

In response to the possible conclusiveness of the Islamization reforms, the court developed its "harmonization doctrine," according to which no specific provision of the constitution stands above any other provision. In a landmark ruling in 1992 (*Hakim Khan v. Government of Pakistan*), the Supreme Court held that the "Islamization amendment" shall not prevail over the other articles of the constitution, as the amendment possessed the same weight and status as the other articles of the constitution and therefore "could not be placed on a higher pedestal or treated as a *grund norm*" (Mian 2004, 135). The court's subsequent judgments of this key issue have firmly precluded and strongly warned against an interpretation of the Islamization amendments that would "raise it to the point of being a litmus test for gauging, evaluating, and potentially justifying the judiciary to strike down any other constitutional provisions" (Siddique and Hayat 2008, 368). Any reading of the amendments as elevated "special clauses" would undermine the entire constitution. The constitution as a whole must be interpreted in a harmonious fashion so that specific provisions are read as an integral part of the entire constitution, not as standing above it. In the words of the court: "It may be observed that the principles for interpreting constitutional documents as laid down by this Court are that all provisions should be read together and harmonious construction should be placed on such provisions so that no provision is rendered nugatory" (*Qazi Hussain Ahmed et al. v. General Pervez Musharraf* 2002).

In addition to its refusal to accept the Islamization amendments as a supra-constitutional norm, the court has retained its overarching jurisdictional authority, including its de facto appellate capacity over the Shari'at Appellate Bench at the Supreme Court. This has proved time and again to be a safety valve for secular interests. In 2002, for example, the Supreme Court ordered the Shari'at Appellate Bench to reconsider its 1999 ruling that interest or usury (*riba*) in any form contravened Shari'a principles and was therefore impermissible (*United Bank Ltd. v. M/S Farooq Brothers* 2002). The Supreme Court accepted the government's argument that the transition to a *riba*-free economy, as it had been defined by the Shari'at Appellate Bench, was effectively infeasible. It noted concerns about the economic stability of Pakistan should the reforms occur and stated that they were simply impractical. The court also accepted the government's claim that the reasoning employed by the Shari'at Appellate Bench misinterpreted both the Qur'an and Sunna, had invoked only one conception of *riba*, and thus lacked the objectivity needed to render an adequate verdict in the case.

The court therefore ordered the Shari'at Appellate Bench to "to conduct thorough and elaborate research, and comparative study of the financial systems which are prevalent in the contemporary Muslim countries of the world" (ibid., 815–16).

In 2003, to give another example, the Pakistani Supreme Court ruled that the Hudood Ordinances (adopted in 1979 to introduce harsh penalties for offences described in the Qur'an) had been drafted hastily, had many gaps, were defective, and were the source of many challenges to the establishment of human rights in the country. The enforcement of the ordinances, stated the court, was not in line with the justice-seeking purpose of enforcing Islamic law. In 2004, the Supreme Court went on to curtail the Federal Shari'at Court's competence to overturn any legislation judged to be inconsistent with the tenets of Islam. The court held that any Shari'a-related jurisprudence that involves significant constitutional law aspects must take a cohesive view of Pakistan's constitutional law as well as the supremacy of federal legislation over provincial legislation (*Muhammad Siddique et al. v. Government of Pakistan* 2004). In other words, Pakistan has seen official support for Shari'a-based national tribunals at the front door, alongside curtailment of these tribunals' jurisdiction by the Supreme Court at the back door.

Principles of federalism have also aided the court in its mission to contain radical religion. In July 2005 and again in December 2006, for example, the SCP blocked attempts to enact laws to enforce Islamic morality in the NWFP, which was governed by an alliance of religious parties sympathetic to the Taliban from 2003 to 2008. Specifically, the NWFP Islamization bill (also known as the Hisba [Accountability] Act, 2005) aimed at implementing greater Islamic regulation in the NWFP by establishing a government agency headed by a special cleric given the title of *mohtasib* (ombudsman). This agency was responsible for overseeing the Islamization of everyday life in the province, including many aspects of private life. To that end, the act created an enforcement force – essentially a religious police squad – that would help ensure the moral and virtuous conduct of Muslims in the province. President Musharraf, whose administration supported an enlightened, moderate form of Islam, denounced the bill as a fundamental breach of human rights that, accordingly, would violate federal legislation and constitutional rights. Upon Musharraf's request and on these grounds, Pakistan's attorney general challenged the constitutionality of the proposed Islamization bill, using the constitutional reference procedure that allows the executive branch to refer constitutional questions to the

Supreme Court in its advisory jurisdiction (Section 186 of the constitution). The main question the court was asked to address was "whether the Hisba Bill or any of its provisions would be constitutionally invalid if enacted" (*In Re: NWFP Hisba Bill* 2005).

The Supreme Court unanimously agreed and ordered the NWFP governor not to sign the Hisba Bill into law: "The Governor of the North-West Frontier Province may not assent to Hisba Bill in its present form as its various Sections ... have been declared *ultra vires* the Constitution of the Islamic Republic of Pakistan, 1973" (ibid.). The court ruled that "Islamic jurists are unanimous on the point that except for *sallat* [prayer] and *zakat* [alms] no other religious obligation stipulated by Islam can be enforced by the state" (ibid.). In other words, the court suggested that even within Islamic jurisprudence there is no agreement that state enforcement of religious values is warranted. The decision again contained a conflation of Islamic and secular constitutional law, suggesting that the functions of the *mohtasib* would interfere in the citizens' "personal life, freedom of assembly, liberty, dignity, and privacy which is strictly prohibited in Islam" (ibid.). The bill was sent back to the NWFP Assembly for redrafting and was subsequently passed in a diluted version, which the Supreme Court later struck down again in December 2006. In short, while falling short of advancing a truly progressive human rights agenda by western standards, the Supreme Court has nonetheless served as a bastion of relative cosmopolitanism in an otherwise increasingly religious Pakistan. It has thus allowed moderately religious politicians to talk the talk of strong commitment to religion while transferring the costs of not implementing that talk to the courts.

Conclusion

In light of the diversity of federal political arrangements worldwide and the importance of context in shaping their effects, the answer to the question "is federalism a centralizing or decentralizing mechanism?" must necessarily be "it depends." Indeed, as Richard Simeon notes, "it often appears that for every generalization one might make about federalism, an equally convincing counter-generalization can be made" (2010, 9). But when it comes to assessing the viability of federalism in addressing the theocratic challenge, at least one observation may be made with some confidence. Based on the widely documented constitutional experience of several leading federal countries where religion is prevalent (e.g., the United States and India), as well as the constitutional jurisprudence of the less frequently explored, religion-laden countries discussed in this chapter, we can safely say that more than promoting diversity within regional boundaries, principles of federalism in religion-laden settings – most notably the notion of constitutional supremacy and national high courts' overarching review, or "right of final word" capacity – have been consistently drawn upon by those who object to theocratic government, to contain religion and its traditional interlocutors, spread a notion of state-controlled, institutionalized religion, or advance secularizing solutions to religion and state problems. This broad pattern may well reflect the rule of law's embedded inclination to assert itself as the ultimate source of authority in any given polity.[6] Federal systems, however, offer a ready-made institutional hierarchy that allows accommodation of alternative sources of authority at the sub-national level while maintaining the status of constitutional law and courts at the apex of a given polity's legal system.

NOTES

1 A prominent exponent of this line of thought is Arend Lijphart (see, e.g., Lijphart 1977).
2 One of the perennial bones of contention in the Indian context is the struggle between advocates of universal secularism (and by extension, the adoption of a uniform civil code) and proponents of the *status quo*, in which religious minorities, most notably Muslims, enjoy certain jurisdictional autonomy in matters of personal status, primarily marriage and divorce. The leading Supreme Court of India ruling on the matter is *Mohammed Ahmed Khan v. Shah Bano Begum* (1985), which brought about a major political backlash culminating in the court's watered-down ruling in *Danial Latifi* (2001).
3 The twelve states are Bauchi, Borno, Gombe, Jigawa, Kaduna, Kano, Katsina, Kebbi, Niger, Sokoto, Yobe, and Zamfara.
4 For a detailed discussion see Butt (2010).
5 Women have served as Islamic court judges in Indonesia since the 1960s. Indonesian religious scholars concluded that women may serve as Islamic court judges in all but criminal cases, which in any event are not tried in the Islamic court system.
6 For a detailed elaboration and comparative examination of this argument, see Hirschl and Shachar (2009).

REFERENCES

BBC News. 2002. Nigeria Sharia Architecht Defends Law. 21 March. Available at http://news.bbc.co.uk/2/hi/africa/1885052.stm

Bolaji, M.H.A. 2009. Shari'ah in Northern Nigeria in the Light of Asymmetrical Federalism. *Publius: The Journal of Federalism* 40(1):114–35.

Bose, Amitabha. 2004. Do All Roads Lead To Islamic Radicalism? A Comparison of Islamic Laws in India and Nigeria. *Georgia Journal of International and Comparative Law* 32:779–812.

Brubaker, Rogers. 2004. *Ethnicity without Groups*. Cambridge, MA: Harvard University Press.

Brubaker, Rogers, and Frederick Cooper. 2000. Beyond "Identity." *Theory and Society* 29:1–47.

Brubaker, Rogers, Margit Fox, Jon Fox, and Liana Grancea. 2008. *Nationalist Politics and Everyday Ethnicity in a Transylvanian Town*. Princeton: Princeton University Press.

Butler, Judith. 2004. Interview in *Ha'Aretz*. 6 January.

Butt, Simon. 2010. Islam, the State and the Constitutional Court in Indonesia. *Pacific Rim Law & Policy Journal* 19:279–301.

Cammack, Mark E. 2007. The Indonesian Islamic Judiciary. In *Islamic Law in Contemporary Indonesia: Ideas and Institutions,* edited by Michael Feener and Mark Cammack. Cambridge: Harvard University Press.

Hirschl, Ran. 2010. *Constitutional Theocracy*. Cambridge: Harvard University Press.

Hirschl, Ran, and Ayelet Shachar. 2009. The New Wall of Separation: Permitting Diversity, Restricting Competition. *Cardozo Law Review* 30:2535–60.

Horowitz, Donald. 1985. *Ethnic Groups in Conflict*. Berkeley and Los Angeles: University of California Press.

Huntington, Samuel. 1996. *The Clash of Civilizations and the Remaking of World Order*. New York: Simon and Schuster.

Iwobi, Andrew Ubaka. 2004. Tiptoeing through a Constitutional Minefield: The Great Sharia Controversy in Nigeria. *Journal of African Law* 48(2):111–64;

Jacobsohn, Gary. 2003. *The Wheel of Law: India's Secularism in Comparative Constitutional Context*. Princeton: Princeton University Press.

Khosla, Madhav. 2012. *The Indian Constitution*. New York: Oxford University Press.

Laitin, David. 1982. The Sharia Debate and the Origins of Nigeria's Second Republic. *Journal of Modern African Studies* 20(3):411–30.

Lijphart. Arend. 1977. *Democracy in Plural Societies: A Comparative Exploration*. Princeton: Yale University Press.

Lijphart, Arend. 2004. Constitutional Design for Divided Societies. *Journal of Democracy* 15:96–109.

Marshall, Paul. 2005. Nigeria: Shari'a in a Fragmented Country. In *Radical Islam's Rules: The Worldwide Spread of Extreme Sharia Law*, edited by Paul Marshall. Lanham: Rowman & Littlefield.

Mian, Ajmal. 2004. *A Judge Speaks Out*. Oxford: Oxford University Press.

Nmehielle, Vincent Obisienunwo Orlu. 2004. Sharia Law in the Northern States of Nigeria: To Implement or Not to Implement, the Constitutionality Is the Question. *Human Rights Quarterly* 26(3):730–59.

Nwauche, Enyinna S. 2008. Law, Religion and Human Rights in Nigeria. *African Human Rights Law Journal* 8:568–95.

Otto, Jan Michiel. 2009. Rule of Law, Adat Law, and Sharia: 1901, 2001, and Monitoring the Next Phase. *Hague Journal on the Rule of Law* 1:15–20.

Siddique, Osama, and Zahra Hayat. 2008. Unholy Speech and Holy Laws: Blasphemy Laws in Pakistan – Controversial Origins, Design Defects, and Free Speech Implication. *Minnesota Journal of International Law* 17:303–85.

Simeon, Richard. 2010. Is Federalism Like Snow? And, Is It Exportable? Some Cautionary Notes on the Study of Federalism. Lecture at Leiden University, 11 June.

COURT RULINGS

Abdul Kahar bin Ahmad v. Kerajaan Negeri Selangor Darul Ehsan; Kerajaan Malaysia & Anor (Interveners). 2008 4 CLJ 309 [Malaysia].

Amina Lawal v. The State. Case No. KTS/SCA/FT/86/2002 (Shari'a Court of Appeal of Katsina State, Sept. 25, 2003) [Nigeria].

Attorney-General of Kano State v. Attorney-General of the Federation. S.C. 26/2006, (2007) 3 NILR 23 (Mar. 2, 2007) [Nigeria].

Blasphemy Law Case I (Constitutional Court Decision No 140/PUU-VII/2009) [Indonesia].

Blasphemy Law Case II (Constitutional Court Decision No 84/PUU-X/2012) [Indonesia].

Che Omar bin Che Soh v. Public Prosecutor. 1984 1 MLJ 113 [Malaysia].

Danial Latifi v. Union of India. AIR 2001 SC 3958 [India].

Hakim Khan v. Government of Pakistan. PLD 1992 S.C. 595 [Pakistan].

In Re: NWFP Hisba Bill. Reference 2/2005, PLD 2005 S.C. 873 [Pakistan].

Lina Joy v. Majlis Agama Islam Wilayah Persekutuan. 2007 4 MLJ 585 [Malaysia].

Latifa Mat Zin v. Rosmawati Binti Sharibun et al 2007 5 MLJ 101 [Malaysia].

M. Indira Gandhi v. Pengarah Jabatan Agama Islam Perak et al., JR 25/10/2009 (High Court of Malaya in Ipoh, Perak; decision released July 25, 2013) [Malaysia].

Mohammed Ahmed Khan v. Shah Bano Begum. AIR 1985 SC 985 [India].

Muhammad Siddique et al. v. Government of Pakistan (decision released on Nov. 5, 2004) [Pakistan].

Polygamy Case (Constitutional Court Decision No 12/PUU-V/2007) [Indonesia].

Qazi Hussain Ahmed et al. v. General Pervez Musharraf, Chief Executive and Another, P.L.D. 2002 S.C. 853 [Pakistan].

Religious Court Law Case (Constitutional Court Decision No 19/PUU-VI/2008) [Indonesia].

Safi yatu Hussaini Tungar Tudu v. Attorney-General Sokoto State. Appeal No. SCA/GW/28/2001 (Shari'a Court of Appeal of Sokoto State, Mar. 25, 2002) [Nigeria].

Sarla Mugdal v. Union of India. AIR 1995 SC 1531 [India].

S.R. Bommai v. Union of India. AIR 1994 S.C. 1918 [India].

Subashini v. Saravanan and other. 2008 2 MLJ 147 [Malaysia].

United Bank Ltd. v. M/S Farooq Brothers. PLD 2002 S.C. 800 [Pakistan].

Vallamattom v. Union of India. AIR 2003 SC 384 [India].

7 Ideology, Identity, Majoritarianism: On the Politics of Federalism

ALAIN NOËL

In this chapter, I want to highlight the profoundly political underpinnings of federalism and argue that, more than a set of institutions and practices, federalism is also very much an object of contention between the left and the right, between different national identities and, in multinational federations, between majorities and minorities. Hence, federalism always constitutes a contentious, historically situated project, and it has to be appreciated as a genuinely political undertaking, at least in democratic societies.

This argument is not unlike that of Richard Simeon and Ian Robinson, who base their *State, Society, and the Development of Canadian Federalism* on the premise that to understand the evolution of Canadian federalism, one must pay close attention to "the organization, mobilization and activities of collective interests and identities" and to the "political parties, interest groups and governments that shape and express them" (1990, 4). This chapter, however, makes a more specific claim, to emphasize the relevance of key social cleavages, often neglected by accounts focused too closely on the rules and institutions of federalism, on particular actors, or on discrete sets of events (Pontusson 1995; Erk and Koning 2010). Three dimensions of political conflict seem most important. The first two are drawn from the comparative literature on party politics, which suggests that in electoral democracies, the political space "essentially boils down to two dimensions": a first aspect that is socio-economic and expresses class divisions over social change and distributive issues, and a second that is more cultural and captures important religious or identity differences (Kriesi et al. 2008, 11). A third dimension can be associated with this cultural division, but is distinctive and defines a line of conflict more specific to multinational federations; this dimension opposes national majorities and minorities (Simeon and Conway 2001, 338).

The chapter draws on the existing literature in different disciplines to present a theoretical account of the main lines of political conflict in federations, with a particular concern for multinational federations. It is organized around three stories or personal recollections about Quebec and Canadian politics, which are used to introduce the key dimensions of conflict and to show how an awareness of their presence and of the underlying cleavages they express is useful in making sense of the politics of federalism. This narrative procedure is meant not to demonstrate or test rigorously one or a few causal relationships, but simply to point to significant and important theoretical and political considerations that can enhance our understanding of the Canadian federation and of federalism in general.

My first story is about Quebec politics, and it reminds us that the politics of federalism is always, as well, a politics of left and right. This is hardly surprising, since the left-right cleavage is the most universal cleavage, a ubiquitous division that tends to encompass all other political dimensions, and has done so for decades, across the world (Noël and Thérien 2008). Still, this dimension is notoriously absent in discussions of Canadian federalism, perhaps because Canadian political scientists have long believed that in their country class politics was not as important as elsewhere (Carty and Cross 2010, 193). The second story brings in politics in my own department, at the Université de Montréal – a rarely studied question – and leads us beyond the politics of left and right, and into the politics of identity. Finally, the third story goes back to Mont-Tremblant in 1999, and it stands at the intersection between Canadian and world politics, to help us to see the cleavage that, in multinational federations, separates the national majority from national minorities and, in this context, to ponder with some realism the "global promise of federalism" for divided societies.

All three stories remind us that federalism is, in all circumstances, very much a political affair. There is certainly a vast literature on the relationship between federalism, democracy, and social justice (see, e.g., Obinger, Castles, and Leibfried 2005; Simeon 2006; Noël 2006a). This literature, however, mostly concerns policy consequences, and it does not say all that much about the politics of federalism or, to borrow a classic political science concept, about the mobilization of bias associated with federalism. How, indeed, does federalism interact with existing social cleavages? Does it favour majorities or minorities? Does it accommodate and diffuse identity differences, or does it reinforce and entrench them? Above all, is federalism left or right? Let us begin with the last question. To do so, I will introduce first a story, about Quebec politics.

Federalists as Conservatives

I grew up, in Montreal, thinking of federalists as small-c (and sometimes big-C) conservatives. Quebec federalists, I thought, were persons who did not like social change and had little trust in collective action, did not care all that much about social justice, placed their personal interests ahead of their principles (assuming everybody did the same), and, to tell the truth, appeared prone to cheating and corruption. For these guys, I thought, the end always seemed to justify the means. I was young then and relatively ignorant, but I was not necessarily wrong. Indeed, in Quebec politics not all federalists were on the right, but the right was federalist, and not all sovereignists were on the left, but the left favoured sovereignty. By and large, this equation remains true.

Overall, then, in Quebec politics, those who professed an attachment to Canadian federalism were to be found in parties of the right or centre-right; they prevailed in the chambers of commerce and business meetings and expressed their views in mainstream, conservative newspapers. In trade unions, student associations, women's groups, and community organizations, federalists remained few and far between. After all, how could someone on the left feel at ease with the close connection between the federal idea, its local intellectual and political champions, and a conglomerate like Power Corporation?

These relatively predictable alignments always made sense to me. Those who worried about change and distrusted collective action found the existing federal arrangement preferable to an unpredictable transformation, and they naturally rallied around the federal idea. Voting in favour of Quebec sovereignty in 1995, Conservative leader Jean Charest liked to say, would plunge us all into a "black hole" of uncertainty (Pratte 1998, 261).

Stéphane Dion candidly explained this reality to me, once, when we were still colleagues at the Université de Montréal. If Quebec had already been a country, he said in substance, and we had been offered an arrangement whereby we would become one among ten equal provinces, on a par, say, with Prince Edward Island, of course I would have stood against it, he said. But Quebec is not a country; it is a province within Canada. This situation may not be ideal, but it must be accepted in a realist way, as a fact of life. Undoing Canada would be simply too costly and troublesome.

Pierre Elliott Trudeau did not say anything different in his early writings, when he acknowledged that only the circumstances of history and the exercise of power could explain that Ireland and Nicaragua were countries, but not Scotland and Quebec (1968, 187). Existing frontiers nevertheless had to be accepted, to avoid unnecessary conflicts and an infinite regress toward smaller and less and less sustainable units (ibid., 157–8). Reason should prevail over emotions, wrote Trudeau, and this appeared especially true for a people "not well enough educated, not rich enough, nor, above all, numerous enough, to man and finance a government possessing all the necessary means for both war and peace" (ibid., 170). Robert Bourassa gave the same stance a rather appalling connotation when in 1970 he invented the idea of profitable federalism ("le fédéralisme rentable"; Lisée 2012, 65).

Federalism, then, was the shape of our status quo, not an ideal, but a suitable arrangement for those who preferred their social and political institutions secure, stable, and "profitable." To take one anecdotal but revealing example, during the 1995 referendum campaign, the Hell's Angels favoured the No, while the nuns involved in community action naturally supported the Yes (Presse canadienne 1995; Baillargeon 1995). For someone who grew up thinking the world was neither fair nor particularly well governed, this preference for the status quo obviously held little appeal.

This is where my first story meets political science. In the work I did with my colleague Jean-Philippe Thérien on the left and the right in global politics, we emphasized differences over equality. There was something else, however, to the debate that divided the left and the right – something we saw and mentioned in our work, but did not explore thoroughly. The cleavage between the left and the right was indeed anchored in contrasting views of human nature.

In *Left and Right in Global Politics*, Jean-Philippe and I captured these contrasting views by pointing to the optimism of the left, which went back to Jean-Jacques Rousseau's idea of human nature as intrinsically good and compassionate, and the pessimism of the right, anchored in Thomas Hobbes's view of the state of nature as a situation "where every man is enemy to every man" and life is condemned to remain "solitary, poor, nasty, brutish, and short" (Noël and Thérien 2008, 21). The right's pessimism about human nature sustained a relatively satisfied outlook on society: life could be so much worse; and the optimism of the left fostered a critical stance on everything: collectively, we could do so much better. In our book, we more or less left it at that, somewhere among other distinctions, such as the right's preference for downhill over cross-country skiing and the left's choice, in France, of Renault over Peugeot (ibid., 23). This question, however, kept bugging me. What was exactly the relationship between these opposite views of human nature and attitudes toward equality?

I cannot expand too much on this question here, but interesting insights in this respect are offered by recent studies in psychology. John Jost and his co-authors, in particular, find a close connection between attitudes toward social change and views about inequality (Jost, Nosek, and Gosling 2008, 128). Conservatives fear insecurity and dislike uncertainty. As a consequence, they tend to favour tradition and social order over social change, they more readily adopt system-justifying attitudes, and they are inclined to accept, and even celebrate, existing hierarchies and inequalities. Individuals on the left, on the other hand, appear more secure, open minded, and comfortable with change and are thus more critical of existing injustice and inequalities. These consistent differences in attitudes, explain Jost and his colleagues, are anchored in deep predispositions, which can be traced back to childhood: confident and self-reliant children tend to become liberals, and insecure and fearful children tend to end up as conservatives (Jost, Federico, and Napier 2009, 318). Our preschool years are, so to speak, our own little state of nature. For some, these years appear Hobbesian; for others, they evoke the world of Rousseau! Of course, events later in life also affect and reshape our attitudes. Severe social disorder and threatening situations, in particular, tend to make persons shift to the right (ibid., 321). And the right always keeps an advantage because humans naturally appreciate certainty: a conservative response to change may well be the "default" and most common position. Indeed, in experiments where the context of decision is manipulated, it seems "much easier to get a liberal to behave like a conservative than it is to get a conservative to behave like a liberal" (Skitka et al. 2002, 484; quoted in ibid., 319).

The division between the left and the right, then, is about equality and social justice, but it is also about personal feelings of security and insecurity, and more generally about attitudes toward change. In the psychology lab, Hobbes and Rousseau still make sense, and their contrasting outlooks on life predict fairly well individual views about equality.

This is exactly how the politics of federalism is configured in Quebec. It is a politics of left and right, not only or merely in terms of equality and inequality, but also and more importantly in reference to a deeper opposition between the preservation of the status quo and the promotion of social change. The question of federalism, in this context, reaches beyond public policy. It is political through and through and concerns the mobilization of bias in a fundamental way.

This is where, for instance, Pierre Elliott Trudeau and René Lévesque, two reformists in their youth, parted ways. Trudeau, explained Reg Whitaker in what may well be the best analysis of his thought, was a "Hobbesian liberal" preoccupied by a world of "conflict, violence, insecurity and death" (1992, 138, 158). As mentioned above, state boundaries had been "established and maintained largely by the threat of or the use of force" (Trudeau 1968, 186). In this context, "the idea that the nation must necessarily be sovereign" constituted a dangerous illusion and ultimately a source of disorder and war (ibid., 151, 157–8). There was obviously rhetorical excess, observed Whitaker, when Trudeau portrayed "the nationalism of a tiny Quebec struggling to maintain its language and culture in the vast Anglophone sea of North America as exactly the same phenomenon as the nationalism of Nazi Germany," but this analogy also stemmed from a coherent, if stark, view of the world (ibid., 150). To this sombre, realist outlook, Trudeau added a profound pessimism about the possibilities of renovation and collective action within Quebec, which led him, in the end, to become a staunch defender of the federal and social status quo (ibid., 148; Heintzman 1983, 42; Noël 2008, 142–3). René Lévesque, who accompanied the American troops when they entered Dachau in 1945, was no stranger to human evil (Godin 1994, 169–70). But he drew different conclusions from his encounter with war and genocide: he balanced his initial bias in favour of the underdog with an ever-present and strong reluctance to condone any form of ideological and political excess. Lévesque nevertheless kept an enduring faith in the possibility of human progress and in the ideal of equality, in Quebec and in the world arena. "From the jungle to civilization," he observed in the wartime part of his memoirs, "there is only one step to take" (1986, 155; my translation;). Trudeau and Lévesque; fear and hope, status quo and equality, right and left: for the last 50 years, this profound antinomy defined the politics of federalism in Quebec.

Federalists as Nationalists

Elsewhere in Canada, federalism and the politics of left and right in-

Figure 7.1

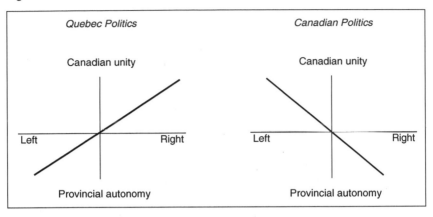

tersected differently. Compared with Quebeckers, Canadians experienced less a world of either/or, or of status quo versus change, than one of more or less, where the country's unity and national standards were opposed to provincial autonomy and decentralization, a world where usually the left favoured national unity and the right provincial autonomy. In this second intellectual and political world, I have been, oddly enough, on the side of autonomy, arguing, against many on the left, that the federal principle and decentralization were not necessarily inimical to social justice. This stance was not so surprising, since, as can be seen in Figure 7.1, the main axis of debate was different in Quebec and in Canada. Thinking about federalism from Quebec, I ended up in an unlikely spot in Canada, the lower-left quadrant.

The progressive argument against federalism and decentralization is well known. Federations, it is argued, deprive the central government of the powers, financial resources, and administrative capacities necessary to develop generous, encompassing, countrywide social policies. They also divide social forces and fragment the political process, leading to races to the bottom and lower common denominator social policies. Federations may also multiply veto points in the centre, rendering cohesive policy-making difficult (Obinger, Castles, and Leibfried 2005, 42). And the more decentralized a federation is, the more these difficulties become manifest. Conservative scholars make similar arguments, but they appreciate, of course, what they see as the "market-preserving" virtues of federalism (Weingast 1995). Federalism, approves Aaron

Wildavsky, "means inequality" (1998, 39–54). On the left, evaluations are similar but less sanguine. "A decentralized Canada," worries Keith Banting, "would have been a more unequal Canada" (2005, 135).

I have argued, along with Richard Simeon and other comparative scholars, that the inhibiting effects of federalism and decentralization on the welfare state remain, in fact, limited and marginal compared with other social and institutional determinants (Noël 1999, 2006a; Simeon 2006; Leibfried, Castles, and Obinger 2005, 338–9; Treisman 2007, 274). The consensus now, even among scholars who favour centralization, is that the effects of federalism and decentralization remain relatively modest and conditioned by a host of other factors. Why then are Canadian scholars so preoccupied by the distributive consequences of federalism and decentralization? Is social justice really harmed, as Richard Simeon asks in reference to Keith Banting's image of a sick child not being treated in the same way everywhere, "if a province chooses to improve upon the national standard?" (2006, 39–40). At this point, we leave the world of left and right and enter that of identity politics. This is what my second story is about.

I do many things during departmental meetings. Once, a few years ago, after I had run out of to-do lists and outlines for this or that, and while the debate was still raging on a critical issue probably involving the department's photocopier, I undertook to draw a two by two matrix to classify my colleagues according to their political views. I started, of course, with a horizontal left-right axis and, being in Quebec, added a vertical federalist/sovereignist line, to obtain a table similar to those presented in Figure 7.1. It was quite easy to fill in my four boxes, especially since I was alone in deciding whether my colleagues were left or right, federalist or sovereignist, regardless of their publicly expressed views.

As I completed this quick research project, I realized that the left-right division was by far the best predictor of the core cleavages within the department (over hiring decisions, for instance). My allies on most matters of significance stood on the left, whether they were sovereignists or federalists, and my habitual opponents were located on the right.

Note, before I go further, that the fact that all boxes of this matrix were occupied does not contradict the macro-level trends outlined in the previous section. Indeed, at the individual level, all positions remain theoretically possible. Still, in the political life of Quebec, federalism belongs to the right, for reasons already explained. My federalist colleagues on the left are thus political orphans in the province. In federal politics, on the other hand, they have more than one party to choose from. Worst off, my colleagues who are conservative sovereignists stand poorly represented everywhere and usually are forced to rally to left-leaning sovereignist parties. A few voices among Quebec intellectuals now deplore this situation (Bédard 2011; Bock-Côté 2012). Institutions of political representation never capture all possible political stances. As I considered my sketchy matrix, I was impressed by the predictive power of the left-right division, which practically always trumped the vertical axis in departmental politics. Isn't it amazing, I thought, that so much hinges on the left-right division and so little on the federalism/ sovereignty cleavage? This was, after all, the fall of 1995, on the eve of the referendum. One plausible interpretation, suggested by a colleague, was that the left/right axis expressed reason, whereas the federalist/ sovereignist division remained deeply anchored in emotions. In this perspective, alliances would unite colleagues who think more or less alike, on the same rational ground, leaving emotions aside, as a less tractable, less relevant consideration.

In fact, the distinction between ideology (left and right) and identity (Quebec or Canada) is not as sharp as is often thought. Indeed, "a growing body of evidence suggests that left-right ideological stances reflect, among other things, the influences of heredity, childhood temperament or personality, and both situational and dispositional variability in social, cognitive, and motivational needs to reduce uncertainty and threat" (Jost, Federico, and Napier 2009, 317–18). In other words, left and right positioning are also rooted in emotions.

The main difference between the two types of disposition lies elsewhere. Because it creates a spatial, bipolar continuum – a horizontal axis with two ends – ideology can function as a relatively sophisticated cognitive tool, to guide preferences and choices on a number of different questions (Holmberg 2009, 256). There are always many possible positions on the left, for instance, and various degrees of animosity toward the right, all of them defined in the context of a specific place and of a given time. With all its gradients, the distinction between the left and the right has proven very effective as a heuristic tool and it has become, in modern democracy, the "core currency of political exchange," the grammar that structures most public deliberations (McDonald, Mendes, and Kim 2007, 63; Noël and Thérien 2008). Identity works differently. A social identity links one person's self-concept to a group, which is valued and favoured compared with other groups perceived as significantly different and somehow less close and congenial

(Greene 2002, 182). Identity tells us where we belong and heightens our perceptions of sameness toward the in-group and of distance toward out-groups. Anchored in a person's self-definition, such perceptions are obviously powerful and probably more so than ideology. Indeed, in the study of public opinion, identity usually ranks high in the "funnel of causality" among the root causes of most other attitudes (Johnston 2006; Lewis-Beck et al. 2008, 134). This powerful notion, however, is also a blunt cognitive tool, less flexible and malleable than ideology and less movable from one scale of activity or one domain of interest to another. In departmental politics, for instance, national identities are nearly irrelevant, except perhaps over issues such as the choice of language in academic affairs (a question that arises once in a while at the Université de Montréal). The same may be true for most questions of world politics, where the left-right dichotomy travels much better than national or social identities (Noël and Thérien 2008). This cognitive difference explains why, in my departmental politics story, the left and the right almost always trumped the Canada/Quebec cleavage.

Identity often matters, though, especially when peoples need to define who they are and what they could and should do together. This operation is never as straightforward as it may seem. Indeed, collective identities are not simply derived from pre-existing, primordial cultural traits; they are created and developed through contested political processes, where contending social actors propose and debate plausible but different "stories of peoplehood" along with their corresponding political and institutional projects (Smith 2003, 32–7). The process is necessarily contentious because the affirmation of a political identity requires the denial of other possible identities (Greene 2002, 82; Smith 2003, 56). Multiple identities and allegiances are possible, of course, notably in federations, but they stand in competition and, in the best of cases, their coexistence proves difficult and conflict ridden (Smith 2003, 31).

In Canada, such tensions are familiar and, indeed, existential. In an essay on the federal role in health care, Keith Banting and Robin Boadway (2004) note that social policy disagreements in this country often stem from different conceptions of what constitutes the appropriate sharing community. Some Canadians envision a country-wide sharing community, others prefer provincial sharing communities, and still others would favour a dual scheme combining both country-wide and province-wide elements. While this summary rings true, the notion of sharing community does not go to the heart of the matter because it remains an abstract, dispassionate way of addressing identity. Why indeed do so many Canadians prefer a countrywide sharing community? The answer is because they see such a community as an embodiment of their identity as Canadians. Likewise, many Quebeckers define their province as their main sharing community, in accordance with their national identity. In another essay, Banting himself is very clear on this count, when he presents countrywide social programs "as the social glue holding Canada together" (2005, 134). In this light, social programs have a redistributive purpose – to make Canada a decent and just society – but they are also "breathing life into the sense of a pan-Canadian community." They are the "bonds that tie" (ibid., 134).

In a multinational federation, then, the politics of national identity is ever present. It matters as much as the politics of left and right, albeit in different ways. This explains why disagreements over the effects of federalism and decentralization can become so intense, in spite of the relatively modest size of the presumed effects. Take, once more, Richard Simeon's question about the sick baby being treated above national standards in some jurisdictions of Canada. Why should Canadians care? he asks. Some would say that they should care because the question is purely rhetorical: what worries Canadians is the possibility of substandard, not superior, social services. Perhaps, but go to the other side of the left-right divide and consider, for a moment, the genuine outrage of conservatives who denounce the more favourable social programs of some provinces as unfair to Canadians living in less generous provinces (Eisen and Milke 2010; MacKinnon 2011). Note that these conservatives never advocate lifting up services in less progressive provinces; they want to bring the spirit level down. Their claim is that some provinces, notably Quebec, offer more to their citizens than wealthier provinces like Alberta or Ontario because they benefit from equalization payments. Hence, their citizens get advantages the taxpayers of Alberta and Ontario simply cannot afford. The facts are not kind to such interpretations. Alberta, for instance, without equalization payments and with much lower tax rates, disposes of much more provincial revenues per capita than Quebec ($9,545 per capita in 2011–2012, compared with $8,520 in Quebec; Gouvernement du Québec 2011, A7–A9). If the Alberta government does not offer as many social services to citizens, it is simply because it chooses not to do so. As for Ontario, if it matched the autonomous revenues associated with its fiscal capacity – as defined by the equalization program – by a fiscal effort identical to that assumed by Quebeckers, its provincial revenues per capita and capacity to sustain social services would be practically the same ($8,424 compared with $8,520 in Quebec; ibid., A7–A11). In 2009, in provincial and municipal taxes Quebeckers contributed $23 billion more than they would have if they had paid the average Canadian rates; by comparison, their gain from federal transfers exceeded by only $1 billion what a simple per capita distribution would have yielded (Fortin 2012).

The issue at stake is neither services nor money, but difference and identity. *Calgary Herald* columnist Licia Corbella goes to the heart of the matter when she writes: "Equalization, in case Quebec students are unclear, is a program designed to make the government services available to Canadians equal across the country" (2012). As a matter of fact, equalization is precisely designed to allow provincial governments to do as they wish, with the means "to provide comparable levels of public services at reasonably comparable levels of taxation (Constitution Act 1982, Section 36(2)). The program, noted the 2006 panel on equalization chaired by Al O'Brien, is not conceived "to ensure that common standards in quality or outcomes in public services are achieved," but is intended simply to equalize fiscal capacity (Expert Panel 2006, 26). This is precisely what is galling to someone like Corbella: social programs and services are not "equal across the country." On this point, the Canadian right and the Canadian left almost agree: as Canadians, we should all be treated alike, wherever we live. In a sense, Corbella evokes the same sick child problem that bothers Keith Banting, but in reverse: she does not like difference and wishes Quebec would shrink its social programs to Alberta size.

Cast in this way, the politics of federalism becomes less a matter of hope and fear, equality and competition, or left and right, as discussed earlier, than one of identity. When identity prevails, conflicts over federalism and centralization become debates about peoplehood, about the appropriate sovereign in a given case. Such debates may give rise to claims for formal recognition and accommodation, through encompassing exercises in what Peter Russell called mega-constitutional politics (2004), through more circumscribed negotiations – on self-government for instance – or even through symbolic gestures such as the 2006 House of Commons motion on Quebec as a nation within Canada. If these avenues are closed or difficult, identity politics may work more indirectly, through conflicts over specific, and sometimes mundane, issues or policies. In such cases, identity claims may be muted, but nevertheless effective. The 2005 Agreement on the Quebec Parental Insurance Plan, for instance, was propelled by the nationally anchored conviction, shared by the key social actors and carried by the government, that

Quebec was the right "sharing community" for parental insurance. Largely unnoticed by scholars and practitioners interested in federalism, this agreement was perhaps the most important intergovernmental breakthrough since the creation of the Quebec Pension Plan in 1964. Indeed, it allowed the Quebec government to take back from Ottawa a jurisdiction that practice and court judgments had associated with the federal competence on unemployment insurance, duly accepted by the provinces in 1940. The Quebec government put the 2005 agreement to good use and created its own parental insurance program, which is unique in Canada and far superior to what is offered by the federal employment insurance program (Noël 2012). However conflictual, the politics of identity rarely disappears. Addressed formally or informally, directly or indirectly, it remains at the centre of public deliberations in multinational federations. National identities simply cannot be wished away (Noël 2006b).

Together, ideology and identity capture a good part of the politics of federalism, and they do so in distinctive ways, in given historical and national contexts. In Quebec, for instance, it was the social-democratic left that carried the fight for autonomy and eventually independence, just as it was in Catalonia and Scotland, but not in Flanders. For many years, the main rival of Quebec nationalists on the federal scene was also on the centre-left and promoted a relatively generous pan-Canadian citizenship supported by a strong central government. In comparison, the Canadian right appeared more open to enhanced Quebec autonomy. In Spain and in the United Kingdom, the opposite was true. Bent against a legacy of authoritarian centralism, the Spanish socialists favoured the development of the "autonomic state" and proved much more open to the demands of the "historical nationalities" than a right that looked back and sought to maintain Spain as an unqualified unitary state (Balfour and Quiroga 2007). In the United Kingdom, devolution was also a project of the left: in this case the Labour party, against the preferences of the right (Hopkin and Bradbury 2006).

The left and the right matter for federalism and decentralization, as they do for just about everything. But they do so, and combine with identity politics, in contingent ways. As a result of decisions made at critical junctures, observes Jan Erk, "Walloon nationalism is on the left" and "Flemish nationalism is on the right" (2005, 566). Before the Second World War, Quebec and Catalan nationalism expressed conservative visions; they now carry social-democratic convictions (Guibernau 1999, 95).

Majorities and Minorities

However important expressions of ideology and identity are, politics is not only about convictions and distinctive visions of the good society; it is also, and always, a contest for power (Noël 2006b). And in multinational federations, the exercise of power often means that the majority rules. This fundamental aspect of life in a multinational federation appeared to me most vividly in the fall of 1999, at the founding gathering of the Forum of Federations in Mont-Tremblant, Quebec. This is my third story.

The main purpose of the Mont-Tremblant conference was to promote the federal idea as a fair and enticing vision for a complex world, in a Quebec society still divided in the aftermath of the 1995 referendum. The new Forum of Federations was to be a glamorous, international contribution to Plan A. The project had a rough start, however, because, even though it was launched in the Laurentians, it deliberately avoided addressing the preoccupations of Quebec nationalists. In one session after another, Quebec participants raised questions and tended to spoil the fun. The low point was reached when Premier Lucien Bouchard delivered what was certainly the most sombre after-dinner talk I have ever heard, and he told an embarrassed audience they were not getting the full story. The day after, following a golf game with Jean Chrétien, President Bill Clinton saved a faltering show with a talk where he linked the quest for independence to "the most primitive human failing: the fear of the other and the sense that we can only breathe and function and matter if we are somehow free of the necessity to associate with" others (1999). A long, broad, and very democratic attempt to rethink Canada – a country where the new constitution had been imposed on the main national minority – was reduced to a narrow-minded and mean-spirited tribal impulse. I was disappointed by this shallow and insensitive talk but more disappointed, even, by the reaction of my Canadian colleagues – experts on federalism – who cheered and celebrated a message so dismissive of their country's long and difficult but always democratic and respectful conversation.

To me, this ending said something about the global promise of federalism, a promise that often seemed to work better for the winners than for the losers. George Anderson summed up the idea better than I could when he explained, at a conference in Toronto to honour the career of Richard Simeon, that in a post-conflict situation, federalism is more likely to be established soundly if there is a clear winner. When one side prevails, usually the majority, it may be enlightened enough to make concessions and share power in a federal arrangement. Otherwise, the underlying conflict is likely to continue and to undermine the global promise of federalism. Always the realist, Pierre Elliott Trudeau made a similar point about majorities and minorities. Quebec nationalists who bet on a wake-up signal should know, he warned, that after an initial shock they would be confronted with an opposite nationalist reaction from the majority, with dire consequences; "there is nothing meaner," he wrote, "than the coward recovered from his fright" (1968, 176–7).

Multinational arrangements are inherently conflictual. Indeed, as François Rocher and Philippe Cousineau-Morin note, the very idea of a multinational federation appears contentious: usually the presence of many nations within a state is asserted only by national minorities against a majority that does not readily accept such a representation of the country (2011, 271–5). Most of the time, national majorities do not even see themselves as majorities endowed with their own identity: they speak more naturally the language of undifferentiated citizenship, equality, and universality (Kymlicka 1998; Lecours and Nootens 2011, 7–8; Dieckhoff 2011, 29). James Bickerton sums up this reality nicely when he observes that even when "there is a minority there is not always a majority" (2011, 147).

Multinational federations, then, not only oppose conflicting ideologies and identities. They confront national minorities against a majority that tends to deny being one and, consequently, resists granting recognition and autonomy to internal nations (Lecours and Nootens 2011, 9). The conflicts between these contending visions – multinational versus undifferentiated citizenships – may lead to a number of outcomes, depending on the political context. John Coakley, for instance, suggests that the majority may incorporate, exclude, or ignore national minorities (2011). In democracies, however, the outcome is likely to be a compromise, one that is more or less stable and constantly evolving (Simeon and Conway 2001, 364–5).

This being said, the majority remains the majority. As James Tully explains, in any given situation, "not all members are heard and not all compromises are acceptable to all. The relations of power codified in the prevailing system of misrecognition structure the discussions and negotiations in unequal and unfair ways" (2001, 28). In Canada, for instance, the obstacles to constitutional changes have multiplied since the adoption of the new constitution in 1982 to consolidate the preferences of the majority (Taillon 2007), and a number of reforms and court decisions have run contrary to the idea of a multinational federation (Gagnon 2010, 88–105; Lajoie 2002). In Spain, in June 2010, the Constitutional Court invalidated many elements of Catalonia's new statute of autonomy, approved by both Catalan and Spanish parliaments and by referendum four years earlier. The court adjudicated, in particular, that references to a Catalan nation had no legal weight; constitutionally, only the Spanish nation existed, and its unity remained "indissoluble" (Requejo 2011).

At times, obviously, national minorities make gains (Noël 2012). If this were not the case, multinational federations would not last. However, the relationship between minorities and majorities remains inherently unequal.

In his recent writings, Alain-G. Gagnon makes a plea for a better understanding among scholars and, more broadly, for a new politics of reconciliation, recognition, and habilitation (2011). This perspective is sensible and may point to the best avenue of reform for multinational federations. It may be exceedingly optimistic, however, to expect an open, fair, and even relationship. Indeed, majorities – winners – seldom ask minorities – losers – for insights (see, for some empirical evidence, Rocher 2007). Hence, Quebec scholars of federalism have hardly played a role in the international deployment of the Forum of Federations. Again, relationships between majorities and minorities are rarely egalitarian. Politics, in this way as well, permeates federalism.

Conclusion

In his very first book, Richard Simeon described Canadian intergovernmental relations as a form of federal-provincial diplomacy: the description underlined the conflicts and tensions inherent in a process where the broad, sometimes existential, objectives of political actors were weighted more than the "concrete programmes and policies" they were debating (1972, 312–13). When you think about federalism, he suggested in this book and in subsequent writings, always mind the politics. Federalism gives rise to specific institutions, norms, and rules, but it is also an ever-contentious arrangement, driven by politically motivated actors.

Written from this perspective, this chapter stresses three dimensions that, in a given country and at a given time, are likely to shape the politics of federalism. First, as is the case with most questions, the politics of federalism is always a politics of left and right. In Quebec, the right carried the federal idea, while the left largely vied for sovereignty. For many decades, this basic alignment defined the politics of Quebec society. In Canada, federalism as such was not questioned by political parties, but the left leaned toward more centralized arrangements, and the right favoured provincial autonomy, if only because decentralization was associated with less state intervention. Of course, the overlap between the two political spheres – Quebec and Canada – made for interesting deliberations. Elsewhere in the world, the politics of left and right combined with federalism in different ways, but ideology always remained of prime political importance. Second, the politics of federalism also stems, especially in multinational federations, from the politics of identity. The centrality of identity explains, in particular, why citizens – and scholars or, as Alan Cairns would put it, "citizen scholars" (2008, 247) – care so much about the ins and outs of federalism. Identity accounts, as well, for the intriguing convergence that sometimes brings the left and the right to agree on the contours of the sharing community, whatever they think about the extent of sharing that is necessary. Third, the politics of federalism is also power politics, and it opposes majorities and minorities. The majority/minorities dynamic is not always the main factor in explaining decisions or outcomes, but it often matters. Currently, for instance, Canada is governed, with little in the way of compromises, by a party that obtained practically majority support outside Quebec – 48% of the popular vote – but came only a distant third in Quebec, with 16.5% of the votes and five seats. In this context, majority/minority differences tend to take on an everyday meaning. For the country's aboriginal peoples, the majoritarian impulse of the current government is also very obvious.

Federalism, then, is always an object of contention between the left and the right, between different national or social identities, and between majorities and minorities. More than a set of rules and institutions, it constitutes a concretely situated political project that can never be neutral. This does not mean that federalism does not hold promises. But such promises come in very different forms and shapes, and they are not necessarily promises for everyone. One should remember, starting with the earliest work of Richard Simeon, *Federal-Provincial Diplomacy*, the inherently political and always contested character of federalism. In this light, we seem well advised to keep a sober perspective on the "global promise of federalism."

REFERENCES

Baillargeon, Stéphane. 1995. Les religieuses répondent à l'appel du Oui. *Le Devoir*, 23 October.

Balfour, Sebastian, and Alejandro Quiroga. 2007. *The Reinvention of Spain: Nation and Identity since Democracy*. Oxford: Oxford University Press.

Banting, Keith. 2005. Canada: Nation-Building in a Federal Welfare State. In *Federalism and the Welfare State: New World and European Experiences*, edited by Herbert Obinger, Stephan Leibfried, and Francis G. Castles. Cambridge: Cambridge University Press.

Banting, Keith, and Robin Boadway. 2004. Defining the Sharing Community: The Federal Role in Health Care. In *Money, Politics, and Health Care: Restructuring the Federal-Provincial Relationship*, edited by Harvey Lazar and France St-Hilaire. Montreal and Kingston: Institute for Research on Public Policy and Institute of Intergovernmental Relations.

Bédard, Éric. 2011. La fin du consensus libéral? *Policy Options* 32(6):125–7.

Bickerton, James. 2011. Janus Faces, Rocks, and Hard Places: Majority Nationalism in Canada. In *Contemporary Majority Nationalism*, edited by Alain-G. Gagnon, André Lecours, and Geneviève Nootens. Montreal and Kingston: McGill-Queen's University Press.

Bock-Côté, Mathieu. 2012. *Fin de cycle: aux origines du malaise politique québécois*. Montreal: Boréal.

Cairns, Alan C. 2008. Conclusion: Are We on the Right Track? In *The Comparative Turn in Canadian Political Science*, edited by Linda A. White, Richard Simeon, Robert Vipond, and Jennifer Wallner. Vancouver: UBC Press.

Carty, R. Kenneth, and William Cross. 2010. Political Parties and the Practice of Brokerage Politics. In *The Oxford Handbook of Canadian Politics* edited by John C. Courtney and David E. Smith. Oxford: Oxford University Press.

Clinton, William J. 1999. Remarks to the Forum of Federations Conference in Mont-Tremblant, Canada. 8 October. Available at www.presidency.ucsb.edu/ws/?pid=56687#axzz1wNQMfW62

Coakley, John. 2011. National Majorities in New States: Managing the Challenge of Diversity. In *Contemporary Majority Nationalism*, edited by Alain-G. Gagnon, André Lecours, and Geneviève Nootens. Montreal and Kingston: McGill-Queen's University Press.

Corbella, Licia. 2012. Quebec Students Get Cushy Deal on Tuition – Thanks to Alberta. *Calgary Herald*, 9 March.

Dieckhoff, Alain. 2011. The Paradoxes of Contemporary Nationalism. In *Contemporary Majority Nationalism*, edited by Alain-G. Gagnon, André Lecours, and Geneviève Nootens. Montreal and Kingston: McGill-Queen's University Press.

Eisen, Ben, and Mark Milke. 2010. *The Real Have-Nots in Confederation: Ontario, Alberta and British Columbia. How Canada's Equalization Program Creates Generous Programs and Large Governments in Have-Not Provinces.* Winnipeg: Frontier Centre for Public Policy, FCPP Policy Series 83.

Erk, Jan. 2005. Sub-State Nationalism and the Left-Right Divide: Critical Junctures in the Formation of Nationalist Labour Movements in Belgium. *Nations and Nationalism* 11(4):551–70.

Erk, Jan, and Edward Koning. 2010. New Structuralism and Institutional Change: Federalism Between Centralization and Decentralization. *Comparative Political Studies* 43(3):353–78.

Expert Panel on Equalization and Territorial Formula Financing. 2006. *Achieving a National Purpose: Putting Equalization Back on Track.* Ottawa: Finance Canada.

Fortin, Pierre. 2012. Le Québec vit-il aux crochets du Canada? *L'actualité*, mai.

Gagnon, Alain-G. 2010. *The Case for Multinational Federalism: Beyond the All-Encompassing Nation.* London: Routledge.

Gagnon, Alain-G. 2011. *L'âge des incertitudes: essais sur le fédéralisme et la diversité nationale.* Quebec: Presses de l'Université Laval.

Godin, Pierre. 1994. *René Lévesque : un enfant du siècle (1922–1960).* Montreal: Boréal.

Gouvernement du Québec. 2011. *Budget, 2011–2012: Update on Federal Transfers,* Quebec: Ministère des Finances.

Greene, Steven. 2002. The Social-Psychological Measurement of Partisanship. *Political Behavior* 24(3):171–97.

Guibernau, Montserrat. 1999. *Nations without States: Political Communities in a Global Age.* Cambridge: Polity Press.

Heintzman, Ralph. 1983. The Political Culture of Quebec, 1840–1960. *Canadian Journal of Political Science* 16(1):3–59.

Holmberg, Sören. 2009. Partisanship Reconsidered. In *The Oxford Handbook of Political Behavior,* edited by Russell J. Dalton and Hans-Dieter Klingemann. Oxford: Oxford University Press.

Hopkin, Jonathan, and Jonathan Bradbury. 2006. British Statewide Parties and Multilevel Politics. *Publius: The Journal of Federalism* 36(1):135–52.

Johnston, Richard. 2006. Party Identification: Unmoved Mover or Sum of Preferences. *Annual Review of Political Science* 9:329–51.

Jost, John T., Christopher M. Federico, and Jaime L. Napier. 2009. Political Ideology: Its Structure, Functions, and Elective Affinities. *Annual Review of Psychology* 60:307–37.

Jost, John T., Brian A. Nosek, and Samuel D. Gosling. 2008. Ideology: Its Re-surgence in Social, Personality, and Political Psychology. *Perspectives on Psychological Science.* 3(2):126–36.

Kriesi, Hanspeter, Edgar Grande, Romain Lachat, Martin Dolezal, Simon Bornschier, and Timotheos Frey. 2008. Globalization and its Impact on National Spaces of Competition. In *West European Politics in the Age of Globalization,* edited by H. Kriesi, E. Grande, R. Lachat, M. Dolezal, S. Bornschier and T. Frey. Cambridge: Cambridge University Press.

Kymlicka, Will. 1998. Multinational Federalism in Canada: Rethinking the Partnership. In *Beyond the Impasse: Toward Reconciliation,* edited by Roger Gibbins and Guy Laforest. Montreal: Institute for Research on Public Policy.

Lajoie, Andrée. 2002. *Quand les minorités font la loi.* Paris: PUF.

Lecours, André, and Geneviève Nootens. 2011. Understanding Majority Nationalism. In *Contemporary Majority Nationalism,* edited by Alain-G. Gagnon, André Lecours, and Geneviève Nootens. Montreal and Kingston: McGill-Queen's University Press.

Leibfried, Stephan, Francis G. Castles, and Herbert Obinger. 2005. "Old" and "New Politics" in Federal Welfare States. In *Federalism and the Welfare State,* edited by Herbert Obinger, Stephan Leibfried, and Francis G. Castles. Cambridge: Cambridge University Press.

Lévesque, René. 1986. *Attendez que je me rappelle* .... Montreal: Québec/Amérique.

Lewis-Beck, Michael S., William G. Jacoby, Helmut Norpoth, and Herbert F. Weisberg. 2008. *The American Voter Revisited.* Ann Arbor: University of Michigan Press.

Lisée, Jean-François. 2012. *Le petit tricheur: Robert Bourassa derrière le masque.* Montreal: Québec/Amérique.

MacKinnon, David. 2011. *Dollars & Sense: A Case for Modernizing Canada's Transfer Agreements.* Toronto: Ontario Chamber of Commerce.

McDonald, Michael D., Silvia M. Mendes, and Myunghee Kim. 2007. Cross-Temporal and Cross-National Comparisons of Party Left–Right Positions. *Electoral Studies.* 26(1):62–75.

Noël, Alain. 1999. Is Decentralization Conservative? Federalism and the Contemporary Debate on the Canadian Welfare State. In *Stretching the Federation: The Art of the State in Canada,* edited by Robert Young. Kingston: Queen's University Institute of Intergovernmental Relations.

Noël, Alain. 2006a. Social Justice in Overlapping Sharing Communities. In *Dilemmas of Solidarity: Rethinking Redistribution in the Canadian Federation,* edited by Sujit Choudhry, Jean-François Gaudreault-DeBiens, and Lorne Sossin. Toronto: University of Toronto Press.

Noël, Alain. 2006b. Democratic Deliberation in a Multinational Federation. *Critical Review of International Social and Political Philosophy* 9(3):419–44.

Noël, Alain. 2008. Un homme de gauche? In *René Lévesque: mythes et réalités*, edited by Alexandre Stefanescu. Montreal: vlb éditeur.

Noël, Alain. 2012. Asymmetry at Work: Quebec's Distinct Implementation of Programs for the Unemployed. In *Making EI Work: Research from the Mowat Centre Employment Insurance Task Force*, edited by Keith Banting and Jon Medow. Montreal and Kingston, McGill-Queen¹s University Press. Available at http://mowateitaskforce.ca/sites/default/files/Noel.pdf

Noël, Alain, and Jean-Philippe Thérien. 2008. *Left and Right in Global Politics*. Cambridge: Cambridge University Press.

Obinger, Herbert, Francis G. Castles, and Stephan Leibfried. 2005. Introduction: Federalism and the Welfare State. In *Federalism and the Welfare State: New World and European Experiences*, edited by Herbert Obinger, Stephan Leibfried, and Francis G. Castles. Cambridge: Cambridge University Press.

Pontusson, Jonas. 1995. From Comparative Public Policy to Political Economy: Putting Political Institutions in Their Place and Taking Interests Seriously. *Comparative Political Studies* 28(1):117–47.

Pratte, André. 1998. *L'énigme Charest*. Montreal: Boréal.

Presse canadienne. 1995. Les Hell's Angels voteront Non. *Le Devoir*, 21 October.

Requejo, Ferran. 2011. Reconnaissance politique et autonomie nationale (1979–2010). *L'Action nationale* 101(6–7):143–67.

Rocher, François. 2007. The End of the 'Two Solitudes'? The Presence (or Absence) of the Work of French-Speaking Scholars in Canadian Politics. *Canadian Journal of Political Science* 40(4):833–57.

Rocher, François, and Philippe Cousineau-Morin. 2011. Fédéralisme asymétrique et reconnaissance des nations internes au Canada. Évolution récente dans l'espace québécois ou comment abdiquer l'asymétrie sur l'autel du principe de l'égalité des provinces. In *Le fédéralisme multinational: un modèle viable?* edited by Michel Seymour and Guy Laforest. Brussels: P.I.E. Peter Lang.

Russell, Peter H. 2004. *Constitutional Odyssey: Can Canadians Become a Sovereign People?* 3rd ed. Toronto: University of Toronto Press.

Simeon, Richard. 1972. *Federal-Provincial Diplomacy: The Making of Recent Policy Making in Canada*. Toronto: University of Toronto Press.

Simeon, Richard. 2006. Social Justice: Does Federalism Make a Difference? In *Dilemmas of Solidarity: Rethinking Redistribution in the Canadian Federation*, edited by Sujit Choudhry, Jean-François Gaudreault-DeBiens, and Lorne Sossin. Toronto: University of Toronto Press.

Simeon, Richard, and Daniel-Patrick Conway. 2001. Federalism and the Management of Conflict in Multinational Societies. In *Multinational Democracies*, edited by Alain-G. Gagnon and James Tully. Cambridge: Cambridge University Press.

Simeon, Richard, and Ian Robinson. 1990. *State, Society, and the Development of Canadian Federalism*. Vol. 71. Collected Research Studies. Toronto: University of Toronto Press in cooperation with the Royal Commission on the Economic Union and Development Prospects for Canada and the Canadian Government Publishing Centre, Supply and Services Canada.

Skitka, L.J., E. Mullen, T. Griffin, S. Huchinson, and B. Chamberlin. 2002. Dispositions, Ideological Scripts, or Motivated Correction? Understanding Ideological Differences in Attributions for Social Problems. *Journal of Personality and Social Psychology* 83:470–87.

Smith, Rogers M. 2003. *Stories of Peoplehood: The Politics and Morals of Political Membership*. Cambridge: Cambridge University Press.

Taillon, Patrick. 2007. Les obstacles juridiques à une réforme du fédéralisme. In *Cahier de recherche de l'Institut de recherche sur le Québec*. Montreal: IRQ. Available at www.irq.qc.ca

Treisman, Daniel, 2007. *The Architecture of Government: Rethinking Political Decentralization*. Cambridge: Cambridge University Press.

Trudeau, Pierre Elliott. 1968. *Federalism and the French Canadians*. Toronto: Macmillan.

Tully, James. 2001. Introduction. In *Multinational Democracies*, edited by Alain-G. Gagnon and James Tully. Cambridge: Cambridge University Press.

Weingast, Barry R. 1995. The Economic Role of Political Institutions: Market-Preserving Federalism and Economic Development. *Journal of Law, Economics and Organization* 11(1):1–31.

Whitaker, Reg. 1992. *A Sovereign Idea: Essays on Canada as a Democratic Community*. Montreal and Kingston: McGill-Queen's University Press.

Wildavsky, Aaron. 1998. *Federalism and Political Culture*. New Brunswick: Transaction.

8 Adaptability and Change in Federations: Centralization, Political Parties, and Taxation Authority in Australia and Canada

LUC TURGEON AND JENNIFER WALLNER

What explains patterns of centralization and decentralization in federations? This question has been and continues to be of central concern to students of federalism. Recent scholarship has tended to stress factors such as the demographic make-up of the polity (Erk 2008) or sequences of historical developments (Broschek 2011). According to the former analysis, heterogeneous federations with territorially concentrated national minorities, like Canada, experience greater centrifugal forces that encourage decentralization and constituent unit autonomy. By contrast, homogeneous federations, like Australia, experience greater centripetal forces, as the polity is more willing to accept the overarching authority of the central government. For those emphasizing the significance of historical developments, critical junctures of contingent events take centre stage as long periods of institutional stability are punctuated by brief periods of institutional flux. At these moments, specific events, such as economic disasters, wars, or constitutional renewal, can propel adjustments in the balance of power between the central government and constituent jurisdictions in a federation. Both perspectives have provided stimulating perspectives to account for the evolution of federations. However, in both cases, the role of political actors has tended to be downplayed.

In this chapter, we follow in the footsteps of students of an older generation of political scientists, who stressed the importance of institutional actors such as the courts and political parties to account for the evolution of federal states (Riker 1964; Scott 1937; Chandler 1987). In particular, we believe that the influence of political parties has been underplayed in the recent scholarship on federalism.[1] *Without ignoring or denying the importance of structural factors, such as the features of the polity or critical junctures, in this chapter we argue that the (changing) nature of the party system plays an important role in the fluctuating degree of centralization and decentralization in a federation.* To appreciate the role of political parties in the dynamics of centralization and decentralization in federations, William Riker (1964) advanced a theory that emphasized the organization of political parties, pinpointing the relationship between national and sub-state parties as a key determinant in the ebb and flow of powers among the orders of government. Federations with integrated national and sub-state parties were more likely to centralize. In contrast to his theory, however, here we focus on the ideological dimension of the party system. More specifically, we highlight the importance of left-wing parties as agents of centralization in federations.

Owing to their contrasting trajectories of federal evolution, we use Australia and Canada to advance this proposition. As argued by Bruce Hodgins and his collaborators:

> The British North America (BNA) Act of 1867 provided for a more centralized form of federalism than the Commonwealth of Australia Constitutions Act passed in 1901 and yet over time, despite the expectations of the founding fathers, Canada has tended to *move erratically* towards a much more decentralist operation of government, while Australia has shifted in the opposite direction. (1989, 19; emphasis ours)

Whereas Australia moved uniformly away from decentralization and towards centralization through a series of staggered steps, Canada experienced intermittent periods of centralization and decentralization before coalescing into a decentralized federation. These different endpoints, at odds with the two countries' beginnings, present an interesting puzzle in need of explanation.

A number of metrics can be deployed to measure the degree of centralization and decentralization in a federation. Here we focus on the allocation of taxation authority in the fiscal architectures of the two federations. The allocation of taxation authority lies at the heart of all federal systems, as it determines the relative revenue-raising capacities of the various governments, establishes the degree of autonomy and independence that can be exercised by the respective governments, and directly impacts these governments' ability to act in their respective spheres of competencies (Boadway and Shah 2009). To be sure, taxation authority as a proxy for sub-state autonomy may be confounded by revenue-sharing agreements between the central and sub-state governments, particularly if they rely upon conditional grants where the central government imposes its own priorities and stipulations in exchange for the funds. To account for this problem, we provide data on the significance of conditional grants in our two federations.

Our argument is not that the distinct Australian-Canadian centralization-decentralization trajectories are solely explained by public support for left parties in the two countries' party systems. Rather, we argue that many theoretical explanations to account for patterns of centralization or decentralization *on their own* are insufficient to account for the undulating patterns of centralization and decentralization. To correct for these existing deficiencies, we suggest that the analysis must incorporate a focus on political parties and the party systems. *Parties act as a crucial linchpin that connects critical events to subsequent actions, mediates existing social forces, and provides an important catalyst that shapes the balancing of powers in federations.* More precisely, in this chapter, we argue that a strong left party in Australia's generally stable party system resulted in support at both the Commonwealth and the state levels for the centralization of taxation powers over time, making the latter possible. In Canada, in contrast, undulating support for left-wing parties at the national and provincial levels fostered fluctuations in the centralization and decentralization of taxation autonomy in the federation.

We advance this argument in four sections. Our chapter opens with a snapshot of the puzzle and a critique of the different approaches that have been used to account for divergent patterns of federal evolution. The second section presents the chapter's theoretical framework, detailing the importance of left-wing parties as potential agents of centralization. The third outlines the role of the distinct Australian and Canadian party systems on the allocation of taxation authority in the two countries. We conclude with a discussion of our findings, considering why Australia and Canada have had such markedly different party systems and outlining an agenda for future research.

The Puzzle

The designers of federations face a multitude of choices as they endeavour to create a central government that is simultaneously strong and limited while striking a balance between centrifugal and centripetal forces. Of all the decision points, crafting the fiscal architecture carries considerable weight in the balance of power, and federations differ widely in the ways in which they have chosen to apportion revenue-raising responsibilities (see Watts 2008; Boadway and Shah 2009).

Today, Australia and Canada fall on opposite ends of the centralized-decentralized continuum. Australian states have no direct access to income, corporate, or general sales taxes, and they rely extensively on grants from the Commonwealth government. The Canadian provinces, in contrast, can access essentially the same taxes as the federal government, from personal income taxes and corporate taxes to social insurance and sales taxes (Boadway and Shah 2009, 157). Canadian provinces, moreover, have complete control over the tax rates and tax base for provincial taxes, while Australian states have discretion only over roughly half, the remainder being determined through tax-sharing agreements with the Commonwealth government (OECD 2008, 37).

The variations in the fiscal architectures translate into markedly different results when we examine the data on sub-state revenues. For example, Australian states generate only the equivalent of 4.6% in GDP from taxes over which they have full discretion, while Canadian provinces generate the equivalent of 12.3% of GDP from autonomous taxes (Wallner and Boychuck 2014). In the meantime, as a proportion of sub-state revenues, conditional transfers make up 21.3% of Australian state revenues and only 15.8% for Canada (Watts 2005, 55). Finally, without getting into the details, the conditions affixed to federal transfers are less onerous in Canada than in Australia.[2] Australian states thus enjoy little fiscal autonomy from the Commonwealth, while the Canadian provinces can determine an impressive proportion of their own fiscal destinies: "The capacity of the Canadian provinces to pay for their expenditure responsibilities from their own revenue sources is greater than that of their counterparts in most other federal systems" (Bakvis, Baier, and Brown 2009, 140). How can we account for these dramatic differences?

The first explanation would ask us to consider the original configuration of the fiscal architectures. If Australian states saw their taxing authority circumscribed while Canadian provinces enjoyed expansive fiscal independence, the current conditions would be neither unexpected nor interesting. An examination of the initial constitutional accords, however, demonstrates that states and provinces in both federations had access to similar taxation authority. It thus seems that "knowledge of the formal legal framework for the assignment of fiscal power does not appear to be a useful basis for predicting the actual, contemporary assignment of either tax or expenditure responsibilities" (Winer 2002, 96).

We could also consider the societal attributes of the two federations. Jan Erk (2008), for example, has argued that over time federations gradually evolve so that they come to be congruent with the underlying sociolinguistic structure of a federal polity. Those with territorially based linguistic heterogeneity tend to decentralize, while linguistically homogeneous ones centralize. When we use this analysis, Australia's centralized taxation arrangements have thus emerged, owing to its relatively homogeneous population and mono-national identity, while Canada's tax architecture has gradually transformed to become more congruent with its bilingual and multinational polity.

Probing into Canada's history, however, we uncover facts that lead us to nuance this narrative. Some of the earliest and staunchest defenders of provincial rights came from the anglophone provinces and certain premiers were later fierce defenders of provincial autonomy (Russell 2010, 26). While Quebec was undeniably the most stalwart opponent of federal incursions, it consistently had a number of important allies in other provinces. The history of federalism in Canada thus cannot be reduced to a simple fight between a federal government and nine predominantly anglophone provinces promoting greater centralization and a Quebec government impeding such development (Simeon and Robinson 1990). Moreover, whereas Erk argues that federations gradually evolve over time to become congruent with their underlying sociolinguistic structure, Canada has gone through alternate periods of centralization and decentralization. Consequently, while the enduring features of the polity can exert particular pressures for centralization and decentralization, these features alone cannot account for undulating or changing patterns in the allocation of powers in a federation.

Finally, with regard to the role of political actors, differences in the evolutionary trajectories could be the result of court decisions. A common argument in Canada is that the Judicial Committee of the Privy Council contributed to the decentralization of Canada's federal union (Scott 1937, 1951; Tuck 1941), while in Australia, analysts pin centralization on the High Court of Australia (Saywell 2002). Certain scholars have nevertheless challenged the emphasis on courts. Alan Cairns, for one, argued: "it is impossible to believe that a few elderly men in London deciding two or three constitutional cases a year precipitated, sustained and caused the development of Canada in a federalist direction that the country would not otherwise have taken" (1971, 319). It seems that, while the courts have undoubtedly played a role, there are two important limits to this interpretation.

First, as argued by Patrick Monahan, "it is *always* possible to do indirectly what you cannot do directly" (quoted in Baier 2006, 162). Court decisions do not preclude the emergence of political bargains and adjustments. The 1984 decision of the Supreme Court of Canada that offshore oil was a federal responsibility, for example, did not prevent the Conservative Mulroney government and the province of Newfoundland from negotiating an agreement that granted control to the province over this resource. Second, such a perspective depicts courts as isolated from debates in the political sphere, including the discourse advanced by political parties, when they are in fact not immune from such pressures. Reflecting on the Australian case, Gerald Baier opines: "the High Court's balanced centralism was always a pressure release for the more overt centralism coming from the political process, *particularly during the periods of Labor Party Rule*" (2006, 53; emphasis ours). Consequently, court rulings are not the lone explanatory variable.

Given that initial constitutions, societal attributes, and a specific institutional actor individually cannot explain the divergent evolutions, how then can we account for the contrasting patterns in these two federations? *Without denying the importance of many of these factors, we suggest that a missing piece in contemporary work is the political parties and the party system that are at work within a federation.* Drawing on the work of an older generation of federal scholars, in the subsequent section we outline the ways in which political parties and the party system can influence the distribution of powers in a federation and help us account for patterns of the centralization and decentralization of power and authority among the orders of government over time.

Party Systems and the Evolution of Federations

In the study of federalism there is a long tradition of focusing on political parties as an agent of centralization or decentralization. In the Canadian context, James Mallory argued more than half-century ago that "change in the party machine [was] one of the most important causes of the shift in the centre of power in the federal system away from the Dominion and towards increasing provincial autonomy" (1954, 43).

Mallory's work anticipated William Riker's contribution to the study of federalism. For Riker, "the proximate cause of variants in the degree of centralization (or decentralization) in the constitutional structure of a federation is the variation in degree of party centralization" (1964, 129). He believed that if the same, organizationally connected parties existed at both the national and the state levels, where officials at the central level might have a role to play in the selection of subordinate leaders, such a party system would undermine the independent action of the constituent members, contributing over time to greater centralization. Riker's approach is nevertheless ill suited to explain Australia. In Australia, the degree of centralization of the federal system – including the fiscal architecture – is much greater than the degree of centralization of the party system, where national and state parties are organizationally independent (Sharman 1994). Consequently, while the structure of party systems plays a role, we need to add a further ingredient to understand the impact of political parties.

The complementary approach we advance here considers the ideologies of political parties represented in a country's party system and builds on an important body of literature that has found a strong correlation between the presence and strength of left parties and high levels of state intervention.[3] The power resource school in welfare studies, for example, has found systematic and statistical evidence that confirms the importance of labour movements and left-wing parties in building "generous, universalistic, and redistributive welfare states" (Huber and Stephens 2001, 10). Left-wing political parties, however, not only promoted greater public spending for most of the twentieth century, but also privileged a greater degree of political centralization.[4] In a study of the British Labour Party's stand on local governments, W.A. Robson presented the case for why socialists came to favour centralization: "One reason is probably an extreme emphasis on equality: if socialists regard the provision of more or better services in one area than another as indefensible anomalies ... they have ceased to believe in local government as regards these services" (1953, 52).

Moreover, many socialist thinkers and socialist parties viewed centralization as desirable because they regarded decentralized authority as incapable of meeting the challenges of the twentieth century. This was certainly the view of the British Labour politician and political historian, Harold Laski, who influenced a generation of left thinkers. According to Laski (1939), both Keynesian economic management as well as the construction of the welfare state required centralized forms of governance because the fragmentation of authority with federalism created weak and ineffective governments at both the national and the sub-state level.

Theoretically, the impact of left-wing parties favouring centralization can be felt in two ways. First, if elected to govern, such parties can use the opportunity to pass major reforms that can become a lasting legacy in federations. Second, even when out of office, left-wing parties can influence the discourse and ideological currents that flow throughout the party system by elevating the salience of socialist ideas and, perhaps, encouraging other parties to adopt them. This insight draws from the consequences of party competition associated with the work of Anthony Downs (1957). By assuming that voters would support the party closest to their ideal point, Downs located a median voter and predicted that the parties would converge to that voter's ideal until there were just enough differences between the two parties that the voter would not be indifferent between the two. In their analysis of welfare state regimes, Huber and Stephens, for example found that "competition between left and centrist parties pushes centrist parties to adopt more generous welfare state legislation" (2001, 20). As such, dedicated left-wing political parties can exert influence even when out of office.

Australia and Canada present interesting cases to test the impact of the presence of left parties on the degree of centralization in a federation and the evolution of the balance of taxation authority between the two orders of government. Since the late nineteenth century, the Australian Labor Party (ALP) has been one of the two dominant parties that claimed power both nationally and at the state level. In return, the growing strength of the ALP led parties of the right either to join forces (leading to the creation of the Liberal Party) or to form coalitions against Labor (the Liberal-Country Party coalition, in which the Liberal Party represented urban liberal and conservative voters, and the Country Party represented conservative rural voters).

The ALP had the dual purposes of nation-building and economic justice, articulated during the 1905 convention.

a) The cultivation of an Australian sentiment based upon the maintenance of racial purity and the development in Australia of an enlightened and self-reliant community.
b) The securing of the full results of their industry to all producers by the collective ownerships of the monopolies and the extension of the industrial and economic function of the state and the municipality.[5]

The growing national and social discourse of the ALP helped radicalize the Commonwealth legislature. As argued by Norris, a more radical-ized legislature "put conservatism on the defensive, made progressive social measures – emanating from whatever source – more likely, and increased the prospects of success" (1978, 273). It would be a mistake to see the Liberal Party's support for centralization as only a reaction to the rise of the ALP. While the Liberal Party rejected the abolition of the federal system proposed by the ALP, it nevertheless continued to favour centralization of the federal system, owing to the popularity for most of the twentieth century of "socially liberal" ideas.

In contrast to Australia, Canada did not have a strong left or social-ist party at the outset. Instead, Canada's party system tended to fo-cus on the needs of the business class (Porter 1965). What is more, the different regional economic interests and the linguistic and religious heterogeneous character of its population made it necessary for the Liberal and Conservative parties to balance a number of interests, en-gaging in what has come to be known in Canada as brokerage politics (Brodie and Jenson 1988). Unlike the ALP, these parties were not char-acterized by their commitment to any specific ideology, which meant that the party system was not "locked into" the same pattern of in-terest aggregation, generating markedly different party systems over time (Haddow 2008, 232; Patten 2007; Carty, Cross, and Young 2000). Furthermore, the parties' need to engage in coalition building to ac-commodate individuals on both sides of the social divide "minimized the differences between the parties rather than polarizing them on big issues" (Carty, Cross, and Young 2000, 15). While social-democratic parties, including the Cooperative Commonwealth Federation (CCF) in the 1930s and its successor, the New Democratic Party (NDP) in the 1960s, eventually emerged, their fortunes varied over time. As dem-onstrated in the next section, whereas in Australia the presence of a strong left contributed to centralization, alterations in Canada's party system contributed to oscillations between centralization and decen-tralization in the allocation of taxation authority between the federal and provincial governments.

Party Systems and Taxation Authority in Australia and Canada

Australia

When the Australian federation was created, the states retained control of land and income taxes, whereas the Commonwealth gained control over customs and excise taxes. However, this allocation of taxation authority created a major fiscal imbalance, since most resources came from customs and excise duties. To resolve this situation, the Commonwealth adopted the Braddon Clause. Under its terms, for the first 10 years after federation, the federal government kept one-quarter of customs and excise revenues and distributed the remainder to the states; in addition, states received any surpluses that the Commonwealth government received that went beyond its expenditures (Reinhart and Steel 2006, 6). Within a few years, however, it became quickly apparent that this fiscal arrangement would cede greater control to the Commonwealth at the expense of state fiscal autonomy.

Measures adopted to increase the fiscal capacity of the Commonwealth were defended on the grounds of a "national agenda." As articulated by the burgeoning ALP, these measures included old-age pension, maternity allowance, and workers' compensation. Indeed, the Commonwealth's taxation policy cannot be dissociated from the ambitious agenda pursued by the ALP in the early years of the federation. These expenditures by the national government, however, translated into lower revenues for the states, since they decreased Commonwealth surpluses and thus also decreased transfers to the states, further weakening sub-state fiscal autonomy. Moreover, in light of the popularity of a proposed national pension plan by the ALP,[6] the Commonwealth legislature adopted the Surplus Revenue Act in 1908, largely to finance the plan adopted later that year following the election of the first ALP minority government. Rather than automatically transferring surplus funds to the states, the act provided for these revenues to be consolidated into the Commonwealth Trust Funds and controlled by federal decision-makers (Hancock and Smith 2001, 24). The first ALP majority government, elected in 1910, continued to increase social spending on pensions and maternity allowances while increasing taxation revenues through the Commonwealth land tax. Firmly on a centralizing trajectory, some members of the ALP, including the party leader Andrew Fisher, went even further, calling for the transfer of complete legislative authority to the national parliament with or without the abolition of state legislatures (McMullin 1991, 79–80).

Following the expiration of the Braddon clause, over the next 30 years the Commonwealth adopted different measures to ensure that states would have adequate revenues. These measures, which ranged from per capita transfers to fixed payments, proved insufficient and states were forced to levy income taxes. Owing to the fact that the Commonwealth had been occupying that tax field since 1915, this taxation imperative created significant resentment from poorer states, such as Tasmania, Western Australia, and Queensland, that had less revenue-raising capacity and had to tax their citizens at higher rates than their wealthier counterparts (Hancock and Smith 2001, 27). To ameliorate this inequality, during the 1920s and 1930s considerable efforts were made to harmonize Commonwealth and state taxation. In general, the smaller states came to support centralized taxation, as they would benefit, while the larger ones registered some unease with the plan (ibid., 28). Nevertheless, any reticence was overcome as centralized income taxation was also supported by a large section of the ALP, which increasingly perceived territorial disparities as contributing to inequality and inefficiency (McMullin 1991, 220).

World War II provided an impetus to centralize control over tax instruments. In 1942, the Labor-led government gave the Commonwealth an effective monopoly over income taxation when it passed the Income Tax Act and the States Grants (Income Tax Reimbursement) Act. Under the terms of the legislation, the first act levied uniform income taxes across the country, while the second act called for the Commonwealth to reimburse the states an equivalent amount on the condition that they permanently vacate the tax space. While a state could continue to impose its income tax, it would pay a double price, having to impose an increased burden on its citizens and losing federal government grants (Reinhart and Steel 2006, 8).

Although some states challenged centralization, members of the ALP at the state level nevertheless impeded the battle against the Commonwealth by successfully blocking any sustained opposition. "ALP advocates of state rights had a hard time when unificationist tendencies were entrenched not only in many Labor minds but in the party platform as well" (McMullin 1991, 220). To demonstrate, during the 1942 party conference, the members of the New South Wales Labor Party rejected Premier William McKell's proposal to contest the tax scheme in the courts.

After World War II, the Labor government decided to maintain control over income tax. For Prime Minister Ben Chifley, central control over progressive taxation was akin to redistribution from wealthier states to poorer states (quoted in Hancock and Smith 2001, 35). It must be stressed that there was an all-party consensus on the maintenance of Commonwealth control over taxation. As argued by McClean, "in the bipartisan welfarist climate of the 1950s and 1960s nobody except the

State governments opposed the income tax power staying at Commonwealth level" (2004, 24). States twice challenged the constitutionality of the act, but in both cases the High Court found that the legislation was legitimate, as it was deemed to be non-compelling, since states could essentially opt out. The High Court argued that control over taxation was a political question. According to Chief Justice Latham: "The determination of the propriety of any such policy must rest with the Commonwealth and parliament and ultimately with the people. The remedy for alleged abuse of power ... is to be found in the political arena and not in the courts" (quoted in Baier 2006, 52).

Key to the political maintenance of Commonwealth control over income tax was that it was used to finance new popular social programs. In 1943, using revenues from the uniform income tax and a payroll tax, the Labor government had created the National Welfare Fund. It substantially increased taxation rates, especially for low-income earners, to develop a national system of income security that included unemployment benefits, widow's pensions, and child endowment, funded at the expense of revenues for the states (Hancock and Smith 2001, 35). As argued by Francis Castles, while war provided the impetus for the centralization of income taxes, "it was popular sentiment favouring welfare reform that underpinned these changes and made them, effectively, irreversible" (2005, 76). It was also made possible by an egalitarian philosophy, promoted by the Labor Party, which valued uniformity above diversity (Commonwealth Grants Commission 2008, 82). Indeed, the ALP discourse had profound consequences for public opinion. A 1941 poll found that 60% of Australians believed that states should be abolished, while only 22% favoured their retention (McMullin 1991, 229). Such public sentiments thus revealed a favourable climate for greater centralization.

This is not to say that no proposals were subsequently put forward to diminish the level of centralization in the Australian federation. One opportunity for change arose during the 1975 Commonwealth election campaign, when the Liberal-National Party (L-NP) coalition advocated a rebalancing of revenue-raising responsibilities, arguing against what they referred to as "centralist authority control ... [and] undue concentration of power" (Mathews and Grewal 1995, 14). The party's platform further specified that under an L-NP coalition government, the states would be given a specified share of personal income tax revenues to increase their budgetary flexibility and autonomy, inculcating degrees of fiscal decentralization into the Australian federation.

Upon gaining office, the new conservative government introduced legislation that allowed the states either to impose a surcharge on a given percentage of personal income tax or to grant a rebate, thus tentatively affording the states greater fiscal independence from the Commonwealth government. In practice, however, this initiative failed to induce any meaningful decentralization, as none of the states took advantage of the opportunity. The reason for this failure was straightforward: "the Commonwealth did not make tax room available by reducing its own tax rate" (Mathews and Grewal 1995, 17). It seemed that once the Commonwealth had occupied the tax room and laid claim to the fiscal resources, even the conservative coalition lacked the necessary willpower to voluntarily diminish their fiscal clout. As a result, the Australian federation has come to be characterized by a considerable vertical fiscal imbalance: "a highly centralised revenue-raising system enabling the Commonwealth Government to raise nearly 80 per cent of the national tax revenue, and a fairly decentralised system of public outlays which are shared almost equally between the Commonwealth and the States" (Grewal 1995, 5)

Ultimately, two important reforms have been adopted in areas other than income tax to address the significant vertical fiscal imbalance in Australia. In 1971, payroll taxes were transferred to the states, and in 2000, a number of state taxes were abolished or phased out and replaced by a goods and service tax collected by the Commonwealth but subsequently transferred to the states. None of those measures, however, has significantly challenged the centralization of taxation in Australia (ibid.; de Mello 2000; OECD 2008).

Now that we have detailed this trajectory of centralization in Australia, we examine the dynamics of the evolution of the Canadian federation.

Canada

During the early years of the Canadian federation, it was the provinces, not the federal government, whose fiscal prowess increased (Winer 2002). Provincial expenditures between 1896 and 1913 ballooned, as provinces accessed lucrative revenue sources to cover their rising costs. Many provinces began to levy direct taxes to cover expenditures: personal income taxes, real and personal property taxes, corporate taxes, and succession duties. Put together, these activities strengthened the independent fiscal capacity of the provinces by generating 26% of total

provincial revenues. But the value of these tax sources varied regionally, constituting only 9% of provincial revenues in the Prairies and 8%
in the Maritimes, but more than double that percentage in Ontario and
Quebec (Smiley 1963, 106).

Somewhat counterbalancing the decentralizing momentum, during
World War I the federal government started levying taxes on personal
incomes and corporate profits. Financing the war thus provided the
immediate stimulus for centralization. Centralization was also buoyed
by emergent nationalistic sentiments in English Canada. The Conservative Party, led by Prime Minister Sir Robert Borden, indicated that personal and corporate income taxes were temporary measures to increase
federal coffers. Following the war, however, regional and other salient
cleavages reappeared with a vengeance, hindering the emergence of
a clear consensus on a common taxation policy (Mallory 1954, 42). So,
under the leadership of the Liberal Party, Ottawa began to scale back its
rate of taxation, freeing up some space for the provinces to reclaim. This
federal withdrawal marked the first instance of the pattern of centralization followed by decentralization in the Canadian fiscal architecture.
How can we account for this oscillation of taxation authority during
these initial decades of the Canadian federation?

Dynamics in the prevailing party system played a key role in these
policy decisions. Whereas Australia already had a strong left-wing tradition operating at both state and Commonwealth levels, such parties
had not materialized in Canada. Instead, political contests played out
largely between the Conservative and Liberal parties, which shared
many ideological predilections and eschewed policies that reflected
socially inspired ideas. During the opening years of the Canadian federation, in lieu of direct state provision, for example, capitalists carried out much of Canada's infrastructure development, where even
Canada's railway was not built by the state: "the half-hearted policy
of building it piecemeal as a public work was discarded and in 1880
a group of capitalists agreed to undertake an all-Canadian railway to
the Pacific as a private enterprise" (Smiley 1963, 68). This propensity to
turn to the private sector reflected the prevailing ideological currents
shared between the two dominant parties. Where the ALP pursued
policies that made Australia a welfare pioneer, the Liberals pursued
a "negative policy, avoiding new obligations and striving to cut down
existing ones" (ibid., 146), further confirming the absence of an influential left-wing voice in the Canadian party system prior to World
War I.

While the Conservatives and Liberals demonstrated common ideological predilections, one key point of difference between the two parties revolved around the preferred balance of powers in the federation. During this first party system, the more right-leaning Conservatives favoured a strong central government, while the Liberals advocated for provincial rights (Dawson 1948, 506). Hence, it was the Conservative prime minister, Sir Robert Borden, who instituted federal income taxes during World War I, entering into the arena of direct taxation and somewhat centralizing the fiscal architecture, while the Liberal government voluntarily reduced its rates after the war was over, ushering in a decentralizing dynamic.

Circumstances nevertheless changed in the 1940s, when Canada embarked on a more determined pathway towards fiscal centralization. Once again, the onset of a war acted as a critical juncture when in World War II the federal government assumed a dominant position in taxation (Winer 2002, 100). The need to finance the war created a window of opportunity for federal politicians to encourage the provinces to give up their personal and corporate income tax systems in exchange for tax rental payments. Although war was the immediate trigger, federal ascendancy was reflective of changing material and ideological factors, which stretched back to the 1920s.

From the federal perspective, the percentage of Dominion revenues from indirect taxes fell drastically through the first half of the twentieth century. From the provincial perspective, between 1920 and 1940 a sizable imbalance emerged between provinces' expenditures and their capacity to cover costs. This problem was particularly acute in the smaller, poorer provinces, especially in eastern Canada, which could not provide their citizens with services of a comparable quality to those in other parts of the country. The Great Depression, moreover, had "revealed Canada's vulnerability to adverse economic circumstances" (Smiley 1975, 45) and further legitimized the idea of centralizing the fiscal architecture of the country.

Changing conditions in the party system also encouraged centralization. Federally, leaders of the Liberal Party had begun to integrate new ideas on state action. "Mackenzie King's views," wrote Joseph Wearing, "reflected the new positive liberalism of T.H. Greene and L.T. Hobhouse in seeing the necessity for state intervention as a means of enhancing the individual liberty of society's weakest members" (1997, 180). However, as many observers of the Liberal Party have argued, "these steps to the left [were] taken more with a spirit of opportunism than from a basic orientation to social progress and change" (Porter 1965, 373; see also Wearing 1997). What pushed the Liberal Party, a party that had long been the defender of provincial interests, to pursue left-wing policies that subsequently required an increase in the fiscal powers of the federal government?

By the 1940s, the "political left was finding its feet" (Banting 2005, 101), when populist and progressive parties had emerged on provincial stages and broke into the national arena. While these parties did not coalesce either politically or intellectually, they challenged the prevailing approaches to "federalism, capitalism, the financial institutions, and the monetary system" (Bradford 1998, 28). The CCF's party literature, for example, included calls for increased expenditures on education, public ownership of utilities, collective bargaining for workers, old-age pensions, and socialized health services (Lipset 1968, chap. 7). These types of initiative require concerted central government action supported through regular and stable financing. As such, parties like the CCF "became an instrument of social change and a progressive force not only in the one province but in the country as a whole where it became a pacesetter in reform legislation" (Porter 1965, 368). During the latter stages of World War II, polls showing a stunning surge in support for the CCF inspired Prime Minister Mackenzie King to move leftward (Young 1997, 223). As Banting writes: "The long-term Liberal Prime Minister, Mackenzie King, was haunted by the prospect of a British-style polarization between left and right, squeezing out the centrist liberal party. At moments of left strength, the Liberals therefore refashioned themselves as a party of social reform" (2005, 102). It therefore seems that while the CCF lacked the necessary pragmatism to cope with the variety of attitudes and interests flowing throughout the Canadian population and to secure a majority in the House of Commons (Young 1997, 221; Banting 2005), the party and its ideals managed to shift the Liberals' platform and encourage centralization in the Canadian federation.

This post-war period marked the pinnacle of fiscal centralization in Canada when, in 1955, Ottawa levied approximately 70% of all taxes (Bakvis, Baier, and Brown 2009, 142). With its newfound fiscal clout, Ottawa began to fashion the scaffolding of what became the Canadian welfare state (Banting 1987). The reaction of the premiers to this pattern of centralization, however, "was mixed, reflecting the varying economic interests of the provinces, different views about the nature of the federation, and partisan party political considerations" (Lazar 2010, 115). The smaller, economically weaker Anglophone provinces tended to welcome centralization, whereas the larger, economically stronger provinces, in tandem with Quebec, often opposed Ottawa's interventions.

The case of Quebec is particularly salient here. When headed by the Godbout government, which was institutionally connected to the federal Liberals, Quebec had agreed to temporarily transfer taxation authority to Ottawa, thus permitting centralization to occur. When led by Duplessis's Union Nationale, which was not dependent on any federal party, Quebec's acquiescence to centralization towards Ottawa disappeared and the province decided to re-institute its own income tax scheme. Perhaps inspired by Quebec's innovativeness, Ontario later pressed for a new deal in the tax rental agreements, demanding 50% of all the major tax sources and subsequently reintroducing their own corporate tax system in 1957 (Winer 2002, 100). Put together, this contributed to an agenda for decentralization in the Canadian federation.

Centralized fiscal relations nevertheless failed to endure, and shifts in the party system once again played a role. Federally, the centrist-leaning Liberals lost control of the House of Commons in 1957, when the Progressive Conservative government of John Diefenbaker took office. Canadian politics also shifted to the right as the CCF saw their support fall to a single Saskatchewan seat. The new prime minister from western Canada had campaigned on an explicitly decentralist platform: "We believe there can be no national unity in this nation until there is a realization that Federal-Provincial matters have handcuffed the provinces of this nation." Particularly sensitive to the interests of the western provinces, Diefenbaker further opined: "We believe that the Federal system is today being challenged by the centralization complex of the St. Laurent Government, and that a healthy division and balance of revenues, as between the Federal and Provincial Governments, must be assured" (1957, n.p).

Prime Minister Diefenbaker thus ushered in a renewed discourse of decentralization. After operating for 20 years, the tax rental system was dramatically altered when the Progressive Conservatives introduced a new regime whereby the federal government instituted tax abatements and block grants. Instead of collecting 100% of the standard taxes, the federal government left room for the provinces to begin collecting their own taxes. Under the new regime, moreover, provinces could either collect these taxes themselves or have the federal government shoulder the administrative costs.[7] The tide of centralization had thus somewhat abated in favour of provincial autonomy, reflecting the shifts in the party system. This tide, however, was not to last.

The undulating pattern of centralization and decentralization persisted through the 1960s and 1970s, propelled by the shifting electoral fortunes of left-wing parties and the salience of certain economic ideas – particularly Keynesian – on the federal parties. In an effort to distinguish itself from Diefenbaker's Conservatives, the Liberal Party initially chose to become the "more aggressive champion of social policy expansion" (Simeon and Robinson 1990, 162). The Liberal Party as champion of the left proved temporary, however, and the 1970s acted as a watershed in Canada's fiscal architecture. The Trudeau Liberals lowered the federal government's rates of personal and corporate taxes in order to make room for higher provincial rates. The April 1977 Established Programs Financing Act reduced federal personal income taxes by nine points. Subsequently, the "proportion of provincial expenditures financed by own-source revenues has been gradually increasing … because provinces have been occupying more and more of the tax room" (Boadway 2007, 111). What factors encouraged the Liberal Party to move away from increasing the power of the national government in the 1970s?

In economic terms, economic stagnation and rising deficits had forced the federal government to scale back its fiscal support of the welfare state, thus transferring the burden to the provinces (Brown 2008). Political events also intervened to shift Canada towards decentralization. In the early 1970s, the minority Liberals had to rely on the support of the NDP to continue governing. When the Liberals first announced their intention to reduce corporate tax rates to stimulate the economy, the NDP voted against the budget, triggering the 1974 election (Simeon and Robinson 1990). Following the election, the New Democratic Party's share of seats in the House of Commons dropped from 31 to 16. Returned to office with a majority and a mandate to reduce corporate taxes, the Liberals "were freed from the need to maintain NDP support for their policies" (ibid., 219). Furthermore, the rise and salience of the nationalist movement in Quebec was a determined force against federal centralization throughout the 1980s and 1990s. The Parti Québécois, the party supporting Quebec independence and centralization of power in the government of Quebec, was in office between 1976 and 1985 and again between 1994 and 2003. It strongly opposed any greater intervention.[8] Furthermore, under the leadership of Robert Bourassa, the Quebec Liberal Party (ostensibly federalist), which was in power between 1985 and 1994, also adopted a nationalist position to grant Quebec more power in the Canadian federation.

Yet Quebec was not the only obstacle to greater centralization during that period. In the late 1970s, further conflict regarding energy policy generated tough bargaining with the western provinces and subsequently encouraged the Liberals to consider decentralizing strategies. The creation of the Reform Party in the late 1980s, moreover, ushered in a new political discourse inspired by neoliberalism and the reduction of state intervention, delegitimizing the idea of government programs pulling the other parties towards the right: "The Reform party's major achievement is arguably to have pulled political discourse and policy debate substantially to the right over the past decade" (Laycock 2002, 140). Put together, these factors and forces spawned a dramatic realignment in the Canadian party system that continues to privilege decentralization in the federation.

Conclusion

Why did Australia, initially designed as a decentralized federation, evolve incrementally into a centralized federation, while Canada, structured as a centralized federation, transformed unevenly over time into a decentralized federation? More specifically, why do Canadian provinces have access to a far wider array of taxation authorities compared with their Australian counterparts? Conventional accounts would have us consider the original allocation of authority, characteristics of the polity (mono-national/lingual or multinational/lingual), or decisions of the courts. We have argued that, individually, none of these explanations sufficiently accounts for the interesting and unexpected patterns of evolution in these two federations.

We have argued instead that, in order to explain the unique and diverging patterns of federal evolution in taxation authority, differences in the strength of the left party for most of the history of both federations must also be taken into consideration. While the ALP was and still is one of Australia's most powerful parties, Canada experienced only intermittent periods of influential left-wing parties at the national and provincial levels. Given that left-wing parties have tended to favour centralization over decentralization for most of the twentieth century, the greater presence of the left in Australia was a key factor in explaining the gradual process of centralization, while the fluctuating strength of the left in Canada helps us understand why the country has gone through both periods of centralization and periods of decentralization.

As Riker argued, party systems are essentially intervening variables "between background social conditions and the specific nature of the federal bargain" (1964, 136). But this chapter opens the door to another interesting question: why were left-wing parties more successful in Australia than in Canada, fashioning a markedly different ideological spectrum for the party system? While it was not our objective to outline the variables that explain the rise of a strong left political party in Australia in comparison with Canada, a number of factors can be outlined. First, as argued almost 50 years ago by John Porter (1965), in Canada the linguistic division of the country and its focus on issues of national unity has constituted an impediment to the organization of Canadian politics along a left and right axis; conversely, we could hypothesize that the homogeneity of the Australian polity created a more hospitable climate for the discourse of collective, universal solidarity promoted by the left to take hold.[9] Second, another important factor is the differences in the political economies of the two countries, another variable that has been neglected recently in the study of federalism. Australia's system of industrial relations and economic development contributed to the growth of one of the world's most powerful union movement in the late nineteenth century, while Canada's regionally truncated economy and American-influenced model of industrial relations impeded the development of a strong union movement that was the basis in almost all western countries for the development of strong national labour or socialist parties. In this chapter we have focused on the role of specific political actors, but more attention needs to be paid to such political economy variables. We need to heed the advice of Richard Simeon:

> To fully explain change we are driven to revive our interest in societal forces and in political economy. It is these forces – domestic and international – which provide much of the energy and raw material which elites mobilize. It is impossible to understand major shifts in the federal system without exploring such factors as global economic forces as they interact with the regionally differentiated domestic economy and territorially defined institutions ... Nor can we understand federalism without looking at changes in the domestic society and economy. (1989, 418–19)

While we hope to have contributed to a better understanding of the evolution of two federal states, the challenge of developing theoretical models that can incorporate structural factors and agency is ongoing.

NOTES

1 There is, however, a growing literature on the impact of federalism on party systems and party politics. For some recent examples see Thorlakson (2009) and Detterbeck (2011).
2 For an extensive comparative discussion of conditionality in Canadian and Australian transfers see Watts (2008).
3 On the left's impact on social policy-making, see Esping-Andersen (1990). On the impact of the left on economic policy-making, see Boix (1998).
4 This stands in contrast to the position of late twentieth-century left-libertarian parties that have been more open to decentralization and devolution. For more on this transformation see Kitschelt (1988).
5 Quoted in Farell (1985, 127).
6 The prospect of a national old-age pension plan had been an important element of support for the creation of a federal union (Hancock and Smith 2001, 23).
7 Although the focus here is on taxation, it should also be mentioned that the government of Canada introduced equalization payments at this time. These unconditional payments can also be understood as a decentralizing fiscal measure.
8 Left-wing politics in Quebec has pushed for increased sovereignty, thus pushing decentralization from Ottawa. However, if we look within that province, the PQ has established a highly interventionist and centralized regime to govern Quebec, confirming that left-wing parties can drive centralization towards the level of government that is accepted as the legitimate "national" authority. It should also be noted that, before being a left-wing party, the Parti Québécois was a coalition of nationalists, which explains why many of its members were and still are more on the right of the political spectrum
9 It must be stressed, though, that linguistic division did not constitute a similar impediment in other multilingual countries, such as Belgium and Switzerland, where strong socialist parties emerged.

REFERENCES

Baier, Gerald. 2006. *Courts and Federalism: Judicial Doctrine in the United States, Australia, and Canada*. Vancouver: UBC Press.
Bakvis, Herman, Gerald Baier, and Douglas Brown. 2009. *Contested Federalism: Certainty and Ambiguity in the Canadian Federation*. Don Mills: Oxford University Press.

Banting, Keith. 1987. *The Welfare State and Canadian Federalism*. 2nd ed. Kingston and Montreal: McGill-Queen's University Press.

Banting, Keith. 2005. Canada: Nation-Building in a Federal Welfare State. In *Federalism and the Welfare State: New World and European Experiences*, edited by Herbert Obinger, Stephan Leibfried, and Francis G. Castles. Cambridge: Cambridge University Press.

Boadway, Robin. 2007. Canada. In *The Practice of Fiscal Federalism: Comparative Perspectives*, edited by Anwar Shah. Montreal and Kingston: McGill-Queen's University Press.

Boadway, Robin, and Anwar Shah. 2009. *Fiscal Federalism: Principles and Practice of Multiorder Governance*. Cambridge: Cambridge University Press.

Boix, Charles. 1998. *Political Parties, Growth and Equality*. New York: Cambridge University Press.

Bradford, Neil. 1998. *Commissioning Ideas: Canadian National Policy Innovation in Comparative Perspective*. Toronto: Oxford University Press.

Brodie, Janine, and Jane Jenson. 1988. *Crisis, Challenge and Change: Parties and Class in Canada Revisited*. Rev. ed. Ottawa: Carleton University Press.

Broschek, Jörg. 2010. Federalism and Political Change: Canada and Germany in Historical-Institutionalist Perspective. *Canadian Journal of Political Science* 43(1):1–24.

Broschek, Jörg. 2011. Conceptualizing and Theorizing Constitutional Change in Federal Systems: Insights from Historical Institutionalism. *Regional and Federal Studies* 21(4):539–59.

Brown, Douglas M. 2008. Fiscal Federalism: Searching for Balance. In *Canadian Federalism: Performance, Effectiveness, and Legitimacy*, edited by Herman Bakvis and Grace Skogstad. Don Mills: Oxford University Press.

Cairns, Alan. 1971. The Judicial Committee and Its Critics. *Canadian Journal of Political Science* 4(3):301–45.

Carty, R. Kenneth, William Cross, and Lisa Young. 2000. *Rebuilding Canadian Party Politics*. Vancouver: UBC Press.

Castles, Francis G. 1996. Needs-Based Strategies of Social Protection in Australia and New Zealand. In *Welfare States in Transition: National Adaptations in Global Economies*, edited by Gosta Esping-Andersen. London: Sage.

Castles, Francis G. 2005. *Federalism and the Welfare State*. Cambridge: Cambridge University Press.

Chandler, William. 1987. Federalism and Political Parties. In *Federalism and the Role of the State*, edited by Herman Bakvis and William M. Chandler. Toronto: University of Toronto Press.

Commonwealth Grants Commission. 2008. *The Commonwealth Grants Commission: The Last 25 Years*. Online publication. Accessed 24 April 2012. Available

at https://cgc.gov.au/attachments/article/147/75_Anniversary_Report_
Website.pdf

Dawson, R.M. 1948. *The Government of Canada*. Toronto: University of Toronto
Press.

de Mello, Luiz, Jr. 2000. Fiscal Decentralization and Intergovernmental Fiscal
Relations: A Cross-Country Analysis. *World Development* 28(2):365–80.

Detterbeck, Klaus. 2011. Party Careers in Federal Systems. Vertical Linkages
within Australian, German, Canadian and Austrian Parties. *Regional and
Federal Studies* 21(2):245–70.

Diefenbaker, John. 1957. Major Campaign Speech Number 1. Massey Hall,
Toronto, 25 April 1957. Accessed 18 April 2012. Available at http://www
.usask.ca/diefenbaker/galleries/virtual_exhibit/federal_elections_
1957–1958/campaign_speech_1957.php

Downs, Anthony. 1957. *An Economic Theory of Democracy*. New York:
Harper.

Erk, Jan. 2008. *Explaining Federalism: State, Society and Congruence in Austria,
Belgium, Canada, Germany and Switzerland*. London: Routledge.

Esping-Andersen, Gosta. 1990. *The Three Worlds of Welfare Capitalism*. Cambridge: Polity.

Farell, Frank. 1985. Socialism, Internationalism, and the Australian Labour
Movement. *Labour/Le Travail* 15(Spring):125–44.

Grewal, Bhajan. 1995. Vertical Fiscal Imbalance in Australia: A Problem for Tax
Structure, Not For Revenue Sharing. CSES Working Paper No. 2. March.
Accessed 3 July 2012. Available at http://vuir.vu.edu.au/68/1/wp2_1995_
grewal.pdf

Haddow, Rodney. 2008. How Can Comparative Political Economy Explain
Variable Change? Lessons for, and from, Canada. In *The Comparative Turn
in Canadian Political Science*, edited by Linda White et al. Vancouver: UBC
Press.

Hancock, Jim, and Julie Smith. 2001. *Financing the Federation*. Adelaide: South
Australian Centre for Economic Studies.

Hodgins, Bruce, et al. 1989. Dynamic Federalism in Canada and Australia:
Continuity and Change. In *Federalism in Canada and Australia: Historical Perspectives, 1920–40*, edited by Bruce Hodgins et al. Peterborough: Frost Centre
for Canadian Heritage and Development Studies.

Huber, Evelyn, and John D. Stephens. 2001. *Development and Crisis of the Welfare State: Parties and Policies in Global Markets*. Chicago: University of Chicago Press.

Kitschelt, Herbert P. 1988. Left-Libertarian Parties: Explaining Innovation in
Competitive Party Systems. *World Politics* 40(2):194–234.

Laski, Harold. 1939. The Obsolescence of Federalism. *New Republic* 98(3 May): 367–9

Laycock, David. 2002. Making Sense of Reform as a Western Party. In *Regionalism and Party Politics in Canada*, edited by Lisa Young and Keith Archer. Oxford: Oxford University Press.

Lazar, Harvey. 2010. Intergovernmental Fiscal Relations: Workhorse of the Federation. In *The Oxford Handbook of Canadian Politics*, edited by John C. Courtney and David E. Smith. Oxford: Oxford University Press.

Lipset, Seymour Martin. 1968. *Agrarian Socialism: The Cooperative Commonwealth Federation in Saskatchewan. A Study in Political Sociology*. Rev. ed. New York: Anchor Books.

Maier, Peter. 1997. *Party System Change: Approaches and Interpretation*. Oxford: Clarendon Press.

Mallory, J.R. 1954. *Social Credit and the Federal Power in Canada*. Toronto: University of Toronto Press.

Mathews, Russell, and Bhajan Grewal. 1995. *Fiscal Federalism in Australia: From Keating to Whitlam*. CSES Working Paper No. 1. March. Online publication. Available at http://www.cfses.com/documents/wp1cses.pdf

McClean, Iain. 2004. Fiscal Federalism in Australia. *Public Administration* 82(1):21–38.

McMullin, Ross. 1991. *The Light on the Hill: The Australian Labor Party, 1891–1991*. Oxford: Oxford University Press.

Norris, Ronald. 1978. Towards a Federal Union. In *Federalism in Canada and Australia: the Early Years*, edited by Bruce W. Hodgins, Don Wright, and W.H. Heick. Waterloo: Wilfrid Laurier University Press.

Organisation for Economic Cooperation and Development. 2008. *Revenue Statistics, 1965–2007*. Paris: OECD.

Patten, Steve. 2007. The Evolution of the Canadian Party System. In *Canadian Parties in Transition*, edited by Alain-G. Gagnon and A. Brian Tanguay. Peterborough: Broadview Press.

Porter, John. 1965. *The Vertical Mosaic: An Analysis of Social Class and Power in Canada*. Toronto: University of Toronto Press.

Reinhart, Sam, and Lee Steel. 2006. A Brief History of Australia's Tax System. *Treasury Economic Roundup* (Winter). Online publication. Accessed on 24 April. Available at http://archive.treasury.gov.au/documents/1156/PDF/Winter2006.pdf

Riker, William H. 1964. *Federalism: Origin, Operation, Significance*. Boston: Little, Brown.

Robson, W.A. 1953. Labour and Local Government. *Political Quarterly* 24(1):39–55.

Russell, Peter. 2010. Constitution. In *The Oxford Handbook of Canadian Politics*, edited by John C. Courtney and David E. Smith. Oxford: Oxford University Press.

Saywell, John T. 2002. *The Lawmakers: Judicial Power and the Shaping of Canadian Federalism*. Toronto: University of Toronto Press.

Scott, F.R. 1937. The Consequences of the Privy Council Decisions. *Canadian Bar Review* 15(6):485–94.

Scott, F.R. 1951. Centralization and Decentralization in Canadian Federalism. *Canadian Bar Review* 29(10):1095–125.

Sharman, Campbell. 1994. Discipline and Disharmony: Party and the Operation of the Federal System. In *Parties and Federalism in Australia and Canada*, edited by Campbell Sharman. Canberra: Federalism Research Centre, Australian National University.

Simeon, Richard. 1989. We Are All Smiley's People: Some Observations on Donald Smiley and the Study of Federalism. In *Federalism and Political Community: Essays in Honour of Donald Smiley*, edited by David P. Shugarman and Reg Whitaker. Peterborough: Broadview Press.

Simeon, Richard, and Ian Robinson. 1990. *State, Society, and the Development of Canadian Federalism*. Toronto: University of Toronto Press.

Smiley, D.V, ed. 1963. *The Rowell-Sirois Report: An Abridgement of Book 1 of the Royal Commission Report on Dominion-Provincial Relations*. Toronto: McClelland and Stewart.

Smiley, D.V. 1975. Canada and the Quest for a National Policy. *Canadian Journal of Political Science* 8(1):40–62.

Thorlakson, Lori. 2009. Patterns of Party Integration, Influence and Autonomy in Seven Federations. *Party Politics* 15(2):155–77.

Tuck, Raphael. 1941. Canada and the Judicial Committee of the Privy Council. *University of Toronto Law Journal* 4(1):3–75.

Wallner, Jennifer, and Gerard Boychuck. 2014. Comparing Federations: Testing the Model of Market-Preserving Federalism on Canada, Australia and the United States. In *Comparing Canada: Methods and Perspectives on Canadian Politics*, edited by Luc Turgeon, Martin Papillon, Jennifer Wallner, and Stephen White. Vancouver: UBC Press.

Watts, Ronald. 2005. *Autonomy or Dependence: Intergovernmental Financial Relations in Eleven Countries*. Kingston: Institute of Intergovernmental Relations.

Watts, Ronald. 2008. *Comparing Federal Systems*. 3rd ed. Montreal and Kingston: McGill-Queen's University Press.

Wearing, Joseph. 1997. The Liberal Party. In *Canadian Political Party Systems: A Reader*, edited by R.K. Carty. Peterborough: Broadview Press.

Winer, Stanley L. 2002. On the Reassignment of Fiscal Powers in a Federal State. In *Political Economy in Federal States: Selected Essays of Stanley L. Winer*, edited by Stanley L. Winer. Cheltenham: Edward Elgar.

Young, W. 1997. A Party-Movement: The CCF and the Rejection of Brokerage Politics. In *Canadian Political Party Systems: A Reader*, edited by R.K. Carty. Peterborough: Broadview Press.

9 Living with Contradictions in Federalism: Goals and Outcomes of Recent Constitutional and Financial Reforms in the Spanish *Estado autonómico*

CÉSAR COLINO

> ... federalism is not a value in itself. Like any other set of institutions, it must be evaluated in terms of its consequences for other, more fundamental, values and principles.
>
> Simeon (2006a)

Introduction: Tensions and Contradictions in the Goals of Federalism

The three emblematic goals or values that most federal polities usually seek to achieve through their constitutional principles and institutions are equity, accommodation of diversity, and democracy (Simeon 2006a, 2006b, 2010; Simeon and Swinton 1995). These three crucial goals are pursued by federal arrangements and contemporary governance in general, and, as three manifestations of social justice, represent yardsticks by which federal designs should be evaluated.

Equity refers here to distributive justice and is manifested in economic equality and high-quality public services for all citizens. *Accommodation of diversity* occurs through the *recognition and protection* of cultural or ethnic diversity; the empowerment and recognition of minorities and their values; opportunities for sub-national communities to participate in the centre; and policies of asymmetry. *Democracy* or procedural justice manifests itself in high accountability, fair and equal representation in and access to the political process, respect for individual rights, government responsiveness, and transparency of decision-making. All these democratic practices encourage citizen participation (Simeon 2006a). However, as Richard Simeon himself has reminded us, federal arrangements are Janus-faced, in the sense that "under different circumstances and with different designs, [they] can promote or undercut equity, promote or undercut democracy, facilitate or erode harmony in divided societies" (ibid., 19).

In this contribution, I take up Simeon's suggestion that we evaluate federalism and its consequences and accomplishments by how it attains the above goals/values and his recognition that they may be realized to different degrees in different federal systems. I focus not only on the relative realization of these three values in federations, but also on the question of whether they can be achieved simultaneously. I intend not so much to establish whether and how some federal arrangements may have negative or positive consequences for equity, accommodation, and democracy, but how these three values may be incompatible and/or difficult to balance when we try to change or adapt federal institutions. My main questions are the following. Are there tensions or trade-offs among equity, accommodation of diversity, and democracy? How do these tensions or trade-offs specifically feature in plural or so-called multinational federations? How do different federations cope with those tensions? How does the balance across these three values determine the legitimacy and therefore the stability or adjustment path of existing federal arrangements?

To answer these questions, I examine the recent reforms in the constitutional setting and financial arrangements of the Spanish *Estado autonómico*.[1] In providing a new interpretation of the recent round of reforms and the evolution and prospects of the Spanish model of federalism, I add to the more general discussion of the global promise of federalism.

I am not the first, of course, to note possible tensions between specific and coexisting goals of federations and to suggest the apparent triumph of some goals over others. To name just a few examples, Watts (2006) has pointed out how the objective of all federal systems is to balance equity and diversity and the difficulties such balancing implies. Banting (2006) has also shown how the logic of social citizenship in the welfare state seems to be in deep tension with, or has predominated over, the logic of federalism or regional diversity within some federations. Bird and Ebel (2006) have pointed out the inherent conflict between subsidiarity and solidarity, and between local autonomy and national redistribution. More recently, Enderlein (2009) has argued that it is possible to achieve only two of the three main principles or goals of all fiscal federalism systems: fiscal equivalence, power-sharing, and equality of living conditions. One goal tends to be sacrificed. The result is three different "worlds of fiscal federalism" within which countries are bound to stay despite reform attempts.

We also know that the value tensions and contradictory forces present in multinational federations in particular derive from their attempt to make compatible different nation-building projects within one state. Federations use various formal and informal institutional devices and strategies, with varying degrees of success, to try to manage diversity. Some of these strategies attempt to protect and promote diverse social and economic conditions while simultaneously fostering equal social citizenship and cohesion and the unity of the country (Simeon and Conway 2001; Simeon 2008, 2011; McGarry, O'Leary, and Simeon 2008).

Institutions and rules for the territorial distribution of authority, re-quirements for the participation of sub-units in central institutions, the symbolic recognition of some constituent units, and fiscal federalism usually seek to enhance one or all of these goals at once. These three ob-jectives of equity, accommodation of diversity, and high-quality demo-cratic government are also enshrined in constitutions as legal principles. In the Spanish case, for example, the constitution refers to the goal of protecting cultural diversity, the equality of citizens, the principle of solidarity among the regions, social citizenship, and the democratic principle. As well, institutions and rules of fiscal federalism are usu-ally designed in constitutions or statutes to achieve these three goals. In Spain, according to the constitution, the funding arrangements are sup-posed to ensure and conciliate the three basic constitutional principles: autonomy, equality, and the democratic ideal of accountability. The ju-risprudence has also established the principle of co-ordination with the central government and the principle of solidarity among all Spanish citizens (De la Fuente 2011; Blöchinger and Vammalle 2012).

Despite the relevance of such constitutional principles, this chapter illustrates the tensions that exist among the three goals and the diffi-culty of reconciling them simultaneously. By looking at recent reforms of the power distribution and the institutions and practices of fiscal fed-eralism in Spain, the chapter's main argument is that "you can't have it all." Federal arrangements are not only Janus-faced in different fed-eral settings regarding their possible effects on equity, recognition of social diversity, and democracy, but these three values frequently may be incompatible or in deep tension among themselves within a specific federal polity. This incompatibility can make reforms to achieve a new balance among these goals a difficult task. The tensions or trade-offs tend to be solved by an actor, such as the central government or the

Constitutional Court, with the capacity to prioritize and sacrifice one or two of these goals to achieve what seems the most important outcome at that point in time.

The recent reforms of the Spanish *estado autonómico* illustrate well the way federal institutions evolve under these contradictory forces and the tensions and trade-offs among these three goals. The recent reform of several regional statutes of autonomy of autonomous communities (hereafter ACs) and the reform of the funding arrangements sought to achieve all three goals at once. I will argue that both reforms pursued aims that may be deemed contradictory or incompatible, a fact that may explain why they failed to achieve some of their original goals. The intervention of other external actors, such as the Constitutional Court, and exogenous circumstances, such as the financial crisis, forced the central government to prioritize the goals of equity over those of accommodation and democracy in the two cases.

The chapter proceeds by first discussing the Spanish federalism model and its evolution until the beginning of recent reforms. It then presents brief accounts of the recent reforms to the regional statutes of autonomy and in the financial arrangements. The chapter then assesses the contradictory forces and tensions behind each of the reforms and the consequences for the attainment of the goals of accommodating diversity, achieving equity, and improving the quality of democracy.

The Evolution and Characteristics of the Spanish Federal Arrangements and the Context of Recent Reforms

The current decentralization model in the Spanish Constitution of 1978 is based largely on provisions establishing the principle of autonomy for the nationalities and regions and on rules about how this autonomy was to be exercised. These provisions and rules were inspired by the principle of choice or voluntariness (the so-called *principio dispositivo*). It left the initiative to accede to devolution to the very territorial entities benefiting from it. The regional statutes of autonomy – ultimately approved by the national parliament – were left to flesh out the main aspects of autonomy, such as competences and the internal organization of each region. Autonomy had to occur within the framework of some exclusive central powers and the basic constitutional principles of unity, equality, and solidarity. These regional charters or statutes of autonomy thus acquired the quality of being both national organic laws and basic institutional – quasi-constitutional – norms of the regional entities. They could not be unilaterally amended by the Spanish parliament and were utilized to complete what the constitution had left open for the sake of successful consensus-building. The regional statutes had to be approved and reformed through a procedure that for many represented a kind of federal pact between the regional parliaments and the Spanish parliament.

This design operated in favour of diversity and some de jure asymmetries were constitutionally entrenched – primarily in issues of fiscal arrangements, language, culture and civil law – and the Spanish *estado autonómico* evolved through the repeated adaptation of some regional statutes, by political praxis or non-constitutional renewal, and through the interpretation of the constitutional court. It became a virtually symmetrical cooperative federal model, federal in all but name (Watts 2009); shared competences and finance were the system's prevailing modus operandi. The distribution of powers, largely accomplished through the intervention of the Constitutional Court in the course of resolving conflicts, became increasingly coherent and clear for political actors.

In sum, the main characteristic of the system when the recent round of reforms began were the following (Colino and Olmeda 2012):

- The territorial distribution of powers was not completely spelled out in the constitution, which contained only general principles and a general distribution of powers among levels.
- Strong nationalist movements and parties existed in two of the autonomous communities (Basque Country and Catalonia), which were recognized in the constitution through extensive and quick devolution and the establishment of some asymmetries.
- An asymmetrical dual equilibrium has given rise to a symmetrical cooperative equilibrium in the absence of even a single formal amendment to the very rigid constitution. Constitutional change has been effected by political agreements, judicial interpretation, and amendments to sub-national charters or statutes of autonomy.
- The system reached a relatively high degree of decentralization, in terms of public spending and authority, with a dominance of shared powers and revenues.
- The Spanish model has operated as a devolutionary federalism, which has produced centrifugal and differentiating tendencies within it that have coexisted with centripetal and equalizing pressures. These two opposing forces are reflected in the party system, featuring both state-wide and regional parties.

To be sure, the evolving model, despite its relative success, was never without opponents. There were always discontent and criticisms regarding its operation, as well as frustration from regional nationalist parties and governments that, paradoxically, had been the main beneficiaries of the system. Until 2003, this discontent never translated into proposals to reform regional statutes of autonomy or the constitution. In the last eight years, however, owing to a confluence of political, ideological, and conjunctural factors at both the regional level and the central level and also because of the institutional conditions and rules of the system, several initiatives to reform the regional statutes of autonomy were enacted by regional parliaments in eight ACs.

They were aimed at deepening the decentralization of powers and resources, improving recognition of diversity, and modernizing the institutional design of regional governments 30 years after their creation. Some regional statutes of autonomy have been amended or even drafted anew: Valencia (2006), Catalonia (2006), Balearic Islands (2007), Andalucía (2007), Aragón (2007), Castile and León (2007), Navarra (2010), and Extremadura (2011) have amended their statutes of autonomy. Some other ACs have debated proposals and drafts but have not found party-political consensus at the regional level as of yet, for example, Canary Islands, Castile-La Mancha, and Galicia. In the Basque Country the reform failed in 2005.

Most of the reform process has been triggered and influenced by the initiative and discussion on the Catalan statute reform (on the Catalan reform, see Castellà 2010; Viver Pi-Sunyer 2009; Colino 2009; De Carreras 2008; Corcuera 2009). For the first time, regional parties and parliaments have set the agenda for reform of their statutes without previous consensus or agreement among the main national political forces regarding the orientation and goals of the reform. In fact, although most reforms ultimately have been approved by the two main Spanish parties in the regional and national arenas, these parties have not pursued in general any global plan or scheme concerning the Spanish territorial model to be achieved. The intervention of the Constitutional Court was triggered by the most controversial reform, the Catalan one, where the main national opposition party challenged some aspects of the Catalan amended statute.

Thus, in a landmark and controversial 2010 ruling, the Spanish Constitutional Court rejected most of the new interpretations of the 1978 constitution made by Catalonia's and the other amended regional statutes of autonomy. The court thus invalidated the political pact for implicit constitutional change that had been reached by the Spanish parliament in 2006. The protracted process of reform and the final intervention by the Constitutional Court was accompanied by the debate on the emergence of a new model of federalism in Spain. Observers disagree on just what this model entails and its merits (for the debate see Cruz 2006; Roig 2006; Tudela and Kölling 2009; Sánchez Ferriz 2009). For some, it is a model characterized by a lack of integration and stability due to excessive asymmetry, bilateralism, and "protoconfederal traits" (Blanco 2006), especially evident in the Catalan statute. For others, the regional statutes' reforms and the ensuing Constitutional Court's judgment may have enabled the constitutional territorial model to enter a new phase of better integration as a result of further decentralization and increased recognition of diversity. This optimistic account views the court's intervention as redressing a problematic reform and thus safeguarding the previous constitutional consensus (see Corcuera 2010; De la Quadra-Salcedo 2011; Tudela 2011). Most constitutional lawyers from Catalonia, however, are much more pessimistic about the consequences of the court's ruling. The intervention of the Constitutional Court, in their view, has diluted or annulled most of the original goals of the Catalan reform (e.g., more national recognition, through symbols and language protection; safeguarding of regional competences against central encroachments; additional fiscal resources; decentralization of the judicial power). Despite the decentralization, for many in Catalonia, the model emerging after the court's ruling means the end of constitutional flexibility and forecloses the traditional openness of the model. The resulting model will be incapable of satisfying the demands of a true plurinational state and will prove to be just a new step towards increased demands for shared sovereignty or outright secession.

Regarding the system of fiscal federalism and financial equalization, reforms in 2001 increased the resources and fiscal autonomy of ACs, whose revenues since then are based mainly on tax-sharing and some unconditional central equalization transfers. However, reforms did not end demands for more resources from all the regions. Wealthy ACs, such as Catalonia, have long tried to establish a link between their constitutional status as a nationality and more financial powers; examples are the Basque Country and Navarre, which enjoy a high degree of constitutionally entrenched fiscal power. Politicians in Catalonia also began to protest about the so-called fiscal imbalance or deficit, that is, the excessive equalizing effects of the funding system and the negative balance between their region's contribution to central revenues and what it was receiving from the central government in central public expenditure. In this context, and considering the innovative and controversial financial clauses in the regional statutes, most ACs were already complaining before the current financial crisis that they lacked sufficient resources to manage their competences, especially those dealing with welfare services such as health and education. Some experts also pointed to the fiscal arrangements' inequity in terms of per capita funding in different ACs (see Herrero and Tránchez 2011). The wealthiest ACs complained about the "over-equalizing" effects of the financial equalization arrangements. For some academics and politicians in those wealthier regions, such as Catalonia or the Balearic Islands and Madrid, the system was far too redistributive and lacked clear distributive criteria and incentives for subsidized regions to improve their performance. Catalonia began to advocate for a limitation of the existing solidarity and redistribution mechanisms among ACs; these redistributive mechanisms are the tax system, social security, and the central government's public investments in all regions.

Additionally, several Catalan politicians and academics, such as public economists – notably the former Catalan finance minister, a well-known expert in fiscal federalism – began to document and publicly denounce the privileged fiscal situation of Basque Country and Navarra (with a per capita funding of 1.6 to 1.8 times the resources of other communities). Paradoxically, however, despite denouncing this asymmetry as a privilege of these two ACs, the political class in Catalonia, as reflected in their regional statute proposal, decided to act just as other ACs in the system had traditionally acted, by asking for a system similar to that of Basque and Navarra, although showing their willingness to contribute to inter-territorial solidarity. They repeatedly sought to gain greater control of the taxes raised in their territory and to put limits to the solidarity within the common system of financial equalization.

The current financial crisis since 2008 caused a deteriorating budget situation for both the central government and the ACs. The latter saw their revenues sharply reduced, owing to the bursting of the housing bubble and the collapse of the tax yield from real estate taxes. Partly because of their budgetary imbalances prior to the crisis, the greater weight of indirect taxes, the greater exposure to real estate, and a population growth above the average, the hardest hit by the crisis in terms of deficit and debt were the Balearic Islands, Castile-La Mancha, Catalonia, and the Valencian Community. This entire situation afforded the context for the renegotiation of the funding arrangements that was provided for in the amended Catalan statute of autonomy (see Colino 2013). The state of the model has been evaluated negatively in terms of the three mentioned values or goals of federalism. One expert in Spanish fiscal federalism recently complained: "our funding system does not guarantee the effective implementation of the constitutional principle of equality, unnecessarily restricts regional autonomy (especially in its revenue side) and does not provide the correct and transparent accountability of the various authorities to their citizens" (De la Fuente 2011).

The Goals, Contents, and Results of the Recent Reforms

Following the Catalan path, amendments to other regional charters of autonomy dealt with several areas: symbolic and identity issues, competences, regional institutions, and fiscal arrangements (see Colino 2009; Tudela 2011). The reform of the eight regional statutes of autonomy and the funding arrangements has brought about increased devolution of competences and resources, some institutional updating or modernizing, the inclusion of regional bills of rights, and some additional recognition of identity features as legitimation of regional governments. Most of these reforms have been upheld by the Constitutional Court. However, the currently prevailing view in Catalonia is that the reforms have not fulfilled most of the traditional nationalists' demands.

The Reform of the Regional Statutes of Autonomy and the Constitutional Court's Ruling on the Catalan Amended Statute

We can group the goals behind the reforms of regional statutes into the three categories mentioned above and highlighted in Simeon's work. First, the reforms sought to achieve accommodation of national diversity for Catalonia through symbolic declarations, further decentralization, participation in central/Spanish and European policies and decisions, protection of minority languages, recognition through asymmetry, and bilateral institutions. Second, they also sought equity or distributive justice goals, albeit here the objectives differed between wealthy and poor regions. Some wanted more autonomous fiscal resources and less solidarity and equalization, while others wanted to keep redistribution high to guarantee welfare benefits and services. Regions also wanted to introduce more citizens' rights and bills of rights in their regional statutes of autonomy. Finally, some goals, such as the disentanglement of competences and the increasing participation in central institutions, could be said to pursue enhanced democracy and accountability. Let us examine them in more detail.

The most debated issues were the self-identification clauses. In previous statutes, both Catalonia and Andalusia defined themselves as "nationalities" in the sense of Article 2 of the Spanish Constitution. Not satisfied with this definition, Catalan politicians proposed the term "nation" in several articles of their statute proposal, but their effort was ultimately deemed incompatible with the Constitution by most Spanish politicians. It was a very delicate issue for the leaders of the ruling party in the central government, who tried to avoid it. The final compromise was an indirect formulation in the Preamble of the Catalan statute of autonomy; it alludes to the definition of Catalonia as a nation by the Catalan parliament according to the ample will of its population.

Since this clause in the Preamble was challenged by the main opposition party, the Constitutional Court had to respond to the issue of how to recognize the distinctness of Catalonia and its national character. The court's ruling accepted the declaration of Catalonia as a nation in the Preamble of the statute and the use of the adjective *national* related to the "national symbols" of Catalonia in Article 8. However, the court stated that the Spanish legal system is based on the principle of popular sovereignty, and that the only holder of sovereignty is the Spanish people writ large. In this fashion, the court sought to deprive the declaration of Catalonia as a nation of any interpretive force (Colino 2011).

Regarding the accommodation of language diversity, the new Catalan statute enshrined the main elements of traditional nationalist language policy in Catalonia, that is, positive discrimination or normalization in favour of Catalan through "linguistic exposure." The statute established Catalan as the language of preferential use in public administration bodies and the public media and as the language of normal use for teaching and learning in the entire education system. An additional novelty was Article 6, establishing the duty to know the regional language; this article gave the Catalan language the same constitutional status as that of Castilian in the Spanish Constitution. It also introduced the obligation of "linguistic availability," or the obligation for businesses and establishments that are open to the public in Catalonia to reply to users or consumers in the language of their choice.

In its ruling, the Constitutional Court largely upheld the existing model of Catalan as the language of normal use in the education system – insofar as this does not involve the exclusion of Castilian as the teaching language – but struck down the term "preferential" as unconstitutional as applied to the use of Catalan in public administration and media.

Another innovation of the Catalan statute of autonomy, which the Andalusian and other regional statutes virtually copied, attempted to separate or disentangle competences by "shielding" regional competences from the usual encroachments of the central government through its use of concurrent framework legislation. To that end, there has been an effort to enshrine in the regional statutes of autonomy some of the most pro-regionalist interpretations of constitutional jurisprudence, employing a detailed definition and typology of competences – exclusive, shared, and executive – and specifying the sub-matters or issues that each competence includes. In addition, some new competences – many of them to execute national legislation – have been incorporated in matters of agriculture, water and hydraulic works, commerce and trade fairs, popular consultations, cooperatives and the social economy, emergencies and civil protection, immigration, the environment, natural areas and meteorology, religious entities, public safety, social security, transport, work and labour relations, universities, and judicial administration.

In its ruling, the Constitutional Court accepted the devolution of those powers but rejected the initiatives in the Catalan statute, and by implication those of the other ACs, to limit the shared powers of the central government and shield regional competences. The court declared that a regional statute of autonomy may not limit the scope or the substance of the central government's competences. At the same time, it rejected the attempts to limit the framework powers of the central government to the "minimum standards of regulation." In sum, the Constitutional Court embraced and reinforced a view whereby in practice most regional competences are shared and not exclusive (see Colino 2011).

Many amended statutes have introduced charters of citizens' rights, focused mainly on social, participation, and gender rights, which were already contemplated in regional legislation. They have also regulated most details of their regional political institutions, which had been contained in ordinary regional laws until then. All of them have also reasserted the elements of regional identity, particularistic history, and self-definition. Finally, the Constitutional Court upheld those reforms aimed at promoting regional participation in central decisions. They include, through the bilateral joint commissions established in the statutes of autonomy, the right of initiative to sign international treaties, the right to be informed, the right to make proposals for the composition of different central state bodies, and the right to participate in the exercise of several exclusive competences of the central government, such as economic planning, road transportation, and the determination of the immigration quota.

The Reform of Funding Arrangements in 2009

The objectives of the finance reform can also be understood in terms of the same three central goals. The first is the accommodation of diversity through increased fiscal autonomy, reduction of vertical fiscal imbalances, and more revenue autonomy. The second is equity in the form of equalization payments that reduce horizontal fiscal imbalances through personal and territorial redistribution and provide enough resources for all citizens to have access to public services under regional jurisdiction. The third is democracy in the form of fiscal equivalence and independent revenues to ensure that all governments are properly accountable and responsive to their citizens and have the appropriate incentives to maximize their welfare.

The 2009 reform of the financial arrangements was already predetermined and even scheduled in the new statutes of autonomy, especially in the Catalan reform. Regional statute reforms included some new principles to regulate sources of regional revenues, criteria for financial equalization and solidarity, and some obligatory public investment clauses for the central government in regional infrastructures (De la Fuente and Gundín 2007). The new Catalan statute included two innovative aspects, which have been partly reproduced in some of the other new statutes. One was an increase in the AC's tax autonomy and revenues by way of sharing a larger amount of taxes and control over them with the central government (e.g., 50% of income tax, 50% of VAT). The other was partial equalization: setting limits to redistribution among territories and abandoning the objective of total equalization. It also included the so-called ordinality principle, by virtue of which equalization mechanisms will not alter Catalonia's position among the ACs in terms of per capita income before equalization.

An additional provision, also emulated by other statutes, imposed a seven-year budgetary obligation on the central government to spend money on public investments in infrastructure in Catalonia proportionate to Catalonia's share of the Spanish GDP (18%). Other regions proposed different criteria, such as population or territory, in their statutes for determining the amount of the central government's public investment in their regions.

In 2010, the Constitutional Court's ruling on the Catalan statute downgraded most of the provisions on financial issues to mere normative proposals. In practice, however, its main principles were subsequently incorporated in the 2009 reform of the funding arrangements. In any case, the court rejected the possibility for regional statutes to establish the criteria for determining the fiscal contribution of the ACs to the common purse. It said doing so would encroach on the central parliament's competence to regulate the exercise of financial powers of the ACs and set the levels of its contribution to the equalization system and to solidarity.

As in previous rounds of funding arrangement reforms, the negotiations proceeded first bilaterally and then multilaterally. For the first time, though, some of the elements of the new funding model were predetermined by provisions in the new regional statutes. Before the deadline established by the Catalan statute expired in August 2008, the central finance minister presented a proposal in July, which was unanimously rejected by Catalonia and the other ACs. The Spanish Ministry of Finance began contacts with all the regional governments in several rounds until November. When these talks produced little consensus and seemed headed for deadlock, Prime Minister José Luis Zapatero began bilateral meetings with all the regional presidents in December 2008 and January 2009. Each leader presented demands and Prime Minister Zapatero pledged to satisfy most of them (see Colino 2013).

After this round, on 30 December the central finance minister presented a new proposal incorporating the principles of the new system, but without concrete figures on final assignations. The central government's promise that no region would be worse off under the new system meant that the prospects for a real reform were limited, since ACs who benefited from the system opposed real changes. To achieve this promise and at the same time make concessions to the aspirations of Catalonia for a less equalizing system with additional resources, the central government decided to inject additional monies and create several special funds in the finance scheme to compensate both the poorest ACs and the richest ones for changes to the model's design. The result was an increase in shared taxes, raising the personal income tax from

33% to 50%, the value-added tax from 35% to 50%, and the excise tax from 40% to 58%. Of these taxes, 75% is allocated to the Equalization Fund to Guarantee Public Services, which is divided among the ACs according to adjusted population criteria. The remaining 25% is allocated to the AC where the taxes were generated. The equalization system thus changed to a system that equalizes only partially (80% of needs), but is frequently adjusted (see Blöchliger and Vammalle 2012).

In this fashion, the funding arrangements, finally adopted as statutory law by the central parliament at the end of 2009, retained the basic features of the previous model. Population was the main allocating principle, there was a guarantee of financial equalization in essential public services (partial equalization, as desired by Catalonia), and financial sufficiency was linked to regional competences. The arrangements also provided additional resources of around €11,000 million, injected through two funds seeking complementary goals: the so-called Competitiveness Fund, to offset the imbalances affecting the most dynamic ACs; and the Cooperation Fund, to support growth and development of more economically backward ACs.

Evaluating the Tensions and the Results of Reform

How adequately have the reforms to regional statutes and financial arrangements served goals of accommodating diversity, promoting equity or social citizenship, and enhancing democracy? How have the tensions among these values played out in these two reforms? Which goals have been promoted and which, if any, have been sacrificed?

The Reform of Regional Statutes: The Demise of Accommodation

The reforms reveal several tensions and trade-offs among values. For instance, the goal of accommodation (entailing symbolic recognition, further decentralization, asymmetry, positive discrimination of the Catalan language, bilateralism, and limits to solidarity and redistribution by the central government) has been in tension with the goal of equity by means of wealth redistribution and policy coordination at the state-wide level. As well, the goal of accommodation has been in tension with the goal of democracy as procedural justice (participation, accountability, equal representation, and individual rights, for example, the right to use one's own language in education). Of course, the degree to which any of these values is attained, as well as the extent to which these values are in tension, can be judged differently by different actors or from different vantage points. We evaluate them from the point of view of the Spanish system as a whole.

It seems evident that the promotion of equity and redistribution at the state-wide level through central investments and welfare benefits is in tension with the goal of recognition and accommodation through financial concessions to some regions. In terms of accountability and representation, one could argue that the dual federalism aspired to by the Catalan statute may be incompatible with the "participation" federalism striven for in other provisions. Moreover, the desired fiscal special treatment and bilateral mechanisms and fora may also pose problems for democracy. Many of the new statutes of autonomy create bilateral participation of ACs in bodies of central decision-making, but seek at the same time to reduce any legislative or executive intervention of the central government in those ACs. The result is the problem known in the UK as the "West Lothian question" (Pemán Gavín 2009). For example, Catalonia may enjoy a position that other regions do not, since the Catalan government and MPs in the central parliament may decide on all issues affecting all Spaniards, but the rest of the representatives would lose any capacity through the central institutions to decide on issues affecting Catalonia.

We could argue that the regional statutes reform and the Constitutional Court's ruling have improved regional empowerment and autonomy, through both some building-in and some building-out mechanisms (Simeon 2008). Some competences in key areas, such as immigration, labour inspection, and public transportation, have been decentralized. Funding arrangements to ensure the sufficiency of resources, as well as a clearer delimitation of the Catalan and other wealthy regions' contribution to the Spanish territorial solidarity scheme, however, do not seem to have contributed to further accommodation of diversity in the system.

At the same time, the extension of the reform initiatives to several ACs with similar demands forced the central government to devolve increasing powers and resources and made the tensions between accommodation and equity more evident. Even if the language policy model of Catalonia has been entrenched in the regional statute and largely upheld by the Constitutional Court, it is doubtful that a further and satisfactory national recognition of Catalonia and of the multinational character of the Spanish state has been achieved, given the nationalist aspirations. In fact, after the reform process, the accommodation of

Catalonia is perceived by many as having worsened with evidence of increased support for secessionism among political actors from Catalonia and some signs of confrontation with the rest of Spain. Two of three Catalans now claim that the level of autonomy of Catalonia is insufficient. On the other hand, for some Spanish-speaking people in Catalonia, the official language policy of positive discrimination for the Catalan language, now enshrined in the statute, will also prove problematic. Despite some lip service to bilingualism in the text, the policy may affect, for example, the effective right of citizens in Catalonia to raise their children in Castilian-Spanish if they wish.

The Constitutional Court seems to have resolved these existing tensions by striking down the most accommodation-oriented aspects of the reforms but upholding decentralization and regional bills of rights. It has thus enhanced the goals of equity and democracy for all, but sacrificed or watered down the goal of accommodation where the latter requires asymmetry for one AC. This outcome, of course, has led to renewed instability and increased reformist or secessionist demands from Catalonia.

The Reform of the Funding Arrangements: Redistributing Misery in Times of Austerity

The reform of the funding arrangements also shows some tensions among the three goals. The goal of increasing accommodation through the reduction of the vertical imbalance and the limitation of redistribution (through only partial equalization or through fiscal asymmetric treatment or fiscal privilege) seems clearly incompatible with equity goals. This tension could only be solved momentarily through the injection of €11,000 million, a move that led all ACs to accept the agreement and the reform. Given the usual difficulty in reaching agreements on the reform of funding arrangements, the final system is extremely complex and visibly incompatible with the democratic values of accountability, fiscal equivalence, and transparency.

Critics of the regional statutes and funding arrangements reforms predicted the demise of solidarity and equality under the new system (Tajadura 2007; De Carreras 2008). Some observe a qualitative change in the philosophy of the financing system from a multilateral agreement model, oriented towards full equalization, to a bilateral system with restrictions on the degree of equalization. Also, this system of fiscal federalism "à la carte" and based on bilateral negotiations, it is argued, goes against the principle that what concerns all should be decided by all (De la Fuente and Gundín 2007).

Regarding the actual results in terms of distributive equity, recent studies (Bosch 2012) show that the new funding arrangements have already had an impact on the equity of the equalization system, which was one of the main criticisms addressed to the funding model. The Community of Madrid, for example, has now gone from being the fourth-worst-off AC in terms of per capita funding to being the third highest in per capita resources. Catalonia, for the first time, has been above the average of the ACs in terms of per capita funding after equalization. Even though it still receives funds, Andalusia, for the first time, has remained below the average in per capita resources after equalization.

The debt crisis from 2010 onwards offset the growth of tax and revenue sharing and the increased equalizing transfers injected into the system, and it bluntly revealed the contradictions among the three goals embedded in the reform. In its austerity measures, the central government sacrificed the goal of accommodation of the wealthiest ACs and tried to secure goals of equalization and policy coordination to comply with the EU-imposed budget consolidation targets. This strategy seems to have neutralized the goals achieved earlier of more revenue autonomy and more accountability of regional governments. In 2011, the central parliament approved a constitutional reform to force ACs to comply with budget consolidation and debt ceilings under the threat of intervention. This initiative has clearly implied centralization and proved to contradict the goals of accommodation, although it might have enhanced the capacity of the centre to pursue redistribution and equity.

Conclusions

This chapter has shown some of the typical features of the Spanish version of federalism and recent efforts to respond to the internal tensions and underlying demands that are typical of other federations, especially multinational federations. It has described reforms undertaken by regional statutes of autonomy led by the Catalan initiative and also by the central government in negotiation with the ACs to renew and update the regional funding arrangements. Finally, it has assessed those reforms in terms of their consequences for several goals that are associated with federations.

The scope, direction, and effects of Spanish reforms are far from clear at this stage. Nonetheless, a substantial transformation of Spanish federalism seems to be under way. It is accompanied by a growing sense of the failure to realize the original goals of the Spanish federalism model. This perception is strong among nationalist forces in Catalonia and the Basque Country, which are increasingly tending towards secessionism, but it also exists in the rest of Spain. The reforms, the mood of failure, and the current financial and fiscal crisis affecting all orders of government in Spain have consequences for the future balance of power between the central government and the ACs and the capacity, stability, and cohesion of the Spanish state for some years to come. These factors have also exacerbated and highlighted some of the typical contradictions present in federations among values such as diversity, equity, and democratic accountability.

Although this reform phase could have opened up a period of stability regarding the integration of Catalonia, the prospects of its having achieved sufficient accommodation of Catalan nationalism are not very good. Despite the clear decentralization and some increased asymmetry they imply, the current reforms do not seem to have solved any of the traditional problems and tensions. For nationalists in Catalonia, reforms are just a new step in the direction of sovereignty, some of them announcing a self-determination referendum along the way. The Constitutional Court's ruling confirmed their worst expectations about their desired accommodation goals. This ruling has given many nationalists an alibi for permanent dissatisfaction and grievance and a future agenda for years to come. More and more Catalans will continue striving for independence. The state may be running out of competences or financial resources to devolve in the next rounds of reform, and the country may be headed forever towards adversarial politics and what Canadians call "megaconstitutional" politics (Russell 2004).

NOTE

1 An English translation of the term *estado autonómico* is a state composed of self-managing or autonomous communities.

REFERENCES

Banting, Keith. 2006. Social Citizenship and Federalism: Is a Federal Welfare State a Contradiction in Terms? In *Territory, Democracy and Justice*, edited by Scott Greer. London: Palgrave Macmillan.

Bird, Richard M., and Robert D. Ebel. 2006. Fiscal Federalism and National Unity. In *Handbook of Fiscal Federalism*, edited by Ehtisham Ahmad and Giorgio Brosio. Cheltenham: Edward Elgar.

Blanco, Roberto. 2006. El estatuto catalán: texto y pretextos. *Claves de la razón práctica* 162:20–7.

Blöchliger, Hansjörg, and Camila Vammalle. 2012. Spain: Reforming the Funding of Autonomous Communities. In *Reforming Fiscal Federalism and Local Government: Beyond the Zero-Sum Game*. OECD Fiscal Federalism Studies. Paris: OECD.

Bosch, Núria. 2012. Horizontal Equity in the 2009 Regional Financing Model. In *Report on Fiscal Federalism 2011*, edited by IEB. Barcelona: IEB.

Castellà, Josep M. 2010. La sentencia del Tribunal Constitucional 31/2010, sobre el estatuto de autonomía de *Cataluña* y su significado para el futuro del estado autonómico. Fundación Ciudadanía y Valores.

Colino, César. 2009. Constitutional Change without Constitutional Reform: Spanish Federalism and the Revision of Catalonia's Statute of Autonomy. *Publius: The Journal of Federalism* 39(2):262–88.

Colino, César. 2011. What Now for the Autonomic State? Muddling through Growing Tensions amidst the Aftermath of the Court's Ruling and the Painful Fiscal Crisis. In *Jahrbuch des Föderalismus 2011*. EZFF Tübingen. Baden-Baden: Nomos Verlag.

Colino, César. 2013. The State of Autonomies between the Economic Crisis and Enduring Nationalist Tensions. In *Politics and Society in Contemporary Spain: From Zapatero to Rajoy*, edited by Bonnie N. Field and Alfonso Botti. New York: Palgrave Macmillan.

Colino, César, and José A. Olmeda. 2012. The Limits of Flexibility for Constitutional Change and the Uses of Subnational Constitutional Space: The Case of Spain. In *Changing Federal Constitutions: Lessons from International Comparison*, edited by A. Benz and F. Knüpling. Opladen: Verlag Barbara Budrich.

Corcuera, Javier. 2009. Las reformas del modelo territorial en Alemania y en España: dos lógicas diferentes. In *La reforma del Estado Autonómico Español y del Estado Federal Alemán*, edited by J. Tudela and M. Kölling. Madrid: Fundación Manuel Giménez Abad-Centro de Estudios Políticos y Constitucionales.

Corcuera, Javier. 2010. El modelo de Estado Autonómico español tras la STC 31/2010 sobre el Estatuto de Autonomía de Cataluña. *JADO: Academia Vasca de Derecho Boletín* 9(20):11–38.

Cruz Villalón, Pedro. 2006. La reforma del Estado de las autonomías. *Revista d'Estudis Autonòmics i Federals* 2:77–99.

De Carreras, Francesc. 2008. El dilema del estado de las autonomías ¿cierre del modelo o apertura indefinida? *Claves de Razón Práctica* 188:10–19.

De la Fuente, Angel. 2011. La financiación territorial en España: situación actual y propuestas de reforma. In *Reformas necesarias para potenciar el crecimiento de la economía española*. Vol. I: *Civitas*. Madrid: Thomson Reuters.

De la Fuente, Angel, and Maria Gundín. 2007. La financiación autonómica en los nuevos estatutos regionales. *FEDEA, Estudios sobre la Economía Española*.

De la Quadra-Salcedo, Tomás. 2011. El estatuto de Cataluña y el Estado autonómico tras las sentencias del Tribunal Constitucional. *Revista de Administración Pública* 184:41–77.

Enderlein, Henrik. 2009. Three Worlds of Fiscal Federalism. Solving the Trilemma of Multi-Layered Fiscal Frameworks in Industrialized Countries. Manuscript. Harvard University. Accessed June 2012. Available at www. henrik-enderlein.de

Herrero, Ana, and José Manuel Tránchez. 2011. El desarrollo y evolución del sistema de financiación autonómica. *Presupuesto y Gasto Público* 62:33–65.

McGarry, John, Brendan O'Leary, and Richard Simeon. 2008. Integration or Accommodation: The Enduring Debate in Conflict Regulation. In *Constitutional Design for Divided Societies: Integration or Accommodation?* edited by S. Choudhry. Oxford and New York: Oxford University Press.

Pemán Gavín, Juan. 2009. El sistema español de autonomías territoriales: apuntes para un diagnóstico. *Revista Aragonesa de Administración Pública* 35:11–73.

Roig, Eduard. 2006. La reforma del estado de las autonomías: Ruptura o consolidación del modelo constitucional de 1978? *Revista d'Estudis Autonòmics i Federals* 3:149–85.

Russell, Peter. H. 2004. *Constitutional Odyssey: Can Canadians Become a Sovereign People?* Toronto: University of Toronto Press.

Simeon, Richard. 2006a. Federalism and Social Justice: Thinking Through the Tangle. In *Territory, Democracy and Justice*, edited by Scott Greer. London: Palgrave Macmillan.

Simeon, Richard. 2006b. Social Justice: Does Federalism Make a Difference? In *Dilemmas of Solidarity. Rethinking Redistribution in the Canadian Federation*, edited by Sujit Choudhry, Jean-François Gaudreault-Desbiens, and Lorne Sossin. Toronto: University of Toronto Press.

Simeon, Richard. 2008. Managing Conflicts of Diversity. In *Building on and Accommodating Diversities*, edited by Ron Watts and Rupak Chattopadhyay. Forum of the Federations. New Delhi: Forum of Federations and Viva Books.

Simeon, Richard. 2010. Federalism and Intergovernmental Relations. In *A*

Handbook of Canadian Public Administration, edited by Christopher Dunn. 2nd ed. Oxford: Oxford University Press.

Simeon, Richard. 2011. Preconditions and Prerequisites: Can Anyone Make Federalism Work? In *The Federal Idea: Essays in Honour of Ronald L. Watts*, edited by T.J. Courchene, J.R. Allan, C. Leuprecht, and N. Verrelli. Kingston and Montreal: Institute of Intergovernmental Relations.

Simeon, Richard, and Daniel-Patrick Conway. 2001. Federalism and the Management of Conflict in Multinational Societies. In *Multinational Democracies*, edited by Alain-G. Gagnon and James Tully. Cambridge: Cambridge University Press.

Simeon, Richard, and Christina Murray. 2008. Recognition Without Empowerment: Minorities in a Democratic South Africa. In *Constitutional Design for Divided Societies. Integration or Accommodation?* edited by Sujit Choudhry. New York: Oxford University Press.

Simeon, Richard, and K. Swinton. 1995. Introduction: Rethinking Federalism in a Changing World. In *Rethinking Federalism. Citizens, Markets, and Governments in a Changing World*, edited by K. Knop, S. Ostry, R. Simeon, and K. Swinton. Vancouver: UBC Press.

Tajadura, Javier. 2007. Reformas territoriales y Estado Social *Sistema* 196:49–73.

Tudela, José. 2010. Heterogeneidad y asimetría en un estado indefinido. Una aceptación de la diversidad que es una puerta de future. In *España y modelos de federalism*, edited by J. Tudela and Felix Knüpling. Madrid: CEPC/Gimenez Abad.

Tudela, José. 2011. Reforma constitucional en clave federal? (sistematización de problemas generados por las reformas y posibles soluciones). *Revista de Estudios Políticos* 151:231–79.

Tudela, José, and Felix Knüpling, eds. 2010. *España y modelos de federalismo*, Madrid: CEPC/Fundación Manuel Giménez Abad.

Tudela, José, and Mario Kölling, eds. 2009. *La reforma del Estado Autonómico Español y del Estado Federal Alemán*, Madrid: Fundación Manuel Giménez Abad-Centro de Estudios Políticos y Constitucionales.

Uriel, Ezequiel, and Ramón Barberán. 2007. *Las balanzas fiscales de las comunidades autónomas con la Administración Pública Central, 1991–2005*. Bilbao: Fundación BBVA.

Viver Pi-Sunyer, Carles. 2009. Grandes reformas o pequeñospasos? Una perspectiva desde Cataluña. In *La reforma del Estado Autonómico Español y del Estado Federal Alemán*, edited by J. Tudela and M. Kölling. Madrid: Fundación Manuel Giménez Abad-Centro de Estudios Políticos y Constitucionales.

Watts, Ron L. 2006. Origins of Cooperative and Competitive Federalism. In *Territory, Democracy and Justice,* edited by Scott Greer. London: Palgrave Macmillan.

Watts, Ron L. 2009. Spain: A Multinational Federation in Disguise? Paper read at the conference, The Federalization of Spain-Deficits of Horizontal Cooperation, 27–28 March, Saragossa, Spain.

10 Spatial Rescaling, Federalization, and Interest Representation

MICHAEL KEATING

Federalism and Its Relatives

The term "federalism" is used in a multiplicity of ways. For some, federalism is a precise juridical concept, confined to the realm of government and to be distinguished from other ways of dividing power, including separation-of-powers, devolution, regional government or decentralization. At the other extreme, it is used as a sociological concept, embracing civil society and even culture and behaviour. Even confining the term to the political realm, it is difficult to find a clear shared meaning, especially in Europe, where we have effectively federal states that are not officially federations (like Spain) and formally federal states that are more unitary (like Austria). Federal language and concepts are also used to describe and analyse the European Union itself. Matters are further complicated by the strong normative charge of the term in various contexts. So for the British right, federalism conjures up the spectre both of a centralized European "super-state" and of a disintegrated United Kingdom. The term is out of order in France, while in Italy it has been adopted by right and left as a useful slogan but without much agreed substance. In eastern and central Europe it is often seen as giving licence for secession, while in Spain the minority nationalists consider it too constraining and centralizing.

The usefulness and outcomes of these definitional debates will depend on the purpose for which we are using the term. So it may be important for jurists to distinguish among legal forms of dividing and sharing power. The normative concept of federalism may be useful as a guide for Europhiles or for those seeking principles for a constitutional equilibrium in Spain or the United Kingdom. My interest in the present project is more functional, on the relationship between federalism and public policy and the constitution of sub-state territories as policy systems. Specifically, the aim is to understand the ways in which policy systems adapt to governmental rescaling. The focus is on the emergence in Europe of an intermediate or "meso" level of government with some constitutional entrenchment, its own competences, and a role in public policy-making. These systems are variously labelled as federalism (Germany, Austria, Belgium), as regional government (France, Italy), as devolution (the United Kingdom), or as the state of the autonomies (Spain). My interest is less in the legal distinctions than in the fact that for our purposes (analysis of policy) they can all be seen as varieties of federalism. The question is whether policy systems and interest representation are "federalizing" along the same lines as states.

There is a large literature on federalism or devolution and public policy focused on intergovernmental relations. We know much less about the internal policy processes of European regions and the way in which social and economic interests are refracted at new territorial levels and articulated in policy demands and in relationships.

Spatial Rescaling

The literature on public policy has tended to take the nation-state as its basic unit of analysis. This is true whether the focus is on political parties as policy-makers and elections as policy cues; on corporatist policy-making among nationally based groups and government; or on the weight of the state machine itself in setting and maintaining policy lines. I have argued elsewhere that this has always been somewhat misleading and that territorial cleavages and territorial management have always been part of European statecraft (Keating 1998). Nonetheless, there have been changes recently and a rescaling of various functional systems and policy domains. This has been reported most extensively in relation to economic development, a substantial literature showing how, in a globalized economy, territory has become a more, not less, important resource (Scott 1998; Storper 1997; Cooke and Morgan 1998). The spatial division of prosperity owes less nowadays to traditional factors of production, such as raw materials and proximity to markets, and more to the social constructions of territories themselves and their ability to sustain innovation and entrepreneurship. Regions and localities have been identified not merely as sites of production but as production systems. More contentiously perhaps, such regions are presented as being in competition with each other for investment, technology, and markets, encouraging forms of neo-mercantilism in the search for absolute advantage. The decline in central state regional policies has stimulated a search for endogenous growth policies and policy instruments. Competitive regionalism has been encouraged by what some see as a move from comparative advantage, in which each region has its place in the national or global division of labour, to absolute, or competitive advantage. Others dismiss this as a distorted vision and a reification of the region, since only firms can really compete in a market economy. The idea of competitive regionalism has nevertheless taken hold among policy-makers and international organizations and has been exploited by politicians so as to construct a unified regional interest, which might cut across other sectoral or class interests. Rescaling has also occurred in culture; for example, minority languages rest increasingly on a territorial basis since they require an institutional support base and a community sustaining face-to-face contact.

Policy fields are also rescaling. Social integration is increasingly seen as a local matter (Kazpepov and Barberis 2008). The international tendency to link active labour market policy with social welfare has privileged the meso level, based upon local and regional labour markets and proximity. Agricultural policy is territorializing as a result of reforms to the Common Agricultural Policy and the gradual (and difficult) move to the concept of rural policy. It is also increasingly linked to environmental policy. Higher education and research are internationalizing and regionalizing (Paterson 2001; Piattoni 2010). To a lesser and more uneven degree, the state level is ceasing to be the only level for social solidarity, and there is a search for new levels, especially at the urban level and in historic or national communities below the state level (McEwen and Moreno 2005; Ferrera 2006; Greer 2006). Political behaviour is also showing signs of territorial distinctiveness, partially reversing the "nationalization" of the twentieth century (Hough and Jeffery 2006).[1]

Institutional Change

Much analysis of the effects of rescaling is functionally determinist. There is a rescaling literature derived from neo-Marxist regulation theory that sees capitalism seeking new scales for accumulation and to gain support and escape constraints. A neoliberal literature based on rather similar premises celebrates the end of irksome national regulation and the emergence of "regional states" (Ohmae 1995). Another strand in the rescaling literature has tended towards an idealization of the meso level as a space in which the production-distribution dilemma disappears. Some of this literature, in the Putnam (1993) tradition, reasons directly from individualized citizen attitudes to the performance of regional societies across a range of institutional, social, and economic indicators. Analyses based on public goods theory portray state rescaling as the response to the needs of optimal scales for service delivery and internalization of costs and benefits. There is a widespread tendency to conflate normative with causal arguments here and a fair amount of wishful thinking.

Governance and multilevel governance theories argue that, at new spatial scales, there is a move in modes of regulation, from hierarchy to networks and negotiation (Hooghe and Marks 2001; Bache and Flinders 2004; Piattoni 2010). Multilevel governance (MLG) theories, derived as they are from organization theory and rational choice theory, tend to take as their units of analysis socially unembedded organizations or individual actors rather than social and economic interests. The MLG game often seems divorced from wider consideration of social stratification and social conflict. Functionalist arguments, whether neo-Marxist or neoliberal, downplay the importance of institutions and of the region as an arena of conflict and competition and, critically, of politics. They tend to pay little attention to the way in which new territorial spaces are created and institutionalized as a result of competition among social and political interests with different stakes in the shape and constitution of the new arenas.

In order to understand the effects of rescaling on policy systems, we need to connect policy actors to broader social and economic interests (to re-embed them). Rescaling, at the supranational, transnational, and sub-state levels, is a process that refracts social and economic interests in various ways, altering their definition and articulation. Secondly, it has also led to a search for new institutions, which in their turn have served to reshape the political arena and contributed a new, governmental dimension to rescaling.

Spatial rescaling in Europe has not directly "caused" any changes in the structure of federal or devolved systems, but it has profoundly influenced them. On the one hand, states have sought to regulate the new spaces, seeking coherence and strategic direction, and to link them into state policies. They have also sought to use the regional level to solve wicked problems, for example, linking social and economic policy or rationing and management in health services. This has led to a growth in regional administration, even in a centralized state like France.

On the other hand, social movements, interests that feel that they are losing out, and (more selectively) political parties have sought to politicize the new spaces, broaden the meso-level policy agenda, and introduce electoral politics and accountability. This development is especially likely when the meso level has been constructed around the needs of economic development narrowly defined. In historic, cultural regions or stateless nations, an existing territorial identity has often been politicized to provide a basis for mobilization.

The result is the constitution of a meso level of action in various forms. There are deconcentrated arms of central government, as in France, where the latest reforms have fortified the regional prefect. There are neo-corporatist forms, selectively bringing in key social and economic actors in the management of territory. Then there are elected regional governments. There is a strong tendency for rescaling to end up with this last form of meso-governments or federal-type arrangements. Central governments find them a useful way of offloading responsibilities, managing at a distance, and reducing political pressure and responsibilities. Oppositional movements tend to go for elected government as a way of opening up policy systems. Government also has the standing and legitimacy to take decisions with redistributive implications and to impose taxation. So we now have meso-governments in all the large states of Europe (Germany, Italy, Spain, France, Poland, and, at least partially, the United Kingdom) as well as in some smaller ones (notably Belgium). The only large jurisdiction to escape this tendency is England, where moves to regionalization were started and reversed twice, in the 1960s–1970s and in the 1990s–2000s. Of course, deconcentration, regional corporatism, and elected government are ideal-types and often exist simultaneously, but there is a tendency towards the emergence of federal-type constitutional arrangements. Ironically, considering how often the term "governance" is used for the regional level, this represents a move from governance (if that is understood as non-hierarchical negotiation in networks) to government, a tendency that Goetz (2008) has noted more generally. Government also defines territories more authoritatively (across diverse functions), establishes a stronger territorial boundary around policy-making systems, carries a higher degree of legitimacy, and is open to a broad range of interests through the electoral mechanism. My interest is in exploring how public policy works within these new governmental arenas, bearing in mind that government has always been about the relationships between the public power and private interests (in other words, this is not something that came with "governance"). The present stage of the research involves mapping territorial policy communities at the meso or regional level.

The formation and consolidation of European states has been presented as a process of boundary-building, in which the external border is consolidated, while politics and interest representation turn inwards towards the national arena (Rokkan 1999; Caramani 2004). Spatial rescaling has opened up these boundaries, allowing some interests to operate at multiple levels and engage in "partial exit" from national arenas (Bartolini 2005). We may also be seeing the same thing at the sub-state level, as rescaling and territorial decentralization are constructing new territorial boundaries to social, economic, and political systems, below the level of the state, at the same time as the external boundary is opening. This suggests the emergence of more loosely bounded spatial systems of interest articulation, representation, and intermediation, at multiple spatial scales.

The public policy literature contains a bewildering variety of concepts for analysing the relevant actors and relationships: policy networks, policy communities, epistemic communities, the *référentiel*, and advocacy coalitions (Dowding 2001; Jobert and Müller 1987; Rhodes and Marsh 1992). Some authors use the term "policy network" to denote what others mean by policy community and vice versa. Almost always, however, these terms are defined within the territorial limits of the nation-state. The establishment of regional government creates a new arena and imposes a new spatial boundary on policy actors, drawing them into new patterns of activity and relationships. The same can be said about giving greater powers to federated units and clarifying their role, as has been done, with varying degrees of success, in Germany. This is certainly a weak boundary compared with the old nation-state and it is one that is contested in day to day politics, but the difference is one of degree not of kind. Federal states have frequently experienced tensions over the division of competences and the definition of political community, and this is a staple of relations between states and the European Union. My interest is in what happens to interest articulation and brokerage under the dual conditions of functional rescaling and governmental decentralization.

Without being drawn into the conceptual morass, in this chapter I use the term "policy community" in a broad, descriptive sense, to refer to the set of actors involved in a given policy field and construe the various other characteristics that are usually taken as defining features of the competing "models" as variables. This definition give us four sets of issues. One is the set of actors involved in any given policy field, which some describe as the network and others as the community (and yet others as "stakeholders"). Second is the interests of those actors and the way in which they are constructed and expressed. Third is the balance of power among groups in the competition for policy and resources. Fourth is interaction among groups and with government at various levels. Applying this definition at the meso level of government, I propose the concept of territorial policy communities, referring to the constellation of actors at that level, and then pose a series of questions about them.

Cases and Questions

The study concerns the territorialization of interest representation in six countries, with case-studies in each:

- United Kingdom (Scotland, Wales, Northern Ireland, North-East England).
- Italy (Tuscany, Campania, Lombardy)
- France (Rhône-Alpes, Brittany)
- Spain (Catalonia, Basque Country, Aragon)
- Germany (Bavaria, Saxony)
- Belgium (Flanders, Wallonia)

In each state, we have examples of what are prima facie stronger and weaker regions (to use the term in a generic sense), including functionally based regions and those based on historic and cultural identity. In each case, there has been recent change, through the establishment of devolved/ federal government or its strengthening and reform. The states constitute a universe of European states with a significant meso level, although Poland might be included as a borderline case. The research is based on extensive interviews with representatives of peak interest groups and examination of documents. The present chapter reports on findings from work done in the United Kingdom, Italy, France, and Spain.

The dimensions of change in which I am interested are the following:

1) Organizational: the extent to which groups have territorialized their structures.
2) Cognitive. This has two elements.
   - The way that groups define their interests. It is true by definition that interest groups have interests, but it is not always obvious just what these are. They may be expressed by class (employers and unions), by sector, and/or by territory. Different expressions may be found at different territorial scales.
   - The orientation towards particular territorial levels as a priority and a frame of reference.
3) Relational. This refers to working relationships, collaboration, confrontation and social compromise vertically (among territorial levels) and horizontally (within the territory). It includes relationships with
   - the state-wide level of their own organization;
   - governments;
   - other groups within the same sector;
   - groups in other sectors.

There is a series of possible outcomes of rescaling, which provide a set of competing hypotheses. These are as follows:

1) Institutional isomorphism, in which groups take on the same territorial scale of organization as the state. Governmental decentralization is mirrored by interest groups.
2) The counter-hypothesis, "regions without regionalism,"[2] in which government is decentralized but interest representation is not, so that regions do not become policy arenas and interest intermediation is through the central state, with regional institutions acting at best as relays (Trigilia 1994; Le Galès 1997).
3) A strengthening of territorial lobbies, in which territory at least partially displaces class and sector in the definition of interests and groups cooperate in the promotion of common spatial interests, as one might expect in competitive regionalism.
4) Partial exit, in which some groups can opt out of policy communities by moving to new territorial scales, disengaging from social partnership, or venue-shopping for the scale that suits them best. The result is a fragmentation of existing policy communities

by scale and by sector. Some groups will be privileged over others.

5) The counter-hypothesis to (4), a re-territorialization of policy communities, with a new articulation between class, sector, and territory. There is a move towards regional mediation of interests as a result. At the limit, this could give rise to new forms of regional concertation or neo-corporatism.

The preliminary results are as follows.

Organization

There is a tendency for groups to regionalize in response to devolution, regional government, or regional deconcentration. Sometimes this is a direct result of state policy. For example, France and Italy have obliged their chambers of commerce to establish a regional structure, which has influenced other business bodies, from which it is elected. In other cases, a regional level has been established in recent years to act as an interlocutor with regional government. Regionalization, however, is mediated by a number of factors. There is everywhere a strong path dependency as previous levels of organization are entrenched, such as the *provincia* in Italy and Spain, or the *département* in France. In Spain, chambers of commerce are organized provincially and membership, as from 2011, is no longer compulsory. The regional level, however, has become the key level for policy influence, while the traditional levels remain important for service provision to members. In France, there has been a multiplication of levels (region, *département*, city, *pays*, *territoire*, metropolis, commune), which has made life very difficult for groups.

Some groups have established autonomous regional levels, while in other cases the region is a federation of provincial bodies. Sometimes the regional level has its own funding, but more often it depends on contributions collected at the provincial level. Power relationships vary in important ways. Newly established groups are much more likely to adopt a regional level of organization. Direct political considerations sometimes play a role. The Basque nationalist trade unions, consciously engaged in region- (or nation-) building, are not only independent of the Spanish federations but are also centralized within the Basque Country.

The result is that unions and business groups often have a complex structure, frequently at multiple levels. This structural complexity presents problems of resource constraints, and groups everywhere complain about not being able to be present in all the places that they should be. This need to be in more than one place is particularly constraining for trade unions. The other tension is between combining territorial and sectoral representation within the main union and employer's federations; there are frequent tensions, as sectoral divisions, often coming down from the national level, cut across horizontal cooperation at the regional level.

It is not just that the structure of government influences the organization of groups. The latter also are actors in the politics of rescaling, seeking to mould structures in a way that can maximize their influence, without sacrificing those levels where they are already entrenched.

Orientation

We observe territorial lobbies in places where identity is strong and has been reconstructed around themes of development and competitive regionalism. Examples are found in the UK cases (even NE England), in the Basque Country and Catalonia, in Belgium, and in Spain. However, nobody in Rhône-Alpes and few in Tuscany invoked the idea of a regional interest in competition with other regions.

The region has become an important point of reference in the perception of policy issues. This development is in contrast to interviews I did in France in the 1980s, when the region was always referred to as the territory "of the future" rather than of the present. It also represents a change from the *regioni senza regionalismo* in Italy in the 1980s. There is a territorial spillover from one policy sector to another, as the local implications of sectoral initiatives become apparent. So, for example, active labour market and training policies spill over into other areas of social policy, including social inclusion, housing, and the wider questions of young or older people, broadening the definition of the sector.

Concurrent changes in politics affect the realignment of interest representation. Unions and employers are delinking from political parties and the old subcultural divisions among both employers and unions (Catholic, Socialist, Lay, Communist) are less important. Old networks (such as the Freemasons, Opus Dei, Comunione e Liberazione) within the business community are better entrenched in some regions than in others, but their local connections are challenged by territorial rescaling. Networks are consequently restructuring differently in different territories, most notably in Italy and Spain. In Tuscany, the difference between the post-Communist and Christian Democrat worlds was smaller than elsewhere in Italy and the Partito Democratico is locally hegemonic. In Lombardy, the regional president, Formigoni, was part of Berlusconi's Popolo della Libertà, but enjoyed a certain leeway in an otherwise highly centralized party. However, he faced competition from the Lega Nord, who embrace a more divisive idea of regionalism. They compete for control of the old Christian Democrat networks. Campania remains fragmented, with little political mobilization at the regional level.

Regional decentralization has been politically controversial in the past, both left and right at times supporting and at times opposing it. As it has been established, however, it has gained more support, and almost nobody wishes to reverse the process. Nonetheless, there are different interpretations of what it means and exactly what form it should take. Almost all groups in France, Spain, and Italy support regional devolution in principle but complain about the multiplicity of levels at which they need to operate. They generally favour simplification and a clearer allocation of competences. Business groups in the UK, which previously were hostile to Scottish and Welsh devolution, have now accepted it but remain reluctant to go further. In the early 2000s they were also in favour of regional deconcentration and development agencies in England, although opposed to the moves towards regional government. Catalan business groups, by contrast, have gone from opposition to devolution to active promotion of it.

In fact, both unions and employer groups are cross-pressured. Unions have looked to territorial spaces to expand the scope of their activities beyond workplace negotiation and (usually national) wage bargaining. It is at the territorial level that they can address issues such as youth unemployment, marginalization, precarious and seasonal employment, and the lack of unionization in small firms. A territorial focus enables them to compensate for the very low levels of unionization in small firms. Regionally provided public goods and negotiating arenas are important. Yet at the same time, unions insist on maintaining state-wide employment law and collective bargaining. Their attitude to political decentralization is therefore complex and sometimes contradictory.

Business, for its part, while knowing that production in the modern economy is often linked to territory and collective production goods, seeks to avoid territorial capture, to ensure its own mobility and to venue-shop. It therefore seeks territorial institutions that it can control, or in which it negotiates with the fewest interlocutors, preferring the corporatist mode or, better still, bilateral links with policy-makers. Its orientation may depend on the place of ownership of business, their place of production, the scope of their markets, and the level at which they are regulated. There are also divisions within the business community. Large employers are more inclined to neoliberal ideology than in the past, wary of social concertation and careful to avoid territorial capture, but this does not mean that they are deterritorialized, since territory remains a factor in business strategy. Small businesses are often more dependent on regional public goods and are often more protectionist, but are less well organized and tend to emphasize local rather than regional structures. This produces tensions everywhere between the representatives of large and small business.

In spite of the formal distancing of unions from parties, left-wing regional governments are still more accommodating of trade unions. In Rhône-Alpes, the dominance of the socialists in the last two elections has given the unions more of an entry, while the presence of the Greens in the coalition gives an opening to social movements. Business groups, in response, look more to the central state.

The degree to which groups are obliged to operate within the new meso-level policy systems also depends on the strengths of the devolved government. Where devolved governments have extensive competences, groups are forced into dialogue or lobbying. Partial exit and venue-shopping are more difficult where the devolved government has the legitimacy of a historic nation or cultural community, as in Scotland or Catalonia, although it still does happen there. At the minimum, groups in these places must give verbal respect to the territorial community. At the other extreme, the North-East of England in the 2000s lacked both a strong sense of identity or local patriotism and elected institutions. Business groups thus invested heavily in the regional development agency, on which they had a privileged position, and tried to ignore the indirectly elected regional assembly, drawn largely from local government. Trade unions and voluntary groups, on the other hand, wished to strengthen the assembly, where they had greater access, and to use it to widen the development policy agenda into social issues.

A great deal has been written on the impact of Europe on region-building and regional mobilization. The research shows this impact to be highly variable, as far as interest groups are concerned. Groups in Spain and Italy make regular reference to the European context, although they still tend to approach Europe through their state-level organizations rather than directly or in alliance with regional governments. Groups in Brittany and Rhône-Alpes do so much less, perhaps reflecting growing French Euroscepticism. Europe was a strong theme among the British groups in the early 2000s, but is mentioned less now. This shift reflects a general falling away of the Europe-of-the-Regions movement during the decade (Elias 2008).

Beyond these generalizations, there are important individual traits to be found among unions and among employers' organizations. For historic and political reasons, some are notably more inclined to regionalism than others. In France, the Confédération française démocratique du travail (CFDT) has been regionalist since the 1960s, while Force Ouvrière (FO) pays it little heed, and the Confédération générale du travail (CGT) is somewhere in between. The Scottish Trades Union Congress has supported devolution since the late 1960s, although some individual trades unions have been more reticent. In Spain, Comisiones Obreras (CCOO) is traditionally more decentralist than the Unión General de Trabajadores (UGT).

New Cleavages

The new regionalist literature, presenting regions as engaged in competition for economic advantage, would suggest that territory itself has become an important cleavage, replacing sectoral or class divisions. It is true that meso-level governments place a strong emphasis on cooperation in pursuit of development, but the idea of a common interest is found mostly in places where there is an existing territorial identity. There is a long tradition in Scotland of mobilizing around common economic interests, although this does not in itself necessarily attenuate intra-territorial divisions. Catalonia and the Basque Country similarly have social identities that underpin the notion of a common interest; this has been true of Brittany since the economically based regionalism of the Comité d'Études et de Liaison de Intérêts Bretons (CELIB) in the 1950s. It is less common to hear interest representatives speak of common regional interests in the Italian cases and the theme is completely absent in Rhône-Alpes. While competitive regionalism postulates a common territorial interest, however, the move to regional *government*, that is, multi-functional elected institutions, can have the opposite effect. It constitutes the region as a political arena and policy-making system, which has introduced competition over policy and resources within regions and sometimes caused tensions within former territorial lobbies. This opens up differences over sectoral and spatial priorities in development policy and even over the meaning of development itself, especially over contested ideas like sustainable development.

One effect has been the emergence of a productivist/environmentalist cleavage. Producer groups, both business and unions, line up on one side against environmentalists and conservationists (of both left and right) on the other. More broadly, there has been some fragmentation of policy communities, as old state-bound relations are disrupted and groups look for new opportunities. Reform of the Common Agricultural Policy (CAP), combined with decentralization of the field, is threatening existing patterns of corporatist management of agriculture. The supporters of the old productivist model tend to defend the traditional state-bound structures (within the CAP), while challengers, including organic farmers, neo-ruralists, and those pressing for redefinition of the field may look to regional government. In Scotland and Wales, on the other hand, it is the farmers (who are often small and hill farmers) who have gained support from the devolved governments, against the UK line of radical retrenchment and liberalization of the CAP.

There are also differences in social policy concerning entitlements and how the "deserving poor" are defined and identified. Modes of public service delivery are one of the clearest examples of policy divergence among meso-level governments in Europe. There is a tendency in Lombardy, in Catalonia, and in England towards greater involvement of private actors in service delivery, contracting-out of services, competition, selectivity, and "consumer choice," which is less evident in Tuscany, Campania, Scotland, Wales, and some Spanish autonomous communities. This involvement of private actors is defined by exponents of New Public Management (which is not so new any more) as a matter of efficiency, but there are distributive consequences to the adoption of one model or another. It has, not surprisingly, become a matter of political contestation, often pitching social movements, public sector unions and professional groups against business and the central or local administrative elites.

In some regions, institutionalization and mobilization at the meso level are paralleled at the level of the large city. In all our cases governments have sought to reinforce the metropolitan level for the purposes of planning, development, and infrastructure provision. In some places the metropolitan level is emerging as a rival to the meso. Barcelona is in some ways a rival to Catalonia, especially when the two have been controlled by different parties. In Rhône-Alpes, the Lyon metropolitan area competes both with the region and with the smaller metropolis of

Grenoble. The failure of the move to regional government in England was followed by a rediscovery of the concept of the city-region. There is consequently some rescaling of interest representation but in a distinct mode. At the urban or metropolitan level, there is a greater pluralism of representation as social movements challenge roles and strategies of the productivist partners. Forms of social concertation tend to be looser and less stable here.

Interaction and Concertation

Interaction is facilitated where groups share the same level of territorial organization. It is also facilitated where the cognitive meaning of territory is shared and there is a commitment to territory as a frame for public policy, as in obviously territorialized sectors such as economic or urban development. As other sectors territorialize, horizontal interaction also becomes more important. On the other hand, where territorial identity is highly contested, as in the Basque Country, it is less available as a common reference point. The nationalist Basque trade unions (who are the majority there) some years ago broke the existing system of social cooperation in pursuit of both industrial militancy and radical nationalism. Basque employers are divided, to a lesser degree, between those closer to the Partido Popular and those closer to the PNV (Basque Nationalist Party). Cooperation is also difficult in Lombardy because of the Lega Nord, whose model of regionalism is internally divisive. Some regions, like Rhône-Alpes, lack both historic identity and a unified urban structure, being divided among competing metropolitan areas. Brittany has a tradition of cooperation going back to the 1950s, with roots in Christian Democracy and the rise of new regional elites (the *forces vives*) from the 1950s, but this cooperation is not associated with militant nationalism. These examples suggest that the strongest basis for a common lobby might be "weak ties," based on economic interest but without the need for strong common cultural or political identities.

The literature in new regionalism regularly suggests that at this territorial level there is a distinct style of policy-making, based on horizontal coordination, collaboration, and networks, rather than partisanship of pluralist interest politics. This emphasis on horizontal linkages is one of the innumerable interpretations of the move from "government to governance." A closer examination shows a multiplicity of forms of interaction between organized interests and regional government.

All devolved governments have embraced forms of engagement with groups and citizens. Doing so is a consequence of their search for legitimacy and support. It also stems from the nature of their responsibilities, which include economic development and, specifically, training policies. It would be a mistake, however, to generalize from these policy fields, where cooperation is a practical necessity or statutory (by national or European regulation) responsibility, to regional government as a whole. In other words, we cannot conclude that changing scales itself entails a change in the modalities of governing. Groups are drawn into social engagement to varying degrees. Militant unions still sometimes see it as a distraction from the class struggle, but this is a minority view. Some employers disdain it in the name of neoliberalism, but, except for the United Kingdom, most of them embrace it to some degree.

The most minimal engagement is in the form of consultation, which involves governments making policy proposals and asking for input. It is widely criticized, as it seems to promise more than it can deliver and groups do not know what happens to their ideas once expressed. A more formalized mode is through economic and social councils, which are statutory in France, representing employers, unions, and civil society. In Campania, the Tavolo di Partenariato Economico e Sociale is convened three to four times a year by the regional government to consult all relevant interest groups on key economic legislation. Catalonia and Rhône-Alpes have economic and social councils, but in the Basque Country, councils have been largely paralysed as a result of a boycott on the part of the nationalist unions. These bodies provide a place of encounter for business and unions, although not for common action. There is some evidence of their providing a mode of socialization, in that representatives of groups get to know each other and share a common spatial perspective. In some of the non-national Spanish regions, however, they appear to be little more than ritualistic, since the social partners hardly exist.

A more structured form of engagement is through "parity" institutions, allowing the social partners to manage training policy, some labour market matters, and some social welfare functions. Training and active labour market policies have been regionalized widely, the region providing both a new territorial scale that is closer to labour markets and a place of encounter between economic and social policy. The sphere of regional encounters expands as active labour market policy interacts with the domain of social inclusion and welfare. Trade unions have seen regionalized training and employment bodies as a mechanism to expand the agenda of collective bargaining to incorporate externalities and a range of social issues. In this way, they seek to use territory to compensate for their weakness in the workplace and the decline of national-level bargaining as well as to extend their reach to non-unionized sectors of society. Some unions (such as the Comisiones Obreras in Spain and the Confédération française démocratique du travail in France) are more committed to this strategy and more territorialized than others. Employers are more sceptical about this expansion and seek to confine the regional agenda to development narrowly defined. Small and medium-sized enterprises, while needing the public goods provided by such partnerships, are often poorly organized and thus unable effectively to contribute.

Economic development partnerships exist widely at the local level, including regional and local governments and employers. Unions have consistently sought entry into these partnerships, although business has not always welcomed them. In Italy, local pacts have been promoted with European encouragement. While these various partnerships tend to be at a sub-regional level, regional governments have increasingly sought to define these arenas, sometimes in competition with the state. The result, in some places, is a proliferation of territorial arenas and a stretching of the resources of interest groups.

There are instances of broader social concertation, or weak forms of neo-corporatism. In Tuscany the regional government has an elaborate system of concertation through *tavoli di concertazione*, representing the social partners, which discuss policy proposals. This concertation system is separate from the consultative processes of the regional council and is vaunted by the region as a distinct Tuscan model. Lombardy, too, has its own model, based on Christian Democratic notions of subsidiarity, although there is much less social concertation than in Tuscany and it tends to be more sporadic. Catalonia has a formal system of social dialogue on the basic lines of social and economic policy, as did the Basque Country before the nationalist unions broke it. Such systems are unlikely to emerge in France as long as the regional council has such weak powers. There is also a national effect here, as it seems to be countries that have a tradition of social concertation at the state-wide level that are most easily able to reproduce it at the devolved level; hence the weakness of social concertation in Scotland. The Rhône-Alpes regional council is committed to social dialogue, but respondents constantly complain about the historic weakness of the practice in France. Many of the non-historic Spanish autonomous communities have regular social and economic pacts and plans, but these appear to have little effect, being vague statements of intent.

Another concept, which has had a number of labels but is now widely known as co-production, involves engagement by professional providers and users of public services. This practice has become an important theme recently in Scotland to describe the policy style in public services. It perhaps predates devolution, but it has been strengthened by it and contrasts with the emphasis in England on New Public Management, which is focused on competition and contestability.

Although for rhetorical purposes they all are often run together, these practices need to be distinguished from participatory democracy, which involves expanding the number of participants and broadening the agenda. Initiatives for participation are typically found at the local or urban level, where the political agenda is very broad and social movements contest the domination of the policy process by politicians and selected social partners.

Of course, it is dangerous to take regional governments' own descriptions of their modes of policy-making and interest intermediation at their face value. These new governments have sought legitimacy, beyond their electoral mandate, by drawing in groups but also by adopting the fashionable language of subsidiarity, social partnership and "governance." Some of this discourse has been imported from the European Union, and there is some evidence that traditional forms of closed and clientelist politics, or older networks, are being dressed up in new language to gain legitimacy at state and European levels. Moreover, these various forms of group politics and intermediation are in tension with the principle of elective democracy. There is often resistance on the part of elected politicians to corporatist or participative forms of policy-making, and, the stronger the elective element in regional government, the less important corporate modes of policy-making may become.

Representativity

There are serious questions in all our cases about the representativity of organizations speaking for the social partners at the regional level. These organizations tend to be the general-purpose, or intersectoral, interest organizations rather than the sectoral business bodies and unions which are in closest contact with the membership. There is a problem of articulation between the regional level and the sectoral bodies, which are often national or local. The need for an organizational presence at numerous levels means that it is often either full-time officials or retired members who participate in social concertation. They are consequently not always able to commit their own members.

Union membership is often very low, especially in southern European countries, where wage deals are binding, providing incentives to free ride. In some cases, regional representative groups are financially highly dependent on regional governments. This financial dependence exists in France, Italy, and Spain, where unions and some employer groups receive funding for training and social programs, which is often discreetly diverted for representation. In regions with weaker civil societies, representative groups appear to have been created by regional government.

Conclusion

As government functions rescale, with the deconcentration of the central state (as in France), regional agencies (as in England in the 2000s), or elected regional government, there is institutional isomorphism, whereby interest groups mirror the organization of territorial government. However, it is limited by path-dependency. Old structures, which represent power bases both for political elites and for interest representatives, resist. The territorialization of groups is a matter of political contestation. There is more territorialization in Spain, Italy, and the UK (Scotland and Wales) than in France. Regional government, as opposed to various forms of "governance," does make a difference, as it strengthens the territorial boundary of institutions, makes it more difficult for groups to bypass the regional level, and provides a greater legitimacy to regional policy-making.

Territorial lobbying is strongest where there is a historic identity and is not merely the outcome of sectoral interests or functional logic. As has long been known in Scotland, territorial identity coexists with, rather than displacing, class or sectoral loyalties. Interests cannot therefore be reduced to the individual or the firm; territorial interests are also being constructed.

There is cognitive change, as we have encountered regional group leaders who do view sectoral issues through a regional lens and often complain about the lack of understanding of their colleagues in the national capital. In many cases, there are tensions between the functional and territorial perspectives of interest groups, although this research was not able to explore detailed differences among economic sectors, as Coleman and Jacek (1989) do (but only for business associations). These changes are more important where there are other reasons for national policy communities to weaken or restructure, such as a crisis in the old system of representation (Italy) or an externally motivated reform in a policy sector (agriculture, energy).

There are new cleavages and alliances at the regional level as the policy agenda shifts. Shifting territorial scales does not dissolve class or sectoral cleavages or replace the politics of conflict and compromise by those of consensus and collaboration, but it does transform them. There is no general shift at the regional level from government to governance, if the latter is understood as horizontal cooperative policy-making in the absence of hierarchy. Such forms of policy-making have long been characteristic of the sector of economic development, especially under the new regionalist mode of partnership, but economic development does not exhaust the regional policy agenda. The popularity of the idea of governance probably stems from the fact that studies of policy at the regional level have tended to focus on development (under the new regionalist rubric) or EU programs, where social partnership is a statutory requirement. Even within economic development, often presented as a zero-sum game within the region, there are conflicts with environmentalist concerns.

There is evidence of partial exit of venue-shopping, as well-connected groups, notably the big business lobbies, are able to operate at multiple levels. Small business is tied more into local and regional networks, while trade unions are constrained by lack of resources. This difference in the capacity to venue-shop has disrupted some existing local and regional networks, adding to the effects of externally imposed change such as reform of the Common Agricultural Policy and the challenges of competition within the European single market.

The experiences with social dialogue and concertation at the regional level vary by territory and by sector. Nowhere do we find regional corporatism. The Tuscan model of social concertation comes closest. Elsewhere we find social concertation within particular sectors, especially where there is statutory provision. Federalizing tendencies in Europe are thus accompanied by a federalization of policy systems and policy arenas. There is, however, no clearly defined hierarchy of arenas. Territorial policy systems are open, with unequal constraints on different groups. The boundaries of the new arenas themselves remain the objects of contestation.

ACKNOWLEDGMENTS

This work is supported by an ESRC Professorial Fellowship.

NOTES

1 Caramani (2004), however, emphasizes continued nationalization.
2 The expression "regioni senza regionalismo" was used to refer to the Italian regions in the 1970s and 1980s (Pastori 1980).

REFERENCES

Bache, Ian, and Matthew Flinders, eds. 2004. *Multi-level Governance*. Oxford: Oxford University Press.
Bartolini, Stefano. 2005. *Restructuring Europe: Centre Formation, System Building, and Political Structuring between the Nation State and Europe*. Oxford: Oxford University Press.
Caramani, Daniele. 2004. *The Nationalization of Politics: The Formation of National Electorates and Party Systems in Western Europe*. Cambridge: Cambridge University Press.
Coleman, William, and Henry Jacek, eds. 1989. *Regionalism, Business Interests and Public Policy*, London: Sage.
Compston, Hugh. 2002. The Strange Persistence of Policy Concertation. In *Policy Concertation and Social Partnership in Western Europe*, edited by Stefan Berger and Hugh Compston. Oxford: Berghahn.
Cooke, Philip, and Kevin Morgan.1998. *The Associational Economy: Firms, Regions, and Innovation*. Oxford: Oxford University Press.
Dowding, Keith. 2001. There Must Be End to Confusion: Policy Networks, Intellectual Fatigue, and the Need for Political Science Methods Courses in British Universities. *Political Studies* 49(1):89–105.
Elias, Anwen. 2008. Introduction: Whatever Happened to the Europe of the Regions? Revisiting the Regional Dimension of European Politics. *Regional & Federal Studies* 18(5):483–92
Ferrera, Maurizio. 2006. *The Boundaries of Welfare: European Integration and the New Spatial Politics of Solidarity*. Oxford: Oxford University Press.
Goetz, Klaus H. 2008. Governance as a Path to Government. *West European Politics* 31(1–2):258–79.
Greer, Scott, ed. 2006. *Territory, Democracy and Justice. Federalism and Regionalism in Western Democracies*. London: Palgrave Macmillan.

Hooghe, Liesbet, and Gary Marks. 2001. *Multi-Level Governance and European Integration*. Lanham: Rowman & Littlefield.

Hough, Dan, and Charlie Jeffery. 2006. An Introduction to Multi-Level Electoral Competition. In *Devolution and Electoral Politics*, edited by Dan Hough and Charlie Jeffery. Manchester: Manchester University Press.

Jobert, B., and P. Müller. 1987. *L'état en action*. Paris: Les Presses Universitaires de France.

Kazepov, Yuri, and Eduardo Barberis. 2008. La dimensione territoriale delle politiche sociali in Europa: alcune riflessioni sui processi di rescaling e governance. *Revista delle Politiche Sociali* 3:51–78.

Keating, Michael. 1998. *The New Regionalism in Western Europe: Territorial Restructuring and Political Change*. Cheltenham: Edward Elgar.

Keating, Michael. 2006. From Functional to Political Regionalism: England in Comparative Perspective. In *The English Question*, edited by Robert Hazel. Manchester: Manchester University Press.

Keating, Michael, Paul Cairney, and Eve Hepburn. 2008. Territorial Policy Communities and Devolution in the United Kingdom. *Cambridge Journal of Regions, Economy and Society* 1(2):1–16.

Le Galès, Patrick. 1997. Gouvernement et Gouvernance des Régions: Faiblesses Structurelles et Nouvelles Mobilisations. In *Les paradoxes des régions en Europe*, edited by Patrick Le Galès and Christian Lesquesne. Paris: La Découverte.

McEwen, Nicola, and Luis Moreno, eds. 2005. *The Territorial Politics of Welfare*. London: Routledge.

Ohmae, Kenichi. 1995. *The End of the Nation State: The Rise of Regional Economies*. New York: Free Press.

Pastori, G. 1980. Le regioni senza regionalism. *Il Mulino* 10(2):268–83.

Paterson, Lindsay. 2001. Higher Education and European Regionalism. *Pedagogy, Culture and Society* 9(2):133–60.

Piattoni, Simona. 2010. *The Theory of Multi-Level Governance: Conceptual, Empirical, and Normative Challenges*. Oxford: Oxford University Press.

Putnam, Robert. 1993. *Making Democracy Work: Civic Traditions in Modern Italy*. Princeton: Princeton University Press.

Rhodes, R.A.W., and David Marsh. 1992. Policy Networks in Britain. In *Policy Networks in British Government*, edited by R.A.W. Rhodes and David Marsh. Oxford: Clarendon.

Rokkan, Stein. 1999. *State Formation, Nation-Building, and Mass Politics in Europe: The Theory of Stein Rokkan*, edited by Peter Flora, Stein Kuhnle, and Derek Urwin. Oxford: Oxford University Press.

Scott, Allen. 1998. *Regions and the World Economy: The Coming Shape of Global Production, Competition, and Political Order*. Oxford: Oxford University Press.

Storper, Michael. 1997. *The Regional World: Territorial Development in a Global Economy*. New York and London: Guildford.

Trigilia, Carlo. 1994. The Paradox of the Region: Economic Regulation and the Representation of Interests. *Economy and Society* 20(3):306–27.

11 *Engagé* Intellectuals, Technocratic Experts, and Scholars

JAN ERK

primum non nocere (first, do no harm)

Over the centuries following the original Hippocratic Oath of fifth-century BC, the Latin admonition *primum non nocere* came to define the key ethical element in the medical profession Hippocrates himself had envisioned: *first, do no harm*. This prudent rather than activist principle reminds physicians to exercise humility in the efficacy of the tools, technology, and talent available to them. In every generation of the profession, some have been enticed by the new advances, willing to impetuously apply them in order to undo the previous generation's inaction. But before any action is taken, it is imperative we make sure this fundamental ethical principle is met. Our knowledge for accurate diagnosis and effective treatment is still incomplete. Multiple immediate causes could be interacting with long-term structural causes, accompanied by additional factors medical science has not yet fully uncovered. In order to make sure that the patient's well-being is paramount, uncertainty dictates prudence before an action is taken.[1]

In the last decade, various federal models have been prescribed to cure the ills of deeply divided societies. These prescriptions always take the form of institutional/constitutional engineering that has a direct bearing on the well-being of individuals and communities. At best, the consequences of not getting it right could lead to unforeseen problems appearing elsewhere in the political system, or federal designs that are simply unworkable in the political context they are cut-and-pasted upon. At worst, the consequences of institutional/constitutional engineering cover an unseemly spectrum ranging from human suffering to economic/social/environmental devastation.

The main focus of this chapter is the relationship between analytic and applied comparative federalism – particularly in the context of new institutionalism where emphasis is on the formal distribution of political power across orders of government – and the risks of prescribing federalism (based on this analytic perspective that overlooks uncodified factors at the expense of institutional/constitutional ones). All variants of new institutionalism in the social sciences (i.e., rational choice, sociological and historical) share an analytical emphasis on institutional arrangements that distribute political power among political and social actors and, by extension, shape political strategies. The risk this chapter seeks to expose does not automatically cast a negative verdict on new institutionalism as an explanatory theoretical framework. The very nature of scientific theorizing relies on emphasizing certain general explanatory factors through an analytic framework that brings an intellectual order to an array of otherwise unrelated outcomes. By definition, this is a deliberately reductionist exercise, aimed at presenting a stylized reproduction of political and social phenomena by putting the spotlight on the generalizable and relegating the idiosyncratic to the background.

In fact, new institutionalism has been a major factor behind the scholarly growth in comparative federalism (Erk and Swenden 2009a). In due course, the sub-field's earlier normative preference for Jeffersonian small government has been replaced by a commitment to analytical scholarship. Contemporary federalism scholars influenced by the teachings of new institutionalism tend to be more analytical in their approaches than previous generations of federalism researchers, whose work was often informed by a normative attachment to the merits of divided political authority (e.g., Elazar 1987). New institutionalism has brought a level of conceptual and theoretical clarity to our sub-field as well as allowing scholarly links to other areas of study informed by similar perspectives. Put differently, those who study federalism are no longer confined to a collection of federalism partisans. In terms of diagnosis, our findings based on the federations of the industrialized world are increasingly more systematic and cumulative. Yet does this gain justify prescribing a one-size-fits-all federal treatment for the developing world?

The goal of this chapter is to expose the risks in automatically translating the teachings of what is, by definition, an explanatory perspective into a prescriptive blueprint for new federations. But such a discussion on comparative federalism cannot be isolated from bigger philosophical questions on the scholarly vocation.

Comparative Federalism and Exporting Federalism

Federalism – the vertical division of political authority among orders of government – has experienced a remarkable comeback in recent decades. From the margins, the study of federalism has moved to the dynamic centre of scholarly enquiry, linking up literatures that had remained separate from one another. As the dominant explanatory perspective, new institutionalism has played an important role in bringing about this growth and consolidation of the sub-field (Erk 2007a).

Comparative federalism now studies varied phenomena – in both the developed and the industrializing world – such as power-sharing arrangements, democratic accountability in multilevel settings, public policy effectiveness, and economic performance. Parallel to the theoretical growth, there has been an increase in the global supply of federalism as new federal constitutions are prescribed as cures for ethnic conflict, macro-economic performance, and democratic consolidation (Erk 2006). Comparative federalism is thus no longer a solely explanatory sub-field, but a prescriptive one too.

Prescriptions of federalism inevitably reflect the institutionalist perspectives guiding the diagnosis. In analytical terms, scholarly focus has been on how political authority is divided, shared, or dispersed among two or more orders of government. As a sub-field with origins in constitutional studies, many students of federalism were often *avant la lettre* new institutionalists anyway. The new institutionalist wave in the social sciences broadened the possibilities for systematic comparative analyses of federal institutions/constitutions. Of course, one of the main practical advantages of institutionalist analysis is the easy operationalization across cases based on comparable institutional benchmarks and readily available data. There is thus some risk that feasibility and availability determine how things are done, while explanatory factors that don't lend themselves to such convenience might be overlooked. In a piece on constitutional courts and federalism, I use the following metaphor to portray institutional/constitutional analyses: "this might be a bit like the proverbial drunk who is looking for his car keys under the streetlight; not necessarily because the keys were lost there, but because the light is better" (Erk 2011, 525). Answers might very well be found away from where the light can shine satisfactorily.

From the appointment of judges to the Supreme Court of Canada to Swiss cabinet formation, federalism in the developed world relies a great deal on custom and informal practices that have established themselves over the *longue durée*. That is, the workings of the federal systems of the industrialized world reflect long-term patterns that cannot be delivered (or indeed predicted) by instant institutional/constitutional designs. Yet, as new federal constitutions are devised, emphasis tends to be on getting the formal institutional boilerplate right at the expense of the harder-to-operationalize uncodified aspects of federalism. In addition to the prevalence of informal practices that accompany – and sometimes trump – institutional/constitutional procedures, the workings of federalism can be captured only after uncodified factors such as ethnicity, language, demographics, culture, and class structure are brought into the picture. The fact that there are explanatory factors that don't come with easily operationalizable comparable benchmarks and readily available data should not result in their explanatory role being ignored. This shortcoming is not unique to new institutionalism; it exists whenever the analytical and the applied get mixed up.

The *Engagé* and the Expert

There are a number of angles from which to examine the relationship between the analytical and the applied. This paper approaches the question through its practitioner: the *engagé* intellectual, the technocratic expert, and the scholar.[2] A foundational question on the role of the academic lies at the heart of this angle: whether there is indeed a responsibility for *engagé* politics. This question was particularly pressing for academics who lived and worked during ideologically dark times. It was not necessarily whether one was a student of politics, philosophy, history, or law that created the expectations for involvement, but *engagé* behaviour was expected of all academics – from classicists to mathematicians – who had the courage to stand up. Their knowledge and societal impact was too big to be squandered in ivory towers away from the existential challenges liberal democratic free societies faced. The opposite view questioned this elitist sense of entitlement for moral leadership; academic credentials should grant no special rank to those joining their fellow citizens in manning the barricades of liberal democracy.

While the most acute form of the dilemma of *engagé* politics was experienced in the face of the two despotic ideologies of fascism and communism in Europe during the twentieth century, the question of the moral responsibility for political involvement versus the self-appointed leadership of intellectual elites continues to have contemporary resonance. The question thus remains contested: regardless of one's academic specialization, is there a special moral responsibility for scholars to stand up in defence of liberal democratic freedom against despotic political tendencies?

In his essay entitled "The Lure of Syracuse" (with reference to Plato's unsuccessful attempt to educate the tyrant ruler of Syracuse, Dionysius the Younger, into a philosopher-king), Mark Lilla contrasts French and German attitudes to *engagé* academia. While nineteenth-century French intellectual life was characterized by a romantic commitment to political causes, "east of the Rhine the assumption in the nineteenth and early twentieth centuries had been that professors were engaged in timeless *Wissenschaft* [knowledge] in the secluded university, that writers pursued private *Bildung* [formation] as they wrote their works, and that journalists dared to write about politics, and they were untrustworthy" (Lilla 2007, 204). Himself an *émigré* German academic chased away by National Socialists to Britain, owing to his *engagé* activities, after the war Norbert Elias advised academics to tread a fine balance between "involvement" and "detachment" (1956). More recently, the renowned student of International Relations, Robert Keohane, has shown how our times might still call for the *engagé* academic: "[As citizen-scholars], our first obligation is to take advantage of our academic freedom to speak out on controversial public issues, especially when others, less well protected, may fail to do so" (2009, 127). While the broader relevance of these moral questions is self-evident to an investigation on the relationship between analytical and applied comparative federalism, this philosophical debate is not new and it is not the main focus of this chapter.

Our focus is not about the philosophical trials and tribulations of the romantic *engagé* academic. However, without explicit recognition, the *engagé*'s less flamboyant technocratic contemporary sibling, that is, the *expert*, has been facing comparable conflicting dynamics. The relationship between the analytical and the applied is still at the core of these conflicting dynamics, but this time the question is not about the academic's involvement in political causes. Rather, it is about the application of their analytical expertise to real-life political problems ranging from reforming provincial electoral systems to designing new federal constitutions.

In his *Expert Political Judgment: How Good Is It? How Can We Know?* Philip Tetlock offers a number of benchmarks to evaluate the reliability of "expert political judgement." However, the bigger foundational questions about the desirability of such scholarly behaviour and the potential risks of corrupting the findings are not part of his investigation (Tetlock 2005). For Craig Calhoun, on the other hand, applied political science comes with fears of distorted academic autonomy and concern about potential complicity in causing harm (2010, 1101). Lending one's technocratic expertise to contemporary political projects often comes with a price – particularly if one happens to have career plans in politics. As Robert Keohane puts it: "'speaking truth to power' is harder for people with political ambitions than those without them" (2009, 126). In the context of the 2003 Iraq War, Keohane derisively observes:

> Academic IR specialists who were not seeking future government positions were almost unanimously opposed to the war – from Samuel Huntington to John Mearsheimer to myself. Academics with policy ambitions tended to be conditionally supportive of the invasion or to mute their criticism until they saw which way the political winds would blow. (ibid., 127)

While Keohane might be settling past scores, his observations about the problems associated with the intersection of the applied and the analytical have relevance beyond the American international relations community.

The Lure of Policy Relevance

At first glance, it seems entirely reasonable to expect academic research to generate dividends for society at large. After all, considerable public money is spent on research, and society deserves to benefit from it. Little objection can be levelled at those who call for more applied (and relevant) social science. While the quest for knowledge in itself might be seen as a dividend, the benefits are diffuse, long-term, and not necessarily problem specific. It is difficult to dismiss demands that all this (often publicly funded) research done by dusty dons in ivory towers should now start delivering practical dividends for the rest of the society. However, the assumption behind this call for more applied research is that the insights of analytical social science automatically deliver on real-life political puzzles as well. The following discussion will show how this assumption does not necessarily hold.

The intellectual goals of analytical and applied social science do not point in the same direction. One, that is, analytical social science, is about the search for generalizable (but probabilistic) explanations for political and social phenomena driven by the use of deliberately reductionist (and therefore, by definition, descriptively incomplete) analytical perspectives. The other, that is, applied social science, is about "solving" practical political problems through the use of the theoretical and conceptual toolkit the disciplines have accumulated. One is generalist in outlook; the other is puzzle driven, relying on an ad hoc mix of theories and concepts, backed by a firm grasp of the idiosyncrasies of the political context. The theoretical physicist toiling away in his controlled lab in search of scientific laws might not the best person to call to fix a clogged toilet ... not unlike the dusty don in the ivory tower recruited to put together a new federal prescription that will flush out all previous political ills.

The differences in intellectual goals (generalist theorizing vs. problem-driven puzzle-solving) are independent of the choice of research. But once the applied and analytical get entangled, the very choice of research topic can be influenced by this confusion. The end-justified nature of applied science sets it apart from analytical science, which is driven by explanatory rather than pragmatic goals. According to Jerome Ravetz, the expectations from experts are particularly pressing when "the facts are uncertain, values in dispute, stakes high, and decisions urgent" (1999, 649). Earlier, in his *The Merger of Knowledge and Power*, Ravetz brought attention to the risks involved in applied science driven by real-life problems: "once there are external influences on the choice of problems (and hence of results), the objectivity of science loses an important dimension" (1990, 25). It is these situations where "strong political and economic forces come into play to pull the researcher into different directions, threatening the integrity of the research process" (Elzinga 2004, 10). As a result, "the growth of knowledge might be hobbled by the stifling consequences of pragmatic agendas" (Nimic 2000, 22). The lure of policy relevance might then entice some to market their technocratic expertise in areas that otherwise would not have been their first choice of academic research.

One of the fathers of the realist school in international relations – and a Jewish *émigré* scholar who had witnessed the collusion between politics and science in his native Germany – Hans Morgenthau was particularly aware of how pragmatic concerns could come to dictate the research agendas of academics. Lyndon B. Johnson's expansion of American involvement in Vietnam had coincided with a growth in government research funds – and the accompanying financial and professional allure of applied research. Morgenthau was conscious, of course, of the risks when political power and the intellectual search for truth intersected to create an

> academic-political complex in which the interests of the government are inextricably intertwined with the interests of large groups of academics.

> These ties are both formal and informal, and the latter are more dangerous to intellectual freedom, as they consist in the intellectuals' unconscious adaptation to imperceptible social and political pressures. (1970, 25)

Across the Atlantic, Morgenthau's views were shared by a vocal opponent of realism, the father of the so-called English school of international relations, Hedley Bull. According to Bull, it was especially the behaviouralist school "who attracted huge research grants because their 'scientific' approach posed no kind of ideological threat to US foreign policy, rather promising to be able to make it more effective" (1966). The memoirs of Dean Acheson, the author of what came to be known as the Truman doctrine, the architect of the Marshall program, and the future secretary of state, show how correct Morgenthau's and Bull's fears were:

> [The] task of a public officer seeking to explain and gain support for a major policy is not that of the writer of a doctoral thesis. Qualification must give way to simplicity of statement, nicety and nuance to bluntness, almost brutality, in carrying home a point ... If we made our points *clearer than truth*, we did not differ from most other educators and could hardly do otherwise. (1969; italics added)

Most social scientists are aware, of course, that our theories are idealized, reductionist, half-pictures providing probabilistic explanations (Walt 2005, 32). However, the enticing pull of policy relevance privileges those who can project technocratic expertise at the expense of those who transparently admit the probabilistic and incomplete state of our knowledge. The lure of policy relevance can sometimes coexist with material incentives, leading some academic entrepreneurs to peddle their technocratic expertise under Kafkaesque titles like "power-sharing expert in the stand-by team of the mediation support unit."

Technocratic Expertise

In this context, works that project confidence and certainty (while sweeping inconvenient theoretical/methodological/substantive/normative issues under the carpet) seem to have a better chance of conveying a sense of technocratic expertise to grant agencies, bureaucrats, and politicians. As Donald McCloskey characterizes it: "The social engineer promises to run the economy or the war or the culture with godlike expertise" (1990, 3). New institutionalism – precisely because it sounds technical rather than intellectual – is particularly helpful in giving that expert gloss designed to impress the uninitiated. Consequently, new institutionalist research heavy on techniques rather than ideas has colonized the research grant industry. Writing in 1953, Barrington Moore Jr was able to presage where things might end up:

> technique alone cannot define what is scientifically worth investigating. Larger problems of the social milieu and, ultimately, of philosophy enter into any defensible judgment of scientifically significant problems. Ill at ease in such questions, many technicians *search for pseudo-security in a form of pseudo-precision*. (125; italics added)

Moore's contemporary, another influential sociologist, C. Wright Mills, observed the way such emphasis on technique now started to figure prominently in the planning of research projects:

> [This practice] is bound to in some degree be salesmanship, and, given prevailing expectations, very likely to result in painstaking pretensions; the project is likely to be "presented," rounded in some arbitrary manner long before it ought to be; it is often a contrived thing, aimed at getting money for ulterior purposes, however valuable, as well as for the research presented. (1959, 7-2)

The projection of technocratic expertise best fits the expectations of applied and relevant social science. Yet the emphasis on technique obscures the fact that there is often a political choice in policy relevance; for example, do we want more income equality with lower economic growth or more inequality with higher growth? Politicians have electoral accountability, bureaucrats follow the political will, but for academics things are different. Political prescriptions inevitably include a hierarchy of political goals and choices among different political priorities. This might sound rather mundane, but decisions that have a direct bearing on the well-being of individuals and communities should be taken by those who can be held accountable for their behaviour. The outsourcing of politics to the expertise of neutral third parties (in this case academia) inevitably results in circumventing the very nature of political accountability in modern representative democracies. Scholarly erudition and even-handed reflection are one thing; offering institutional engineering as a technocratic expert without accountability is another. Be that as it may, the current global economic crisis is slowly exposing how the electoral cycle might be too short of a check on accountability. Many representative democracies of the industrialized world need long-term structural economic changes, but their politicians are naturally drawn to short-term patching-up jobs in order to ensure re-election. Yet flying into post-conflict societies, prescribing a constitution, and then flying out is not an answer to problems with political accountability in the developing world.

All Eggs in One Basket

The projection of technical expertise requires a discipline defined by a paradigmatic consensus; that is, the foundational principles should be beyond contention, so that experts can focus on applied techniques (and not some epistemological soul-searching). Among social science disciplines, economics for long was dominated by a single paradigm that allowed the formulation of elegant and parsimonious theories. Yet, as George DeMartino puts it:

> Despite the strides made in economics over the past century, the economist today does not know and cannot control whether any particular policy will succeed; nor does she know with certainty what harms may be caused by the policy in the event of its success of failure, etc. There is a danger of ignorance here; there is uncertainty on many levels, and as a consequence there is risk of policy failure. (2009, 14)

Gerald Epstein and Jessica Carrick-Hagenbarth seem to be on the same critical wavelength as DeMartino when they claim that "economists were so busy with elegant models, which explained and resolved market problems perfectly, they were incapable of seeing real world messes" (2010, 3). The global financial crisis of 2008 took the academic discipline of economics by surprise. As Paul Krugman put it in his *New York Times* op-ed piece at the time: "the economics profession went astray because economists, as a group, mistook beauty, clad in impressive-looking mathematics, for truth" (2009, MM36). A handful had foreseen the impending problem, but the overwhelming majority had failed to see the unintended real-life consequences when all the theoretical models of the discipline were originating from the same dominant paradigm. Essentially, this produced only thinking-inside-the-box. There is a similar risk in comparative federalism: the dominance of new institutionalism comes at the expense of the omission of perspectives from other theoretical schools. As Albert Hirschmann observed decades ago: "ordinarily social scientists are happy enough when they have gotten hold of one paradigm or line of causation. As a result, their guesses are often farther off the mark than those of the established politician whose intuition is more likely to take a variety of forces into account (1970, 341).

Extending federalism models from the developed world to the industrializing tends to come with the similar risk of putting all our eggs in the institutional/constitutional basket. The new institutionalist dominance in comparative federalism allows for the confident language of technical expertise, while harder to pin down uncodified factors and inconvenient normative issues are left out; long-term patterns are reduced to instant solutions. By favouring technique over thinking, the paradigmatic consensus can also prevent thinking-outside-the-box.

Thinkers and Tinkerers

In a piece written 40 years ago, Robert Merton explored how "insiders" and "outsiders" contributed to knowledge (1972). Both presented different advantages, but not necessarily pointing in the same direction. A paradigmatic consensus is usually something that unites insider experts as they hone their technical adroitness to take on real-life problems. Owing to the prevailing consensus, change is small-scale and comes only in the form of tinkering with the dominant perspective. Creative thinking, on the other hand, is a closer friend of the leave-no-stone-unturned attitude of thinking-outside-the-box. As C. Wright Mills put it:

> There is a playfulness of mind back of such combining as well as a truly fierce drive to make sense of the world, which the technician as such usually lacks. Perhaps he is too well trained, too precisely trained. Since one can be trained only in what is already known, training sometimes incapacitates one from learning new ways; it makes one rebel against what is bound to be at first loose and even sloppy. (1959, 7–9)

Because of its end-justified *raison d'être*, applied research is often about the competent execution of techniques. Hans Morgenthau believed applied research sapped creativity. In fact, he was sceptical about "whether scientific creativity can flourish if the scientific mind is tied to a practical purpose extraneous to itself, and is thereby deprived of the uncommitted speculative curiosity from which great scientific discoveries of the past have flourished" (Morgenthau 1972, 8). Innovative thinking, on the other hand, tends to flourish when it is unbound from a specific end. In a piece subtitled "The Siren Song of Policy Relevance," Christopher Hill argues that "managerial notions of productivity and 'usefulness' are spreading throughout higher education and imposing subtle pressures on researchers not to follow interests whose harvest might only be gleaned indirectly or in the longer term" (1994, 6). Ronald Krebs believes such emphases on the contemporary and the applied are particularly pronounced in international relations:

> [International Relations'] obsession with relevance contributes to the field's abiding presentism. Prediction is of course more than can reasonably be asked of a social science like international relations, but a less presentist discipline would be better positioned when the unexpected occurred – to make sense of those events and to advise unprepared policymakers – simply because it had spread its intellectual bets more widely. (2010, 1115)

End-justified applied research is bound to follow established and agreed-upon paths in turning expert opinion into policy. But originality and creativity are not the obvious offshoots of the type of "safe" research that characterizes applied social science. In his provocatively titled 1939 article, "The Usefulness of Useless Knowledge," American educational reformer and the founder of the Institute for Advanced Studies at Princeton University, Abraham Flexner, highlights the relationship between scholarly innovation and free thinking:

> that they had done their work without thought of use and that throughout the whole history of science most of the really great discoveries which had ultimately proved to be beneficial to mankind had been made by men and women who were driven not by the desire to be useful but merely the desire to satisfy their curiosity ... curiosity, which may or may not eventuate in something useful, is probably the outstanding characteristic of modern thinking. It is not new. It goes back to Galileo, Bacon, and to Sir Isaac Newton, and it must be absolutely unhampered. Institutions of learning should be devoted to the cultivation of curiosity and the less they are deflected by considerations of immediacy of application, the more likely they are to contribute not only to human welfare but to the equally important satis-

faction of intellectual interest which may indeed be said to have become the ruling passion of intellectual life in modern times. (1939, 545)

Sir Francis Galton's Problem with All This

During the presentation of the findings of a large-n study on the institution of marriage in tribal societies, at the Royal Anthropological Institute in London 1889, Sir Francis Galton made an interjection, highlighting a problem with methodology and evidence that came to be named after him. The study in question had found remarkable parallels between the 350 cases under investigation, and from these parallels he inferred evidence of a shared evolutionary logic in the institutions of marriage in tribal societies. Sir Francis was sceptical of this conclusion, since most convergence could be explained by the borrowing of cultural practices between tribes and/or shared cultural roots. In other words, what seemed to be endogenous in each and every case in fact included both phenomena from within as well those originating from the outside.

The enthusiasm of the comparative federalism expert for prescribing federal institutions/constitutions also presents a challenge to social science methodology. Other than a post-modern minority, most contemporary students of comparative federalism seem to use broadly positivist research methods and language. Yet a foundational principle of positivism in the social sciences is, of course, an assumption that there are social facts independent of the observer waiting to be unearthed. By influencing the nature of the observed (i.e., increasing the supply of new federations designed through prioritizing the institutional/constitutional factors), the observer thus runs the risk of violating a core positivist tenet.

One example of this pattern is the prescription of a continental European-style federal boilerplate to new federations. This model is much neater than trying to capture the workings of (common-law inspired) Anglo-Saxon federalism through the examination of the bewildering complexity of custom and informal practices, as well as uncodified factors such as ethnicity, language, demographics, culture, and class structure. The clearly written and codified formal structure of (Roman-law inspired) European federalism is easier to export. Of course, whether or not these institutions carry all the answers for federalism deserves further examination (Erk 2006; Erk and Koning 2010). But the risk of prescribing federalism based on one model is a Galton's problem for the study of federalism and democracy; that is, the "n" does not reflect endogenous patterns (and distorts the case selection because one type of federalism is more likely to be exported).

"The Treason of the Learned" and "Conspiracies against the Laity"

In 1927, Julien Benda published his controversial *La trahison de clercs* (the treason of the learned), accusing academics and intellectuals of acting as apologists for politicians and political ideologies (1927). Benda's criticism was particularly directed at European intellectuals of the late nineteenth century and early twentieth century, whose work had been influenced (and corrupted) by political concerns. The English translation of the original title in French cannot fully capture the connotations behind Benda's choice of the word *clerc*. Sharing the same etymological origin with the word *cleric*, it suggests a philosopher-priest class whose members devote their lives to knowledge as an end in itself. Benda's learned, however, betray their vocation the moment knowledge becomes a tool for a practical end.

While the initial euphoria of prescribing federalism as a one-size-all-fits-all solution to all political and economic problems seems to have slowed down (Erk and Swenden 2009b), institutional and constitutional reforms in federations are likely to keep analytical and applied comparative federalism in contact with one another. Will the contemporary "learned" betray their scholarly vocation the way Benda's contemporaries did, or will prudence prevail? The doyen of comparative federalism, Richard Simeon, had seen the writing on the wall 35 years earlier:

> There is something of a danger that the lure of influence for academics, and the desire of the federal government to promote mission-oriented contract research, especially in sensitive policy areas, will lead students to a concentration on technique and relevance which will inhibit the development of more sophisticated understanding of policy ... Prescription, moreover, is to a large extent made possible only by explanation: the danger is that we are being asked to run before we can walk, with the resulting possibility of misleading both ourselves and the governments. However, without better understanding of the general process and without the attempt to uncover basic assumptions and constraints, "applied" research and concentration on technique become no more than ad hoc response to transient events, and risk degeneration into more fundamental irrelevance. (1976, 554)

Later on in his career Simeon did lend his erudition to various initiatives on the applied side of comparative federalism, but his contributions were always marked by even-handed reflection and prudence, not a technocratic zeal for political engineering. While making his scholarly wisdom available during the course of successive constitutional crises in Canada and helping post-conflict societies find ways to deal with their divisions, Simeon also acknowledged complexity and uncertainty. His contributions were never about institutional tinkering, instant solutions, and inflated promises.

In her contribution to the 2008 International Studies Association Annual Conference round table on the policy-academy divide, Janice Gross Stein reflects on how "professional civil servants – socialised never to admit ignorance – always answered the questions with assurance" (2009, 121). But this is precisely where scholars can help deflate the claims of institutional/constitutional prescriptions to cure the ills of deeply divided societies:

> scholars can be most useful when they help policymakers to understand what they cannot know, to puncture the policy environment of false certainty that is characteristic of so much decision-making. Ironically, our greatest value may not be in what we know – this will vary across fields – but in our awareness of what we do not know. We are most valuable as sceptics all the way up the chain of knowledge. (ibid., 122)

It is here where the expert's – feigned or felt – confidence clashes with the scholar's scepticism. Instead of expertly fitting the pipes or manicuring the lawn, scholars deal with broad foundational pillars of federalism.

If we take this scepticism of technocratic expertise to its logical extreme, we might end up concurring with George Bernard Shaw's blanket statement: "[all professions] are all conspiracies against the laity" (1909, Preface). Shaw's first target in this statement was the exclusivity and protectionism professional associations and guilds employ in shielding their members from commoners, that is, the laity. He also targeted professions' deliberate use of jargon to feign technical expertise and intimidate potential critics. This chapter began with the Hippocratic Oath of the medical profession. It is worthwhile noting that Shaw's caustic assertion about all professions is in fact from the preface to his play *The Doctor's Dilemma*. Similar to contemporary social scientists prescribing federal constitutions with abandon, Shaw's contemporaries within the medical profession had been enticed by the new advances in their field: they were fashionably adopting new "discoveries" in remedies and impetuously prescribing "scientific" operations to cure all ills; *primum non nocere* it was not.

Scholars, Uncodified Factors, and the *longue durée*

In his influential 1958 article, the French historian Fernand Braudel, a prominent member of the *Annales* school of historiography, outlined what came to be known as the *longue durée* approach to social sciences and history. The *Annales* school, emphazising the role of large-scale social factors in history, took the name from their flagship journal, *Annales d'histoire économique et sociale*, but it was Fernand Braudel who articulated the commonalities of the approach in a coherent form. Braudel called for a holistic history examining long-term patterns, rather than the more common historical oeuvre chronicling specific events and emphasizing the leading personalities involved in them (1958, 727–9). Emphasis on long-term patterns across time inevitably came with an interest in uncodified social, political, and economic structures which accounted for the longevity of such patterns (ibid., 731–3).

In constitutional politics Andrew Reynolds advocates a comparable holistic approach – but this time with an intellectual debt to clinical medicine and without an emphasis on long-term structural factors. The holistic approach in medicine takes into account various causal factors, the interaction between these factors and their timing, and further consequences of the cures prescribed to ailments, while acknowledging the potential unknowns. Altogether these can create causal patterns difficult to reduce to an isolated causal relationship between a dependent and an independent variable: "Like medicine, constitutional therapy must be about more than treating particular ailments, considered in isolation. Therapy, whether medical or political, must consider the patient as a whole" (Reynolds 2005, 60). Thomas Carothers is in favour of a similar holistic approach to aid policy, where social, economic, and political factors are combined (1999, 345). But when it comes to the prescriptions of applied comparative federalism, the long-term holistic view is underplayed in the dominant institutional/constitutional boilerplates that are frequently exported to new federations.

Students of comparative federalism committed to scholarly analytical goals have an innate understanding of how federalism in the developed world has evolved over the *longue durée*, leading to informal practices that have come to be part of the day-to-day functioning of federal systems. Furthermore, branches of analytical comparative federalism examine how federal constitutions acquire their working dynamics from interaction with uncodified factors such as ethnicity, language, demographics, culture, and the economy (Erk 2007b). There is, thus, an awareness of the incomplete state of our knowledge in comparative federalism and the probabilistic nature of our theories of federalism. Perfecting representation in the second chambers will not magically deliver better federal politics; neither will tinkering with decentralized institutions suddenly lead to "peace by design." Those who hold holistic long-term views also recognize the importance of extra-institutional factors for the success (or failure) of federalism. In addition to obvious factors such as free and fair elections, freedom of expression, and economic development, other structural factors play a key role: a functioning system of law and order that protects life and property, the impersonal application of the rule of law by the courts, and a sizeable middle class that can act as the main stakeholders of the new federal order and who can help minimize the disruption of politically connected speculative wealth-creation that economic liberalization and political democratization frequently produce in the short term.

Yet the lure of policy relevance can sometimes lead to the repacking of various analytical findings into constitutional/institutional prescriptions that project a false sense of confidence and clarity. True, many post-conflict societies around the globe are in immediate need of federal solutions that could provide quick paths to reconcile unity and diversity. In these cases, of course, one does not have the luxury of long-term scholarly reflection. But there is a real risk of oversell (and subsequent disappointment) when we put all our eggs in the institutional/constitutional basket and expect immediate results from constitutional engineering. To quote a prominent student of Canadian federalism, Keith Banting: "political institutions are much too important to have their policy significance exaggerated" (1987, 180).

NOTES

1 A scholar who has further explored parallels between medicine and designing constitutions is Andrew Reynolds (2005).
2 Of course, the *engagé*, the expert, and the scholar also happen to have a fourth sibling in the family composed of those who blend different doses of

the analytical and the applied, that is, the *partisan*. But since the makings of the partisan academic ideal-type are fairly straightforward and self-evident, the discussion will focus on the other three.

REFERENCES

Acheson, Dean. 1969. *Present at the Creation: My Years in the State Department*. New York: Norton.

Banting, Keith. 1987. *The Welfare State and Canadian Federalism*. Montreal and Kingston: McGill-Queen's University Press.

Benda, Julien. 1927. *La trahison des clercs*. Paris: Éditions Bernard Grasset.

Braudel, Fernand. 1958. Histoire et sciences sociales: La longue durée. *Annales, Économies, Sociétés, Civilisations* 13(4):725–53.

Bull, Hedley. 1966. International Theory: the Case for a Classical Approach. *World Politics* 18(3):361–77.

Calhoun, Craig. 2010. Social Science Research and Military Agendas: Safe Distance or Bridging a Troubling Divide? *Perspectives in Politics* 8(4):1101–6.

Carothers, Thomas. 1999. *Aiding Democracy Abroad: The Learning Curve*. Washington, DC: Carnegie Endowment for International Peace.

DeMartino, George. 2009. On the Need for Professional Economic Ethics. *Challenge* 54(4):6–15.

Elazar, Daniel. 1987. *Exploring Federalism*. Tuscaloosa: University of Alabama Press.

Elias, Norbert. 1956. Involvement and Detachment. *British Journal of Sociology*. 7(3):226–52.

Elzinga, Aant. 2004. The New Production of Particularism in Models Relating to Research Policy: A Critique of Mode 2 and Triple Helix. Paper presented at the EEAST Conference, 26–28 August. Institute for History of Ideas and Theory of Science University of Göteborg, Sweden.

Epstein, Gerald, and Jessica Carrick-Hagenbarth. 2010. *Financial Economists, Financial Interests and Dark Corners of the Meltdown: It's Time to Set Ethical Standards for the Economics Profession*. Political Economy Research Institute Working Paper 239, University of Massachusetts.

Erk, Jan. 2006. Does Federalism Really Matter? *Comparative Politics* 39(1):103–20.

Erk, Jan. 2007a. Federalism as a Growth Industry. *Publius: The Journal of Federalism* 37(2):262–78.

Erk, Jan. 2007b. *Explaining Federalism: State, Society and Congruence in Austria, Belgium, Canada, Germany and Switzerland*. London: Routledge.

Erk, Jan. 2011. The Sociology of Constitutional Politics: Demos, Legitimacy, and Constitutional Courts in Canada and Germany. *Regional and Federal Studies* 21(4/5):523–38.

Erk, Jan, and Edward Koning. 2010. New Structuralism and Institutional Change: Federalism between Centralization and Decentralization. *Comparative Political Studies* 43(3):353–78.

Erk, Jan, and Wilfried Swenden. 2009a. The New Wave of Federalism Scholarship: An Analytical Framework. In *New Directions in Federalism Studies,* edited by Jan Erk and Wilfried Swenden. London: Routledge.

Erk, Jan, and Wilfried Swenden. 2009b. Taking Stock during Times of Change. In *New Directions in Federalism Studies,* edited by Jan Erk and Wilfried Swenden. London: Routledge.

Flexner, Abraham. 1939. The Usefulness of Useless Knowledge. *Harper's Magazine* 179, June/November.

Hill, Christopher. 1994. Academic International Relations: The Siren Song of Policy Relevance. In *Two Worlds of International Relations: Academics, Practitioners and the Trade in Ideas,* edited by Christopher Hill and Pamela Beshoff. London: Routledge.

Hirschmann, Alfred. 1970. The Search for Paradigms as a Hindrance to Understanding. *World Politics* 22(3):329–43.

Keohane, Robert. 2009. "Beware the Bad Fairy": Cautionary Notes for Academics in the Policy Realm. *Cambridge Review of International Affairs* 22(1):124–8.

Krebs, Ronald R. 2010. Striking the Right Balance: Of High Walls and Divisions of Labor. *Perspectives in Politics* 8(4):1113–16.

Krugman, Paul. 2009. How Did Economists Get It So Wrong? *New York Times,* 6 September.

Lilla, Mark. 2007. *The Reckless Mind: Intellectuals in Politics.* New York: New York Review Books.

McCloskey, Donald. 1990. *If You're So Smart: The Narrative of Economic Expertise.* Chicago: University of Chicago Press.

Merton, Robert K. 1972. Insiders and Outsiders: A Chapter in the Sociology of Knowledge. *American Journal of Sociology* 78(1):9–47.

Mills, Wright C. 1959. On Intellectual Craftsmanship. In *The Sociological Imagination,* edited by Wright C. Mills. Oxford: Oxford University Press.

Moore, Barrington, Jr. 1953. New Scholasticism and the Study of Politics. *World Politics* 6(1):122–38.

Morgenthau, Hans. 1970. *Truth and Power: Essays of a Decade 1960–70.* London: Pall Mall Press.

Morgenthau, Hans. 1972. *Science: Servant or Master?* New York: New York American Library.

Nincic, Miroslav. 2000. Policy Relevance and Theoretical Development: The Terms of the Trade-Off. In *Being Useful: Policy Relevance and International Relations Theory*, edited by Miroslav Nincic and Joseph Lepgold. Ann Arbor: University of Michigan Press.

Ravetz, Jerome. 1990. *The Merger of Knowledge and Power. Essays in Critical Science*. London: Mansell.

Ravetz, Jerome. 1999. What Is Post-Normal Science? *Futures* 31(7):647–53.

Reynolds, Andrew. 2005. Constitutional Medicine. *Journal of Democracy* 16(1):54–68.

Shaw, George Bernard. 1909. *The Doctor's Dilemma: Preface on Doctors*.

Simeon, Richard. 1976. Studying Public Policy. *Canadian Journal of Political Science* 9(4):548–80.

Stein, Janice Gross. 2009. Evolutionary Hubris, False Certainty, and Structural Scepticism: The Academic Policy Divide. *Cambridge Review of International Affairs* 22(1):120–4.

Tetlock, Philip E. 2005. *Expert Political Judgment: How Good Is It? How Can We Know?* Princeton: Princeton University Press.

Walt, Stephen. 2005. The Relationship between Theory and Policy in International Relations. *Annual Review of Political Science* 8(1):23–48.

12 Reflections on a Federalist Life

RICHARD SIMEON

What might lead a grey-flannelled English immigrant kid growing up "British in British Columbia" in Vancouver to become a life-long student of federalism and decentralized governance?[1] The simplest answer is the influence of three professors of political science at the University of British Columbia in the early 1960s, two just starting their academic careers. The eldest, Donald Smiley, was already established as one of Canada's leading students of federalism. He was joined by Alan Cairns, fresh from Oxford, where he had studied British colonialism, but was now teaching Canadian politics and federalism from his most meticulous notes; and by Ed Black, a gritty former small-town newspaperman with a freshly minted PhD from Duke. Ed taught me about the media in class, then edited my copy during summer jobs at the *Vancouver Province*. These three made UBC perhaps the strongest centre for federal studies in Canada at the time and influenced many others of my generation – including David Cameron, Maureen Covell, and Ken McRoberts. It is worth noting that our UBC experience helped produce students with perhaps a greater sympathy for regional concerns and identities than many of our colleagues raised in central Canada.

Then to Yale, where no one knew much about Canada, but where scholars were pioneering new approaches and ideas in political science, through Robert Dahl, Charles Lindblom, Karl Deutsch, and others. And then to Queen's in 1968, the other major centre for federal studies in Canada, where John Deutsch, Alec Corry, John Meisel, and Bill Lederman, among others, deepened my interest in federalism, and Ron Watts handed me the best job of my life in 1976 as director of the Institute of Intergovernmental Relations.[1]

From all of this came some basic themes in my personal, scholarly, and political commitments.

Collaboration and Collegiality

So much of my work has depended on the collaboration of others and on the collegiality of many in academia and elsewhere. Collaboration is about working together to increase understanding and get things done. Outside academia, colleagues in government have been essential. Don Stevenson in Ontario, Peter Meekison in Alberta, Al Johnson in Ottawa, and many others made it possible for the kid from BC to research and write his thesis. My scholarly collaborators, young and old, junior and senior, are almost too many to name. With David Elkins, I helped break new empirical ground in Canadian politics with our article "Regional Political Cultures," and the subsequent book, *Small Worlds*, which traced further dimensions of diversity among Canadian provinces,[2] finding a complex blend of convergence around common values and difference. My partnership with Keith Banting at the Institute of Intergovernmental Relations was wonderfully productive, taking us deeper into Canadian politics, but also starting to build the bridge to comparison with *Redesigning the State: The Politics of Constitutional Change* and *Degrees of Freedom: Canada and the United States in a Changing World*. The Institute was a kind of rolling seminar, where young scholars such as Thomas Hueglin, Doug Brown, Allan Tupper, Herman Bakvis, and others did fine work. Then there was the great team of collaborators at the Macdonald Commission, under Alan Cairns's leadership, about which there are so many stories to tell. The commission's research effort was conducted in the traditional academic silos, separating politics, economics, and law. My fellow research coordinators on federalism, Ken Norrie and Mark Krasnick, said no to that, and we combined our output in a distinct series of books with their covers in a slightly hideous olive colour, but all with multi-disciplinary content. My research assistant, Ian Robinson, soon became a full colleague and we blended institutions, societies, and political economy in our major research contribution, *State, Society and the Evolution of Canadian Federalism*.

The pattern continued after my arrival at the University of Toronto in 1990. Katherine Swinton and I taught and wrote together in the Law School, David Cameron and I renewed earlier work together on federalism and intergovernmental relations. A parade of superb PhD students – Luc Turgeon, Martin Papillon, Jenn Wallner, Julie Simmons,

Josh Hjartason, Alexandre Pelletier, Karlo Basta, and others – taught and wrote with me, and are now reshaping the study of federalism in Canada. The learning curve was always a circle.

Accommodating Difference

What Peter Russell (2004) calls Canada's constitutional odyssey, the result of Quebec's Quiet Revolution and the growth of its sense of national identity, coincided with my political awakening and preoccupied my first decades as a political scientist. Not surprisingly, a protracted debate about the constitution and the very foundation of Canada came to dominate our work on federalism. I may have been one of the few anglophone Canadians who benefited from the election of the PQ in November 1976: suddenly the Institute I headed had a new and important role. We immediately organized a conference of scholars and practitioners to think about how the ROC (the rest of Canada), as it came to be known, might react. The result was *Must Canada Fail?*, perhaps one of the first books to take seriously the possibility of a secession and to think about its consequences. My view then was not so much to take *sides* or go to war for national unity, but rather to help promote mutual recognition and understanding across the linguistic divide. I was criticized for one sentence in the introduction: "There are many values more important to me than lines on a map." I still believe that to be true. And there was much to be excited about in Quebec's modernizing revolution, especially in contrast with the staid and conservative politics of much of the rest of Canada at the time. This search for compromise, consensus, and accommodation, more than any partisan position, was and is my core belief and has shaped my responses not only to many aspects of Canada's linguistic, regional, and Aboriginal differences, but also to many international cases as well. The title *Toolkits and Building Blocks*, a book I co-edited with Mary Janigan for the C.D. Howe Institute, captures much of that spirit, as did *A Citizen's Guide to the Constitutional Debate*, widely distributed and available for a while at grocery store check-outs.

Indeed, I have generally been the committed but slightly distant observer and analyst – seldom comfortable as the partisan or ideologue. I usually look for the middle ground, the compromise and the balance in any controversy. Students once called me "Professor on the one hand this, and on the other hand that." The danger in this approach is that it can so easily be seen as weak and wishy-washy; but I have also noticed that sometimes it takes real courage to stake out the centre when all around you are shouting slogans. The world needs those who push intellectual and theoretical limits; it also needs bridge builders across its divisions. Each needs the other. The scholarly corollary is that I have been more successful as the synthesizer, summarizer, and integrator than as the hard-edge analyst; more interested in complexity than in the parsimonious single-variable explanation. There has been a vigorous debate about how the causal arrows run. Does institutional design shape the character of federal societies (Cairns 1977), or does the federal character of the society shape the institutions (Livingston 1956; Erk 2008)? I have worked on both sides of this street. The answer is clear: the causal arrow flows both ways. Federal states and federal societies are mutually dependent.

So it is more broadly with facts and values. One of my great teachers at Yale was Robert Dahl, a powerful theorist of democracy and at the same time a leader in the behavioural and empirical revolution in political science. This was a heady and powerful combination, which has influenced my thinking ever since.[3] I tell my students that analysis without the underpinning of normative values and goals is simply sterile. Theory without deep attention to the economic, social, and political conditions that sustain or undermine the core principles, and to the institutions that might promote and protect them, is simply utopian.

Public Engagement

With the very future and definition of the country at stake in the constitutional wars, it was hardly a time for academics to remain on the sidelines, and my role at the Institute opened the doors to that. I was never close to the federal government – I was too often the provincialist – but I had the privilege of being an adviser to successive Ontario premiers, from Davis to Rae and Peterson, on the constitutional file. Working as a research coordinator for the Macdonald Commission on the Economic Union under Alan Cairns was another great experience, though we did not always agree. I was always a strong believer in the idea of Quebec as a distinct society or nation; hence, I was not a strong advocate of the Trudeau approach to federalism. Perhaps my most controversially titled book, edited with Keith Banting, was *And No One Cheered*, published as a response to the constitutional settlement of 1982. This was the most important constitutional change of my lifetime, bringing to Canada the patriation of the constitution, an amending formula, and most notably the uniquely Canadian Charter of Rights and Freedoms.

I think at the time, I underestimated its lasting significance. But I was also disturbed by the exclusion of Quebec and by the failure to respond to its dynamics. Hence our title.[4]

Interestingly, both sides got their predictions about the Charter wrong. For Trudeau it was an affirmation of national values, promoted by national institutions, which would help undercut regionalism and provincialism and build unity. For its opponents it would undermine both parliamentary sovereignty and provincial autonomy. The experience is that, yes, Charter values are now deeply entrenched everywhere in the country, but this has not prevented the growth of provincial influence and a declining presence of the federal government in the lives of Canadians.

By contrast, I was an ardent supporter of and advocate for the Meech Lake Accord, perhaps my moment of most partisan political engagement. For all its flaws, I believed then, and believe now, that it was the key to long-term reconciliation with Quebec. Its failure is one of the great disappointments of my political life. I was part of a small advisory group to Ontario Premier David Peterson, who was desperately seeking ways to save the Meech Lake Accord at the final conference in April 1990; it was supposed to last one evening, but ended in failure after more than a week. Late in the week, David Cameron and I took a break with a walk through the market. As we were returning to the National Conference Centre, we passed a parked police car. The officer rolled down his window. "Are you at the conference?" he asked. Yes, we said. "You should call in me and my partner; we're real good at domestics," was the reply. Right.

Increasing Quebec representation at the centre and promotion of bilingualism from sea to sea to sea was one of the great achievements of Pierre Trudeau and his successors, removing a powerful source of Quebec grievance. But it could be no substitute for more autonomy for the province as the primary political expression of a self-conscious people, one that demography destined to be an ever smaller proportion of the Canadian population.

A journalist manqué from my undergraduate days, my public involvement in these issues got me slightly back into the media world, to my great pleasure.

Not Only Federalism

My career, and this book, focus on federalism, and rightly so. But for me federalism has not been the primary end in itself. It is a set of institutions and practices that must be judged and evaluated in terms of what broader values they might sustain or promote. Two broad themes have pervaded my thinking and influenced how I think about federalism.

First is democracy. Easy to say, hard to practise, and always imperfect. Evaluating the quality of Canadian democracy was the dominant theme of my large introductory course on Canada in comparative perspective, taught over many years. As neoliberalism became the dominant ideology, in a short monograph for the C.D. Howe Institute I wrestled with the conundrum: can we make hard decisions as if democracy matters? I am proud that my 1976 article "Studying Public Policy" has remained on course syllabi in several countries ever since. That should have been the framework for a book, but federalism and the Institute of Intergovernmental Relations took over my attention and it was never finished. I have followed the democracy theme most recently in *Imperfect Democracies: The Democratic Deficit in Canada and the United States*, edited with Patti Lenard.

Second is my concern with public policy that is effective in meeting contemporary challenges. The subtitle of *Federal-Provincial Diplomacy* is *The Making of Recent Public Policy*. How does federalism influence policy? Who are the winners, who are the losers? How does federalism matter for equality, for social justice, for addressing contemporary challenges in a timely and effective fashion? All deeply contentious questions, but the right ones to ask of any institutional arrangement, as so well documented for Canada in Herman Bakvis and Grace Skogstad's (2012) excellent edited collection on Canadian federalism and public policy.

Third has been my interest in the intersection of law and politics. Its most concrete expression was my appointment as the first and only non-lawyer to be a member of the Ontario Law Reform Commission. Led by its chair, now justice, Rosalie Abella, and with a group of excellent commissioners, we carved out some new territory, including a report on family law that came very close to endorsing gay marriage and was perhaps the first official body in Canada to do so.

Beyond the Canadian Model

Steeped in the British model of parliamentary government and preoccupied with language and region, the study of federalism in Canada (as elsewhere, it must be said) has been deeply parochial and insular. It is indeed the case that each federal system is deeply embedded in its own context, particularities, and historical legacies, which are the logical and proper concern of its citizens, politicians, and scholars. But gradually things began to change in my own world.

Following the failed constitutional negotiations and the rancour over the 1995 Quebec referendum and the Clarity Act, Canadians had come to realize that their own constitution was essentially impossible to amend, and they developed a severe case of "constitutional fatigue." Surprisingly, the failure of the Charlottetown Accord, designed to broaden the constitutional debate, and then the narrow victory for federalism in the 1995 Quebec referendum did not intensify the conflict in Canada but rather led to a marked diminution in the intensity of our own internal debates. At the same time many came to realize that federalism and decentralized governance more generally might have considerable relevance for other territorially divided societies. The highly centralized models preferred by post-colonial elites in much of the developing world had lost much of their attraction, and new experiments with dispersed authority proliferated. Moreover, Canadian political scientists had become far more attuned to international trends in theory and method that offered at least some purchase for comparative study.

This was all fertile ground for footloose Canadians. We may not have been a sterling success in reforming our own federal institutions (notwithstanding the Charter, the constitutionalization of a sharing federation in equalization, and the insufficient but major advances of Aboriginal rights in recent years, all of which were notable achievements), but we have also proved that we could do a pretty good job of managing our multiple dimensions of difference with relative success. So we took a "comparative turn," beginning to look abroad and to offer our expertise – not only in federalism, but also in the Charter and other areas – with more confidence. This was strongly encouraged by the federal government and its creation of the international Forum of Federations, which was at least partly designed to show Quebecers that federalism was an internationally desirable model.

If the Forum was one important window into the world of comparative federalism, another was the SSHRC-funded project on Ethnicity and Democratic Governance led by Bruce Berman of Queen's with the Université de Québec à Montréal and University of Toronto as partners. We were able to involve scholars and students from around the world in research, networks, seminars, and an extensive set of publications exploring the multiple dimensions of politicized ethnicity. Here too were new collaborations – notably with John McGarry and Marie-Joëlle Zahar, my teacher on conflict resolution.

My first big international experience began with a phone call from Al Johnson, one of the country's finest public servants and one of the architects of the Douglas CCF government in Saskatchewan, who was now established in Johannesburg advising the newly elected democratic government of South Africa on public administration. "Richard," he said, "they are having provinces in the new South Africa, so we had better tell them how provinces work." And so Johnson, Allan Blakeney, and I spent a few great weeks touring the country talking about provinces. That led to a wonderful collaboration with Christina Murray, a University of Cape Town law professor, activist, and constitutional adviser, teaching and writing about comparative federalism and constitutionalism and the troubled evolution of multi-level government in South Africa.

There followed work with the Forum and others in Jordan, Sudan, Ethiopia, and Kenya discussing the potential of federalist ideas in the developing world. And, in the developed world, I have become fascinated by federalist, decentralist, and secessionist debates in advanced countries – Scotland and Britain, Quebec and Canada, Catalonia, the Basque Country and Spain. In the post-war era there was virtual unanimity among scholars in Europe, North America, and newly independent developing countries like India that, as Samuel Beer (1973) put it, "modernization equals centralization." Anglo-Canadian scholars much influenced by Harold Laski (1939) profoundly agreed that in the post-war period federalism was a burden to overcome, a barrier to full social democracy; by no means was it a virtue. A big long-term question is what explains the resurgence of ethnic and regional identities, the emphasis on decentralization, and so on in these advanced democratic societies in recent decades? And what are the consequences of what Tom Courchene (1995) calls "glocalization" – the simultaneous flow of power and influence both downward to localities and upward to supranational entities?

The Global Promise?

And so to the theme of this book, and the conference that gave rise to it. The Global Promise of Federalism. Let us be clear. Federalism is no "light on the hill," no universal solution to the problems of divided societies.[5] Often, federalism, as Donald Smiley (1987) put it, is not a clear

choice of the current generation, but an inherited "condition." Sometimes in post-colonial societies it has been imposed by the outgoing
colonial power with few if any roots in the society itself. Often we are
destined to work within, through, and sometimes around it. It is also
sometimes second best. John A. Macdonald deeply desired that Canada
would be a unitary state, but understood that there could be no Canada
without federalism. The Kurds in Iraq would almost certainly prefer
to be an independent state, but understood that geopolitical realities
made that impossible. Federalism comes next best. Federalism is also
inherently complex as a system of governance, often difficult for citizens to understand in terms of who does what, and who holds whom
accountable. Federal systems are also so varied and so diverse that, as
William Riker (1964), Daniel Treisman (2007), and others have argued,
virtually no robust generalizations can be made about them. Federalism is also a subset of a much larger family of decentralist alternatives
from administrative decentralization to associate states. So, again, clear
generalizations and recommendations are impossible.

There are also more powerful critiques, arguing that federalism en-
trenches and exacerbates the very divisions it is supposed to manage
and equips regional and local elites with the institutional resources to
push for independence (Roeder 2009).

For me, however, these critiques need not paralyse us. We might distinguish between the design of the specific institutional arrangements
associated with federalism on one hand and its underlying principles
on the other. The former will always need to be specific to the context:
the size and character of the component groups; their degree of territorial concentration; their historical legacies; whether they have shared or
divergent values and interests; and their links to other institutions such
as parties, electoral systems, legislatures, executives, and courts. The
outcomes will also always depend on the results of bargaining among
the constituent groups and their elites. Hence the difficulty of spelling
out a priori solutions.

We can perhaps gain a little more traction by focusing on the underlying values, understanding that there will be many institutional forms
to instantiate them. There will be disagreements about these values as
well, but some come to mind for me. I would include the following:

- In divided societies, simple majority rule is the enemy of democracy.
- In divided societies, democracy is served by ensuring significant

autonomy to self-conscious, territorially concentrated groups or nations.

- In divided societies, integrationist strategies of political equality and participation of all in democratic institutions is critical, but they are not sufficient. Some political space for autonomy and self-determination of territorially concentrated minority communities is essential.
- No modern society is hermetically sealed. Sharing, exchange, and interdependence are universal. Hence, federalism's emphasis on Elazar's (1987) self-rule and shared rule is critical.
- Power – shared, dispersed – is inherently better than power concentrated.
- Democracy is served by offering multiple avenues for citizen participation.
- A sustainable, workable settlement in any divided society that does not embody federalist elements is difficult to imagine (Stepan 1999).

If we think of federalism in these terms, we get no simple rules but a way of thinking about its potential promise. But making it work remains an immense challenge. In long-standing federations such as Germany and the US, federalism and intergovernmental relations are part of normal politics. The operation of federalism may engender vigorous debate, but seldom fundamental challenges to the system. It is a different story when the status quo is challenged by powerful social movements: the modernizing Quiet Revolution in Quebec led to a stronger sense of nationalism; autonomy and decentralization as part of the post-Franco democratization process promoted nationalism in Catalonia and the Basque Country; the independence movement in Scotland took on its own dynamic. All these pose the basic question: is federalism the right middle way between secession and a unitary state? Can the "unionist" model be reconstructed? Is formal independence accompanied by extensive collaboration, as envisaged by the Scottish Nationalist Party and captured in the PQ's terms "sovereignty association" and "partnership," workable from either side? Is full separation or independence even possible in this interdependent world? These are all profound political debates. Resolution will draw on the federalist principles mentioned above, but also on a commitment to free exchange, trust, and respect for the other. These ideas, along with democracy, the rule of law, an independent judiciary, and protection for human rights, are often seen as essential elements in any federal system. Can we in good conscience recommend a federal system if these prerequisites are weak or non-existent? Does federalism depend on the initial presence of these values, or might federalism, once established, help promote and sustain them? Clearly, there can be no single persuasive "have I got a model for you."

So, with respect to spreading federalism to the developing world, I remain modest. But I think that we students of federalism do have an array of possibilities, successes, and failures, which may, in the right circumstances, be helpful.

I began with Canada, so let me finish with Canada. As elsewhere, federalism has been contested throughout our history. The simple starting point for me is that there would be no Canada without federalism, as Richard Gwyn (2007, 2011) demonstrates so well in his biographies of Sir John A. It is worth remembering that with paralysis and conflict in the consociational United Colony of Canada, break-up, perhaps even civil war, was not impossible. The "grand bargain" between Macdonald and Cartier, in which through great leadership each was able to win support from their respective linguistic communities, made Canada possible. Although he was a centralist at heart, Macdonald accepted that substantial provincial autonomy was essential if the larger Canada project was to prevail.

And that set the stage for much of the future dynamic of Canadian federalism, though much else was added to the mix with the expansion of the federation to ten provinces and three territories and, more recently, the political mobilization of Aboriginal communities seeking increased self-government. We moved from the initial centralization, to more dynamic provincialism, to the reassertion of federal influence in the Depression, wartime, and post-war experiences; then, to the contemporary experience of continued Quebec nationalism, and more recently, the rapid growth of economic and political power in western Canada and its call for increased political autonomy and a stronger voice at the centre (like many such movements, a dynamic blending of "we want out," and "we want in"). These and other social, economic, political, and cultural changes were profound. They engendered much conflict.

But perhaps the bigger story is that federalism in Canada has proved highly resilient and adaptable, despite the near impossibility of amending our constitution. Whatever the difference in perspective between our anglophone and Quebec backgrounds, Alain Gagnon and I, in a joint portrait of Canada for the Forum of Federations volume on unity and diversity in federal systems (2009), were able to agree on a portrait of the country as a "bargaining" federalism from its very beginning.

Yet we also need to come to terms with the fact that our linguistic communities – and our other regions as well – have quite different images, perceptions, and evaluations of the Canadian model. There are many critiques of federalism in what we used to call "English Canada" – the democratic deficit of closed-door intergovernmental relations; the need for higher national standards in areas such as health care and the environment; weak regional representation at the centre; and the perverse intergovernmental dynamic of dollars, turf protection, and blame avoidance. But again, these debates are part of "normal politics," and the basic accommodations between national purpose and regional diversity have been made, as best expressed in the fiscal equalization program. English Canadians like to think that Canada is the most decentralized federation in the world, and perhaps the one most accommodating to regional linguistic and cultural differences, in terms both of provincial autonomy and of Quebec influence in Ottawa.

However, the ineluctable fact is that in Canada, Quebec, and Franco-Canadians are the (now declining) minority. Hence, it was fully to be expected that Quebec's primary goal from the outset would be to enhance its autonomy, and to protect itself against the imposition of majority interests. Weak representation of Quebec in the corridors of power in Ottawa and, in the nineteenth and early twentieth centuries, overtly anti-French policies in Ontario, Manitoba, Saskatchewan, and Alberta underlined the point that Quebec must look to its own resources and institutions to protect its identity and interests. "French Canadians" became "les Québécois," partly as a result of majority policies elsewhere. Therefore, in Quebec the critique has been more profound. Canada is seen less as a deeply decentralized federation than as one in which the central government historically has imposed its values on Quebec and has resisted expansion of Quebec autonomy or asymmetrical options. The lens through which federalism is viewed sees most federal activity in public policy as a potential threat to its autonomy, an illegitimate "intrusion."

Quebecers and anglophones do indeed weigh the twin elements of federalism – what we do separately, what we do together – somewhat differently. Hence a common mild reproach. The anglophone may suggest to the Quebecer "you are not really a federalist, because your first identity is as a Quebecer, and you see any initiative by Ottawa as a potential threat." The riposte goes the other way: "You Anglo Canadians are not really federalist because your first identity is to Canada as a whole, and you are comfortable with federal initiatives and would like to expand them in some circumstances." But one of the great strengths of federalism is that we can both hold and argue vigorously with our opponents about these differing views without going to war about them. If one of the big problems of federalism is its complexity, doubt, variability, and uncertainty, those very features may be its great virtue. Federalism is in trouble when it comes to a choice between absolutes. You are a federalist or a separatist, and there is a Rubicon between them. In the globalized, post-Westphalian world we now live in, such absolutes no longer exist and federalists understand that. Interestingly, in the Canadian debate, both the federal government and Péquistes in Quebec have taken the Westphalian view that sovereignty is indivisible. This is partly true in the current UK debate as well, but the Scottish Nationalist Party (SNP) plan calls for keeping the British monarchy, its pound, much of its armed forces, and extended coordination of economic and social politics; at the same time, the UK government is happy to explore "devolution max" within the Union. The differences are more semantic and symbolic than real.

So is federalism in Canada perfect? A model for the world? Not in its institutional detail, mostly an inheritance from the nineteenth century. Understanding its weaknesses and explaining them may be as useful in international discussions as our strengths. For example, the dismal record of our Senate is a great point of departure for a discussion of second chambers in federal systems, as is an analysis of the problems of our first past the post electoral system in accentuating regional differences. But the central core remains the underlying values of tolerance, recognition of the other, accommodating multiple and shared values, and peacefully debating difference. Here we may be something of a model. And here is the promise.

Finally, I recall a debate in the US Senate when a member asked a lawyer witness, "Professor, do you support the constitution of the YEWnited States?" To which the witness replied, "Senator, why should I not, it has supported me very well throughout my career." I can say the same thing about federalism.

ACKNOWLEDGMENTS

Richard wishes to express his deep thanks to Grace Skogstad, Keith Banting, David Cameron, and Martin Papillon for their editing of this book and for their role in organizing the Festschrift that gave rise to it. He also thanks all the authors who have contributed such interesting chapters, and the host of colleagues and students who have taught him so much. And to MaryEtta and my family, at the heart of it all.

NOTES

1 As our button put it at one point, "No Sex Please, Our Relations are Intergovernmental."
2 Ailsa Henderson (2010) breathed new life into *Small Worlds* by editing a special issue of *Regional and Federal Studies* devoted to revisiting its themes in Canada and Europe.
3 Dahl was asked in our seminar: "Given a small question with an iron clad methodology, and an important question without such certainty, which is better for us to study?" "The latter" was Dahl's immediate reply.
4 At the time, there was a strong perception that federalism and Charter values were deeply in conflict, and that rights-oriented Canada would displace federalist Canada. But the experience has been that we have successfully blended the two.
5 At the conclusion of the Macdonald Commission, Alan Cairns wrote a limerick for each of his staff. Mine went: "There once was a professor named Simeon / For whom federalism was like a religion / He argued its strength at inordinate length / With a passion close to a sermon."

REFERENCES

Bakvis, Herman, and Grace Skogstad, eds. 2012. *Canadian Federalism: Performance, Effectiveness and Legitimacy*. 3rd ed. Oxford: Oxford University Press.

Beer, Samuel H. 1973. The Modernization of American Federalism. *Publius: The Journal of Federalism* 3:49–76.

Cairns, Alan C. 1977. The Governments and Societies of Canadian Federalism. *Canadian Journal of Political Science* 26(1):3–29.

Courchene, Thomas. 1995. Glocalization: The Regional/International Interface. *Canadian Journal of Regional Science* 18(1):1–20.

Elazar, Daniel J. 1987. *Exploring Federalism*. Tuscaloosa: University of Alabama Press.

Erk, Jan. 2008. *Explaining Federalism: State, Society and Congruence in Austria, Belgium, Canada, Germany and Switzerland*. London: Routledge.

Gagnon, Alain-G., and Richard Simeon. 2009. Unity and Diversity in Canada: A Preliminary Assessment. In *Forum of Federations*. Available at http://www.forumfedorg/libdocs/Global_Dialogue/Booklet_7/BL7-en-ca-gagnon_simeon.pdf.

Gwyn, Richard. 2007. *John A: The Man Who Made Us*. Vol. 1: *1815–1867*. Toronto: Random House Canada.

Gwyn, Richard. 2011. *Nation Maker: Sir John A. Macdonald: His Life, Our Times*. Vol. 2: *1867–1891*. Toronto: Random House Canada.

Henderson, Ailsa. 2010. *Regional and Federal Studies*, Special Issue: Why Regions Matter: Sub-state Polities in Comparative Perspective 20(4–5):471–87.

Laski, Harold. 1939. The Obsolescence of Federalism. *New Republic* 98(3 May):367–9.

Livingston, Walter. S. 1956. *Federalism and Constitutional Change*. Oxford: Clarendon Press.

Riker, William H. 1964. *Federalism: Origin, Operation, Significance*. Boston: Little, Brown.

Roeder, Philip G. 2009. Ethnofederalism and the Mismanagement of Conflicting Nationalisms. *Journal of Regional and Federal Studies* 19(2):203–19.

Russell, Peter H. 2004. *Constitutional Odyssey: Can Canadians Ever Become a Sovereign People?* 3rd ed. Toronto: University of Toronto Press.

Smiley, Donald V. 1987. *The Federal Condition in Canada*. Toronto: McGraw-Hill Ryerson.

Stepan, Alfred. 1999. Federalism and Democracy: Beyond the U.S. Model. *Journal of Democracy* 10(4):19–34.

Treisman, Daniel. 2007. *The Architecture of Government: Rethinking Political Decentralization*. New York: Cambridge University Press.

13 The Collected Works of Richard Simeon

COMPILED BY ANDREW McDOUGALL

Books and Scholarly Monographs

Federal-Provincial Diplomacy: The Making of Recent Policy in Canada. Toronto: University of Toronto Press, 1972. Reissued (2006) with a new introduction. Awarded the Martha Derrick Best Book Award in 2005 by the Federalism and Intergovernmental Relations section of the American Political Science Association.

ed. *Must Canada Fail?* Montreal: McGill-Queen's University Press, 1977.

ed. *Confrontation and Collaboration: Intergovernmental Relations in Canada Today = Confrontation Et Collaboration: Les Relations Intergouvernmentales Dans Le Canada d'aujourd'hui*. Toronto: Institute of Public Administration of Canada, 1979.

and David J. Elkins, eds. *Small Worlds: Provinces and Parties in Canadian Political Life*. Toronto: Methuen, 1980.

and Keith Banting, eds. *And No One Cheered: Federalism, Democracy and the Constitution Act*. Toronto: Methuen, 1983.

Division of Powers and Public Policy. Vol. 61. Collected Research Studies. Toronto: University of Toronto Press in cooperation with the Royal Commission on the Economic Union and Development Prospects for Canada and the Canadian Government Publishing Centre, Supply and Services Canada, 1985.

Intergovernmental Relations. Vol. 63. Collected Research Studies. Toronto: University of Toronto Press in cooperation with the Royal Commission on the Economic Union and Development Prospects for Canada and the Canadian Government Publishing Centre, Supply and Services Canada, 1985.

and Keith Banting, eds. *Redesigning the State: The Politics of Constitutional Change*. Toronto: University of Toronto Press, 1985. Published simultaneously as *Constitutional Change in Industrial Democracies*. Basingstoke: Macmillan.

and Kenneth Norrie and Mark Krasnick. *Federalism and Economic Union in Canada*. Vol. 59. Collected Research Studies. Toronto: University of Toronto Press in cooperation with the Royal Commission on the Economic Union and Development Prospects for Canada and the Canadian Government Publishing Centre, Supply and Services Canada, 1986.

and Ian Robinson. *State, Society, and the Development of Canadian Federalism*. Vol. 71. Collected Research Studies. Toronto: University of Toronto Press in cooperation with the Royal Commission on the Economic Union and Development Prospects for Canada and the Canadian Government Publishing Centre, Supply and Services Canada, 1990.

and Mary Janigan, eds. *Toolkits and Building Blocks: Constructing a New Canada*. Toronto: C.D. Howe Institute, 1990.

In Search of a Social Contract: Hard Decisions As If Democracy Matters? Toronto: C.D. Howe Institute, 1994.

and Karen Knopf, Sylvia Ostry, and Katherine Swinton, eds. *Rethinking Federalism: Citizens, Markets, and Governments in a Changing World*. Vancouver: UBC Press, 1995.

and Janice Stein and David Cameron. *Citizen Engagement in Conflict Resolution*. Toronto: C.D. Howe Institute, 1997.

and Keith Banting and George Hoberg, eds. *Degrees of Freedom: Canada and the United States in a Changing World*. Montreal: McGill-Queen's University Press, 1997.

Political Scientists and the Study of Federalism in Canada: Seven Decades of Scholarly Engagement. Kingston: Institute of Intergovernmental Relations, 2002.

and Linda A. White, Robert Vipond, and Jennifer Wallner, eds. *The Comparative Turn in Canadian Political Science*. Vancouver: UBC Press, 2008.

and David Cameron, eds. *Language Matters: How Canadian Voluntary Associations Manage French and English*. Vancouver: UBC Press, 2009.

and Patti Tamara Lenard, eds. *Imperfect Democracies: Comparing the Democratic Deficit in Canada and the United States*. Vancouver: UBC Press, 2012.

Book Chapters

Scenarios for Separation. In *One Country or Two?* edited by Ronald M. Burns. 74–87. Montreal and Kingston: McGill-Queen's University Press, 1971. Reprinted in *Must Canada Fail?* edited by Richard Simeon. 189–203. Montreal and Kingston: McGill-Queen's University Press, 1977.

Introduction. In *Must Canada Fail?* edited by Richard Simeon. 1–11. Montreal and Kingston: McGill-Queen's University Press, 1977.

Reaching the Lifeboat: The Roles of Leaders and Citizens. In *Must Canada Fail?* edited by Richard Simeon. 177–185. Montreal and Kingston: McGill-Queen's University Press, 1977.

and Peter M. Leslie. The Battle of the Balance Sheets. In *Must Canada Fail?* edited by Richard Simeon. 243–58. Montreal and Kingston: McGill-Queen's University Press, 1977.

The Federal-Provincial Decision Making Process. In *Intergovernmental Relations: Issues and Alternatives, 1977.* 25–38. Toronto: Ontario Economic Council, 1977.

The Future of Federal-Provincial Relations. In *The Future of North America: Canada, the United States and Quebec Nationalism,* edited by Elliott J. Feldman and Neil Nevitte. 143–62. Cambridge and Montreal: Center for Intergovernmental Affairs, Harvard University, and the Institute for Research on Public Policy, 1979.

Intergovernmental Relations in Canada Today – Summary of Discussions. In *Confrontation and Collaboration: Intergovernmental Relations in Canada Today = Confrontation et Collaboration: Les Relations Intergouvernementales dans Le Canada d'aujourd'hui.* 1–16. Toronto: Institute of Public Administration of Canada, 1979.

and David J. Elkins. Conclusion: Province, Nation, Country and Confederation. In *Small Worlds: Provinces and Parties in Canadian Political Life,* edited by Richard Simeon and David J. Elkins. 285–312. Toronto: Methuen, 1980.

and David J. Elkins. Introduction. In *Small Worlds: Provinces and Parties in Canadian Political Life,* edited by Richard Simeon and David J. Elkins. x–xvi. Toronto: Methuen, 1980.

and David J. Elkins. Provincial Political Cultures in Canada. In *Small Worlds: Provinces and Parties in Canadian Political Life,* edited by Richard Simeon and David J. Elkins. 31–76. Toronto: Methuen, 1980.

and David J. Elkins. Regional Preferences: Citizen's Views of Public Policy. In *Small Worlds: Provinces and Parties in Canadian Political Life,* edited by Richard Simeon and David J. Elkins. 77–105. Toronto: Methuen, 1980.

and Robert Miller. Regional Variations in Public Policy. In *Small Worlds: Provinces and Parties in Canadian Political Life*, edited by Richard Simeon and David J. Elkins. 242–84. Toronto: Methuen, 1980.

Constitutional Development and Reform. In *Canadian Politics in the 1980s*, edited by Michael S. Whittington and Glen Williams. 1st ed. 243–59. Toronto: Methuen, 1981.

and Keith Banting. Federalism, Democracy and the Constitution. In *And No One Cheered: Federalism, Democracy and the Constitution Act*, edited by Keith Banting and Richard Simeon. 2–25. Toronto: Methuen, 1983.

and Keith Banting. Federalism, Democracy and the Future. In *And No One Cheered: Federalism, Democracy and the Constitution Act*, edited by Keith Banting and Richard Simeon. 348–59. Toronto: Methuen, 1983.

and Keith Banting. Introduction: The Politics of Constitutional Change. In *Redesigning the State: The Politics of Constitutional Change*, edited by Keith Banting and Richard Simeon. 1–29. Toronto: University of Toronto Press, 1985.

Meech Lake and Visions of Canada. In *Competing Constitutional Visions: The Meech Lake Accord*, edited by Katherine Swinton and C.J. Rogerson. 295–306. Toronto: Carswell, 1988.

We Are All Smiley's People: Some Observations on Donald Smiley and the Study of Federalism. In *Federalism and Political Community: Essays in Honour of Donald Smiley*, edited by David P. Shugarman and Reg Whitaker. 409–21. Peterborough: Broadview, 1989.

Sharing Power: How Can First Nations Government Work? In *Aboriginal Self-Determination*, edited by Frank Cassidy. 99–107. Lantzville: Oolichan Books, 1991.

The Dynamics of Canadian Federalism. In *Canadian Politics*, edited by James Bickerton and Alain-G. Gagnon. 2nd ed. 366–87. Peterborough: Broadview, 1994.

The Political Context for Renegotiating Fiscal Federalism. In *Fiscal Federalism*, edited by Keith Banting and Thomas Courchene. 135–48. Kingston: School of Policy Studies, Queen's University, 1994.

Canada and the United States: Lessons from the North American Experience. In *Rethinking Federalism: Citizens, Markets and Governments in a Changing World*, edited by Karen Knop, Sylvia Ostry, Richard Simeon, and Katherine Swinton. 250–72. Vancouver: UBC Press, 1995.

Globalization, Domestic Societies and Governance. In *Canada's Century: Governance in a Maturing Society*, edited by C.E.S. Franks et al. 25–42. Montreal and Kingston: McGill-Queen's University Press, 1995.

and Katherine Swinton. Introduction: Rethinking Federalism in a Changing World. In *Rethinking Federalism: Citizens, Markets and Governments in a Changing World*, edited by Karen Knop, Sylvia Ostry, Richard Simeon, and Katherine Swinton. 3–14. Vancouver: UBC Press, 1995.

Afterward: New Directions in Canadian Policy Studies. In *Policy Studies in Canada: The State of the Art*, edited by Laurent Dubuzinskis, Michael Howlett, and David Laycock. 375–81. Toronto: University of Toronto Press, 1996.

Aspetti Instituzionali Del Federalismo Canadese. In *L'ordinamento Constituzionale Del Canada*, edited by Nino Olivetti Rason and Lucio Pegoraro. 49–125. Torino: G. Giappichelli Editore, 1997.

and Keith Banting. Changing Economies, Changing Societies. In *Degrees of Freedom: Canada and the United States in a Changing World*, edited by Keith Banting, George Hoberg, and Richard Simeon. 23–70. Montreal and Kingston: McGill-Queen's University Press, 1997.

Citizens and Democracy in the Emerging Global Order. In *The Nation State in a Global/Information Era: Policy Challenges*, edited by Thomas J. Courchene. 299–314. Kingston: John Deutsch Institute for the Study of Economic Policy, 1997.

and Keith Banting, and George Hoberg. Introduction. In *Degrees of Freedom: Canada and the United States in a Changing World*, edited by Keith Banting, George Hoberg, and Richard Simeon. 3–19. Montreal and Kingston: McGill-Queen's University Press, 1997.

and Elaine Willis. Democracy and Performance: Governance in Canada and the United States. In *Degrees of Freedom: Canada and the United States in a Changing World*, edited by Keith Banting, George Hoberg, and Richard Simeon. 150–87. Montreal and Kingston: McGill-Queen's University Press, 1997.

and George Hoberg and Keith Banting. Globalization, Fragmentation, and the Social Contract. In *Degrees of Freedom: Canada and the United States in a Changing World*, edited by Keith Banting, George Hoberg, and Richard Simeon. 389–416. Montreal and Kingston: McGill-Queen's University Press, 1997.

and David Cameron. Ontario in Confederation: The Not-So-Friendly Giant. *The Government and Politics of Ontario*, edited by Graham White. 5th ed. 158–85. Toronto: University of Toronto Press, 1997.

Rethinking Government, Rethinking Federalism. *New Public Management and Public Administration in Canada*, edited by A. Daniels and M. Charih. 69–92. Toronto: Institute of Public Administration of Canada, 1997.

and Janice Stein and David Cameron. Citizen Engagement in Conflict Resolution. In *The Referendum Papers*, edited by David Cameron. 144–95. Toronto: University of Toronto Press, 1999.

and Ian Robinson. The Dynamics of Canadian Federalism. In *Canadian Politics*, edited by James Bickerton and Alain-G. Gagnon. 3rd ed. 239–62. Peterborough: Broadview, 1999.

The Limits of Partnership. In *The Referendum Papers: Essays on Secession and National Unity*, edited by David Cameron. 384–428. Toronto: University of Toronto Press, 1999.

and David Cameron. Intergovernmental Relations and Democratic Citizenship. In *Governing in the Twenty-First Century*, edited by Donald Savoie and B. Guy Peters. 58–118. Montreal and Kingston: McGill-Queen's University Press, 2000.

and David Cameron. Intergovernmental Relations and Democracy: An Oxymoron If There Ever Was One? In *Canadian Federalism: Performance, Effectiveness and Legitimacy*, edited by Herman Bakvis and Grace Skogstad. 278–95. Don Mills: Oxford University Press, 2001.

and Daniel-Patrick Conway. Federalism and the Management of Conflict in Multinational Societies. In *Multinational Democracies*, edited by Alain-G Gagnon and James Tully. 338–65. Cambridge: Cambridge University Press, 2001.

and George Hoberg and Keith Banting. North American Integration and the Scope for Democratic Choice. In *The Scope for Democratic Choice*, edited by George Hoberg. 47–62. Toronto: University of Toronto Press, 2001.

Recent Trends in Federalism and Intergovernmental Relations in Canada. In *The Dynamics of Decentralization*, edited by Trevor C. Salmon and Michael Keating. 47–62. Montreal and Kingston: McGill-Queen's University Press, 2001.

Conclusion. In *Intergovernmental Relations in Federal Countries: Essays on the Practice of Federal Governance*, edited by J. Peter Meekison. 91–105. Ottawa: Forum of the Federations, 2002.

Federalism and Intergovernmental Relations. In *A Handbook of Canadian Public Administration*, edited by Christopher Dunn. 204–24. Don Mills: Oxford University Press, 2002. 2nd ed. 2010.

and Christina Murray. Eight Years of Decentralization in South Africa. In *Decentralization and Power Shift: An Imperative for Good Government*, edited by Alex B. Brillantes. 171–89. Manila: Asian Resource Centre for Decentralization, Institute of Public Administration of Canada, and UNDP Philippines, 2003.

Federalism and Decentralization in Canada. In *Decentralization and Power Shift: An Imperative for Good Governance*, edited by Alex B. Brillantes. 499–532. Manila: Asian Resource Centre for Decentralization, Institute for Public Administration of Canada, and UNDP Philippines, 2003.

Important? Yes. Transformative? No: North American Integration and Canadian Federalism. In *The Impact of Global and Regional Integration on Federal Systems: A Comparative Analysis*, edited by Harvey Lazar, Hamish Telford, and Ronald L. Watts. 125–72. Montreal and Kingston: McGill-Queen's University Press, 2003.

Canada: Federalism, Regionalism and Language Conflict. In *Federalism and Territorial Cleavages*, edited by Ed. Ugo M. Amoretti and Nancy Bermeo. 93–122. Baltimore: Johns Hopkins University Press, 2004.

and Ian Robinson. The Dynamics of Canadian Federalism. In *Canadian Politics*, edited by James Bickerton and Alain-G Gagnon. 4th ed. 101–26. Peterborough: Broadview, 2004.

and Christina Murray. Multilevel Governance in South Africa. In *Ethnicity and Democracy in Africa*, edited by Bruce Berman, Dickson Eyoh, and Will Kymlicka. 277–300. Oxford and Athens: James Curry and Ohio University Press, 2004.

and Martin Papillon. The Weakest Link? First Ministers' Conferences in Canadian Intergovernmental Relations. In *Reconsidering the Institutions of Canadian Federalism*, edited by J. Peter Meekson, Hamish Telford, and Harvey Lazar. 113–40. Kingston: Institute of Intergovernmental Relations, 2004.

Social Justice: Does Federalism Make a Difference? In *Dilemmas of Solidarity: Rethinking Redistribution in the Canadian Federation*, edited by Sujit Choudhry, Jean-François Gaudreault-Desbiens, and Lorne Sossin. 31–44. Toronto: University of Toronto Press, 2006.

and Martin Papillon. Canada. In *Distribution of Powers and Responsibilities in Federal Countries*, edited by Akhtar Ajeed, Ronald L. Watts, and Douglas M. Brown. 91–122. Montreal and Kingston: McGill-Queen's University Press, 2006.

Federalism and Social Justice: Thinking Through the Tangle. In *Ter-*

ritory, Democracy and Justice, edited by Scott Greer. 18–43. London: Palgrave Macmillan, 2006.

and Luc Turgeon. Constitutional Design and the Construction of Democracy: A Citizenship Regime Approach. In *The Construction of Democracy,* edited by Jorge Dominguez and Anthony Jones. 79–102. Baltimore: Johns Hopkins University Press, 2007.

Federal-Provincial Relations. In *The Canadian Encyclopedia,* edited by James H. Marsh. Toronto: Historica Foundation, 2007.

and John McGarry and Brendan O'Leary. Integration or Accommodation? The Enduring Debate in Conflict Regulation. In *Constitutional Design for Divided Societies: Integration or Accommodation?* edited by Sujit Choudhry. 41–88. Oxford: Oxford University Press, 2008.

and Christina Murray. Recognition Without Empowerment: Minorities in a Democratic South Africa. In *Constitutional Design for Divided Societies: Integration or Accommodation?,* edited by Sujit Choudhry. 409–35. Oxford: Oxford University Press, 2008.

and Antoinette Handley and Christina Murray. Learning to Lose, Learning to Win: Government and Opposition in South Africa's Transition to Democracy. In *Political Transitions in a Dominant Party System: Learning to Lose,* edited by Joseph Wong and Edward Friedman. 191–210. London: Routledge, 2008.

Managing Conflicts of Diversity. In *Building on and Accommodating Diversities,* edited by Ronald L. Watts and Rupak Chattopadhyay. Unity and Diversity Series. Vol. 1. 54–69. New Delhi: Forum of the Federations and Viva Books, 2008.

and Amy Nugent. Parliamentary Canada and Intergovernmental Canada: Exploring the Tensions. In *Canadian Federalism: Effectiveness and Legitimacy,* edited by Herman Bakvis and Grace Skogstad. 89–111. Don Mills: Oxford University Press, 2008.

and David Cameron. Accommodation at the Pinnacle: The Special Role of Civil Society's Leaders. In *Language Matters: How Canadian Voluntary Associations Manage French and English,* edited by Richard Simeon and David Cameron. 174–86. Vancouver: UBC Press, 2009.

Associations in the Voluntary Health Sector: The Heart and Stroke Foundations of Canada and the Huntington Societies of Canada and Quebec. In *Language Matters: How Canadian Voluntary Associations Manage French and English,* edited by Richard Simeon and David Cameron. 95–120. Vancouver: UBC Press, 2009.

and David Cameron. Language and the Institutions of Civil Society. In *Language Matters: How Canadian Voluntary Associations Manage*

French and English, edited by Richard Simeon and David Cameron. 3–22. Vancouver: UBC Press, 2009.

and Christina Murray. South Africa: Promises Unmet, Multilevel Government in South Africa. In *Varieties of Federal Governance* edited by Rekha Saxena. 232–60. Cambridge: Cambridge University Press, 2010.

Preconditions and Prerequisites: Can Anyone Make Federalism Work? In *The Federal Idea: Essays in Honour of Ron Watts*, edited by Thomas J. Courchene, John R. Allan, Christian Leuprecht, and Nadia Verrelli. 207–23. Kingston and Montreal: McGill-Queen's University Press, 2011.

and Patti Tamara Lenard. Introduction. In *Imperfect Democracies: Comparing the Democratic Deficit in Canada and the United States*, edited by Patti Tamara Lenard and Richard Simeon. 1–22. Vancouver: UBC Press, 2012.

and Alexandre Pelletier. Groupes linguistiques et société civile: confiance, coopération, et accommodements au sein des associations volontaires au Canada. In *La Dynamique confiance/méfiance dans les démocraties multinationals. Le Canada sous l'angle comparatif*, edited by Dimitrios Karmis and François Rocher. 245–80. Ste-Foy: Presses de l'Université Laval, 2012.

and Amy Nugent and James Pearce. The Resilience of Canadian Federalism. In *The Global Debt Crisis: Haunting U.S. and European Federalism*, edited by Daniel Nadler and Paul E. Peterson. Washington, D.C.: Brookings Institution, 2013.

Journal Articles

Quebec 1970: The Dilemma of Power. *Queen's Quarterly* 79.1(1972): 100–07.

and David J. Elkins. Regional Political Cultures in Canada. *Canadian Journal of Political Science / Revue canadienne de science politique* 7.3(1974):397–437.

The "Overload Thesis" and Canadian Government. *Canadian Public Policy* 2.4(1976): 541–52.

Studying Public Policy. *Canadian Journal of Political Science / Revue canadienne de science politique* 9.4(1976):548–80.

Regionalism and Canadian Political Institutions. *Queen's Quarterly* 82(1975):499–511. Also published in *Canadian Federalism: Myth or Reality*, edited by J. Peter Meekson. 3rd ed. 292–304. Toronto: Methuen, 1977.

and David J. Elkins. A Cause in Search of Its Effect, or What Does Political Culture Explain? *Comparative Politics* 11.2(1979):127–45.

Natural Resource Revenues and Canadian Federalism: A Survey of the Issues. *Canadian Public Policy* 6(1980):182–91.

An Overview of the Trudeau Constitutional Proposals. *Alberta Law Review* 19(1981):391.

Criteria for Choice in Federal Systems. *Queen's Law Journal* 8(1982):131–57.

Fiscal Federalism in Canada: A Review Essay. *Canadian Tax Journal* 30.1(1982):41–51.

Inside the Macdonald Commission. *Studies in Political Economy* 22(1987):167–79.

Considerations on Centralization and Decentralization. *Canadian Public Administration* 29.3(1986):445–61. Reprinted in *Perspectives on Canadian Federalism*, edited by R. Olling and M.W. Westmacott. 367–79. Toronto: Prentice Hall, 1988.

Meech Lake and Shifting Conceptions of Canadian Federalism. *Canadian Public Policy* 14.S1(1988):7–24.

Considerations on the Design of Federations. *SA Public Law* 13(1998):42–72. Also published in Institute of Intergovernmental Relations, Working Papers 1998 (2).

and Christina Murray. From Paper to Practice: The National Council of the Provinces in Its First Year. *SA Public Law* 14(1999):96–141.

and Meric Gertler. Conclusion: Thinking About Regions. *Policy Options* (January–February 2000):98–9.

Let's Get at the Basic Question Indirectly. *Policy Options* (January–February 2000):11–16.

and Christina Murray. South Africa's Financial Constitution: Towards Better Delivery. *SA Public Law* 15(2000):477–504.

Adaptability and Change in Federations. *International Social Science Journal* 53.167(2001):145–52.

and Christina Murray. Multi-Sphere Governance in South Africa: An Interim Assessment. *Publius: The Journal of Federalism* 31.4(2001):65–92.

and David Cameron. Intergovernmental Relations in Canada: The Emergence of Collaborative Federalism. *Publius: The Journal of Federalism* 32.2(2002):49–72.

Plus Ça Change ... Intergovernmental Relations Then and Now. *Policy Options* (March–April 2005):84–7.

and Luc Turgeon. Federalism, Nationalism and Regionalism in Canada. *Revista d'Estudios Autonomics I Federals* 3(2006):11–41.

and Christina Murray. Tagging Bills in Parliament: Section 75 or Section 76. *South African Law Journal* 123(2006):232.

Constitutional Design and Change in Federal Systems: Issues and Questions. *Publius: The Journal of Federalism* 39.2(2009):241–61.

and Beryl A. Radin. Reflections on Comparing Federalisms: Canada and the United States. *Publius: The Journal of Federalism* 40.3(2010):357–65.

and Christina Murray. Reforming Multi-level Government in South Africa. *Canadian Journal of African Studies* 43.3(2010):536–71.

Postscript: Many Small Worlds. *Regional & Federal Studies* 20.4–5(2010):545–8. Also published in *Why Regions Matter: Small Worlds in a Comparative Perspective,* edited by Ailsa Henderson. 107–10. London: Routledge, 2011.

Book Reviews

What Culture? What Heritage? A Study of *Civic Education in Canada* by A.B. Hodgetts. *Canadian Journal of Political Science / Revue canadienne de science politique* 2.4(1969):539–40.

The Maple Leaf Forever: Essays on Nationalism and Politics in Canada by Ramsay Cook. *Canadian Journal of Political Science/ Revue canadienne de science politique* 6.1(1973):158–9.

Elite Accommodation in Canadian Politics by Robert Presthus. *Canadian Journal of Political Science / Revue canadienne de science politique* 7.3(1974):567–71.

Echange/Exchange. *Canadian Journal of Political Science / Revue canadienne de science politique* 9.1(1976):127–31.

Communications – Comment on Vaillancourt's Review (vol. 72, December 1978, pp.1491–92). *American Political Science Review* 73.4(1979):1109–20.

National Politics and Community in Canada by Kenneth Carty and W. Peter Ward. *American Political Science Review* 81.4(1987):1383–4.

The British Tradition of Federalism by Michael Burgess. *Publius* 26.3(1996):206–8.

Reports and Policy Papers

The Regional Distribution of the Benefits of Confederation: A Preliminary Analysis. Kingston: Institute of Intergovernmental Relations, Queen's University, 1976.

Issues in Intergovernmental Relations. Toronto: Ontario Economic Council, 1978.

Opening Statement to the Special Committee on the Constitution. Kingston: Institute of Intergovernmental Relations, 1978.

Federalism and the Politics of a National Strategy. In *The Politics of an Industrial Strategy: A Seminar*. 5–43. Ottawa: Science Council of Canada, 1979.

Intergovernmental Relations and the Challenges to Canadian Federalism, edited by Donald W. Craik, J. Stefan Dupré, Kenneth Kernaghan, James J. Macdonell, James D. McNiven, Donald V. Smiley, Gérard Veilleux, and Kenneth W. Wiltshire. Kingston: Institute of Intergovernmental Relations, Queen's University, 1979.

Intergovernmental Relations and the Challenges to Canadian Federalism. In *Intergovernmental Canada – Government by Conference?* edited by Donald W. Craik, J. Stefan Dupré, Kenneth Kernaghan, James J. Macdonell, James D. McNiven, Richard Simeon, Donald V. Smiley, Gérard Veilleux, and Kenneth W. Wiltshire. Also published as Discussion Paper No. 7 prepared for the Conference of the Institute of Public Administration of Canada, Winnipeg, August 1979. Kingston: Institute of Intergovernmental Relations, Queen's University, 1979.

and Jeff Evenson. The Roots of Discontent. *Proceedings of the Workshop on the Political Economy of Confederation*. Kingston and Ottawa: Donald Gordon Conference Centre for Continuing Education, Institute of Intergovernmental Relations, Queen's University, and Economic Council of Canada, 1979.

A Citizen's Guide to the Constitutional Question. Toronto: Gage, 1980.

Réponse au Québec: Les autres provinces et le débat constitutionnel. Kingston: Institute of Intergovernmental Relations, Queens University, 1980.

The Challenge of Research on the Canadian Communities. In *Proceedings of the Workshop on the Challenge of Research on the Canadian Communities*, edited by Richard Simeon. 1–28. Ottawa: Social Sciences and Humanities Research Council of Canada, 1980.

and Marie-Hélène Bergeron and Douglas Brown, eds. *The Question: The Debate on the Referendum Question, Quebec National Assembly, March 4–20, 1980*. Kingston: Institute of Intergovernmental Relations, Queen's University, 1980.

and Jack Mintz. *Conflict of Taste and Conflict of Claim in Federal Countries*. Discussion Paper 13. Kingston: Institute of Intergovernmental Relations, Queen's University, 1982.

Some Observations on the Powers over the Economy. *A Separate Personal Income Tax: Background Studies,* edited by David Conklin. 365–80.Toronto: Ontario Economic Council, 1984.

Aboriginal Self-Government and Canadian Political Values. *Issues in Entrenching Aboriginal Self-Government: Report on the Workshop Held on February 16–18, 1987,* edited by David C. Hawkes and Evelyn J. Peters. 49–56. Kingston: Institute of Intergovernmental Relations, Queen's University, 1987.

Global Economy/Domestic Society: Competing Challenges to Governance in Canada. In *Canada-Japan: Policy Issues for the Future,* edited by K. Lorne Brownsey. 173–88. Halifax: Institute for Research on Public Policy, 1989.

Parallelism in the Meech Lake Accord and the Free Trade Agreement. In *Re-Forming Canada? The Meaning of the Meech Lake Accord and the Free Trade Agreement for the Canadian State,* edited by John D. Whyte and Ian Peach. Dean's Conference on Law and Policy No. 1. 3–8. Kingston: Institute of Intergovernmental Relations, 1989.

and Keith Banting, Elaine Willis, and Michael Hawes, eds. *Policy Choices: Political Agendas in Canada and the United States.* Published proceedings of the Rethinking North American Relationships Conference. 2–4 November 1989. Kingston: Queen's University School of Policy Studies, 1991.

Introduction: Setting Out The Framework. In *Toolkits and Building Blocks: Constructing a New Canada.* Published proceedings of the Imagining Constitutional Futures Workshop, 17–18 November 1990. 1–7. Toronto: C.D. Howe Institute, 1990.

Concluding Comments. *Canadian Federalism: Meeting Global Economic Challenges?* edited by Douglas M. Brown and M.G. Smith. 285–91. Kingston and Halifax: Institute of Intergovernmental Relations and Institute for Research on Public Policy, 1991.

Globalization and the Canadian Nation-State. *Canada at Risk: Canadian Public Policy in the 1990s,* edited by G. Bruce Doern and Byme B. Purchase. Policy Study 13. 46–58. Ottawa: C.D. Howe Institute, 1991.

Introduction. *Policy Choices: Political Agendas in Canada and the United States,* edited by Keith Banting, Michael Hawes, Richard Simeon, and Elaine Willis. Published proceedings of the Rethinking North American Relationships Conference, 2–4 November 1989. 1–6. Kingston: School of Policy Studies, Queen's University, 1991.

and Mary Janigan, eds. *Toolkits and Building Blocks: Constructing a New*

Canada. Published proceedings of the Imagining Constitutional Futures Workshop, 17–18 November 1990. Toronto: C.D. Howe Institute, 1991.

Federalism in Hard Times: Concluding Comments. In *Fiscal Reform for the 21st Century*, edited by Sherri J. Torjman. 77–80. Ottawa: Caledon Institute of Social Policy, 1993.

The Evolution of Canada and the European Union. In *Canada and the European Union*, edited by J. Christiansen. 38–59. Ottawa: Delegation of the Commission of the European Union, 1995.

and Alan C. Cairns, David Cameron, Gretta Chambers, Thomas J. Courchene, Wendy Dobson, David Elton, Angela Ferrante, et al. *Group of 22: Making Canada Work Better*. Support provided by the C.D. Howe Institute, Canada West Foundation, John Deutsch Institute, the McGill Institute for the Study of Canada, and the Royal Bank of Canada. 1 May 1996.

Is Partnership Possible? Toronto: C.D. Howe Institute, 1998.

Interdependence, not Independence: Institutional and Administrative Dimensions of Judicial Independence. *Setting Judicial Compensation: Multidisciplinary Perspectives*. 83–93. Ottawa: Law Commission of Canada, 1999.

Report: Constitutional Design. Conference held October 2001 in Madrid. Published in *FRIDE, Conference on Democratic Transition and Consolidation*. Madrid: Mehta, 2002.

Lectures and Presentations

The Economic and Social Union and the Division of Powers. Conference on the Charlottetown Accord. Faculty of Law, University of Toronto, October 1992.

Trends in Canadian and American Federalism. Conference on Federalism and the Nation State. University of Toronto, June 1992.

The Lessons of Meech and Charlottetown. Conference on Quebec and Canada. Robarts Centre for Canadian Studies, York University, March 1995.

Models of Federalism and Intergovernmental Relations. Conference entitled Towards a Democratic Constitution for South Africa. Ministry of Constitutional Development, South Africa, July 1995.

The Structures of Intergovernmental Relations. International Roundtable on Democratic Constitutional Development. Pretoria, South Africa, 1995.

Considerations on the Design of Federations. Conference on Hyper-Federalism in Russia. Princeton University, February 1996.

After the Quebec Reference: Next Steps. Human Rights Program, Harvard University Law School. Harvard University, December 1998.

Federalism and Conflict Management in Multinational Societies. Conference on Multinational Societies. McGill University, February 1998.

and David Cameron. Multilevel Governance and Democratic Citizenship. Canadian Political Science Association Annual Meeting. Ottawa, June 1998. Revised edition presented to Israeli Association of Canadian Studies and Canadian Centre for Management Development, Jerusalem, July 1998.

Adaptability and Change in Federations. Background Paper Prepared for the Forum on Federations. Mont Tremblant, Quebec, November 1999.

Recent Trends in Federalism and Intergovernmental Relations: Lessons for the UK? Canada-UK Colloquium on Decentralization, Regionalization and the Role of Government. Belfast, Northern Ireland, November 1999.

Why Success, Why Failure? Cunliffe Centre for Constitutional Studies, Sussex University, May 1999.

Legacies and Innovations: Studying Canadian Federalism. Institute of Intergovernmental Relations, Kingston, Ontario, October 2000. The McGregor Lecture.

Competition and Cooperation in Fiscal Federalism. Conference on Fiscal Wars, Forum of the Federations and Government of Sao Paulo. Sao Paulo, Brazil, May 2001.

Globalization and Canadian Federalism. Conference on Federalism and Globalization, Ottawa, Institute of Intergovernmental Relations, February 2001.

Making Federalism Work: Intergovernmental Coordination and Institutional Capacity. Notes for presentation at the Forum of Federations: International Seminar on Modernization and Fiscal Federalism: Alternatives to Tax Wars: Sustainable Economic Development in Brazil. Sao Paulo, Brazil, 21 June 2001.

Perspectives on Devolution: Democracy, Effectiveness and Diversity. Conference on Workshop on Devolution. Narobi, Kenya, 13 December 2001.

and Martin Papillon. The Weakest Link: First Ministers' Conferences in Canadian Intergovernmental Relations. Conference on The Machinery of Intergovernmental Relations in Canada. Kingston, Institute of Intergovernmental Relations, October 2001.

Club De Madrid, Inaugural Meeting. Participated as member of academic advisory council. Madrid, October 2002.

Federalism and Decentralization in Canada. International Conference on Decentralization. Centre for Local and Regional Governance, University of the Philippines, July 2002.

Questions for Constitutional Engineers. Roundtable on Constitutional Engineering. Annual Meeting of the American Political Science Association, Boston, September 2002.

Addressing the Democratic Deficit in Intergovernmental Relations. Leadership Forum. Arthur Kroeger College of Public Affairs, Carleton University, Ottawa, 11 February 2003.

Federal Systems in North America and Africa. Stability and Viability in Afghanistan Panel at VIII Liechtenstein Colloquium on European and International Affairs. Liechtenstein Institute on Self-Determination, Princeton University, Triesenberg, Liechtenstein, 13–16 March 2003.

Federalism and North American Integration. Federalism and Transborder Integration in North America Conference. Carleton University. 7–8 February 2003. Keynote Address.

Federalism and Social Justice. Constitution Unit, University College London, November 2003.

Building Legislative Federalism. Saskatchewan Institute for Public Policy, March 2004.

Debating Secession Peacefully and Democratically: The Case of Canada. III Annual Congress, the Club of Madrid. November 2004.

Intergovernmental Relations Beyond Our Borders. Annual Conference of the Institute of Public Administration of Canada. Vancouver, August 2004.

Federalism and Social Justice: Thinking Through the Tangle. Conference on Redistribution in the Canadian Federation. Faculty of Law, University of Toronto, 6 February 2005.

Decentralization for Bolivia? Issues and Concepts. Friedrich Ebert Stiftung/ILDIS. La Paz, Bolivia, August 2005.

and Christina Murray. Parachute or Strait-Jacket? The Legacy of South Africa's "Pacted" Constitution. Workshop on Constitutional Politics in Africa. University of Wisconsin, Madison, 26 October 2005.

and Antoinette Handley and Christina Murray. Learning to Lose: Learning to Win: Government and Opposition in South Africa's

Transition to Democracy. Learning to Lose Conference. University of Toronto, 31 March – 1 April 2006.

Is Federalism Like Snow? And, Is It Exportable? Some Cautionary Notes on the Study of Federalism. Lecture given at Leiden University, 11 June 2010. Also presented earlier at the University of Kent, 19 November 2008 and at the Centre for Canadian Studies, University of Edinburgh, 19 May 2009.

Contributors

Keith Banting is a Professor in the Department of Political Studies and the School of Policy Studies at Queen's University, where he holds the Queen's Research Chair in Public Policy.

David Cameron is a Professor of Political Science, former Chair of the Department of Political Science at the University of Toronto, and currently Acting Dean of the Faculty of Arts and Science at the University of Toronto.

César Colino is an Associate Professor in the Department of Political Science and Public Administration at the Spanish National Distance-Learning University (UNED) in Madrid.

Jan Erk is an Associate Professor/Reader in the Department of Political Science at the University of Leiden.

Patrick Fafard is an Associate Professor of Political Science at the University of Ottawa.

Ran Hirschl is a Professor of Political Science in the Department of Political Science at the University of Toronto, where he holds a Canada Research Chair in Constitutionalism, Democracy and Development.

Thomas O. Hueglin is a Professor of Political Science at Wilfrid Laurier University.

Michael Keating is a Professor in the School of Social Sciences at the University of Aberdeen, where he holds a chair in Scottish Politics.

Andrew McDougall is a PhD student at the University of Toronto who is writing a doctoral thesis on the impact of intergovernmental relations on support for the sovereignty movement in Quebec.

John McGarry is a Professor of Political Science at Queen's University, where he holds a Canada Research Chair in Nationalism and Democracy.

Alain Noël is a Professor of Political Science at the Université de Montréal and President of the Canadian Political Science Association (2013–14).

Martin Papillon is an Associate Professor of Political Science at the University of Ottawa.

François Rocher is a Professor of Political Studies at the University of Ottawa.

Richard Simeon is Professor Emeritus at the University of Toronto.

Grace Skogstad is a Professor of Political Science at the University of Toronto and Chair of the Department of Political Science at the University of Toronto Scarborough.

Luc Turgeon is an Assistant Professor of Political Science at the University of Ottawa.

Jenn Wallner is an Assistant Professor of Political Science at the University of Ottawa.

Marie-Joëlle Zahar is an Associate Professor of Political Science at the Université de Montréal.